EMERGING CONCEPTS IN URBAN SPACE DESIGN

The cover illustration shows detail from Luciano Laurana (*c.* 1420–79): *Ideal City*. Painting in the Ducal Palace at Urbino.

EMERGING CONCEPTS IN URBAN SPACE DESIGN

Geoffrey Broadbent
Formerly Professor of Architecture,
University of Portsmouth

E & FN SPON
An Imprint of Chapman & Hall

London · Glasgow · Weinheim · New York · Tokyo · Melbourne · Madras

Published by E & FN Spon, an imprint of Chapman & Hall,
2-6 Boundary Row, London SE1 8HN, UK

Chapman & Hall, 2-6 Boundary Row, London SE1 8HN, UK

Blackie Academic & Professional, Wester Cleddens Road, Bishopbriggs, Glasgow G64 2NZ, UK

Chapman & Hall GmbH, Pappelallee 3, 69469 Weinheim, Germany

Chapman & Hall USA., 115 Fifth Avenue, New York, NY 10003, USA

Chapman & Hall Japan, ITP-Japan, Kyowa Building, 3F, 2-2-1 Hirakawacho, Chiyoda-ku, Tokyo 102, Japan

Chapman & Hall Australia, 102 Dodds Street, South Melbourne, Victoria 3205, Australia

Chapman & Hall India, R. Seshadri, 32 Second Main Road, CIT East, Madras 600 035, India

First edition 1990
Reprinted in paperback 1996

© 1990 Geoffrey Broadbent

Typeset in 10/11½pt Palatino by Scarborough Typesetting Services
Printed in Hong Kong

ISBN 0 419 16150 3

A Catalogue record for this book is available from the British Library

Library of Congress Cataloging-in-Publication Data available

Contents

Acknowledgements

The author and publishers are most grateful to many architects and planners who have been most generous in granting permission for their work to be reproduced and who also, in several cases, have provided original material. These include Ricardo Bofill and the Taller de Arquitectura, Gordon Cullen, Andrés Duany and Elizabeth Plater-Zyberk, David Gosling, Léon Krier, Robert Krier, Sir Leslie Martin, Charles Moore, Rodrigo Pérez d'Arce, Miguel Angel Roca, François Spoerry, James Stirling and Bernard Tschumi.

In many cases this work has appeared in earlier books and journals. These are cited, where appropriate, as aids to those who wish to find further references.

Every effort has been made to trace copyright holders although this has proved difficult where there have been multiple changes of publisher.

PART ONE

HISTORICAL PERSPECTIVES

1

Urban space design in history

The roots of planning

If we are to understand the nature of the city it is useful to remember that the word itself derives from the Latin *civilis* which means 'befitting a citizen'. We should remember also that the same root underlies our word civilization. Civilization is that which takes place in great cities!

Kenneth Clark (1959) opened his television series on 'Civilization' and the associated book by looking at the centre of Paris; at Nôtre Dame, the Louvre, the Institute de France, the town houses and the bookstalls lining the quais of the Seine. Here, he suggested, are all the things which civilization means to us.

As he said, civilization is possible when humankind has reached beyond the level of scratching a bare subsistence and freed from 'the day-to-day struggle for existence and the night-to-night struggle with fear', develops in equilibrium qualities of thought and feeling, ideals of perfection in reasoning, in justice, in physical beauty, and so on.

It's a matter of stability too, or as Clark puts, 'permanence'. The good, solid walls of stone he saw in Paris gave him such permanence, so did the ideas enshrined in the books. Civilization for him was evidence that humankind had extended itself to the utmost, mentally and spiritually.

Some of course will recoil in horror at such elitism. Clark would simply have called them 'uncivilized' but they would do well to read what Frederick Engels said in his funeral oration at the grave-side of Karl Marx (1883).

> 'Marx' he said, 'discovered the law of human history . . . that mankind first of all must eat, drink, have shelter and clothing, before it can pursue politics, science, art, religion etc'.

The latter Marx called the 'superstructure', built onto the economic 'base'. But once society has passed beyond the primitive struggle for existence economic activity itself, of course, becomes part of the 'superstructure'. Which puts into context the origin of the city.

The first cities obviously were built when humankind had got beyond the struggle for mere existence. The earliest known city, Jericho (*c.* 7000 BC) was an oasis near the River Jordan and it has extensive defences whilst Catal Huyuk in Central Anatolia (Asian Turkey *c.* 6500 BC) seems to have flourished on trade (Mellaart, 1967). Both depended on sophisticated agriculture, including the rearing of livestock.

But city-sized populations in general could not be brought together until ways had been found of producing food nearby, in sufficient quantities and transporting it into the city. So it is hardly surprising that traces of the first great cities on the whole are to be found in great river valleys and basins.

Irrigation on the necessary scale seems to have been developed first of all in central Mesopotamia – between the Tigris and the Euphrates – from about 6000 BC. There the first city-scale developments were built in Sumer, at Uruk (*c.* 3500 BC), Ur (*c.* 3100 BC) and Eridu (*c.* 2750 BC). The first Egyptian cities have been found near the estuary of the Nile, at Faiyum (*c.* 4440 BC), and Meride (*c.* 4300 BC). Further south down the Nile beyond Cairo the first two Egyptian capitals were founded, at Memphis (*c.* 3100 BC) and Thebes (*c.* 2080 BC). Further east in the Valley of the Indus there were Mohenjo-daro and Harrappan (both before 2400 BC, whilst further east again on the Yellow River, or its tributaries, there were the early Chinese cities such as Erh'li-t'ou (*c.* 1766 BC) and Cheng-chou (*c.* 1650 BC).

The presence of great rivers made irrigation possible but as Kenyon says (1960) it had to be organized:

> The successful practice of irrigation involves an elaborate control system. A system of main channels feeds subsidiary channels, watering the fields when the necessary sluice gates are closed. Therefore the channels must be planned, the length of time each farmer may take the water by closing the sluice gates must be established, and there must be some sanction to be used against those who contravene the regulations. The implications therefore are that there must be some central communal organization and the beginnings of a code of laws which the organization enforces . . . the evidence that there was an efficient communal organization is to be seen in the great defensive systems.

Power naturally accrued to those who built and controlled the irrigation systems, not to mention the defences. None of this could have been achieved without centralized planning. Small wonder then, that the first cities show evidence of social stratification and the development of craft specializations.

The little town of Beidha, south of Jericho, had individual shops for specialist workers in bone, workers in stone, butchers and so on, whilst the greatest Neolithic city of them all, Çatal Huyuk had very much more detailed specializations (Mellaart, 1967).

There were specialists in flint and obsidian – a black volcanic glass – who made arrowheads, daggers, spearheads, knives, sickles, scrapers and boring tools, not to mention mirrors of polished obsidian. There were jewellers who made beads for necklaces, armlets, bracelets and anklets. There were workers in stone who made adzes, axes, polishers, grinders, chisels, mace heads and palettes; bone-workers who made awls, punches, knives, scrapers, ladles, spoons, bowls, scoops, spatulas, bodkins and belt-hooks. There were wood carvers who made boxes and bowls, weavers who made woollen cloths and rugs. There were reed weavers, who made baskets and mats; potters, painters, sculptors and other artists. Since some of the houses were a good deal larger than others and since some people were buried much more lavishly than others, there is evidence of social stratification.

So, four things in the first place, made the city possible: the separation of the built-up area from the surrounding countryside, possibly by defensive walls; the development of irrigation systems for intensive agriculture; the development of power structures by which the irrigation systems, and other aspects of urban life, could be controlled – usually by kings and priests; and the development of craft-specialities to serve not only the needs or the desires of the urban population but also as bases for trade.

Since cities were founded in these things, it is hardly surprising that cities ever since have been permeated by them or their equivalents.

As for their physical design, cities and parts of cities, have grown in two ways. The first is described by Alexander (1964) as the natural way in which people simply start building, as they still do in the shanty towns of the emerging world. And then there is the artificial way in which a master plan is prepared; streets laid out, squares and urban blocks on to which buildings are then placed according to some planners' sense of order (Stanislawski, 1947).

This contrast will recur many times in the book. So will another contrast: between formality and informality. The 'natural' city tends towards informality, not to mention an apparent disorder whilst the planners will want their conscious decisions to show. Most planners aim for regularities of a kind which show that human minds have been at work; but some aim for a self-conscious irregularity of the kind we call Picturesque. This book is largely about that contrast but of course it will have to be put into context.

Classical planning

Straight streets, meeting at right angles, were known in Nebuchad-nezzar's Babylon which was planned between 1126 and 1105 BC (Fig. 1.1). Aristotle in *Politics* (ii, 5) seems to have thought such planning was invented by Hippodamus of Miletus (479 BC) who, he says: 'discovered the method of dividing cities'. Miletus was planned on a checkerboard or grid as many later cities have been. But so was its neighbour, Priene, built on steeply sloping ground with the main streets running along the contours and the (stepped) minor streets crossing them (Figs 1.2 and 1.3). Indeed, as Kostoff says (1985), the preferred Greek method of planning was *per strigas*, that is to say by bands in which east–west avenues were crossed, at right angles, by one or more north–south streets.

Such ancient texts as survive on city planning are concerned, not so much with the geometry of the streets, as with aspect, prospect and climate. Hippocrates, for instance, suggests (in *Airs, Waters and Places*

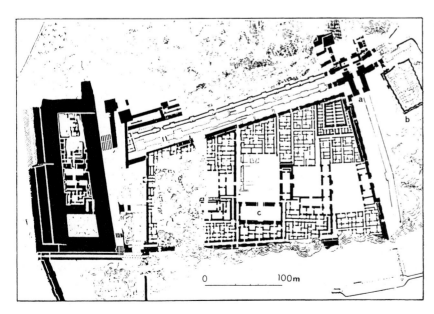

Fig. 1.1 Babylon: Nebuchadnezzar's South Palace (*c.* 1126–1105 BC) (from Oates, 1979, p. 100).

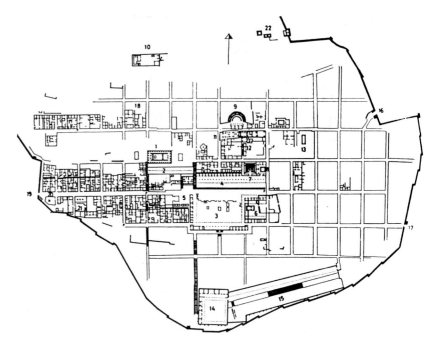

Fig. 1.2 Priene (*c.* 350 BC): Gridiron
plan (from Akurgal, 1978).

iii–iv) that the healthiest aspect will be facing east and Aristotle agrees
(*Politics* vii, 10.1). If it cannot face east then the city should face south.
Vitruvius too is concerned with prevailing wind (I, 6. i): broad streets
will be open to the winds but the smaller alleys should be protected.
'Cold winds are very unpleasant; hot winds ennervating, humid
winds unhealthy.'

Vitruvius, indeed, has much to say about the winds and other
environmental matters in choosing the location for a city (Fig. 1.4). The
first need, he says, is for water. So (VIII, 1. i) one ought, before sunrise,
to fall flat on one's face, supporting one's chin on the ground so 'the
sight will not wander higher than it ought'. Thus one can observe
where moisture 'seems to curl upwards and rise into the air' after
which digging will confirm that indeed there is water to be found.

One should observe what kinds of plants seem to flourish on site for
these will be good climatic indicators, the flavours of the fruits, not to
mention any wine. Above all one should look at the cattle for, as
Vitruvius says (I, IV, 9)

Fig. 1.3 Priene (*c.* 350 BC): the steeply
terraced streets (author's photograph).

Fig. 1.4 Vitruvius: Diagram of the Winds from Rivius, G.H. (1548) (Vitruvius Teutsch, in Rosenau, 1959).

> Our ancestors, when about to build a town or an army post, sacrificed some of the cattle that were wont to feed on the site . . . and examined their livers. If the livers . . . were dark coloured or abnormal, they sacrificed others to see whether the fault was due to disease or food. They never began to build . . . until . . . they had made many such trials and satisfied themselves that good water and food had made the liver sound and firm.

If the livers were not, they moved to a different site.

Rykwert (1976) goes into considerable detail about the ceremonies by which Roman cities were founded and there is no need here to repeat his splendid account.

As for winds, Vitruvius thought there were eight – as represented on the Tower of the Winds in Athens. The Tower is octagonal, facing the eight winds and so, accordingly, should a city be planned.

Since its sides would face the eight winds, Vitruvius says (V, 7) 'let the directions of your streets and alleys be laid down on the lines of division between the quarters of two winds' so no wind would blow directly down them. For if the winds blew directly into the street they would blow even more strongly as they were confined. They would be dispersed, however, if they blew towards the angles of the buildings.

Vitruvius is so proud of this account that he repeats it then goes on to prescribe locations for the major temples, the forum, the basilicas 'which should be in the warmest possible quarter' and so on.

He assumed that the city would be walled, with defensive towers projecting from the walls. Access roads should slope upwards towards the city gates which should be approached from the right so that enemies, carrying their shields in their left hands, would expose their unprotected flanks to the defenders.

Vitruvius suggests (I, V, 2) that towns should be laid out: 'not as an exact square, nor with salient angles, but in circular form, to give views of the enemy from many points'. He is clear that any 'salient angles'

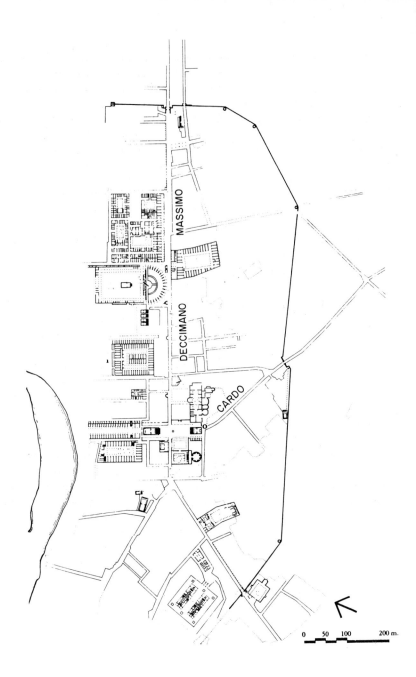

Fig. 1.5 Ostia: cardo maximus and
decumani (from McDonald, 1986).

made defence more difficult because, instead of protecting the
defenders, they protected the approaching enemy.

Despite Vitruvius's predilection for circular cities, most Roman
planning followed the Greek gridiron form.

One Roman surveyor, probably Frontinus, describes the method for
setting out a town (quoted Pennick (1979)): once the centre had been
located, the *augur* identified it as the *omphalos* – from which the city, not
to mention his survey, originated.

He sat at this point facing west and of course the four major
directions could be laid out. In setting out the city, one should start
with an *amussium* – an absolutely level marble slab – on which one
should set a bronze *gnomon*, a 'shadow tracker'. By tracing the
shadows at certain specified times one could plot a line running due
north to south and use this as the basis for setting out one's city.

Agrimensores laid out the lines of two major roads, the *decumanus
maximus* running from north to south and the *cardo maximus* running

from east to west (Fig. 1.5). Along these roads both town and country were laid out in squares although as Dilke (1971) says, the country was 'squared' in *centuriae* of 2400 Roman feet each containing 200 'heritable plots' whilst the town was laid out in urban blocks, *insulae* which varied considerably in size although *acti* squares – a little less than half a mile – were not uncommon. Roman feet were a little larger than their Imperial equivalents and the *decumanus maximus* was made some 40 feet wide and the *cardo* about half this width. Then every 20 *acti* or so lesser roads were built, each only eight feet wide.

They were numbered from the major crossing, the *omphalos*, and every fifth one might be 12 feet wide as a public right of way. The *cardo* and the *decumanus maximus* themselves often were simply sections of major trunk roads, such as the Appian Way, as they passed through the city and across an entire colony.

As Dilke says, a number of Roman maps survive, as illustrations to texts which seem in themselves to have been teaching manuals for surveyors. There are also fragments of a splendid Plan of Rome, the *Forma Urbis Romae* which was carved on stone panels for Septimus Severus between AD 203 and 208 (Fig. 1.6). Originally it was some 18 metres high by 13 metres wide and the scale averages 1:300.

This Plan too is evidence indeed that geometric instruments were used by the Roman surveyors, not just straight edges and squares but also compasses. If such instruments were available for map-making and measured drawings then of course they were also available for designing.

Which one would have concluded anyway from the forms of much Roman planning, at the scales both of individual buildings and of urban spaces (Ward-Perkins, 1970). It is quite inconceivable, for instance, that the great Baths, not to mention the *Fora* of Caesar (c. 46 BC), of Augustus (c. 52 BC) and, especially, of Trajan (early 2nd century AD) could have been built as they were, with their geometric splendours, without their first being planned through the medium of geometric drawings (Fig. 1.7).

As for the urban fabric of Rome, the *insulae* between the major buildings, Trajan's Market, a multi-storey structure in brick with vault and arches represents, together with equivalents at Ostia, the nearest we shall ever see to what most of ancient Rome was really like.

Fig. 1.6 Part of the 'Forma Urbis', the marble Map of Rome set up for Septimus Severus (3rd century AD) (from Bacon, 1967).

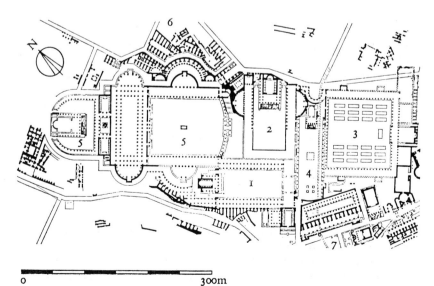

0   300m

Fig. 1.7 Forum Romanum (from Ward-Perkins, 1970).

Since, by the time of Trajan, Rome had been growing over some 900 years, the general urban texture was informal with the large formal projects inserted. But informality too can have its rules.

It is difficult to get the feel of being in a Classical city. So many of them are ruined, with walls, if they have any, no more than a metre high. One gains a general sense of where the buildings are and some idea of the spaces between them, in plan but not in three dimensions. It is true that on the Acropolis (Fig. 1.8) in Athens the Propyleon, the Parthenon, the Erectheion and even the tiny Temple of Athena Nike all stand to their full height. But the Acropolis was by no means a typical part of the city, and as we see it now it lacks the 40 or so steps, terraces, altars, shrines, statues and other features which Pausanius (*c.* 3rd century AD) recorded in his amazing description of what he saw between the Propyleion and the Parthenon alone.

As for the Forum Romanum, that, if anything, is even more ruinous. Again we have to make great leaps of the imagination to see it complete and occupied. So it is with the great baths and other urban monuments. We gain some idea of their size and shape from the naked ruins but no clues as to the treatment of the marble architectural skin with which they were clad in ancient times inside and outside the brick and concrete structures which survive.

The Pantheon gives us a better idea, internally, at least, where the marble architectural lining is still complete. And Trajan's Market gives perhaps the best idea of all of the space, lined with six-storey buildings, which formed a typical Roman street. These too are lacking the various balconies and other projections from their present rather flat façades. Parts of ancient Ostia, too, approach this level of completeness but being somewhat smaller in scale, they do not give the sense of urban claustrophobia which many must have felt in ancient Rome.

In terms of completeness, the monumental centres of remoter Roman cities, less plundered by later builders, give us clearer ideas of what it would have been like to *be* there. Such North African sites as Leptis Magna, and Timgad, for instance, have rather more to show than most but the clearest impression of *walking* real Roman streets is probably offered by Ephesus, very close to the western coast of Turkey.

The upper parts of the city are as ruinous as most, but once one starts to descend the so-called Curetes Street the degree of completeness

Fig. 1.8 Acropolis reconstruction.

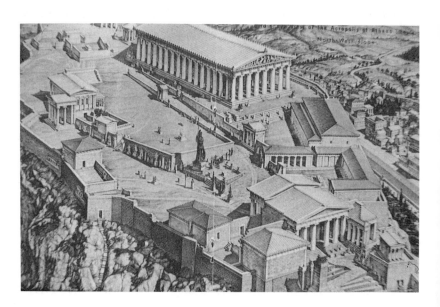

increases markedly and by the time one reaches Marble Street, the Library of Celsius (Fig. 1.9) and the Theatre, these buildings enclose urban spaces much they must have done in Classical times. Pompeii and Herculaneum are even more complete in the parts which have been excavated. One gains a strong sense, literally, of being in the streets but since most of them are lined by single-storey villas, the sense of enclosure is not very great. There are two-storey villas along the Via dell' Abbondanza and they certainly give one a much greater sense of urban enclosure. The large Forum also is surrounded by two-storey colonnades, but with so many empty sites behind them, between the surviving buildings, that again there is not much sense of urban enclosure.

Fig. 1.9 Ephesus: Library of Celsius (*c.* 117–125 AD) (author's photograph).

Islamic planning

Whilst the rules for regular planning were well known in Classical times those for informal planning were developed in quite a different culture, Islam, during that period which we in the West tend to think of as the Dark Ages.

These ages were by no means dark for Islam and, as Nasr points out (1976), as Islam expanded, so whatever seemed appropriate from the cultures of the conquered territories was absorbed and developed. This included medicine, philosophy and the sciences, not only of Greece and Rome but also of the earlier cultures which they in their turn had absorbed. As Nasr says, Islam itself was far more than a 'bridge over which ideas of Antiquity passed to mediaeval Europe'.

Not that any of this was accepted at face value by Islam. It was, rather, filtered through that view of the world which Mohammed had given to the Muslims, a view which he enshrined in the Holy Koran, or *Qur'an* (*c.* AD 625) and which was developed also in the *Sunna* – a record of the Prophet's own – divinely inspired – behaviour. So it is that the *Qu'ran* and the *Sunna* between them provided the bases of the first encoded rules for what we have called 'informal' planning.

For the finest of all informal planning: intricate, complex yet consistent, is to be found in cities, towns and villages which were founded as Islam spread, literally from Spain to India and down into South-East Asia.

As Hakim says (1986) Islamic Law itself was extracted from the *Qu'ran* and the *Summa* by al-Shaffi (died 819), al-Bukhari (died 870) and Muslim (died 875). Once a system of Laws had been encoded, others, such as Isa ben Mousa (996) and Ibn al-Rami (1334) extracted and codified *Akham* or building solutions out of the more general Laws.

Hakim (1986) analyses the Principles behind these 'solutions', finding that each is based, directly, on specific verses from the *Qur'an* or the Prophet's own practices from the *Sunna*. Hakim analyses these in terms of their effects on the form of the Islamic city. He distinguishes between the public street (the *Shari*) which is open to everyone and the cul-de-sac (the *Fina*) giving access to a small group of houses belonging in co-ownership, to those who live along it. The Principles include those of:

1. *Harm:* by which one is encouraged to exercise one's personal rights to the full, provided that in doing so one causes no harm to others.

Guidelines of many kinds were derived from this including those concerned with locations within the city for activities that caused

smoke, created offensive smells, made offensive amounts of noise and
so on. Other Principles included:

2. *Interdependence:* by which people within the city and the structures
   they inhabit are considered interdependent in what we would call
   an ecological sense.
3. *Privacy:* by which every family is entitled to acoustic, visual, and
   other kinds of privacy.

Given the nature of the Muslim family and the way in which the
women had to be protected from the eyes of strangers, there were strict
rules indeed against overlooking of any kind. These affected the
positions of windows including their height above the street so that
people could not see in. Nor should doors or windows face each other
directly across the *Fina* into someone else's doorway or windows.
Above all, visual corridors of any kind had to be avoided, which of
course led inevitably to irregularities in façade design. Nor should one
be able to look into any part of one's neighbour's premises, especially
the courtyard and the roof where his women might be. Even the
Muezzin, as he climbs the minaret of the mosque to call the faithful to
prayer, is forbidden to overlook neighbouring premises.

There are Principles also concerning:

4. *Original usage:* which means that older and established uses such as
   the positioning of windows, party walls and so on, have prior rights
   over any later uses and especially over new proposals.
5. *Building higher:* consisting, surprisingly, of a right to build ventilation towers, and so on, as high as one pleases, provided they are

Fig. 1.10 Tunis: plan of the *Suq* south
of the Zaytuna Mosque (*c.* 668–800 AD)
(from Hakim, 1986).

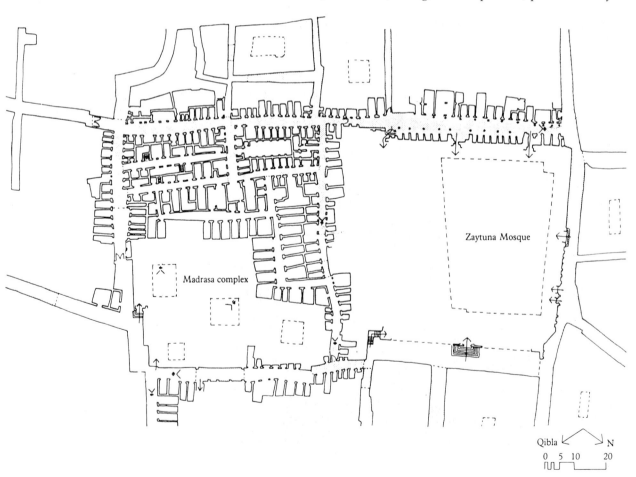

contained within one's own air space. This right applies even if such building will deprive one's neighbours of air and sun. It will be refused, however, where there was evidence of intent to harm one's neighbour(s).

6. *Respect* for the property of others.

7. *Pre-emption:* by which in selling one's property one must, in the interests of keeping building lots together, offer first refusal to one's neighbour(s), adjacent property-owner(s), or even one's partner.

There were Principles too about the widths of thoroughfares and alleys (*sharis* and *finas*) which determined:

8. Seven cubits as the minimum width of public *sharis*. A cubit is about half a metre and this dimension allows two fully laden camels to pass without colliding.

As Hakim points out, a fully laden camel might be seven cubits high which gives a minimum of headroom under any building which spans across the street.

The *fina* of course may be narrower than the *shari* but at least one laden camel should be able to pass down it so the minimum width will have to be four cubits. There are clear rules too as to what may and may not be allowed to encroach on the street, so:

9. Any public thoroughfare should never be obstructed by permanent or even temporary obstructions.

Each owner, however, had a right to use that part of the *fina* immediately outside his house for the loading and unloading of his beasts, and so on, but still he had no right to block the *fina*.

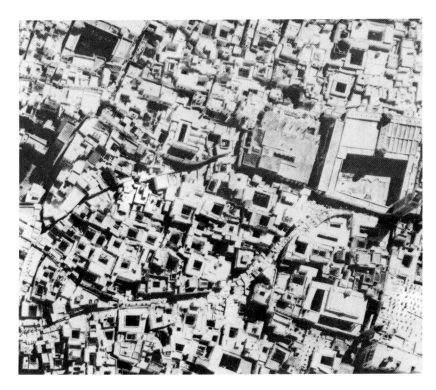

Fig. 1.11 Tunis: aerial view of the *Suq* south of the Zaytuna Mosque (from Hakim, 1986).

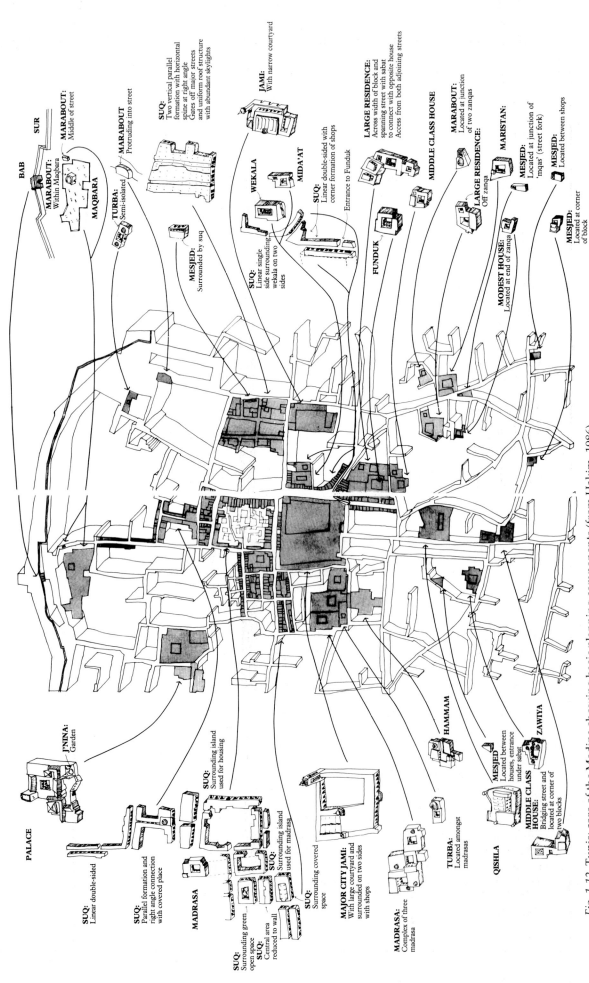

BAB

SUR

MARABOUT: Middle of street

MARABOUT: Within Maqbara

MAQBARA

TURBA: Semi-isolated

MARABOUT Protruding into street

SUQ: Two vertical parallel formation with horizontal spine at right angle Gates off major streets and uniform roof structure with abundant skylights

JAMI: With narrow courtyard

MESJED: Surrounded by suq

WEKALA

MIDA'AT

SUQ: Linear single side surrounding wekala on two sides

SUQ: Linear double-sided with corner formation of shops Entrance to Funduk

LARGE RESIDENCE: Across width of block and spanning street with sabat to connect with opposite house Access from both adjoining streets

FUNDUK

MIDDLE CLASS HOUSE

MARABOUT: Located at junction of two zanqas

LARGE RESIDENCE: Off zanqa

MARISTAN:

MESJED: Located at junction of 'mqas' (street fork)

MODEST HOUSE: Located at end of zanqa

MESJED: Located between shops

MESJED: Located at corner of block

PALACE

J'NINA: Garden

SUQ: Linear double-sided

SUQ: Parallel formation and right angle connection with covered place

MADRASA

SUQ: Surrounding island used for housing

SUQ: Surrounding island used for madrasa

SUQ: Surrounding green open space

SUQ: Central area reduced to wall

MAJOR CITY JAMI: With large courtyard and surrounded on two sides with shops

SUQ: Surrounding covered space

MADRASA: Complex of three madrasa

TURBA: Located amongst madrasas

QISHLA

HAMMAM

MESJED: Located between houses, entrance under sabat

ZAWIYA

MIDDLE CLASS HOUSE: Bridging street and located at corner of two blocks

Fig. 1.12 Tunis: core of the Medina showing basic planning components (from Hakim, 1986).

Naturally enough there are Principles concerning party walls and rights of support. Nor is it surprising, given the origins of Islam in Arabia, that there should be Principles too concerning the use of water, including run-off rainwater and waste, the maintenance of drainage channels and cesspits and, most particularly, the rights of neighbours to make use of any water surplus to the owner's needs.

As Hakim points out, each of these Principles forms part of an urban language and each of them too has a name which is deeply embedded in Arabic. And of course there were regional variations depending on local climate, not to mention indigenous ways of building which would have been established before the Arabs arrived. These were assimilated as appropriate, just as ancient kinds of science had been assimilated into Islam.

Having outlined the bases of Islamic planning law, Hakim then goes on to analyse their applications in the City of Tunis, showing how the layout of the streets, the locations of offensive uses, the avoidance of visual corridors, the niceties of party-wall construction, the drainage of rain and waste water all contributed to the fine-grained planning of the city (Figs 1.10–1.12).

As Hakim shows, it is very much easier to find examples of Islamic planning which still show very clearly the solutions than it is to find examples of Classical planning. One can still find pockets in what were the major cities of Islam in Spain, such as Granada and Seville. Across the Straits of Gibraltar too in Tangier, Fez, Marrakesh, and other Moroccan cities, examples are easy to find as, indeed, they are along the northern coast of Africa as far as, and certainly including, Cairo.

As Hakim also points out, there are regional variations even along the width of this single Continent and as one goes further east into Saudi Arabia and beyond the variations proliferate according to climate, available building materials, and so on.

But the overall impression, one finds, say in the *souks* of Marrakesh, is of an urban labyrinth of tiny streets, often covered, straight for short sections within their length but generally turning, twisting, opening into each other and into obviously private courtyards and so on.

Medieval planning 1: The Dark Ages

It was really the Christian Church that kept civilized values alive in Europe during the Dark Ages, riven as it was by invasions by the Ostrogoths, the Huns, the Visigoths, the Alans, the Sueves, the Slavs and the Vandals. The Vandals even passed across Europe into Spain and, eventually, into North Africa (429) and stayed there until Justinian drove them back (533).

So it is hardly surprising that the first Christian monasteries were set up on the further fringes of Europe, in Ireland including Clonnard (*c.* 520) and Bangor (559), that Irish monks moved north to Iona in 563, east to Lindisfarne (635), Jarrow, Wearmouth and Whitby (664) and then south, across France, to Luxiel (*c.* 590), to Fontaine, Anegry, St Gall in Switzerland (610) and Echternach in Luxemburg (698) (Fig. 1.13). (See Matthew, 1983; Chadwick and Evans, 1987.)

In 597 however Augustine landed in Kent with 40 monks and founded a different kind of religious establishment: the episcopate with its cathedral and its bishopric (the bishop's office). The King of Kent was converted to Christianity and gave his palace to Augustine. His daughter married and brought York into the fold, thus episcopates were established in London (604), York (625), Winchester (676) and Hexham (678).

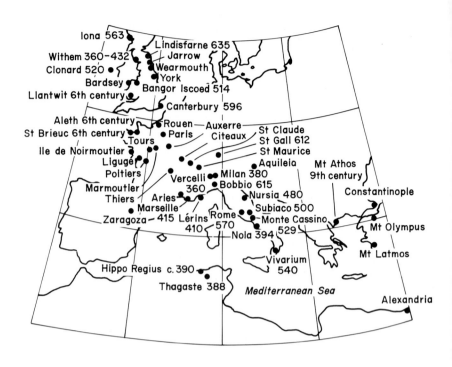

Fig. 1.13 Europe showing the spread
of Monasticism 320–612 AD (based on
Chadwick and Evans, 1987).

● Monastic community
563 date of foundation

Augustine and the other bishops brought with them the ancient
Roman concepts of law and property not to mention an ecclesiastical
hierarchy to administer these things. As Korn says (1953) the Church
imposed on to the peasants' code of living such things as central
control, discipline, written charters and legacies. Eventually the whole
of England was divided into sees, each with its own cathedral and
bishopric. The sees were divided further into parishes, each clustering
around its own church. The bishopric was responsible, not merely for
the spiritual welfare of the citizens but also for their financial and legal
affairs. Nor was its influence confined to the city; it extended, rather,
over the whole diocese.

So once a cathedral had been established, a sizeable community
would grow up around it. As Pirenne says (1925) monasteries would
be built in and around such cities not to mention ecclesiastical schools.
The bishop and his administrative staff, the monks, the teachers and
their students, of course would all need services of various kinds;
which meant that the city also had to have its 'servitors and artisans'.
Everyone needed food so there would be weekly markets to which
peasants and tenant farmers could bring their produce from the
surrounding countryside.

Some cathedrals, such as London, Winchester and York, were built
within the walls of Roman cities and this was much to the advantage of
the bishop. Since the cities were walled, tolls could be collected at the
gates and these were raised on 'everything that came in or went out'.
Saint Peter had been martyred outside the walls of Rome, so his
cathedral had been built outside them too (*c.* AD 155) but that did not
stop the Visigoths from sacking the city itself in 410.

Yet the building of cathedrals, and even monasteries, continued
even in the more vulnerable parts of Europe, almost up to the Slavonic
border. These included cathedrals at Ohrduf (730) and Fulda (744)

whilst some of the most easterly monasteries included Friesing, Passau, Regensburg and Salzburg (all 739).

Arab influences in Europe

We know from history, of course, that Arabs carried Islam along the north coast of Africa (from AD 641 onwards) and converted the Berbers to Islam who, with their converters, came to be known as the Moors. Having moved to the north-west tip of Africa, the Moors crossed the Straits of Gibraltar then moved up and into Spain (from 711) and even into France (where Charles Martel turned them back at Poitiers in 732) (Fig. 1.14). But as the Arabs passed through what is now Tunisia they converted the Carthaginians who, as Saracens, also did their own invading of Europe (see Daniel (1975) for a discussion of these terms).

The precepts of Islam itself, and the nature of family life, forced irregularity on to Moslem urban design and, most particularly, on to the layout of housing. But many cities of medieval Europe also were irregular. Since few cities developed very much during Europe's Dark Ages, it is important that we establish just how much the cities of 'the Recovery' of civilization in Europe owed to Arab precedents. Many of them, but by no means all, were almost as irregular as Islamic cities.

The great Islamic cities on the mainland of Europe, of course, were those which the Moors built in Andalucia. There are substantial, not to say magnificent, remains of their building in Cordoba, Granada and elsewhere.

But apart from 19th century pastiches, there are few signs of Islamic influence on architecture or planning elsewhere in mainland Europe. Since Roman times, indeed, Europe has drawn far more inspiration from Italy than ever it has from Spain.

If we can find traces of Islamic architecture and planning in Italy, however, we might well find that Islam had effects on the design of

Fig. 1.14 Arab expansions across the Near East, North Africa and Europe 634 to 808 AD (based on Kinder and Hilgemann, 1964).

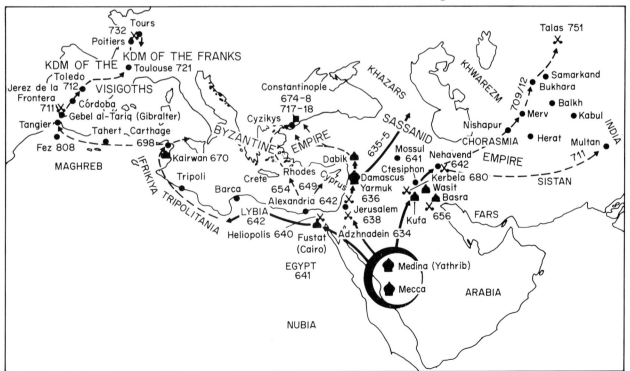

European cities, not to mention individual buildings. So we need to
know whatever we can find of Islamic architecture and planning in
Italy.

We know from the histories anyway that Sardinia was occupied by
Saracens in AD 827. We know also that they occupied Sicily (c. 827)
Corsica (850) and Malta (870). By 891 also a group of Saracens had
seized and fortified a villa at la Garde-Freinet, between Fréjus and St
Tropez, which they used as a base for raiding other parts of Provence,
not to mention the western coast of Italy. Arles, Aix, Fréjus itself and
Genoa were all abandoned after such raids and the raiding continued
for eighty years or so.

Daniel (1975) draws on such medieval historians as Erchembert (of
Monte Casino), Hincmar and Liutprand to paint a picture of almost
continuous Saracen raids, especially on the Ligurian coast, but little in
the way of sustained settlement.

The great river valleys, such as those of the Alanti, the Arno, and the
Arpino provided convenient invasion routes. So did the ancient
Roman Appian Way.

Cities which were so raided along these routes included Pisa and
Florence on the Arno, Siena on the Arbia and Viterbo. Eventually,
according to Hincmar, the Saracens penetrated into the heart of
Umbria as far as Perugia and further over the Appenines to Verona,
Pavia, and even Venice.

Civitavecchia had been besieged as early as 828 but the boldest
Saracen attack was on Rome itself (846).

As Hincmar says (quoted Daniel, 1975):

> The Arabs and the Moors assaulted Rome . . . and when they had
> laid waste the basilica of the blessed Peter . . . and carried off all
> the ornaments and treasures (including) the very altar . . . they
> occupied a strongly fortified hill (on the River Garigliano) a
> hundred miles away from the city. . . .

The Garigliano runs to the sea some 90 miles south of Rome from the
direction of Montecassino. Here the Saracens established a fortress
(which they held until 915) where they could keep their wives, their
children, their prisoners and their goods.

Between Rome and Pisa, the Saracen invasions were essentially
destructive. Montecassino itself was sacked in 883, Farfa in 890, Amalfi
and Sabina in 897. The destruction of Rosselle in 935 encouraged the
development of towns further inland such as Viterbo and Siena.

In the 840s too, according to Liutprand:

> . . . Arabs came from Africa with ships and occupied Calabria,
> Apulia, Benevento and almost all the cities of the Romans, so that
> the Romans held half and the Africans half of each city.

There are indeed, as Daniel says, fine dividing lines between
raiding, destruction, settlement and colonization. And as Guidoni
(1979) says, even if there were clear cultural and economic barriers in
the 9th century, it is difficult for us to trace them now.

So in addition to Saracen military expeditions there was a fair
amount of trading between the areas they occupied, those which were
still part of the (decaying) Byzantine Empire (around Ravenna and
Rome, also southern Italy) and those occupied by the Lombards (from
744).

We do know, however, that Taranto (on the instep of Italy) became a
Saracen Emirate in 842 as did Bari (behind the heel) in 847.

So one would expect to find traces of Saracen occupation in these cities, not to mention Reggio di Calabria, Brindisi and Gallipoli.

Historical records, in any case, tell us only half the story and Guidoni looks for other kinds of evidence including the survival of Arabic words in describing parts of the city. But above all Guidoni looks for physical traces of Saracen building in Italy.

Whilst much of it is overlaid with later planning, including that of the Normans who drove the Arabs out, Guidoni indeed finds many examples of the kind of planning he seeks, in the cities of Sicily, certainly, such as Palermo, Sambuca, Agrigento and Castelvetrano, at Fiumedicini and Agro in Messina, Mineo, Castronovo, Caccama, Salemiu and Sutern.

There are various ways, as Guidoni (1979) says, of looking for evidence of a former Arab presence. He suggests that we might look at traditional costumes, at the survival, 'translated' into Italian, of Islamic legends and traditions. Above all, of course, we should look at urban layouts which display the unmistakable signs of labyrinthine planning, with tortuous, blind alleys, very narrow, often covered and ending in private courtyards. We should look for typically Islamic discontinuities, irregular aggregations of houses, the all-of-a-piece organic planning which is so characteristic of Islam.

We might look at constructional techniques, methods of planning and so on, particularly the hierarchy of various kinds of street. He also looks for typically Islamic distinctions between fortified areas and residential areas, the articulation of the dwelling areas within the Arab *medina* and the various *borghi* called *rabati* in Arabic.

The hierarchy of spaces within Islamic planning corresponds to what Guidoni calls a *quartier* occupied by an ethnic tribal group, or even a family clan.

Even where they were built many such developments have been lost or prove difficult to trace since often they were built on to classical layouts and themselves overlaid by later, Byzantine or Norman constructions. What had been a mosque might well have been converted into a church. Even so, according to Guidoni the necessary traces are to be found in a hundred cities, large and small, in various parts of Italy.

They rarely occur in grand, monumental structures. They survive, rather, in methods of construction (which may still be in use), in the typologies of planning and of actual building, not to mention decorative motifs, however much these may have been distorted over the years.

As in Spain, so in Italy cities which had been almost entirely Islamic might have been changed for various reasons: military, general urban viability – the need, for instance, to accommodate different means of transport – and even for aesthetic reasons. So streets might be widened and straightened, dead-end alleyways opened up, and so on.

Sicily

So it was with ideas of this kind that Guidoni looked, first of all, at cities in Sicily. Naturally he found innumerable examples of what he called the urban labyrinth in Palermo (Fig. 1.15) (de Seta and di Mauro, 1980), Trapani, Marsala, Mazara, Sciacca, Syracuse, Agrigento, Enna and Messina. These all displayed traces of Islamic planning, not only in the physical structures themselves but also in such things as street names. He found many variations also of the Arabic *shari* – or street – such as Sera, Xera, Xuerai, Shera, Seri and so on. Even in the landscape he found evidence of Islamic irrigation systems.

Fig. 1.15 Palermo: survivals of Arabic
Planning (from Lossieux, 1818 in de
Seta and di Mauro, 1980).

Guidoni produces many illustrations of places such as Sambuca
which show alleyways and courtyards clearly Islamic in origin. His
aerial views of Bari also, not to mention Taranto, Brindisi and Amalfi all
reveal their bases in Islamic layouts.

Italian peninsula

Guidoni also shows that Islamic planning underlies the forms of such
cities in Calabria and Basilicata as Sassi, Matera, and above all Taranto
and Bari. He finds similar planning in Lecce, Gallipoli, Bitonto,
Grotaglie, Martina Franca, Massafra, Altamura, Lucera, Ostuni and so
on. In Altamura, for instance, there are several examples of alleyway –
courtyard planning of a thoroughly Islamic kind. Lucera too has a large
Saracenic nucleus.

Some of these cities indeed show the co-existence of Christian and
Islamic cultures – of the kind which Luitprand described, with the
Romans and the Africans living side-by-side in, presumably, peaceful
co-existence. These include various ports from Salerno to Positano not
to mention Amalfi and Naples.

He finds evidence of similar co-existence, the uninterrupted flow of
cultural and economic exchanges in Campania during the 9th and 10th
centuries.

But eventually the Moslems were driven out of Europe. The Pisans,
in particular, took the initiative. Thus they were driven from Reggio
Calabria in 1005, Corsica and Sardinia (1051–52), Palermo (1072) (Fig.
1.15).

As the Pisans and others drove the Saracens out, of course, they
must have found that the Islamic urban labyrinth made their task most
particularly difficult. No doubt they learned from this experience that

complex planning of the kind which the Laws of Islam determined, made for exceedingly good defence. Which may have been one reason why complex planning, not, it is true, identical with Islamic planning, began to permeate the design of many, but by no means all, of the cities of medieval Europe.

The logic of informal space

Whilst it is easy to see that gridded cities must be planned according to geometric rules and the irregular cities of Islam by, as it were, social rules it seems unlikely that rules of any kind underlay the initial development – as distinct from any later regulation by planning laws – of the irregular medieval city.

Such cities seem to be organic growths, dependent on the exigencies of the terrain; the positions of ridges and valleys, rocky outcrops and so on.

Yet Hillier and Hanson argue (1984) that even the most irregular layouts are determined by *The Social Logic of Space*. Their arguments are truly medieval in complexity starting as they do (without defining them) from the biological concepts of genotype – the genetic constitution of a living organism, and phenotype – the organism as it actually appears as distinct from its genetic constitution.

This biological analogy leads them to think of spaces within buildings, and even of buildings themselves – as cells which they see as linked, or otherwise related – according to genotypes. Now clearly there is no DNA, within individual rooms or buildings, for passing instructions from one generation to the next as to how they *should* relate to each other. So Hillier and Hanson look instead for the geometric, or rather topological rules, which seem to determine such relationships.

A cell for them may be one of two things: an enclosed space with a boundary consisting, presumably, of a floor, walls and a ceiling or roof. It has an inside, an outside, an entry and a threshold. The latter two may join their enclosed cell to one of their other kind, an open cell; open, that is, to the sky and defined only by the boundary walls, of whatever closed cells may surround it.

Hillier and Hanson describe certain topological rules by which their cells may, or may not, be connected. An enclosed cell, for instance, may be connected to another one by a 'full facewise join' forming, as it were, a party wall. In that case one would cover the ground with pairs of cells somewhat like semi-detached houses!

But then they add another rule: that 'at least one face of each cell should be free of a facewise join'. Which means that it can have full face connections with up to three other cells as long as each enclosed cell is adjacent to at least one open cell forming, as it were, a courtyard enclosed by cells on two, three or even four sides (Fig. 1.16). Certain ancient cities, such as Catal Huyuk in Asian Turkey – which may be the first of all cities – display planning of this kind in parts.

Hillier and Hanson draw useful parallels between their topological rules for clustering cells together and the rules of syntax which, according to scholars such as Chomsky (1957), we apply, subconsciously when we are speaking or writing grammatically correct sentences.

Having described such rules in the abstract, Hillier and Hanson then look at certain clumps of buildings in the Vaucluse area of Southern France. The smallest of these, such as Crevoulin, consist of no more than six buildings with, as Hillier and Hanson say: 'total heterogeneity

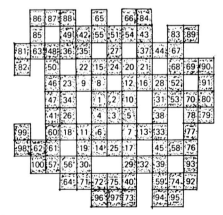

Fig. 1.16 Hillier: Random, full-face aggregation of square cells each with one wall free of other cells (from Hillier and Hanson, 1984, *The Social Logic of Space*, Cambridge University Press).

of plan'. But as they look at larger settlements, 'a certain global regularity seems to appear'. Perrotet, for instance, has some forty buildings which appear irregular on plan. 'Yet as a place to walk about or experience, it seems to possess order of another, more subtle, more intricate kind'.

Such impressions, they say, are reinforced when they enumerate its spatial properties such as:

1. Each building fronts directly, with no intervening boundary, on to some part of the hamlet's general open-space structure.
2. The hamlet is not grouped around a single, central open space; it is, rather, a linear sequence of connected spaces, rather like beads on a string, some wider, some narrower than the others, according to how the buildings enclose them.
3. As the settlement grows larger, the spaces remain connected in this bead-like way but in rings. One of these rings emerges as the strongest global characteristic of the complex but with a growing number of sub-rings.
4. Each beady ring of spaces is formed between an inner clump of buildings and a series of outer clumps.
5. The buildings which form the outer ring of clumps provide a boundary to the settlement which may give it the appearance of a finite, even finished object.
6. Since each building has at least one opening on to one of the beads in the various rings the complex as a whole has a high degree of permeability. What is more the buildings are mutually accessible; there are by definition at least two ways from any building to any other building.

So for Hillier and Hanson this beady ring structure is a genotype for all the settlements in the Vaucluse which they analysed.

Behind it they find a remarkably straightforward explanation. They program their computer with two rules: firstly that each closed cell be linked to an open cell by a full facewise join on the entrance face to form a doublet, and secondly that these doublets are allowed to aggregate randomly in such a way that each new (doublet) added to the surface joins its open cell full facewise on to at least one other open cell. As that program is run, the result is a global beady ring effect which results, not from the imposition of some overall form as in, say, the gridded city, but a spatio-temporal unfolding of the local rule.

Fig. 1.17 'G', a small town in the Var Region of France showing Hillier's aggregation in practice (from Hillier and Hanson, 1984, *The Social Logic of Space*, Cambridge University Press).

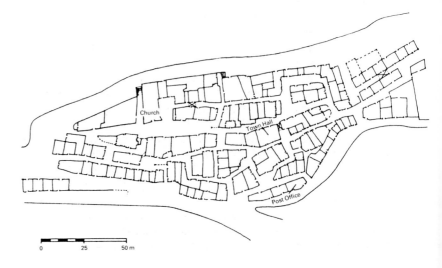

They liken this to the way in which a cloud of midges might form. No midge, obviously, has any sense of a grand design and even if it had, there is no way in which it could convey this grand design to other midges! But 'if each midge moves randomly until half its field of vision is clear of (other) midges then moves in the direction of (the) midges (as a whole) the result will be a stable cloud'.

The crucial point, of course, is that a global form has been generated, but not on the basis of some global plan. The cloud, rather, is 'the global, collective product of a system in which discrete organisms follow a purely local rule . . . a rule relating each . . . only to whatever other individuals happen to be in the vicinity at the time'. So: 'the design of the global object . . . is not located in a particular spatio-temporal region: it is *distributed* through the collection'. So 'global order emerges of its own accord from a . . . locally ordered system' (Fig. 1.17).

Clearly that could happen even on the flattest of sites and once one applies such thinking to the irregular, sloping sites on which so many medieval cities were founded the pressures towards irregular urban planning of course were even stronger.

Medieval planning 2: European recovery

As Europe recovered from her Dark Ages some of the new urban forms came from the invaders themselves. As if invasions in Southern Europe were not enough Vikings who had come from Norway began to attack north-west Europe in 793 with their raid on Lindisfarne. After which much of Britain and the European coasts, from Belgium to Provence, were vulnerable to attack by these Norsemen. And just as the Moslems founded cities in Spain so the Norsemen founded cities in Britain and the Netherlands not to mention Nantes (799) aand Rouen (911).

As trade routes between northern Europe and the Mediterranean were cut by these invasions so many cities were deserted or at least fell into decline. Some of the old Roman cities survived, however, because they were walled.

But by the 9th century, as Pirenne (1925) suggests, these, even with the cathedral cities and the monasteries, were by no means sufficient to resist the various invaders. The walls of existing cities had to be strengthened, rebuilt, and properly fortified.

The Danes for instance surrounded their settlements with defensive earthworks surmounted by stockades and these were called burghs from which our borough derives. And even after the Vikings had settled in north-west France – becoming in the process Normans – they continued to raid the kingdom of the Franks to the south and east of them.

So the local lord would build a fortified house for his family and his retainers. As Hohler points out (1966) there was not much protection in a timber-framed house however well fortified it might be. The Vikings, for instance, used to wait until their hosts were very drunk, then they burned their houses around them. He suggests, indeed, that it would have been considered unsporting to have built in fireproof construction. As early as 992 however Fulk Nerra's two-storey fortified Hall at Langeais in Anjou was built of stone.

In the 9th century indeed Charles the Bald had ordered the Franks to fortify every place that could be used defensively. So they built – mostly timber – towers, on rocky outcrops or natural hills wherever they could. And where there were no such features they built artificial mounds instead, anything from 10 to 200 feet high. These mounds are called mottes and they were encircled by ditches. Of course it occurred to some of the lords that if their towers were big enough, they could live in them, with their families and retainers. These larger defensive towers are called keeps.

Edward the Confessor introduced them into England from France (1042–1066) and, after the invasion of 1066, William the Conquerer built some 49 of them. His barons built another 50 but even at this late date all but four of them were built of timber.

As methods of attack became more sophisticated, the keep on its motte was by no means enough so, as Hohler says, the motte would be surrounded by a ward or bailey with a battlemented curtain wall around it. And thus the castle was formed. The bailey would be more or less circular, according to the exigencies of the site, and in a fully developed castle there might be an outer bailey and an outer curtain wall surrounding all this.

Not that castles of this sophistication were built in western Europe until after the Crusaders had been to the eastern Mediterranean (1096 onwards) and seen for themselves what the Byzantines and the Moslems of that region, the Saracens, had been building (Boase, 1967). There was nothing in the West like the walls of Constantinople (Fig. 1.18); a triple line of moat, outer terrace and wall, inner terrace and an even greater wall with towers up to about 60 feet high built by Theodosius II around 578–582. The Saracens, too, seem to have been building proper castles (in Armenia) as early as 650 or so (see Grabar, 1973).

Like these, the European castles were built for defence but any sizeable community, be it a castle, a cathedral city, a monastery, attracted farmers with their produce and other traders. In the case of castles also people huddled round them for protection. Such a settlement is known as a *burgus*, from which the English word borough derives.

Of course the castellan encouraged such developments. They were in his interests for once a *burgus* had been established he could exercise the kind of financial and legal authority which had been the province of the church.

So a city might have started as a town, old Roman, cathedral, monastic or whatever, or it might have started as a *burgus* round a castle.

But of course the Europeans needed confidence before their cities could be developed any further. This started to grow in Europe again after Otto I had turned back the Magyars near Augsburg in 955. By the end of the 10th century the Moors – and the (Christian) Byzantines – were being driven out of southern Italy. And in 1005 the Pisans even

Fig. 1.18 Walls of Constantinople (from Zorzi, 1980).

defeated the Saracens at sea. By 1015 they had established themselves in Sardinia. They even occupied Bona, North Africa for a while in 1034. Then having occupied Sicily (1058–90) and Corsica (1091) the Pisans began to reassert their Christian presence in, and even to control, the Mediterranean.

So it was that in 1096 the Christians of northern Europe were emboldened to embark on the first Crusade, hoping to recapture the Holy Land from the Saracens. But still for the First and even for the Second Crusade (1147) they found it prudent to treck overland by way of Constantinople.

Once the invasions had been halted, Europe recovered very quickly. In AD 1000 or so, most of the land was covered by forest. With the renewal of confidence, however, villagers in many parts of Europe began to clear the forests around their villages and bring the land into agricultural use. Others, even more hungry for land, migrated to the unoccupied uplands. As more food became available so the population grew. Indeed it has been estimated that whilst the population of Europe may have been 30 million in the year 1000, it had probably grown by 40% during the next 150 years. As the population grew, so abbots and bishops began to plan new towns outside the gates of their monasteries and cathedrals, as did lay lords below the gates of their castles. They realized as entrepreneurs, promoters and speculators that towns could be valuable and continuing sources of income.

Since their walls had gates traffic could be controlled, as in the cathedral cities. Here also duty could be levied on everything that passed through, into or out of the town.

City walls and gates served such purposes at least until the French Revolution (1789) (see Fig. 5.2). Indeed it was the building of a wall and gates by Ledoux that actually triggered the Revolution.

But in the Middle Ages, as Mumford says (1938, 196), the wall served other psychological functions. For given such a wall (p. 54):

> One was either in or out of the city; one belonged or one did not belong. When the town gates were locked at sundown, and the portcullis was drawn, the city was insulated from the outside world. As in a ship, the wall helped create a feeling of unity between the inhabitants: in a siege or famine the morality of the shipwreck – share-and-share-alike – developed easily.

Once individual (burgage) plots had been set out within the new town they would be made available to all comers on a first come and first served basis. Each burgage holder was required to build a house on his plot within a stated time, usually one year.

So new towns were founded and by the 11th century, there was a real commercial revival centred in Venice and on the Flemish coast at Bruges (Beresford, 1967). Bruges was particularly well placed as a centre of trade between northern Europe – including Britain – and the Mediterranean. Indeed Pirenne argues (1925) that the cities of northern Europe, and especially in Flanders which he studied, began to develop and expand specifically because of this international trade. Flanders was well placed for trade across the Baltic, the North Sea and down the River Rhine. So entrepreneurs in Flanders were well placed to import wool from England, weave it to make their very fine cloaks and export these back to England.

But by 1150 they were sending their cloaks to trade fairs in Champagne, south of Paris. These, not to mention furs from northern Europe, could be traded for French wine. But the fairs also attracted merchants from Lombardy, in northern Italy, who brought with them

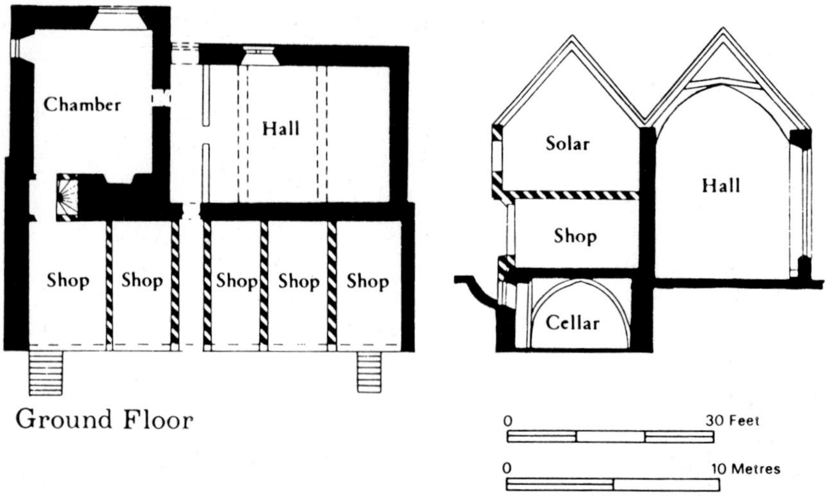

Ground Floor

Fig. 1.19 Oxford: Tackley's Inn. Late
13th or early 14th century.
Reconstruction by A. W. Pantin (from
Platt, 1976).

not only produce from the Mediterranean but also more exotic goods
from the Orient, such as Arab and Byzantine silks imported into Italy
through Venice.

The presence of the merchants naturally attracted artisans and
indeed as Pirenne says (1937) there was a real, if limited, Industrial
Revolution. Thus it was in Flanders particularly that manufacturing
and trading began to be developed side by side which, naturally, had
its effects on the form of the medieval city.

Even though the city may have been started according to a regular
plan, it may have been continued on quite irregular lines. The sites
most desirable for entrepreneurs within the town: merchants, artisans
and so on, were those immediately surrounding the market place. So
rent structures too helped determine the form of the town for rents
naturally varied according to location (see Platt, 1976). According to
Burke (1975) plots adjoining the market place, used for shops,
commanded the highest rents. Indeed as Platt suggests (1976) there
was a premium on sites with desirable frontages which might be taxed
to encourage efficient planning. Platt shows ingenious developments
in King's Lynn, Oxford and other places, planned so that street
frontages were occupied by several shops but with a single large
residence behind them (Fig. 1.19).

Second-best to frontages on the market-place itself were those on
streets which lead to it from the gates: anything else was third-best and
suitable only for housing.

But as Pirenne suggests (1937) as more and more traders flocked into
the cities the sites within them were filled. So they had to settle outside
the city and build for themselves a new burg immediately against the
walls of the old one. Or: to use the term which exactly describes it, a
foris-burgus faubourg, i.e. an outside burg (Fig. 1.20).

The term survives, of course, in the Faubourgs St-Antoine, St-
Germain and St-Honore in Paris. The merchants built their faubourgs,
when they could, just outside the gates of the existing city where they
would form secondary market places (Fig. 1.21).

As the merchants themselves became rich enough, and their
faubourgs grew, so they too built walls or pallisades. Which meant that
others had to start new faubourgs outside theirs and thus the cities
grew in concentric but irregular loops. So it was that close to the old
ecclesiastical towns or feudal fortresses, mercantile agglomerations
were constructed; Hillier-like 'clouds of midges' on a very large scale
indeed.

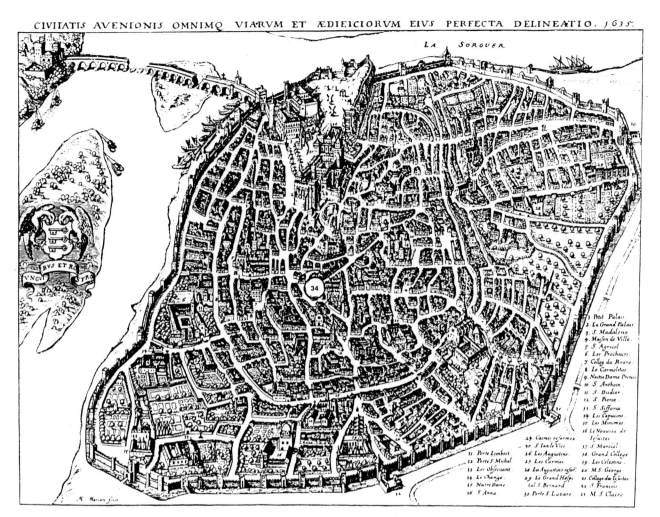

Fig. 1.20 Avignon showing concentric developments within the city walls and faubourgs (from Saalman, n.d.).

Medieval planning 3: Irregular

There were several reasons therefore why so many medieval cities were irregular; including the nature of the sites on which they were built, often initially for defensive purposes, the facts of topology which Hillier and Hanson describe, influences from Islam and so on. As Mumford says (1938) (p. 53) the medieval builders had 'no a priori love for symmetry as such'. Where it was simpler to 'follow nature's contours' they did so rather than grading them down or evening them up.

Nor were regular streets needed to accommodate wheeled vehicles. Mules were used for transport so the streets could be even narrower than those of Islam which had to accommodate laden camels! And since wells or springs were used as sources of water, steep, rocky sites could be just as good as low lying, rather level ones. So, according to Mumford:

> it is by its persistent power of adaption to site and to practical needs that the mediaeval town presented such multiform examples of individuality; the planner made use of the irregular, the accidental, the unexpected; and by the same token, he was not averse to symmetry and regularity when, as in the frontier towns, the plan could be laid out in a single step on fresh land.

Fig. 1.21 Medieval Paris (early 17th
century print) (from Hiorns, 1956).

So it is that the surviving irregularities of many medieval plans 'are
due to streams that have been covered over, trees that have been cut
down, old balks that once defined (the) rural fields'.

But as Kostoff points out (1985), apart from the site itself there were
pressures of other kinds towards building in certain ways. Some of the
first planning statutes, for instance, were enacted for Siena in 1262,
and, as Saalman suggests (n.d.) the public records of towns all over
Europe abound with statutes governing such things as street width,
frontage lines, the minimum heights at which the upper storeys might
be cantilevered over the street and so on.

Indeed there was a tendency, as Saalman says, for owners to
encroach upon the street. They could get away with doing so to the
extent that they held personal political power. In extreme cases, such
as the Venetian *sottoportici* the houses actually were bridged across the
street whilst in others, such as the Shambles in York, the upper storeys
projected until they almost touched.

There were regulations too about materials. As Korn (1953) says
(p. 51) the lord might want to sell his own timber and stone. In some
places too there were regulations about the use of fireproof materials:
brick, stone, tile and so on. For a town of close-packed timber-framed
and thatched houses would be a veritable firetrap.

It will be helpful, if we are to clarify relationships between land
formation, *ad-hoc* building and civic legislation on the form of the
medieval city, to look at one of the prime examples: the city of Siena, in
which the interplay of these forces was shown with particular clarity.

Medieval planning in Siena

As we have seen, certain of the sites on which medieval cities were
built forced irregularity on to the most tidy-minded planners. That was
true, most certainly, of the rocky outcrops on which castles were built
and the basic irregularity often extended to the cities which were
clustered on the slopes around them (Fig. 1.22).

Individual fortified houses too, such as the towers which survive in
San Gimignano, Bologna and elsewhere would be built where the

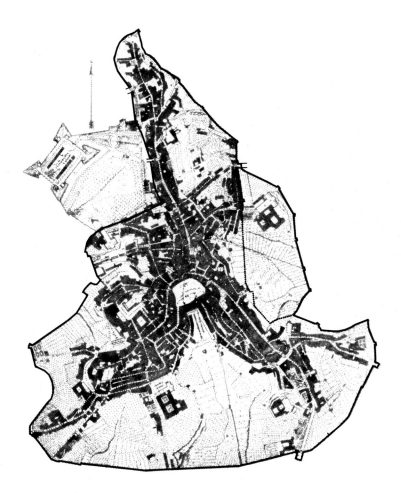

Fig. 1.22 Siena: plan (from Bortolotti, 1983).

ground offered the firmest bearing with no thought for the alignments which any search for urban symmetry and order would have required. Sixteenth century engravings of Siena (see Pellegrini, 1986) show some forty such towers within the city walls and Siena itself is the classic example of a highly irregular city whose forms were dictated, above all, by the exigencies of the site (Fig. 1.23).

Schevill (1909) traced the history of Siena in which, he says, the city clustered originally around the Castel Vecchio built on a ridge to the south of the present city centre.

This ridge drops north and eastwards to meet two others which run in from the north and east. Thus the city is built on a Y-shaped formation of three ridges which radiate, to the south-west, the north-west, and the south-east from the Croce del Travaglio marked, since 1417, by the Loggia della Mercanzia. The roads along these ridges, which start from the Croce are named, in those three orientations, the Via di Cittá, the Banchi di Sopra and the Banchi di Sotto. They pass, with various changes of name, to the three main gates of the city walls: the Porte San Marco to the south-west, Camnolia to the north-west and Romana to the south-east through the three major *Terzi* (Thirds), into which the city is divided: which again in those same orientations are the Terzi di Cittá, di San Martini and di Camollia.

As the Via di Cittá curves southwards from the Croce and di Sotto to the east, they embrace between them the shell-shaped Campo, one of the finest urban spaces in the world (Fig. 1.24). Its scallop-shell form

Fig. 1.23 Siena with Medieval tower-houses (from an engraving by Cock, 1555) (from Pellegrino, 1986).

extends, not merely to its plan – as defined by the buildings which surround it – but also to the dishing of the pavement itself down towards the Palazzo Publico. This dishing amounts to no less than 4.7 metres – over a radius of some 55 metres – and since all the buildings rise sheer from the paving the dishing contributes greatly to the sense of enclosure, of real urban containment that one feels within the Campo of Siena (Fig. 1.25).

In the early days, as Schevill suggests, the 'grandis' of the city built stone or brick houses along the ridges; often rude castles with open courtyards and towers. Engravings from as late as 1555 show some 40 such towers surviving and indeed, Schevill describes one of the *castellare* still standing opposite the Church of Svigilio although it is lacking its tower.

As for the 'common people' they lived, according to Schevill, in rude huts, caves and cellars along the slopes running either side of the ridges.

So in the early days the city would have undulating streets along the ridges, lined with the *castellare*, surrounded on both sides by labyrinths of dark byways.

As for the Campo itself, like many of the world's great urban spaces it is surrounded by buildings which, in themselves, are by no means all distinguished. The Palazzo Publico (started sometime after 1250) is certainly very fine with its stone Gothic arcade at ground level, or, rather, Travertine marble, specifically Sienese because within its pointed arches there are flatter, segmental ones.

The upper stories of the Palazzo are built of brick with Gothic windows each divided, by colonnetes, into three parts. The main block, four bays wide, was completed in 1299 whilst the two-storey wings, each three bays wide and matching the forms of the original, were added between 1305 and 1310. Further stories, supported on cantilevering merlons of brick arches, were added in 1610.

The whole composition was enhanced in 1338–48 when the Torre del Mangio was added at the north-east corner of the extended Palazzo. This rises four-square in brick to a stone turret with battlements, cantilevered on stone merlons, to a total height of 102 metres.

At the foot of the campanile there is the graceful Capella di Piazza, an open loggia started in 1352. This originally was Gothic but in 1468 it was faced with finely chased round Renaissance arches.

The only other building on the Campo to match the Palazzo Publico in style and scale is the Palazzo Sansedoni, built along the north-eastern curve of the scallop shell in 1339. This too has a travertine ground floor – but with rectangular openings and with rectangular openings also to the (brick) first floor. The upper three stories – also brick, however – have the same, tripartite, Gothic windows as those of the Palazzo Publico.

Which is exactly as they should be since in 1297 the Council General of Siena passed an Ordinance to the effect that all the houses on the Campo should have windows 'a colonnelli' to match those of the Palazzo Publico and also 'senza alcuno ballatoio' – that is without any open galleries.

Not that this was by any means the first Ordinance to be passed in Siena with intent to influence the physical form of the city. We like to think that planning legislation, building regulations and bylaws are products of 20th century bureaucracy and that whilst in Classical and Renaissance times architects may well have been constrained by the geometric layouts of their cities, in Europe in the Middle Ages, at least, people were free to build exactly as they pleased, wherever and whenever that may have been. How else can we account for the Picturesque irregularity of the medieval city?

There may well have been haphazard building as Europe recovered from the Dark Ages but even then would-be builders were beholden to some kind of landowner, noble, ecclesiastical or whatever. In the case of Siena the rulers, consecutively, were Lombards, Franks and, by the middle of the 11th century, prince-bishops. But half way through the

Fig. 1.24 Siena: plan of the Campo (from Guidoni, 1971).

Fig. 1.25 Siena: the Campo (author's photograph).

12th century, the prince-bishops were replaced by consuls who set up their own form of government. They in turn were replaced by a Podestà (or mayors) in 1252 and he by a Council of Nine in 1287.

Despite the ever-changeable political position, successive governments of Siena passed: in 1262 a *Costituto*, in 1290 a *Statuto dei Viari* and another *Costituto* in 1308. These contained detailed prescriptions to do with the widths of streets, the forms of windows and other openings on to them, the relationships of buildings to each other, to the street, and so on. Zdekauer (1967), Balestracci and Piccini (n.d.) describe these in some detail.

The *Costituto* of 1262, for instance, clearly was intended to right previous wrongs. Given the nature of the terrain on which they were built, the streets of Siena curved and counter-curved. Individual buildings – particularly private dwellings – projected into them haphazardly. So the *Costituto* prescribes ways in which these could be corrected so that, as far as possible, each street would take a *recta linea* from end to end. This could be achieved by using as a reference point the corner of a building, a pilaster, a tower or whatever; finding another such reference point and stretching a cord between them. Any building which passed beyond this cord, thus forming an obstacle, would be deemed out of line and subject to demolition.

The *Costituto* also prescribed the widths for various kinds of street ranging from six braccia (a braccio is the length from elbow to finger-tip which makes this about three and a half metres) and 8 to 10 braccia (4.7 to 5.9 metres) for more important streets. The main street by the cathedral was considered beautiful and light at 10 braccia, whilst the Cavina di Salicol, larger still, was considered ample, light and luminous.

A *cavina* in this sense was a public street whereas a *treseppio* was a space between two houses – an extremely narrow alley which may be arched over. The *treseppio* according to the *Costituto* of 1309 would be used for household drainage although adjoining owners, apparently, were often 'litigous and pugnacious' about such things. So the *Costituto* of 1309 required drainage channels to be buried and covered over with tiles.

The main streets along the ridges of Siena were paved with stone but this was not necessarily true of the smaller streets which ran parallel, either side of them, along lower contour lines.

Apart from specifying the dimensions of streets, requirements for drainage, and so on, projections over and into the streets were covered by legislation. Projecting galleries, for instance, made narrow streets even darker. So did projecting windows which, in the *Costituto* of 1262, were limited to half a braccia for the six braccia streets.

Like the Arab *fina* too the narrow, Sienese street tended to get cluttered by the users, buying and selling food, craft work and so on. So again in 1357 the Council General introduced penalties for those who encroached on the street too much. As the *Costituto* said, the Council General wanted to confer dignity on their city.

Nor was Siena alone in having such regulations. Bocchi (1987) describes equivalents for a number of medieval cities, including Piacenza, Ferrara, Modena, Bologna, Parma and Regio. In Parma, for instance, streets were to be 10 piedi wide (that is about four metres), in Modena they were 12 piedi, whilst those outside the walls in Ferrara were to be 20 piedi wide.

So, despite appearances, the irregular medieval city was by no means unplanned. Just as Islamic planning law, and practice, determined particular kinds of irregularity, so medieval legislation and practice determined particular – and rather different – kinds.

Medieval regularity

We tend to think of medieval planning, typically, as irregular. But that was by no means always the case; medieval drawings exist of regular, geometric planning. These are plans for monasteries including one for Canterbury (mid 12th century) showing the drainage system and the much earlier design drawing for the Abbey of St Gall (*c.* AD 820–830) (Fig. 1.26). Horn and Born have analysed *The Plan of St Gall* in very great detail (3 volumes from 1979 onwards) and their work is summarized by Lorna Price (1982). As they show, the Plan fits into a 160 foot grid, three squares deep from north to south and four squares wide from east to west. The centre line of the church lies one square in from the northern boundary and the church itself is two squares long.

A large cloister is attached to the south side of the church containing a refectory, quarters for the monks and so on. This central group is

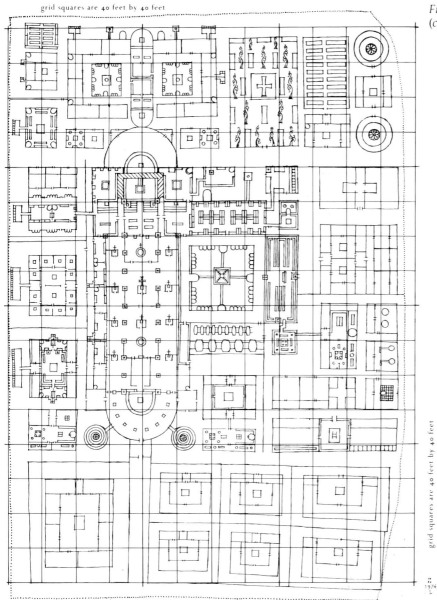

grid squares are 40 feet by 40 feet

grid squares are 40 feet by 40 feet

PLAN OF ST GALL; SHOWING 40 FOOT MODULE SUPERIMPOSED UPON THE ENTIRE SITE OF THE MONASTERY

Fig. 1.26 Monastery of St Gall: plan (*c.* 820–830 AD) (from Price, 1982).

surrounded by many other buildings including an infirmary, quarters for the novices, an abbott's house, a guest house, a hospice for pilgrims and paupers, all with their bath houses, kitchens, bakehouses and brewhouses, workshops, quarters for craftsmen and artisans, a grain store and a mill, orchards and gardens, not to mention houses for hens, geese, sheep and their keepers.

Many of these individual buildings are planned around courtyards; others have fences between them to form rather open blocks. There are streets between some of these blocks so St Gall indeed was planned as a small town might have been. The abbey was never completed to the Plan and what remains these days is heavily encrusted in Baroque.

But (Benedictine) Cluny was even grander (see Conant, 1939, 1954, 1959). It was founded in 910 and the first church there was dedicated around 930. By 1035 there were 20-odd buildings on site (Hourlier, 1964) and during the abbacy of St Hugh (1049–1109) Cluny became the centre of a vast monastic empire stretching as far south as Sicily with some 1100 dependent monasteries in various parts of Europe (Hunt, 1971). But even Cluny was equalled as a monastic centre, if not surpassed, by Citeaux, the heart of St Bernard's (much stricter) Cistercian Order.

At the height of Cistercian expansion, during the 13th century, there were some 742 dependent monasteries and 900 nunneries although some of these were very small. The Cistercians, however, chose to build in remote, if rather beautiful places, and fewer towns, proportionately, were built around their monasteries than those of the more gregarious Benedictines.

So even in the darkest ages monasteries were built, and continued to be built, in enormous numbers. And, according to location they provided the seeds from which many medieval cities grew.

Bastides

The most sophisticated new towns of the Middle Ages were built in the Angevin region of central France. As Korn says (1953), some 300 of them were founded in France between 1220 and 1350. One of the first to build was Alphonse de Poitiers who founded a number of new towns in the Angenais, Central France, between 1253 and 1270.

Since the French word for build is *bâtir* these are known as bastide towns. This part of Périgord was in dispute between the Kings of France and the King of England so these kings also started to build bastides. In return for giving up their land, the owners were granted a town charter, guaranteed protection, freed of military service and given the right of inheritance. Also they elected consuls, although the King's representative, the baillie, collected taxes and dispensed justice.

Raymond VII built some 40 bastides whilst the English King built a dozen of which the most notable, perhaps, are Beaumont (1272), Molieres, Lalinde, Ste-Foy (1255) and Montpazier (1285) (Fig. 1.27).

Beaumont was built around a fortified church whereas Montpazier was a new foundation. According to most urban histories it is the most perfect of the bastides with its rectangular plan, some 400 metres by 220 metres. It is essentially a gridiron plan with five parallel streets and four cross alleys or *carreyrous*. But as Morris shows (1974) this perfect plan never seems to have been achieved. The walls themselves by no means form a perfect rectangle and, or so he suggests, the south-east quarter of the town was never built! There are houses right up to the end walls and one of the four central blocks is given over to an arcaded

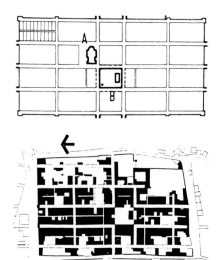

Fig. 1.27 Montpazier, Dordogne (c. 1284). (a) Idealized plan (from Hiorns, 1956) and (b) actual plan (from Morris, 1979).

market place – originally it had a timber roof. There is a church in one of the blocks diagonally adjacent to the market place.

As in other bastides there were narrow gaps between the houses, like the Sienese *treseppii*, called *andrones* and serving as fire-breaks, drains or even latrines. Indeed Morris suggests: 'a ten inch gap between adjoining houses formed a fire-stop and contained the open sewer over which the latrines were corbelled'. The outer walls had gates – opening on to the main streets – and defensive towers at the corners. Indeed as the French and English fought over Périgord, the bastides proved their worth in military and political terms.

But whilst some bastides, such as Montpazier, were laid out in rectangular blocks within rectangular city walls, others were laid out with similar blocks but within circular walls and others again, such as Montsegur, were essentially rectangular but adapted to the contours and also to the natural boundaries of the site.

As Mumford says (1938) rectangular planning has been subject to superficial interpretation: 'particularly by writers who fail to note that the pattern may in fact be as rural in origin as the windings of the most capricious cowpath'.

For of course it may have originated in Roman or later field layouts including, in all probability, the layout of fields in the rectangular strips or plots of feudal agriculture. He sees such layouts as products, not so much of deliberate, geometric planning but as residues of 'plow culture'. Indeed the origins may be even earlier, in rectilinear layouts of post-and-beam construction on which prehistoric lake villages had been built!

Renaissance planning

Alberti

Curiously enough, the most coherent advocate of medieval irregular planning was the first great architectural theorist of the Renaissance: Leone Battista Alberti. In his *De Re Aedificatori* (1485) he says (Book IV ch v):

> . . . if the City is noble and powerful, the Streets should be straight and broad, which carries an Air of Greatness and Majesty; but if it is a small Town or a Fortification, it will be better, and as safe, not for the Streets to run straight to the Gates; but to have them wind about sometimes to the Right, sometimes to the Left, near the Wall, and especially under the Towers upon the Wall; and within the Heart of the Town, it will be handsomer not to have them straight, but winding about several Ways, backwards and forwards, like the Course of a River.

Alberti had several reasons for this:

> . . . by appearing so much the longer, they will add to the idea of the Greatness of the Town, and they likewise conduce very much to Beauty and Convenience, and be a greater Security against all Accidents and Emergencies.

But above all they will give the town a particular kind of beauty, for:

> Moreover, this winding of the Streets will make the Passenger at every Stop discover a new Structure, and the Front and Door of every House will directly face the Middle of the Street . . . it will

be both healthy and pleasant, to have such an open View from every House by Means of the Turn of the Street.

The wide streets of a larger town, by contrast, will be 'unhandsome and unhealthy', as Tacitus found when Nero had widened the streets of Rome. This simply made the city hotter in the summer, for there was no shade, and in the winter they were open to the 'stormy blasts'. Narrow, winding streets will protect people from such things yet there will be no house '. . . but what in some Part of the Day, will enjoy some sun'. Nor, what is more: 'will they ever be without gentle breezes'.

Narrow, winding streets had the further advantage that if some enemy should ever penetrate the town, he would get confused, and lost.

The town should also have its squares as Alberti says (Book IV ch viii): 'some for the exposing of Merchandises to sale in Time of Peace; others for the Exercises proper for Youth; and others for laying up Stores in Time of War, of Timber, Forage, and the like Provisions necessary for the sustaining of a Siege'.

Like Vitruvius before him, Alberti is concerned with the location of the city for the healthiest possible climate (Book 1 ch iii) and he too refers to the taking of *Auspices* as described, so he says, by Varro and Plutarch, and various other Classical authors (Book IV ch ii). He assumes that the city will be walled, with battlements, towers, *cornishes* and gates.

As for the ideal shape, he finds this impossible to specify. As he says (Book IV ch iii): 'it must be various according to the Variety of Places'. One could plan with a perfectly circular, square or other regular form if one were building on a level site but that would be impossible on a hill. Vitruvius, of course, had condemned 'all Angles jutting out from the naked of the Wall' on the grounds that they made the city vulnerable to the forms of attack which were possible in his day. But as Alberti points out they could be useful to the city on a hill especially if 'they are set just answering to the Streets'.

So Alberti's vision of the city is emphatically not what most people have in mind when they think of the Renaissance city. These derive rather from editions of Vitruvius illustrated, and published, by Alberti's successors such as Fra Giocondo (1511), and Cesariano (1521), not to mention paintings by Luciano Laurana, Piero della Francesca and others. Indeed a painting in the Ducal Palace at Urbino (Fig. 1.28), now attributed to Luciano represents for most of us the ideal of the Renaissance city, centred as it is about a three-storey circular temple. Yet all is by no means what it seems. There are wells, mirror-images of each other about the central axis and buildings which, on the left side at least conform, in strict perspective, to a regular building line. But

Fig. 1.28 Luciano Laurana (*c.* 1420–79): *Ideal City*. Painting in the Ducal Palace at Urbino.

whilst each of these is symmetrical in itself they vary in height from four, rather low individual storeys, to three rather higher ones and, in one case, to a single-storey link between two buildings.

Those to the right of the axis are even more irregular. A three and a four-storey building match each other in height but the latter projects well in front of the building line whilst on this same side, behind the central temple, there is a Basilican church with an axis parallel to, but otherwise firmly independent of the main one.

Such Renaissance city plans as have survived, however, suggest greater regularities than these. Indeed the earliest we have is by Filarete (n.d.) who described and illustrated his fictitious City of Sforzinda in the *Codex Maggliabecchianus* (*c.* 1457–64) which remained, unpublished, in Florence until well into the 20th century (Fig. 1.29).

The city was intended for a patron, Count Sforza, hence the curious name Sforzinda. Rosenau describes it in some detail (1959) and, not surprisingly, it is based on a Vitruvian circular plan and with a Vitruvian response to the winds in the layout of the streets. But the circle seems to be merely a base or a plinth for an eight-pointed regular star with defensive towers at the points and gates at the internal angles.

There is a (rectangular) main square at the centre with two subsidiary piazzas one with the cathedral and the Prince's Palace, the other with the bank, the mint and the Podesta's Palace. Other public buildings were to surround these connected, by a Vitruvian arrangement of streets, to some 16 subsidiary squares serving, alternately, churches and markets. The main piazza was connected to the outlying areas by canals, and every second street was a canal in the manner of Venice. The main squares and streets were to be colonnaded.

In addition to his layout for the city as a whole, Filarete also designed individual buildings, including schools, hospitals and prisons, ranging in scale from the 10-storey 'House of Vice and Virtue' to single-storey artisan's dwellings. Vice was represented in his 10-storey building by a brothel, contained within the square plinth, above which rose his cylindrical building towards the virtues of learning in the higher storeys. The highest of the virtues was astrology, whilst the whole edifice was to be crowned by a statue of Virtue herself.

Rosenau traces the further development of the ideal city during the Renaissance through the work of Francesco di Giorgio, Leonardo da Vinci, Michelangelo, Raphael and Dürer who all drew cities, or parts of cities. She looks at Thomas More's *Utopia* and at ideal city plans by Cataneo (1554), Maggi and Castriotto (1564) and Scamozzi (1615). Their more or less fortified plans tend to be variations on Vitruvian themes, or, rather, on Filaretean ones (Lazzaroni and Muñoz, 1972). Most of them are star-shaped with a central plaza which, in Cataneo's case, has six smaller plazas grouped around it and, in Scammozzi's case, four.

None of them agreed with Alberti's thesis, that undulating streets made for greater beauty *and* for greater convenience. Indeed within their walls the cities are variations on the gridiron theme with piazzas grouped symmetrically within the grid. Which of course makes for awkward sites where these gridded streets meet the 12-sided (Scammozzi), 7-sided (Cataneo) or other polygonal perimeter walls within their star-shaped defences.

One city, of course, was built along these lines: the fortress city for Venice, Palmanova (Fig. 1.30). This was started in 1593 and has been attributed to Scammozzi. But as Rosenau says it owes much to Filarete and perhaps even more to Maggi and Castriotto. It is a nine-pointed star reducing, by a series of defensive walls, to a regular nonagon.

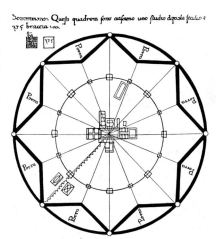

Fig. 1.29 Filarete: plan for Sforzinda (*c.* 1457–64) (from Rosenau, 1959).

There is a central piazza but instead of being planned on a gridiron the streets of Palmanova radiate from the centre which, in a sense, means that *all* the sites are awkward.

So at first sight it seems that the results of all this Renaissance theorizing was one perfect city, Palmanova, which itself is now something of an urban backwater (Fig. 1.30). Yet as Crouch, Garr and Mundigo suggest (1982), more plans were to be drawn, and built according to Renaissance concepts, than to any other ways of planning in the entire history of cities.

Baroque

Before we consider these, however, we ought to look at the final flowering of Renaissance planning in Europe, that is to say the Baroque.

Baroque urban planning was first manifest in spaces between groups of buildings, such as Michelangelo's Piazza del Campidoglio (Fig. 1.31) in Rome (started 1536) and the space between the two parallel wings of the Uffizi in Florence which Vasari built – with advice from Michelangelo – between 1560 and 1574. Siegfried Giedion analyses these (1941) pointing out that Michelangelo's Piazza was built on the site of the ancient Roman Capitol, on the 50 metre Capitoline Hill overlooking the fora from the east. The ancient Romans of course had approached the Capitol from the fora but Michelangelo orientated his scheme to the west where medieval Rome had been developed.

As Bacon shows (1967) there was already an irregular, medieval Campidoglio when Michelangelo started work with a (castellated) Palazzo del Senatore forming its eastern side – that is the side away from Michelangelo's approach – and, slanting inwards towards the Senatore, the Palazzo dei Conservatori defining the southern side.

Michelangelo started to tidy this up by defining an east/west axis, centred on the Palazzo del Senatori. He then gave this Palazzo a new, symmetrical façade articulated by massive Corinthian pilasters supported by a great basement, and approached by grand flights of stairs.

Fig. 1.30 Scamozzi: Palmanova (*c.* 1593). Plan showing defenses in 1713. *Third International Exhibition of Architecture*, Biennale di Venezia, 1985, Electra Editrice.

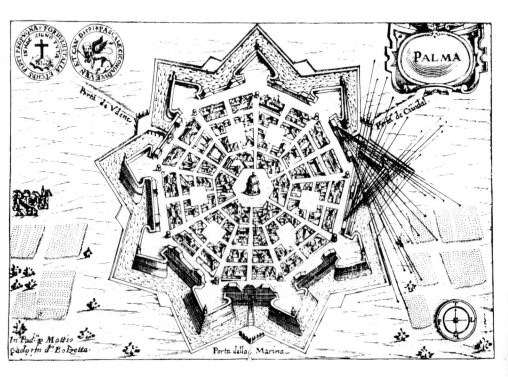

He then faced the Palazzo dei Conservatori with a rather less grand façade and matched it, on the northern side of the axis, with the Museo Capitolini.

North and south, therefore, the two Palazzi are aligned to enclose a tapering Piazza, tapering, that is towards the west which Michelangelo left open, apart from a ballustrade. The whole thing is centred on an equestrian statue – probably dating from the 2nd century – of Marcus Aurelius.

Michelangelo designed a massive flight of stairs, la Cordonata as his approach to the Piazza and work was started on this in 1536. As one approaches up la Cordonata, of course, Michelangelo's tapering Piazza presents one with false perspectives. These perspectives are further enriched, or complicated, by Michelangelo's paving which is centred on the Marcus Aurelius. His statue, with its plinth, stands on a twelve-pointed star in the middle of a large paved Oval. This Oval is lower, by two steps, than the general level of the Piazza. This Oval of paving curves upwards towards the statue and curved lines radiate in plan to fill the entire Oval. Although it was designed by Michelangelo, this paving was completed only in the 1940s. Giedion (1941), the chief exponent of simple, abstract Modernism waxes most lyrical about all this. As he says (p. 68):

> . . . the stripes radiate out in fingerlike beams . . . to form a twelve pointed star of flattened, intersecting curves. Their fantastic pattern enflames the whole frenzied interplay of contrasts: oval, trapezoid, the background of Roman and mediaeval tradition, the subtly shifting interplay of Baroque light and shadow that models the walls, the grandiose gesture of the great stairway – all combine to form a single all-embracing harmony. . . .

That may be so as Venturi says (1953), if one ignores the extraordinarily clumsy juxtaposition of the Michelangelo's Piazza and his Cordonata with the adjacent but higher Church of Santa Maria in Aracoeli with its rather more dominant staircase and beyond that Sacconi's crushing Monument (1885) to Vittorio Emmanuele II (Fig. 1.32).

Fig. 1.31 Michelangelo: (from 1536) Piazza del Campidoglio, Rome. Perspective by Stephano (1596) (from Ackerman, 1961).

Fig. 1.32 Rome: (left) Monument to
Vittorio Emmanuele, (centre) Church
of Santa Maria in Aracoeli and (right)
La Cordonata – Michelangelo's
stairway to the Campidoglio. One can
only perceive Michelangelo's
composition as a 'unified whole' by
ignoring its overpowering neighbours
(author's photograph).

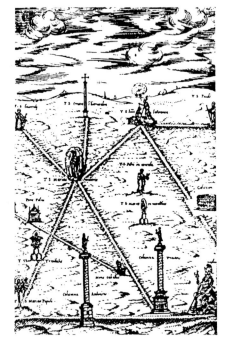

Fig. 1.33 Bordino: sketch plan (1588)
showing Sextus's connections
between the Holy Places of Rome
(from Giedion, 1941).

There are problems, clearly, when one tries to combine the medieval
and even Roman irregularities of the Capitoline Hill with geometric
pattern-making, not to mention symmetries, of a kind which can only
work on level sites. Clearly there were reasons why the medieval
builders left their piazza open towards the church. Obviously Michelangelo was aware of these; his solutions to the problems his symmetry
imposes are immensely ingenious but the overall result, dominated by
Santa Maria, is hardly 'a single all-embracing harmony'.

Nor, given its site on seven hills, and almost two-and-a-half
thousand years of previous development, could Rome as a whole be
unified in the ways that, say, the Château of Versailles could be unified
by Le Vau (1662–70) and Mansart (1678–1708) or its gardens by Le
Notre (from 1668).

Sixtus V certainly did what he could to unify Rome during his five
years as Pope (1585–90) (Fig. 1.33). He was seeking not so much a
visual, architectural unity as an ecclesiastical coherence for the city. For
as Giedion says, his aim was to link the seven major churches and
shrines of Rome with roads by which pilgrims could make their circuits
of them all in a single day.

These sites were mostly within the walls of ancient Rome, at least
those built by Aurelian (AD 270–275), but the most important church of
all, Saint Peter's, was remote from most of the others on the far side of
the River Tiber beyond the Castel Sant' Angelo. Earlier Popes had
connected Saint Peter's and the Castel which was linked across the
Tiber to medieval Rome by bridge, the Ponte Sant' Angelo. They had
established a bridgehead on the southern bank of the Tiber as the Plate
Pontis with road fanning eastwards and south-eastwards through
medieval Rome itself. North-east of this they had made another fan of
roads radiating from the Piazza del Popolo. Given these developments
by his predecessors, Sixtus, as his Architect, Domenico Fontana, put it
(1612):

. . . wishing to ease the way for those who, prompted by devotion
or by vows, are accustomed to visit frequently the most holy
places of the City of Rome, and in particular the seven churches so
celebrated for their great indulgences and relics, opened many
most commodious and straight streets in many places, Thus one

can by foot, by horse, or in a carriage, start from whatever place in Rome one may wish, and continue virtually in a straight line to the most famous devotions.

As Bordino shows in his Map of 1588 Sixtus could achieve this by building another road south-eastwards from the Piazza del Popolo to S. Maria Maggiore – the Strada Felice – which could form the first ray of a star radiating from S. Maria towards S. Lorenzo, S. Croce, S. Giovanni in Laterano and back to the ancient Forum at Trajan's Column. Another fan at S. Giovanni in Laterano could connect it with S. Paolo and the Colosseum, whilst a diagonal, cutting across the Strada Felice, could connect the Quirinal and the Porta Pia in Aurelian's Wall. Which is more or less what Sixtus did.

Apart from the buildings which Sixtus's roads connected their most important destinations were marked by (Egyptian) Obelisks, in the Piazzas of Saint Peter's, S. Maria Maggiore, S. Giovanni in Laterano and the Piazza del Popolo (see Batta, 1986). Others added further Obelisks so, altogether, Rome now has some 14 in all which, even though they confuse Sixtus's original scheme, greatly enliven the piazzas in which they were erected.

As Giedion points out, Sixtus – and Fontana – were making their roads at the very time when coaches and carriages were coming into general use. Which of course meant that the streets had to be wide enough for carriages to pass. So they had to be much wider than they would have been for people on foot, on horseback or being carried, by others, in sedan chairs. As Fontana went on to say:

The most celebrated is the street called Felice, which originates at the church of Santa Croce . . . passes the church of Santa Maria Maggiore, and then continues on to the Trinita dei Monte from where one descends to the Porto di Popolo; which in all comprises a distance of two miles and a half, and throughout (it is as) straight as a plumb line and wide enough to allow five carriages to ride abreast.

Truth to tell this axis was somewhat compromised by the facts of ancient Rome. The great Basilicas, S. Croce, S. Maria Maggiore, S. Trinita had been built on sacred sites and were not quite aligned in the first place although part of the Strada Felice, from S. Croce to S. Maria, survives as the Via di S. Croce whilst Sixtus's cross-axis, from the Porta Pia to the Quirinale, remains as the Via Venti Settembre. But there is not much sign of the Felice between S. Maria and the Piazza del Popolo. The nearest approximation: the Vias Sistina/delle Quatro Fontane/Agostino Depretis stop well short of the Piazza and even S. Maria. If they represent Sixtus's Strada then they start too far to the south and finish too far to the north!

So it is difficult for us to gain from Rome any sense of Baroque city planning except at the scale of spaces-between-buildings represented by Michelangelo's Piazza del Campidoglio.

As for the far bank of the Tiber, Sixtus started his own new town, the Borgo Nuovo, between Saint Peter's (with the Vatican), and the Castel.

So one has to look to Versailles as the model of what Baroque planning could be. Le Nôtre's axis, of canals with fountains centred on the palace, with its parterress, avenues and walks was some two-and-a-half kilometres long. At first sight it may seem strange to think of a garden, however large, as offering any kind of model for urban planning.

But Le Nôtre himself applied the same principles to his completion of the Champs Elysées in Paris (1664) which in turn had direct influences on city planning elsewhere including Greenwich (Wren), the Amalienburg in Copenhagen (Eigtved, 1749), the Mall in Washington DC (L'Enfant 1791–2) and so on.

As we shall see also, Le Nôtre's method of designing was to be taken as a model for urban design by the most influential of 18th century architectural theorists, the Abbé Laugier.

Laws of the Indies

Those who colonized other continents of course took European models of city planning with them. Thus by the middle of the 15th century the Portugese had founded Arguin, now Agadir in what is now Morocco, modelling it on medieval Lisbon as a hill-top town with a trading post at sea level. They founded Elmina, on the Gold Coast, a similar form (1482), and by 1510 they were Lisbonizing Goa, halfway down the eastern coast of India (Smith, 1955).

Similarly, after Columbus's arrival, in 1492, the Spanish imposed Spanish models of city planning on to the Island of Hispaniola (Santo Domingo and Haiti), Cuba and the other Antilles, not to mention the coasts of Venezuela, Columbia, Mexico and the North American coast of the Gulf of Mexico. As Crouch, Garr and Mundigo say (1982, p. xx), like colonial cities of the Roman Empire those of the Spanish Empire too 'were conceived and executed as propaganda vehicles, symbolizing and incarnating civilization'.

Others had different ways of doing this. There were clashes of interests, for instance, between the French, the Spanish and the Portuguese down the Atlantic coast of Brazil. The latter planned their cities with a Baroque axiality, organized hierarchically, to incarnate civilization and also to symbolize the integration of the native Indians, not to mention Black African slaves, into the Portuguese scheme of things.

But as Crouch, Carr and Mundigo are at pains to point out, the Spanish mode of planning was imposed, not just in South America and the Caribbean – including Mexico – but also up into North America including parts of California, Arizona, New Mexico, Texas and Florida. So they think it important that future comparisons be made between Spanish and Portuguese patterns of colonial settlement, the influence

Fig. 1.34 Santo Domingo: House of Diego Columbus (*c.* 1520) (author's photograph).

of Islamic planning law on Spanish urban thought, the nature of indigenous, Indian planning before the arrival of the Spanish, the different types of colonial city: seaport, fortress, capital city and so on, detailed comparisons of Spanish settlements in different parts of the Americas and comparisons too between Graeco–Roman colonization around the Mediterranean and Spanish colonization in the Americas. Since as they say the Spanish built over 350 cities in the Americas between the founding of their first settlement of Santo Domingo (1493) (Fig. 1.34) and the founding of their last in California (1801), their planning methods probably extended to more places, on a larger scale, over a greater span of time, than any other planning practices including Roman. Except that, as Stanislawski says (1947), they were actually based on Roman, indeed specifically Vitruvian principles.

Crouch, Garr and Mundigo suggest (p. 37) the Spanish learned the virtues of living in towns again as they drove the Moors southwards: from Toledo (1085 by El Cid), Seville (1284) until finally from Granada in 1492. Of course these Moorish cities had been developed according to Islamic planning law.

But certain Spanish cities dated from Roman times retaining vestiges, at least, of their Roman plans. These included Barcelona, not to mention Merida (which name itself derived from Emerita Augusta) and Zaragoza (from Caesar Augusta) (Violich, 1962). The Spanish Kings themselves, or rather their advisers, seem to have thought that since Rome represented the most successful of empires before their own, they would do well to base the planning of their cities on Roman precedents.

Which is why the Spanish Planning Ordinances required regular, not to say rectilinear, gridded city plans. They go on to suggest that the Spanish learned the virtues of such planning from the cities they conquered in the Indies and especially from Montezuma's capital, Tenochtitlan, over which they built Mexico City itself.

Bernal Diaz, who was there, with Hernando Cortés, says of Tenochtitlan:

> The plan of the city, shows the original area divided into four symmetrical parts. Each ward contained . . . remnants of an older organisation . . . on which the imperial state had been superimposed. The boundaries of the four . . . wards met at a single point, which was the area occupied by the great temple, the imperial palaces, and the homes of some of the lords. From each of the four gates of the . . . great temple . . . ran a street that marked one of the boundaries of the wards. Three of these streets became causeways . . . (which) . . . crossed the (lake – in which Tenochtitlan was built) to the mainland.

Cortés and his men first saw this amazing city late in 1519 and they conquered it, finally, early in 1521, promptly razing the Aztec city to the ground and replacing it with their Spanish one. Which seems strange if they admired the Aztec city as much as they said they did, except that it was dominated by the Temple of the Sun and other great pyramids, scenes of brutal human sacrifice and other practices which, despite what they did themselves, were anathema to the Christian Spaniards.

The first Royal Ordinances for planning Spanish cities in the Indies were sent from Seville as early as 1513, that is only twenty years or so after Columbus arrived and six years before Cortez. Each city was to have a gridiron plan with a plaza at the centre around which were to be built the church and other public buildings.

In the case of Tenochtitlan, Cortés himself took over Montezuma's Palace and had the Temple of the Sun torn down to make a platform for the Catholic cathedral. His own City, Mexico, was laid out by a geometer named Alfonso Garcia Bravo whilst the Indians were given their own new capital at Tlatelolco with its government building and plaza beyond which lay their much more irregular residential quarters.

So, as Kostoff (1985) says, the Spanish colonization took place most rapidly in Mexico. The first Franciscan friars arrived in 1524; soon to be followed by Augustinians and Dominicans. These friars planned most of the towns, built the first churches and were responsible generally for setting up Spanish government.

The Ordinances were elaborated over the years until in 1573 Don Felipe, King of Castile, promulgated the Laws of the Indies on which all future plans were to be based (Nuttall, 1921, 1922).

Their 148 articles dealt with every aspect of site selection, planning and political organization. Apart from affording the settlers an environment that was recognizably Spanish, they were to be specifically *Christian* cities, cities which would encourage the native Indians to renounce their pagan ways and embrace Christianity. This would be reflected, of course, by such things as the place of the Church within the city.

So attempts were to be made to pacify the Indians, indeed to build the new towns in ways which caused least harm to the Indian population (Ordinance 5). But whilst the Indians were to be treated in a friendly way the settlers should also look out for available metals (15), local foods (16), the possibilities of religious indoctrination (17), and so on. Indeed it is stated later (Ordinance 36) that 'this is the principal objective for which we mandate that these discoveries and settlements be made'.

In deciding where to build an actual settlement, the following conditions should be taken into account (Ordinance 34):

> the health of the area, which will be known from the abundance of old men or of young men of good complexion, natural fitness and colour, and without illness: and in the abundance of healthy animals of sufficient size, and or healthy fruits and fields where no toxic and noxious things are grown, but that it be of good climate, the sky clear and benign, the air pure and soft, . . . and of good temperature, without excessive heat or cold, and (in the event of) having to decide, it is better that it be cold.

There should be water nearby not to mention existing towns from which building materials could be taken for re-use (39). They should not be too high for high sites are windy and difficult of access (40) nor should maritime locations be chosen, except for harbours, since they were subject to pirate attack nor would there be enough land for cultivation, or natives to be trained in the arts of cultivation (41). If there was a river, then the city should be sited on its eastern bank so the sun in the morning struck the town before it struck the water.

Like Vitruvius some 1500 years earlier Felipe and his advisers were concerned with wind direction, the quality of water and so on. The town should not be located near lagoons or marshes since they might be the haunts of poisonous animals, not to mention polluted air and polluted water (111).

As for population, at least 30 neighbours were needed to start a town and, certainly, never less than 12, including 10 married men (100). Within some specified term – usually a year – each of the 30 neighbours was to have built his own house and, on the same site, accommodation

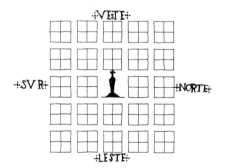

Fig. 1.35 Mendoza, Argentina. Original layout (from CEDEX, 1985).

for 'ten cows, four oxen, or two oxen and two young bulls, and a mare, five pigs, six chickens, (and) twenty sheep from Castille . . .' (89). Also there should be a clergyman who if he failed to build a church, and open it within the specified time for divine service, would be fined 1000 gold pesos.

Once the location of a town had been agreed four major divisions should be planned (90), one for the founder and his 30 neighbours (he would take a quarter of this and they the other three-quarters, one for the settlers he attracted to the town, one for common land for grazing, and one for the indigenous population).

As for the detailed planning methods, these are described in Ordinance 110 as follows:

> On arriving at the place where the new settlement is to be
> founded . . . a plan for the site is to be made, dividing it into
> squares, streets, and building lots, using cord and ruler,
> beginning with the main square from which streets are to run to
> the gates and principal roads . . . leaving sufficient open space so
> that even if the town grows, it can always spread in the same
> manner. . . . (Fig. 1.35).

The main plaza (Fig. 1.36) should never be less than 200 feet by 300 feet nor larger than 532 by 800 feet. Indeed a 'good proportion' was 600 feet by 400 feet (113) which gave a good shape for fiestas, especially where horses were to be used (112).

Its corners should face the principal winds 'because in this manner, the streets running from the plaza will not be exposed to the principal winds' (114). There should be four principal streets, one running from the centre of each side and two more, at right angles to each other, running from each of the four corners (114). As a 'considerable convenience to the merchants who generally gather there', there were to be arcades (*portales*) surrounding the plaza and along the principal streets although they were to stop short at the corners so as not to interrupt the streets that entered there (115).

The streets could be wide in cold locations whereas in hot places they should be narrow although they may need to be wide where horses were used for defence (116).

In coastal towns, the main church should be placed where it would form an effective sea-marker (120) whereas in an inland town, the church should be placed on a prominent, preferably raised, site adjacent to but not actually on the main plaza. It should have a site to itself so as to be visible from all sides (124) whilst the royal council, the *cabildo* (town hall), and in a seaport, the customs house and arsenal should be around the main plaza also but sited in a way which did not 'embarrass' the church. Hospitals for the (non-infectious) poor should be placed nearby.

Hospitals for contagious diseases, not to mention such producers of noxious matter as slaughter houses, fisheries, tanneries and so on should be 'placed where the filth can easily be disposed of' (122).

Here and there within the city, smaller plazas should be built, as settings for smaller churches, monasteries and so on such that everything: 'may be distributed in good proportion for the instruction of religion' (118).

The sites around the plaza should be used for buildings associated with the church, the royal house and so on and the settlers would all contribute to the building of shops and houses for the merchants (127). Other sites would be allocated by lottery (127).

As with the bastide towns, these colonial cities were to be laid out in

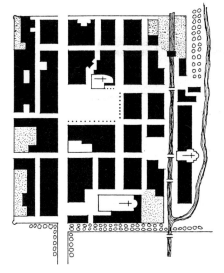

Fig. 1.36 Santiago da Chile: city centre with porticoed Plaza and Church (from Crouch, Carr and Mundigo, 1982).

regular plots. Each settler was allocated a maximum of five *peonias*, for grazing and other purposes, each 50 feet by 100 feet (102) and three *caballerias* or house-building plots each 100 feet by 200 feet. Settlers were expected to bring tents with them for use when they first arrived (128) failing which they could make huts of easily available local materials (128) a tradition, of course, which continues to this day in the building of shanty-towns.

On arrival also the settlers were given seeds which they were expected to plant (131). They were also expected to make arrangements for their cattle (132) and to start work as soon as possible on their permanent houses. They had to build these with great care and efficiency to which end they were provided with moulds, planks and tools (132). Their houses were to be orientated to take advantage of the north and south winds (133) and each house was to have its yards and corrals for animals as large as possible for health and cleanliness (133).

As for architectural forms, as Ordinance 134 prescribed: 'They shall try as far as possible to have buildings all of one type for the sake of the beauty of the town'. Indeed architects and other executors were deputed to ensure that these Ordinances were applied by the 'most careful overseeing' (135).

After which the last 12 Ordinances were concerned with ways in which the Indians were to be brought into the Christian fold, the town itself being a symbol to them of Christian superiority.

Whilst this pattern of settlement worked well enough in Mexico itself, and in various parts of South America, it became increasingly difficult as the Spanish moved northwards from Mexico City into Nueva Galicia and Nueva Vizcaya. Some of the Indians, such as the Hopi were already living, settled, in *pueblos* but others, such as the Apache, most certainly were not. It was proving too expensive, not to say hazardous, to subdue them by force so in 1584 the Bishop of Guadalajara suggested a more modest procedure in which two or three friars should be sent out to found a monastery, protected by eight soldiers or so and their families, together with a group of Christianized Mexican Indians to act, not only as settlers, but also as tribute-collectors and song leaders in religious services.

This seemed to work and fifteen years later some 8000 people were living in small settlements of this kind 1000 miles north of Mexico City in what is now New Mexico. Thus it was that in 1610 Don Pedro de Peralta was able to found La Villa Reale de la Santa Fe as a proper city: a seat of political and military, not to mention religious authority, according to the Laws of the Indies. It was built of local materials, such as stone, adobe mud walls with wooden roof beams and by 1633, 200 people were living in the city itself, of which 50 were Spanish, and by 1859, when the area passed into American control, the population was not quite 5000.

Not that Santa Fe was by any means the furthest north, or the last Spanish settlement to be built in what are now the United States. Crouch, Garr and Mundigo trace the histories also of St Louis and Los Angeles. Maxent, Laclede, a French fur company, had located a trading post on the site of St Louis as late as 1763, across the river from a Peoria Indian village. But already in 1762 the French Governor had ceded Upper Louisiana to the Spanish. So St Louis was first laid out on the general pattern of New Orleans and in 1770, Captain Pedro Piernas actually came to take possession. He had pallisades built, and defensive towers, to protect the town from marauding Indians and gradually the pattern of streets, not to mention the distribution of building and other plots, were brought more into conformity with the Laws of the Indies.

Not that Spanish control of St Louis lasted very long. For in 1800, under a Bourbon Family Pact St Louis was returned to French control and in 1803, of course, Thomas Jefferson actually purchased Louisiana from Napoleon Bonaparte.

The Spanish also built fortresses up the California coast, at San Diego (1769), Monterey (1770), San Francisco (1776) and, further south again, Santa Barbara (1786). They also built some 20 missions, including those at San Antonio de Padua (1771), San Luis Obispo (1772), San Juan Capistrano (1776), Santa Cruz (1791) and San Jose (1797). The last of these, around the Bay Area of San Francisco, were built as late as 1817 (San Rafael Arcangel) and even 1823 (San Francisco de Solano).

But already by 1777 the then Governor of California, Felipe de Neve, had decided to found new settlements of rather a different kind in which the Church would have a lesser role. Indeed he did not see them as centres from which the Indians could be converted to Christianity and was quite content for the Indians to continue living in their own villages.

He saw them, rather, as agricultural centres. They included San Jose and Nuestra Senora La Reina de Los Angeles de Porciuncola which was actually founded in 1781. As Crouch, Garr and Mandigo suggest de Neve applied certain of the Laws with great precision, especially those to do with healthy sites (34), fertile ground (35), an (amenable) indigenous population (36), accessibility by land (37), the availability of water and reusable building materials (39).

Initially Los Angeles was about as small as it could be. For it was started by 11 families – some 44 individuals – in various personal permutations of Spanish, Indian and Black. de Neve respected various other laws to do with the allocation of fields and lots for houses although these were smaller than the standard *peonias* and *caballerias*. There was a plaza as required by the Laws although this too was smaller than it should have been, not to mention a government house, a chapel, a guard house, a granary and so on. The plaza itself had collonades and so did the three main streets which lead from it.

According to Crouch, Carr and Mundigo, lots were still being allocated around Los Angeles according to the Spanish Laws as late as the 1830s. And in 1835 the Mexican Government raised Los Angeles to the status of State capital. But it did not have the necessary buildings and after the war with Mexico in 1846–48 California became American territory and Los Angeles lost its status as capital.

Lieutenant Ord was asked to survey the city with a view to defining the number of lots which could be sold to replenish the coffers of the city. His intentions – perhaps intentionally – were ambiguous – for the city was supposed to be two-leagues square. But Ord surveyed an area of 16 square leagues, much to the city's advantage!

Los Angeles, of course, has grown out of all recognition since then to form one of the largest conurbations in the world in terms, at least, of area.

In some ways too New York looks like a 'Laws of the Indies' city, at least in so far as its gridiron plan is concerned. Not that it was, by any means. Its founders: first of all the Dutch, and then the English, were concerned much more with setting up as trading post than with converting the North American Indians to Christianity. The city grew as a centre for the kind of entrepreneurial enterprise that its founders most certainly would have approved. Indeed by the end of the 19th century it had become the very model, in built urban form, of the entrepreneurial, that is to say the Capitalist city.

Even now, for many people, it represents the essence of what they

expect of the 20th century city, a position which, as we shall see
(Chapter 2), it seems to have been losing to other North American
cities. In terms of city development, however, it represents such a
significant example that we ought to explore it in considerable detail.
This we shall do shortly, but before we do that we ought to look at
what, for many people, are the finest urban spaces in the World; the
Piazza di San Marco in Venice and the Place Stanislas in Nancy.

2

Paradigms

Piazza di San Marco

Consider the following spaces within cities: the Piazza di San Marco in
Venice and the Place Stanislas in Nancy. In each case, the space – or
place – is surrounded by buildings, but one, the Place Stanislas, is axial
and regular whilst the other, the Piazza di San Marco, is highly varied,
asymmetrical, and irregular. This is hardly surprising, for the Piazza
grew to its present form by a process of growth and change over almost
a thousand years (880 to 1810), whilst received opinion has it that the
Place was planned all of a piece by the same architect, Emmanuel Héré
de Corny, at a particular moment in time (1752). What Héré did,
naturally, was consistent within itself although, as we shall see, it was
also consistent with other things. In the overall concept, certainly, each
piece has its part to play in Héré's geometric hierarchy, whilst in the
case of the buildings surrounding the Piazza, each architect responded
to the work of his distinguished predecessors by deciding to blend in
with or to react against it, according to the taste of his time.

The result for most urbanists is one of Europe's more breathtaking
spaces. Kidder Smith (1955) quotes a range of descriptions, from
Napoleon's 'the most beautiful drawing room in Europe' to Saarinen's
'Correlation of individual buildings into a magnificent architectural
ensemble . . . into . . . a lasting symphony of architectural forms'. He
quotes Sitte to the effect that '. . . no painter ever conceived an
architectural background more perfect. . . . No theater ever created a
more sublime tableau', and Hopkinson Smith's 'There is but one grand
piazza the world over, and that lies today in front of the church of San
Marco' (1896), which makes his own comment that 'next to the
Acropolis (St Mark's Square in Venice is) the finest example of
town-planning-and-architecture to be found in the world . . .' seem a
trifle ungenerous to the Piazza.

For the Piazza as it now exists provides a living – and working –
environment for thousands of people, a place of resort, a place to eat
and drink, a place to listen to music, a place to shop, whilst the
Acropolis – a mere shadow of its former self – is just a place for tourists.
A marvellous place, it is true, and most dramatically sited, but the
spaces *between* the buildings – which is what concerns us here – are
simply travesties of what they used to be with the features Pausanius
describes between the Propyleon and the Parthenon. Without them
the spaces between the buildings are just left-over spaces.

We can imagine 20th century concepts of space into them, as
Wycherly (1949) and Doxiadis (1972) did, but they are singularly
lacking in enclosure, which must be the first requirement for anything
that is called an *urban* space. Napoleon's drawing *room* had only the sky
for a ceiling but he saw it, nevertheless, as a room. And a room such as

that has walls: greatly varied in the case of the Piazza, more unified and uniform in the case of the Place. Those uniformities extend to things like cornice height, number of storeys and, most particularly, to architectural language which is unequivocally Classical, or, to be specific, Renaissance. That is to say it is an architecture of walls, with rectangular openings in them for doors and windows, with sills, architraves and pediments. The grander buildings: the Hôtel de Ville (Town Hall) and the Palais de la Gouvernement Provinciale (Palace of the Provincial Government) are fronted by (attached) colonnades and they have central pediments. There is a triumphal arch between the Place Stanislas itself and the longer Place de la Carrière and there are semicircular colonnades defining a frontispiece, as it were, to the Palais. The geometry of the whole system extends beyond that Palace into a (highly formalized) garden.

The Piazza as we see it today was developed in something like 30 phases (Fig. 2.1). It is roughly L-shaped, with the main Piazza running west–east towards the Basilica of San Marco itself, and the smaller Piazzetta running southwards from there, past the Doge's Palace and open, at its southern end, to the Grand Canal across which one has distant views of Palladio's S. Giorgio Maggiore (1565–80) (Moretti, 1831). As it were, the Piazza is hinged into the Piazzetta by the earliest surviving building; surviving, that is, in form if not in substance.

The original Campanile had been built in 888 to 912, rebuilt by Bon in 1511–14 and rebuilt again, after the collapse of 1902, as exactly as possible from photographs, by Beltrami and Moretti. Its total height of 323 feet is made up of a shaft whose verticality is emphasized by buttresses, surmounted by a square stone bell-chamber and that in its turn by a pyramidal spire. It acts as a focal point which unifies, most successfully, the irregular plan of the Piazza, Piazzetta and the disparate forms of the buildings which surround them.

The Campanile at first marked the western extent of the Piazza, where the actual boundary was formed by a canal. But this was filled around 1176 and the church which had been built against it was moved westwards to give the Piazza its present length.

Fig. 2.1 Philip Hirst (1935). Plan of the Piazza di San Marco (courtesy British School at Rome).

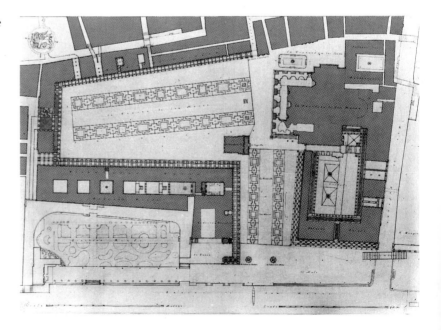

Fig. 2.2 Piazza di San Marco and Campanile (author's photograph).

Apart from the Campanile (Fig. 2.2), the oldest structures in the complex are the two monolithic columns brought from the Levant and erected at the canalside end of the Piazzetta towards the end of the 12th century. One bears a sculpted lion, which may be Persian or Assyrian whilst the other has a statue of Theodore, the first patron saint of Venice. They hint at a screen which frames marvellous views of S. Giorgio and prevents the space of the Piazzetta from leaking out completely into the canal.

As for the Basilica of S. Marco itself, this too represents the result of several rebuildings (828, 976 and, substantially in its present five-dome centralized form, 1063–73). Its ancestors obviously are Santa Sophia and the other great churches of Byzantium, especially the (now destroyed) Church of the Apostles, whilst the marble and mosaic decorations – which were started late in the 11th century – also are of Byzantine inspiration. The elaborately carved ogival pediments which surmount each bay of the façade, the turrets between them, not to mention the onion domes, give the whole thing an exotic flavour which reminds us that Venice was far to the east in Europe, whilst the four gilded copper bronze horses over the central arch, although of Greek origin, were actually brought from Byzantium in 1200.

The Doge's Palace (Fig. 2.3), too, went through many transformations. It was started in 814, rebuilt after fires in 976 and 1105, and remodelled in its present form in 1309 and 1404 (south, or canal side) and in 1424–42 (west, or Piazzetta side). Although the interiors and courtyards are Renaissance and rococo in form, the Palace presents to the external world – including the Piazza and the Piazzetta – a unique form of Venetian Gothic with a massive arcade of 36 columns, and pointed arches at ground level, a more delicate loggia of 71 columns, pointed arches and fretted, quatrefoil openings at first floor level and

Fig. 2.3 Doge's Palace (author's photograph).

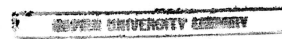

Fig. 2.4 Bon (1480–1517). Procuratie Vecchie (author's photograph).

Fig. 2.5 Jacopo Sansovini (from 1536): Libraria di San Marco (author's photograph).

blank façades above these of pink and white marble laid in diagonal patterns – a modern refacing by Bottasso. These pierced by large pointed windows and smaller bulls-eyes, as appropriate for what is going on behind them. The whole is surmounted by a fretwork marble cresting. It was linked to S. Marco by the Porta della Carta which Bartolomeo and Giovanni Bon added in 1438–42.

The north, west and south sides of the Piazza itself are lined largely with Procuratie, that is houses for the Procurators who looked after the fabric of S. Marco. The northern side, the oldest, was originally built by a younger Bon in 1480–1517. It was reconstructed after a fire in 1512 by Bergamesco, the younger Bon, and Sansovino westwards from Coducci's clock tower, the Torre dell' Orologio (1496–99) which, with Lombardo's oddly unmatching wings (1506), apparently had survived the fire. The Procuratie Vecchie (Fig. 2.4) are formed from three superimposed Renaissance arcades of which the lowest, which is open, has fifty arches, whilst the upper two each have 100, containing windows. Sansovino completed the western end of the Piazza with his Church of San Geminiano.

Leopardi, a goldsmith, placed his three bronze pylons in front of the Basilica in 1505.

Sansovino also was responsible for the two finest Renaissance buildings in the Piazza – the Libraria di San Marco (Fig. 2.5) (started in 1536) which forms the western side of the Piazzetta, and the Loggetta – a meeting place for the patrician *nobih* – at the foot of the Campanile where the Piazza turns into the Piazzetta. Palladio believed Sansovino's Libraria, which was completed by Scammozi (1582–88), to be the most beautiful building since antiquity. It has a strong horizontal emphasis, with pronounced and elaborately carved entablatures over both the ground and first floor colonnades. This horizontality is emphasized by open balustrades at first floor and roof levels, whilst each bay is emphasized along the roof line by a standing statue.

The Loggetta, which is only half the height of the Libraria, consists of three triumphal arches side by side, with piers at either end and between them. The piers are penetrated by niches, with statues of Apollo, Mercury, Peace and Minerva, which themselves are contained by pairs of projecting Corinthian columns. It is surmounted by a windowless attic with plaques carved in high relief over the arches and the piers between them; this, in its turn, supports an open balustrade.

Fig. 2.6 Luigi Moretti (1831). West end of the Piazza di San Marco as it was, with Sansovino's Church of San Giminiano before Soli's A la Napoleonica was built (1807) (from Keller, 1979).

Some think the Loggetta the finest jewel of all, whilst others find its complexity and elaboration – not to mention the coloured marble – verging, shall we say, on the vulgar.

Shortly after taking over Sansovino's Libraria, Scammozi started the Procuratie Nuove along the southern side of the Piazza. He placed it some 20 feet south of the buildings which had lined the southern side which, among other things, left the Campanile standing free at the hinge. He modelled the Procuratie Nuove on Sansovino's Libraria, at least as far as bay-spacings were concerned, but he added an upper storey with pedimented windows – alternating triangular and segmental pediments. Thus the whole thing is somewhat higher than the Procuratie Vecchie which it faces. Scammozi built only ten bays of the Procuratie Nuove, to the width of the Libraria; the westward extension of 29 bays, matching Scammozi's originals, were added by Longhena who completed them in 1640. These brought the Piazza to almost its present form, except for Sansovino's church at the western end.

The Procuratie Nuove were converted into a Royal Palace for Napoleon, who seeking some way to extend this, had Sansovino's church (Fig. 2.6) demolished (1807) to make way for the so-called A la Napoleonica which Soli designed for him. The two lower floors are modelled on the Procuratie Nuove but with archways opening through giving access into the Piazza from the west, whilst Gius used a windowless attic, fronted by statues of the Roman Emperors, to resolve the discrepancy in height between the two Procurateii (Fig. 2.7).

And so the Piazza was more or less completed, although by this time it lacked some of its most compelling details, for the (Greek) bronze horses of S. Marco had been taken to Paris for Napoleon in 1797 where they drew a statue of him, standing in a chariot, on the smaller Arc de Triomphe which Percier and Fontaine had designed for him outside the Louvre in Paris. After Napoleon's defeat, the Duke of Wellington saw to their return in 1815.

And so, with the addition of 19th century lamp-posts, the Piazza was completed in something like 30 phases. The result is so complex that it demands many kinds of study: the dynamic experience of moving through, as Kidder Smith describes it (1955) and more static contemplation from various places, such as one of the café tables: Florian's during the day because, spilling out from the Procuratie Nuove, they are shaded from the southern sun; Quadri's after sundown because

Fig. 2.7 Awkward junction: Bon's Procuratie Vecchie and Soli's A la Napoleonica (author's photograph).

the music is less sentimental; the seats around Sansovino's Loggietta, the bases of the Piazzetta columns, and so on. One should certainly experience it in the spring, the summer and the autumn but whether one's devotion should extend to the winter, with its fogs, its chill winds off the Adriatic and catwalks across the Piazza to protect one's feet from the floodwater, of course is a personal matter. No doubt the Piazza reveals further secrets when the floodwater is even higher and one can explore it by boat (Fig. 2.8a and b).

Place Stanislas

The curious thing is that whilst the Place Stanislas seems so much simpler in concept and much easier to understand – its very symmetry means that when one has understood one side one has also understood its mirror image – yet, curiously enough, it was almost as long in formation as the Piazza di San Marco itself. As Bacon shows (1967) the linear Place de la Carrière – the crucial heart of the Place Stanislas concept – had been a jousting ground in medieval times, hence its overall form – a long, thin avenue lined with buildings. Nancy had been fortified early in the 17th century but its basic topography and its somewhat amorphous medieval shape meant that, unlike, say, those of Palma Nova (*c.* 1500), its defensive walls could not take the form of a geometrically perfect star. Instead it was planned as two elongated and overlapping stars, but these had served their purpose in the 1750s and land became available as the defensive walls were demolished. The then Duke of Lorraine, Stanislas Laczinski – who had been King of Poland – decided that his son-in-law, Louis XV of France, deserved a commemorative statue, and that the statue deserved a worthy setting.

He therefore instructed his architect Emmanuel Héré de Corny to design a Place Royale (Fig. 2.9) on the site of the old city wall, that is south of the Place de la Carrière and at the opposite end from his own Ducal Palace and its garden. The new complex was to be terminated at its northern end by a new Palace for the Provincial Government (Fig. 2.10) – with gardens within the Duke's own – and at its southern end by a new Hôtel de Ville.

Fig. 2.9 Héré de Corny: Royal Palace with Statue of Stanislas (author's photograph).

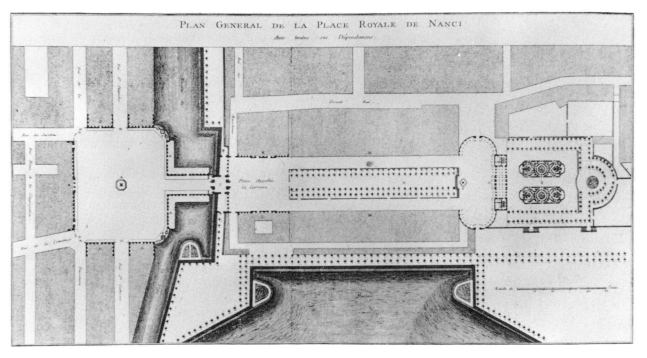

(a)

Fig. 2.8(a) Patte (1765): Plan of the Place Stanislas, Nancy. *(b)* Philip Hirst: Plan of the Piazza di San Marco (1831) to the same scale.

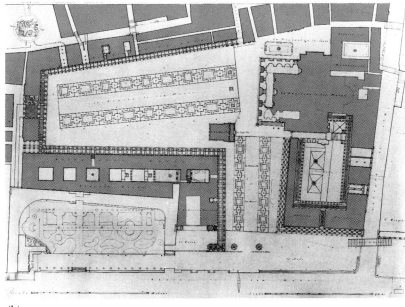

(b)

Naturally these had to be monumental, symmetrical buildings but the question was, what kind of monumentality? Héré took his cue from a house which existed already, at the south-east corner of the Place de la Carrière: the Hôtel de Beauvau-Craon which Boffrand had built in 1715 (Fig. 2.11). Not only did that set the style of Héré's development, it also set the width and alignment of his new Place de la Carrière. For he built a mirror image on the other side of his main axis and then reused Boffrand's bay spacings, columns, window and other forms in his own monumental buildings, simplified in the terraces which line his Place de la Carrière and elaborated for the Palace and the Hôtel de Ville.

The centre section of Boffrand's Beauvau-Craon consisted of a rusticated ground floor, supporting a 2-storey colonnade of Corinthian pilasters, which in turn supported an entablature. His ground and first floors had arched window openings with semicircular arches, whilst his upper floor had segmental arches. Héré elaborated this scheme for his Palais and his Hotel by clustering the columns to suggest, in each case, a central block, connecting wings and end pavilions, adding pediments to his central blocks and, running full length in each case, a crowning balustrade with urns, sculptured figures and coats of arms. These separated the bays on the upper storeys. Héré took Boffrand's basic scheme, elaborating it for this Hôtel de Ville and his Palace – each of which has a pedimented centre section and projected bays.

He repeated the same basic bay form in the six other buildings which surround the Place Royale, closing the otherwise open corners with Jean Lamour's curved wrought-iron screens. Lamour also made the gilded balconies, gates, lanterns and grilles which give to the whole complex its characteristic rococo lightness.

The Place Royale opens towards the Place de la Carrière along the main axis through a comparatively narrow gap opposite the Hôtel de Ville. The transition between the two Places is marked by a Triumphal Arch (Fig. 2.12), linked by rusticated single-storey buildings – matching Boffrand's ground floor – whilst the two large sides of the Carrière are lined with rather plainer facades – but still to Boffrand's bay spacing – built to replace the existing houses at Stanislas's expense. The linear direction of the Carrière is emphasized by avenues of trees, whilst their northern ends are marked by square pavilions, symmetrical about the

Fig. 2.10 Héré de Corny (1752–55): Palace of Provincial Government (author's photograph).

main axis. These are linked to the Palais by semicircular colonnades, or hemicycles, and the axis is finally completed by the formal garden beyond the Palais, with its symmetrical, not to say geometrical, parterres and the lined avenues which sweep round, finally, in another great hemicycle.

So whilst it is true that the Place Stanislas complex (Fig. 2.13) shows the work of one organizing mind, that is to say Héré's, he achieved his apparent unity by using to maximum advantage the things which were given him, the linear form of the Carrière and, more particularly, the details of Boffrand's Beauvau-Craon. Héré's matching of what Boffrand had done, and his working of variations on it, are no different in kind, or in intent, from Scammozi's reworking of Sansovino, Longhena's continuation of Scammozi and so on.

The backs of the Place Stanislas (Fig. 2.14) are even more irregular than anything in the Piazza for, like the Woods in Bath, Héré built merely façades behind which others then built as they pleased.

Despite any similarities, the Piazza and the Place obviously represent different overall strategies in the design of urban space. The Piazza resulted, in a sense, from a series of happy accidents over time, whilst, even though Héré incorporated certain accidents into the design of the Place, such as the length of the Carrière, the position of Hôtel Beauvau-Craon and so on, he did so in such a way that they became part of his overall composition.

There is a sameness, an all-of-a-piece quality about the Place which makes it quite different from the Piazza. And this is emphasized by their differences in size, for the total distance from the Palais to the Hôtel de Ville at Nancy is some 500 metres. The Place de la Carrière itself is 250 metres long, whereas the longest dimension of the Piazza – from the A la Napoleonica to the Doge's Palace is only 200 metres. The Piazza is 75 metres wide at its widest point, whilst the Place de la Carrière is almost the same width for the whole of its length. Given that this is longer than the whole of the Piazza, it is hardly surprising that its east and west façades greatly exceed those of the Venetian Procuratie which are respectively 160 metres (Procuratie Vecchie) and 150 metres (Procuratie Nuovi).

So there's boldness about Héré's geometry which is not matched by any single architectural gesture in the Piazza. The Venetian architects

Fig. 2.11 Boffrand (1715): Hôtel Beauveau-Craon, Nancy (author's photograph).

had a different kind of confidence. It could be said, indeed, that Héré was so lacking confidence that he couldn't even invent a façade; he chose instead to draw on Boffrand. The Venetians by contrast each knew – or believed – that what he had to offer was good of its kind, fit to stand comparison with the work of his predecessors, however different that might be in kind. Occasionally that work was demolished, as when Scammozi moved back the Procuratie Nuovi but obviously he did that out of respect for Sansovino. Gius – or Napoleon – had no such scruples when they caused Sansovino's church to be demolished, but in general there is a feeling at Venice that at each stage the architects of the Piazza looked at what was there already and they decided how they would respond to it. Whilst we know that Héré also did this, there is a feeling that he would have done what he did in any case. If he had been building on a virgin site, then the Place de la Carrière might have been a little shorter. If Boffrand had not been available to provide him with a model, then he might have chosen Mansart instead. For underlying Héré's approach there is an appeal, as it were, to authority; the authority given to him by the exigencies of Nancy itself, the authority of Boffrand for his architecture and, above all, the authority of geometry for his layout. This results in a sober architecture – relieved, it is true, by Jean-Baptiste Lamour's gilded ironwork – but there is nothing in the Place Stanislas to match the sensory indulgence of S. Marco itself. The sugar pink of the Doge's Palace, the clock tower and Sansovino's Loggetta. The Venetian architects have aimed for – and achieved – what Robert Venturi undoubtedly would call a 'difficult whole' aided, it must be said, by that firm anchor the Campanile. Given such a dominant vertical feature at this position close, as it were, to the centre of gravity, it is conceivable that *any* feasible grouping of buildings would be drawn into a visual unity.

For the appeal of the Piazza undoubtedly is a *sensory* appeal and, what is more, it appeals to many senses. Visually, of course, it is stunning, but one's total impression depends on a blending of impressions from many senses: the smell of Florian's coffee, the contrasts of sun and shade, the contrasts of still air and moving air as one moves from place to place in the Piazza, the sensations of that movement in itself which some call haptic and others call kinaesthetic.

Fig. 2.12 Héré de Corny: Place Stanislas, Nancy: Triumphal Arch (author's photograph).

Fig. 2.13 Héré de Corny: Place Stanislas, Nancy (author's photograph).

And certainly there are contrasts of sound. One cannot pretend that the sentimental numbers which Florian's have to offer, or Quadri's somewhat bland rock, offer anything like a profound musical experience, except perhaps when they clash in the manner of Charles Ives. But one should not forget that S. Marco itself inspired the Gabriellis to write some of the earliest, and most effective, of antiphonal music, in which orchestra answered orchestra across the vast dome, and that the courtyard of the Palace itself makes a very fine setting for music.

Such a blending of sensory delights simply does not come to mind when one contemplates the Place Stanislas. It is an intellectual architecture; indeed the contemplation of Patte's marvellous plan gives as much – if not more – pleasure than walking the actual pavements of the Place.

Fig. 2.14 Place Stanislas: the backs. As with so many 18th century urban layouts the architect designed and built only the façades. Others built as they pleased behind them (author's photograph).

3

Twentieth century city

New York

Just as the Piazza di San Marco is a splendid example of sensory-based Empiricist design, the Place Stanislas of Rationalist, so the City of New York shows, more clearly than any other, the forces of Pragmatism at work.

Our purpose here is to look at those things which make New York uniquely *the* city of the 20th century; that is to say a city which would have been quite impossible in any other epoch. We shall look in turn at the developments which, literally, made New York what it is. But before we do that we ought to look, briefly, at the history of the city. For New York has had its own dynamic, quite unlike that of any other city, which made it quite exceptionally equipped to take advantage of these developments at a particular place over a particular period of time.

But of course New York had begun to grow long before ways of generating and using electricity had been developed. Parts of its early history are enshrined in the streets. For instance the earliest settlers, the Algonquin Indians, had a track running from Albany, some 130 miles northwards in New York State, to the southern tip of Manhattan Island which survives to this day as Broadway.

And the Dutch who bought Manhattan from the Algonquin in 1626 for 60 guilders' (25 dollars) worth of gewgaws founded New Amsterdam and built a defensive wall across the southern tip (Fig. 3.1). This proved so ineffective that the then Governor, William Kieft, had a road for ease of movement built immediately to the north, the line of which is still called Wall Street. And in 1789 a group of merchants who had been meeting under a tree at 68 Wall Street instituted the New York Stock Exchange. Wall Street ever since has been the centre of New York's Financial District.

Then in 1803 New York acquired a new and ambitious Mayor, de Witt Clinton whose ten terms of office were to have more profound effects than anything else on the urban-form of New York City (Fig. 3.2).

This was drawn up in 1807 by Commissioners whom Clinton had appointed and their model, clearly, was the gridiron Plan prepared by L'Enfant for Washington, DC.

But whilst Washington had its great vistas along the grand, monumental Mall and the great diagonals of Pennsylvania and Maryland Avenues, the whole point of planning New York, as Stephen Games says (1985) was to divide Manhattan into saleable lots, 'to make the control and acquisition of real estate easier . . . '.

It was intended to prevent the process which, in Europe, had enabled the rich and powerful to buy more and more urban land at the expense of the public in general and of the poor in particular. So Clinton's Commissioners included no public squares in their Plan, no diagonals – apart from Broadway – and certainly no Mall. So New York has no vistas or as Games puts it: '. . . when you stand on a sidewalk and look into the distance, what you see is Nothing, just empty sky; the prospect, as it were, open-ended'.

Manhattan was divided into rectangular blocks by 100 foot avenues, running north to south, and rather narrower cross streets running east to west. These streets were 200 feet apart whilst the avenues were anything from 650 feet to 920 feet apart. So whilst the blocks were of constant width north/south they varied in length from East to West. Most of the avenues run right up Manhattan Island all the way into Harlem and initially these were numbered from First to Twelfth. The cross-streets also were numbered, starting with First, just north of Houston – which itself had been laid some 26 blocks north of Wall Street, and finishing with 155th which indeed is right up in Harlem. As housing was forced further and further north more and more traffic was needed to move people north and south, so new Avenues, such as Madison and Lexington, were added to the basic grid.

Fig. 3.1 Cortelyou (1660) with later additions by Stokes: Plan of New Amsterdam (from Kouwenhoven, 1953).

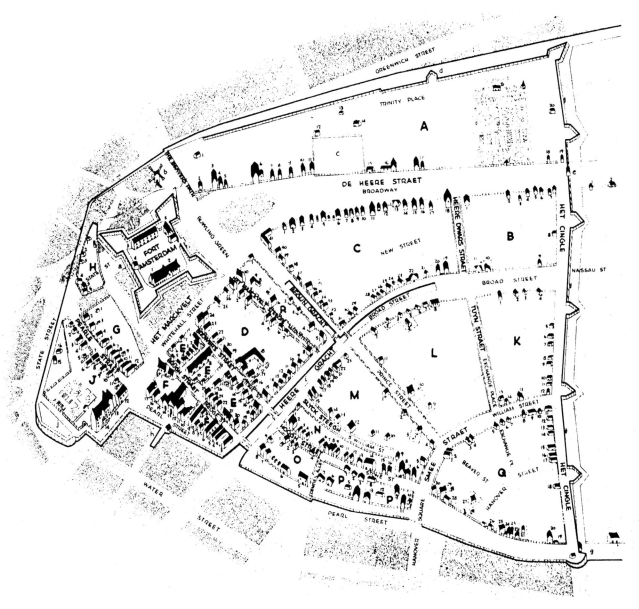

Surface transport

Once the north–south Avenues had been set out, according to the Plan of 1811, tracks could be laid for horse-drawn trams and indeed by 1831 – only a year after Stephenson's Liverpool and Manchester Railway – New York too had its first railroad, running northwards from Downtown into Harlem.

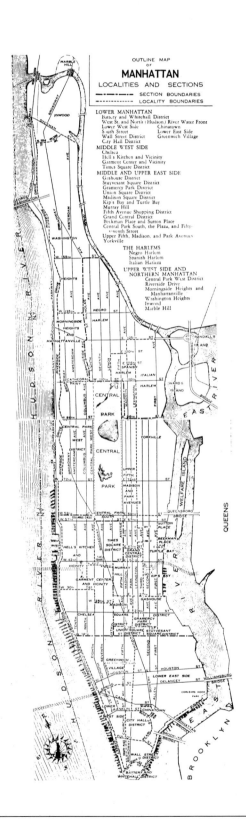

Fig. 3.2 William Bridges (1811). Official plan of Manhattan (from *The Federal Writers Project Guide to 1930s New York* (Pantheon Books, 1939).

By 1825 Clinton, having become Governor of New York State, achieved his long-term ambition of linking New York with the rich farmlands of the mid-West by building a canal between Lake Erie and the Hudson at Albany. Firmly and finally this established New York's pre-eminence as *the* port for the North Atlantic.

The elongated form of Manhattan, too – it is some 16 miles long and only two miles wide – meant that it had long shorelines connected easily by the cross-streets.

In the first half of 1825 alone – the year the canal was opened – some 1500 new merchants set themselves up in New York and 12 new banks were established. These were by no means enough to handle the burgeoning trade and 27 more banks applied for charters. The 10 insurance companies which existed at the time simply could not cope with the vast increase in maritime traffic and 31 more were set up.

The office building

This commercial activity needed new buildings, and indeed new building types. One of these, of course, the office block, was quite crucial and in the 1840s Richard Upjohn built the first: the Trinity Corporation Building on Broadway at Trinity Church Yard.

Not that Upjohn invented the office as a building type. Purpose-made, fire-resisting buildings had been needed in London by the companies which insured the mills of the early Industrial Revolution. The very first had been Robert Abraham's County Fire Office in Regent Street (1819) and naturally he used the iron-frame construction which had been developed for the early fireproof mills such as Bage's at Shrewsbury (1786).

It was in London too that a culturally acceptable style had been developed for the new commercial buildings. Charles Barry had demonstrated with his Travellers' Club (1829) that the Italian Renaissance Palazzo offered by far the greatest flexibility in terms of building form: possible height, number of floors, width, depth, window size and proportion in relation to internal planning, room arrangements and so on. A. T. Stewart brought Barry's ideas to New York with his marble fronted Sun Building which still stands at 280 Broadway (Tauranac, 1979). So the Italianate arrived.

It was timely because 17 blocks of New York had been destroyed in the Fire of 1835. Which Fire inspired architects and engineers, such as James Bogardus, to search for a fireproof construction. Bogardus designed a prefabricated system of columns, beams, entablatures, arches, spandrels and so on all cast in his Iron Foundry.

He chose Italianate for his system, as demonstrated in his own factory at Centre Street and in the five-storey Milhau Pharmacy at 183 Broadway (1848). These were the first all-iron buildings in New York and they were to be followed by many others, by Bogardus himself, by Badger, Johnson, Cornell, Stewart, Gilsey and others. Some 250 of their buildings still stand (see Gayle and Gillon, 1975) mostly in SoHo (*So*uth of *Ho*uston) but only a single Bogardus remains, somewhat decrepit, at 85 Leonard Street.

Further growth of the city

Between 1841 and 1850 New York absorbed some 1 713 251 immigrants, from Ireland, Scotland, England, Germany and other parts of north-west Europe. They were placed in the worst of lodging houses where there was no piped water, no sanitation and no heating. So it is hardly surprising that by 1867 legislation was passed which required all tenements to be built with adequate lighting, means of escape from fire and proper ventilation. It was ignored.

The elevator

Four years after Bogardus's Pharmacy Elisha Graves Otis demonstrated the second of those inventions which more than any others were to transform the physical form of New York. For of course it was Otis's Elevator, together with further developments in metal-frame construction which enabled the construction of that quintessential New York building form, the skyscraper.

Otis made his first (safety) elevator in 1852 and he demonstrated his invention, every day, in the Crystal Palace of the New York World Exhibition of 1853 (Fig. 3.3).

Nor was Otis's elevator the only foretaste of the way things were to go in New York. Opposite the Crystal Palace there was Latting's Ice Cream Parlour over which rose his Observatory, a narrow cone of metal-braced timber some 360 feet high. There were viewing platforms to which visitors could be hoisted by an often balky steam engine whilst if they chose to climb to the top, to the Observatory itself, then as Koolhaas says (1978): 'the inhabitants of Manhattan, for the first time, could inspect their domain from the air'. He quotes a World's Fair Guide Book of 1939 to the effect that: 'If we except the Tower of Babel then (the Observatory) may perhaps be called the World's first skyscraper.'

Latting's Observatory gave New Yorkers a taste, as it were, for higher things and as Koolhaas says, various towers were built as amusements on Coney Island in 1876, 1904 and 1906. Latting had also demonstrated that if one were prepared to dig down 40 feet or so the schist which underlies Manhattan offers splendid bearing for tall buildings.

It is by no means surprising that in the later 1850s inventions which had now become available such as the elevator, the metal frame, and the penchant for building tall, were put to more permanent use.

The race for world's tallest building seems to have started with the old Fifth Avenue Hotel of 1859 which had one of Otis Tuft's vertical screw elevators, yet, curiously enough, none were to be installed in New York office buildings for another ten years.

Industry

Prior to the Civil War New York had depended almost entirely on trade, inland and foreign. But after the war many kinds of industry were set up in the city, especially the manufacture of clothing, especially furs and accessories including jewellery. Publishing and printing were established of newspapers, books, music and so on, not to mention food production including bread and confectionery, drinks, alcoholic and non-alcoholic, metal working, from boilers to ornamental iron work, textiles, wood products, chemicals, stone, clay and glassware, of paper and paper products, tobacco products, and wide ranges of other goods.

Transport

As distances increased from where people lived to where they worked, New York had to think more deeply about how they could be

Fig. 3.3 Otis and his Safety Elevator (1853) (from Giedion, 1941).

transported. Already, by 1860 the horse-drawn streetcars had been hauling some 600 000 000 passengers a year and the streets were becoming so choked that alternatives had to be found. By 1863, London had the first purpose-built steam-driven underground railway, anywhere in the world, the Metropolitan.

New York could have gone underground, burrowing through the schist, but different choices were made after Charles Harvey argued, in 1867, that overhead railways would be cheaper and less disruptive to traffic than horse-drawn trams.

New York's first, steam driven, Elevated Railway – along Third Avenue – was opened in 1878 to be followed by lines along Second, Sixth and Ninth Avenues.

Electricity

Yet already, in 1866, Werner von Siemens had invented his rotary Dynamo, and once he had applied rotation to the generation of electricity, Siemens could then use it to drive rotating motors. He demonstrated his first electric railway at a Berlin Exhibition in 1879 and once motors were powerful enough to drive railways they could, of course, be used for many other things: for driving the machines which industry needed, machines, elevators, fans for moving large volumes of air, and so on.

Nor was this the only environmental conditioning which mains electricity enabled. It could be used specifically for lighting. By 1880 Swan in England and Edison in the United States had made good enough electric lamps and in September 1882 Edison opened *his* (Direct Current) Station at Pearl Street in New York. As late as 1932 when the Rockefeller Center was being designed, New York's Grand Central District still had the original DC supply!

So the potential was there by the early 1880s for a further round of developments of the kind which have helped shape New York. Behind their application, however, there was still one motivating factor. If there was money in it for New Yorkers they were interested; if there was not they were not.

In 1868 for instance George B. Post designed the first New York office building to have an elevator, the old Equitable on Broadway. Its 130 feet were soon to be exceeded by Post's Western Union Building (1872–75) which reached 230 feet, surpassed even while it was being built by R. M. Hunt's Tribune Building at 260 feet. By 1893 Napoleon Le Brun was planning the Metropolitan Life Insurance at 348 feet – it finished up considerably taller – whilst by 1890 G. M. Post's World (or Pulitzer) Building had reached 360 feet and nine years later, R. H. Robertson's Park Row Building was up to 382 feet.

Tall as these buildings may have been they were not true skyscrapers, according to Pevsner (1976) and others for the very simple reason that they were built with loadbearing walls. Their tops may have been in the clouds from time to time but that was not the point. A skyscraper for those historians had to have a steel frame.

Steel-framed building

New York architects were forbidden by Building Laws in the 1880s to use metal framing in any external walls. The cast-iron buildings had proved quite vulnerable when their contents caught fire.

Iron – and then steel – frames were being adopted because as loadbearing buildings went higher, the structures themselves took up more and more of the available space. Rule-of-thumb had it that a masonry wall should be thickened by four inches for every storey which meant that with, say, a 64-storey building 24 foot walls would be needed at basement level leaving no room for offices at all!

So all the ingredients were there for a fireproof framed construction. They were first assembled, as we know them, by William Le Baron Jenney of Chicago in the Home Insurance Building of 1883. Jenney had an extraordinary mixed construction including, in the upper five floors at least, the new rolled steel I-sections for columns and beams, made by the Bessemer process, which had just become available from Pittsburgh (Fig. 3.4).

Whilst the steel frame and the elevator solved the technical problems of building tall they did little to solve the architectural ones. For even though it may be built to five or six storeys, the Renaissance Palace on which the Italianate was based is essentially a horizontal building. As indeed is all Classical building. The three major elements of the Classical orders: *crepidoma* (steps), colonnade and entablature are essentially horizontal.

So it is hardly surprising that the first true skyscraper in New York, the Saint Paul's Building of 1899, should consist of storey piled on storey each complete as a horizontal building-in-itself.

There are better ways of building Classical *and* tall. The easiest is to design the building itself as a single, large column – as Adolph Loos did for the Chicago Tribune Competition (1923) – but this leads clearly to problems of internal planning. Or one can use a three-part composition in which the building itself has base, shaft and capital as a single column would. Louis Sullivan thought along these lines for his Wainwright Building in St Louis (1891) and the Guaranty now Prudential Buffalo (1894).

Having built these he described his aims in an Essay on *The Tall Office Building Artistically Considered* (1896). The two or three storey base should contain entrances, an entrance hall and shops; the multistorey shaft should contain repetitive floors of offices and the capital – with its cornice – should contain the various services.

Fig. 3.4 William le Baron Jenney: Fair Store, Chicago (1890–91), an early example of a structural frame in rolled steel sections (from Condit, 1964).

Sullivan himself built the Condict – now Bayard – Building (1898) in New York – not one of his best – but the building which attracted most attention, as the first true skyscraper in New York, was D. H. Burnham's Fuller Building of 1901 – now known as the Flatiron because of its triangular site where the diagonal of Broadway meets Fifth Avenue. The Flatiron is 21 storeys high, steel framed and stone clad. Here Burnham designed to Sullivan's three-part formula with (rather heavy) Italianate detail (Tauranac, 1979).

Developments in transport

In 1900 too the Elevated Railway on Third Avenue, which had been disgorging soot, cinders and even live coals since 1878 was electrified and two years later, all the lines had been electrified. But by then also the competition was growing for in 1900 the first contract had been awarded, to John B. MacDonald, for a subway system, running northwards from City Hall into the Bronx.

The first subway was opened in 1904, from Brooklyn Bridge northwards to 145th Street. As the subway was extended so housing, including luxury housing, could be built further and further to the north.

Air-conditioning

By 1907 however Willis Carrier was working out the principles of what he called: 'Man made weather!' Stuart Cramer described such things as air-conditioning in various lectures (1904). The principles seem to have been applied, at the luxury end of the market, by Trowbridge and Livingston, also in 1904 at the St Regis–Sheraton Hotel on East 55th Street (Tauranac, 1979; Stern *et al.* 1983). The client, Colonel Arnott, required that each room have a thermostat and wall ducts through which heated, cooled, dried or moistened air could be blown from plant rooms on the 3rd, the 7th and the 12th floors. Each room also had a socket for a hose connected by pipes to a large Kenney vacuum cleaner in the basement.

Such amenities were by no means available to office workers at the time. Just as they had been expected to walk up stairs for ten years after Otis's first elevator, so it was to be another 40 years before New York had a fully air-conditioned office building, the Universal Pictures of 1947 (Banham, 1969).

New York's office builders were more concerned with symbols – and profit – than with the comfort of their workers and soon the battle was on for higher and higher buildings.

In 1909 for instance Napoleon Le Brun designed the Metropolitan Life Tower on Madison Avenue. It would have been the tallest in the world, even at the original 500 feet, but its height was increased during construction to 700 feet. The tower itself rises out of a nine-storey block, which covers the whole of the site and with its tapering, pyramidal top, the tower derives clearly from the (Romanesque) Campanile of St Mark's in Venice, an ingenious alternative to Sullivan's three-part classical arrangement (Tauranac, 1979; Stern *et al.* 1983).

And then the race was on. Frank Woolworth wanted an office tower to symbolize the success of his five-and-dime stores. He approached Metropolitan Life for a loan but they refused him. So he determined that whatever else it might be, his tower would be taller than theirs. It went up to 792 feet (60 storeys) (Fig. 3.5). Woolworth also shared with his architect, Cass Gilbert, an enthusiasm for Barry's Houses of

Fig. 3.5 Cass Gilbert (1913) Woolworth's Building (author's photograph).

Parliament in London. So just as Le Brun's tower reflects the Campanile in Venice, so Gilbert's reflects Big Ben. Gilbert's Gothic, indeed, has been seen as the most appropriate treatment for a tall building, far more natural than Sullivan's Classical. Although the lower parts of his building hunch behind Gilbert's tower it is extraordinarily elegant with its (Perpendicular) Gothic detail modelled in terra cotta which has endured the New York climate exceedingly well. Nothing else could have given Gilbert the combination of delicacy and durability which are so crucial to the Woolworth's continuing success.

Whilst Woolworth was content for Gilbert to waste available space by building only a slender tower others were by no means so generous to New York. Graham, Anderson, Probst and White for instance covered their entire site of their H-plan Equitable Building (1915) to a height of 537 feet. They packed it out to 40 storeys, each of 30 000 square feet, and if such greed had become the norm, then the streets of Manhattan could have become quite uninhabitable canyons (Fig. 3.6). Others were nearly as bad. The Liberty Tower, for instance, occupied its entire plot; 58 feet by 82 feet, to a height of 401 feet.

So new Zoning Laws were passed in 1916. The city was divided into commercial and residential zones where the heights, and the volumes, of buildings were prescribed. On any given street façades could rise vertically to a prescribed height above which buildings had to be set back. Setbacks were determined, for a given site, by drawing an imaginary plane from the centre line of the street to the cornice or parapet line, as specified, of the façade and beyond. Anything higher then had to be set back behind the pyramidal envelope formed as these imaginary planes from the different sides of the building intersected. Towers could rise out of the pyramid provided that they covered no more than 25% of the site.

Impact of the Zoning Laws

There was much study of these Zoning Laws including Papers by Corbett and others including his *Zoning and the Envelope. . .* (1922) notable for the illustrative diagrams by Hugh Ferriss.

There were five Ferriss drawings altogether rendered, dramatically to show, first of all, the permissible building envelope. In subsequent drawings that envelope was compromised, successively against the need for daylight penetration, the realities of steel-frame construction, the realities of renting and finally, against the architectural needs of a Sullivan-like three-part composition (Fig. 3.7).

Art deco

By the early 1920s other forces were at work to determine the forms which New York buildings took. In 1919, for instance, a branch of the Wiener Werkstatte was opened in New York. There designs by Vienna Secession architects, such as Joseph Moffman, Joseph Olbrich and Otto Wagner were sold in the forms of jewellery, fabrics, china and other objects. This seems to have stimulated New Yorkers into that blending of geometric patterns from Frank Lloyd Wright, Mayan Temples, Pueblo patterns, not to mention Cubism, Expressionism, Constructivism and on on (Bletter, 1975) which has come to be known as Art Deco.

It was being used before long for the most commercial of buildings such as Sloan and Robertson's for Fred F. French (1927) not to mention such architectural *tours de force* as William van Allen's Chrysler

Fig. 3.6 Graham, Anderson, Probst and White (1915). Equitable Building, New York; an H-shaped block which covers the entire site to a height of 537 ft (author's photograph).

Fig. 3.7 Zoning Laws of 1916 as interpreted (1922) by Hugh Ferriss (from Ferriss, 1980).

Building (1928). This was started as a speculation and van Allen knew that at 925 feet his building was competing with 40 Wall Street for the title of: 'World's Tallest'. But then he found a client in Walter P. Chrysler, who, like Woolworth before him, wanted a distinctive building. Chrysler made automobiles so van Allen designed automobile crestings for the plinth with front wheels and mudguards in brick with real hub caps and (oversize) winged radiator caps at the corners.

And then van Allen went higher to make an even bolder symbol, replacing the original glass dome with a stainless steel spire of saw-tooth crescents like radiator grilles. This was prefabricated in secret and, once installed, it brought the Chrysler Building up to 1048 feet, 64 feet higher even than the Eiffel Tower.

But in 1931 the title of World's Tallest passed to Shreve, Lamb and Harmon's Empire State Building. They started by designing within the volume that the Zoning Laws allowed and then kept whittling away the lower parts and adding them to the top until, at 86 storeys and 1100 feet, the Empire State was some 50 feet higher than the Chrysler. But the client, Arthur Smith, a failed Presidential candidate wanted to secure the record for all time. The Germans were planning to use Zeppelins on the Transatlantic route so he had a mooring mast added, taking the Empire State to 1250 feet.

So the plinth covers the site – at Fifth Avenue between 33rd and 34th Streets – to five storeys after which a major setback forms a 60 foot terrace around the tower. There are further setbacks towards the top of the tower itself, not to mention grooves, some three bays wide, down the northern and southern façades. These give the Empire State its soaring verticality, reinforced by the stainless-steel mullions which frame the vertical bands of windows, flush with their limestone spandrels.

Rockefeller Center

By the time Empire State was completed, Wall Street had crashed in the great Depression. Which did not deter John D. Rockefeller who had set his heart on building a vast Center in the heart of mid-town Manhattan, between Fifth and Sixth Avenues (Balfour, 1978; Kinsky, 1978). Rockefeller's aim, as he said in 1939, was to 'make the square and the immediate surroundings (into) the most valuable shopping district in the world'.

Since Reinhard and Hofmeister had designed an aborted Opera House with a Plaza for the site they were retained as overall planners. But the scheme included 13 buildings so other architects were brought in. The Master Plan still included a Plaza, parallel to Fifth and Sixth Avenues and running between them. It was connected to Fifth by the leg as it were of a 'T' forming Channel Gardens which runs, appropriately enough, between La Maison Francais and the British Empire Building (Fig. 3.8). For the first time ever, anywhere, sky-scrapers were to be grouped with consciously designed urban spaces between, a practice which, even now, has rarely been emulated. The vista westwards along Channel Gardens is firmly closed by Reinhard and Hood's 70-storey RCA Building. This could be built to 850 feet within the Zoning Laws because the Plaza and the Gardens together gave sufficient open space. Other tall buildings in the Center include the 54-storey Exxon at 740 feet, the 51-storey McGraw Hill at 670 feet, the 48-storey Time Life at 587 feet and the 41-storey International Building northwards of the British Empire Building.

Fig. 3.8 Reinhard and Hood (1931). RCA Building seen along the Channel Gardens of Reinhard and Hofmeister's Rockefeller Center (author's photograph).

The Plaza itself with its fountain, sunken skating rink and shopping mall is one of the most loved, and most used urban spaces, not just in New York, but anywhere in the world.

Radio City Music Hall lay behind the International Building and north of the RCA. It was fully air-conditioned, a comfort job of the kind which had become standard for large auditoria since Willis Carrier installed one in Graumann's Metropolitan Theatre, Los Angeles in 1922. Cool air was brought in at high level and the vitiated air extracted through grilles under the seats.

The RCA Building itself had air-conditioned studios, not to mention a shopping mall. The offices too could have been air conditioned, but Hood chose not to condition his offices even in the RCA. He argued that office workers ought to have natural light and natural ventilation, that this could be achieved by sensible planning. So, according to Hood: 'we have eliminated every dark corner, there is not a single point in the rentable area . . . that is more than 22 feet away from a window'.

Fig. 3.9 Kahn and Jacobs: Universal Pictures (1947): the first air-conditioned office building in New York (author's photograph).

Post Rockefeller

After the Rockefeller Center there was no more spectacular building until the late 1940s, for in 1942, America had engaged in World War II. The first of New York's post-war office buildings, Universal Pictures of 1947 was also the first to have full air-conditioning (Fig. 3.9).

1952 saw the completion of an influential set of buildings: for the United Nations. The site was along the East River, from 42nd Street to 45th and the complex was designed by a truly multinational team, including Bassov, Brunfaut, Cornier, Ssu-Ch'eng Liang, Markelius, Niemeyer, Robertson, Souileux and Villamajo. The Executive Architects were Harrison and Abramovitz but the overall concept was Le Corbusier's. Indeed it was the first realization of his City in a Park ideal with three individual pavilions: the General Assembly, a Conference Building and the Hammarskjöld Library, grouped around a large open courtyard at the foot of the Secretariat (Fig. 3.10).

This latter was developed from that first of all glass-walled sky-scrapers: the Ministry of Education in Rio de Janeiro for which Le Corbusier had been Consultant (1936) to a team of Brazilian architects including Costa, Niemeyer, Reidy and others.

The office slab of the Ministry has solid ends but the sides are completely glazed with curtain walling. So does the Secretariat but there is a fundamental difference. The Ministry's glazed walls face north and south and since Rio is in the Southern Hemisphere, Le Corbusier insisted that the northern facade, which faces directly into the sun, should be faced with sun-shading of the kind he had been developing as *brize soleil* (Le Corbusier, 1937).

Having solved the problem of solar heat-gain for the tropics, Le Corbusier designed a similar *brize soleil* for the glazed walls, facing east and west of the Secretariat. In developing Le Corbusier's overall concept, however, Harrison left off the *brize soleil* on the grounds that solar heat gain could be controlled entirely by air-conditioning (Banham, 1975). Le Corbusier protested with great vigour (Le Corbusier, 1948) but despite his protests that such a solution would be dangerous, very seriously dangerous, Harrison left off the *brize soleil*.

Critics such as Mumford were horrified (1952) by the sheer inhumanity of such a working environment but whereas in 1925, Art Deco had triumphed over the geometric abstractions of the Bauhaus, de Stijl and Purism, the tables were now being turned. Pure, unadorned

Fig. 3.10 Harrison and others to a concept of Le Corbusier's United Nations Buildings, New York (author's photograph).

rectilinear geometry was to become the basis for everything that was serious in post-war design from the scale of radios and fan-heaters to, most certainly, the scale of buildings, not to mention the spaces between them.

New York was a fertile breeding ground for such abstraction since in 1947 Philip Johnson had exhibited, at the Museum of Modern Art, the work of Mies van der Rohe – largely unknown until then – describing his Barcelona Pavilion, for instance, as: '. . . one of the milestones of modern architecture . . . truly one of the few manifestations of the contemporary spirit that justifies comparison with the great architecture of the past. . .'.

After the Secretariat, competition developed between Mies's pupils as to who could build the first office tower with all four façades of glass. Mies, after all, had shown one way in his Apartments at 860 Lake Shore Drive in Chicago, completed in 1951. The winner was Martin Vegas of Caracas who, with Jose Miguel Gallia completed the Polar (Soft Drinks) Office Building also in 1951.

A year later, another Mies pupil, Gordon Bunshaft, of Skidmore, Owings and Merrill completed Lever House on Park Avenue, New York (Fig. 3.11). It has an open courtyard at street level surrounded by *piloti* supporting a single-storey horizontal slab, or, rather a hollow square at first floor level. Bunshaft could have designed a set-back building, filling the permissible envelope, but he chose instead to build a slender, 20-storey slab occupying 25% of the site north of his open court. It reached the set-back line at the 17th storey, but since he had given up so much of the permitted envelope Bunshaft was allowed to build beyond it for another four storeys and a cooling tower.

The three most visible sides of this slab are clad with a curtain walling but the west side, away from Park Avenue, is a solid buff-brick tower of escape stairs and service ducts.

So Bunshaft broke the street-line of Park Avenue by offering his open public plaza; a bleak and rather windswept space which, unlike the Rockefeller Plaza is used only in the summer by those who wish to escape the rigours of their air-conditioned offices.

For like the clear glass of United Nations the light green glass of Lever House gave all the problems one might expect of solar heat gain, heat loss and so on. Yet Mumford (1954) saw it as an exquisite 'House of Glass' in which such problems would be unimportant.

Mies van der Rohe and Philip Johnson still had faith in glass cladding when they were designing 375 Park Avenue (formerly the Seagram Building) (Fig. 3.12). By this time (1958) the manufacturers claimed to have solved the problems of excessive glazing with their bronze glass. Seagram was covered with this both for windows and for infilling spandrels.

Like Lever House it had a major set-back in front, of 90 feet from the building line leaving an open plaza facing on to Park Avenue. The 37-storey tower, 500 feet high rises sheer from this plaza but it is T-shaped on plan for most of its height and there are rather more complex set-backs to the rear.

Yet the abstractions of Lever House and Seagram provided models for skyscraper design, not just in New York itself, but throughout the Western world. As New Yorkers were to learn after the oil crisis of 1973 they represented the most energy-inefficient buildings ever conceived (Fig. 3.13). Later Philip Johnson was to express the gravest of reservations concerning Mies's approach in his *Non-Miesian Directions* (1959). And later still, of course, he was to demonstrate alternatives with such buildings as his AT&T (Fig. 3.14).

One gets the impression, both inside and between their buildings,

Fig. 3.11 Bunshaft of Skidmore, Owings and Merrill (1952): Lever House, New York's first curtain-walled office tower (author's photograph).

Fig. 3.12 Mies with Johnson (1954). Seagram Building (now 375 Park Avenue), New York (author's photograph).

that the abstractionists of the 1950s were quite incapable of thinking of space as something which can be modelled in three dimensions. Internally their spaces simply were the volumes clamped between their horizontal floors and their horizontal ceilings interrupted, as necessary, by columns. Externally, too, space seemed to be simply that which was left over between their rectilinear slabs.

Yet in New York itself the city planners seem to have seen the Seagram Plaza, even though it broke the street-line, as some kind of bonus. So, in 1961, the Zoning Laws were revised yet again to permit any building which occupied only 40% of its site to rise more or less vertically in the air to any height. And if it were set behind a plaza, then the volume of the building itself could be increased by a further 20%.

There was not much of a fight with market forces since by this time it was becoming clear that if it was too far from a window, office space would be difficult to let. At 270 Park Avenue for instance (formerly Union Carbide 1960), Skidmore's sacrificed some 200 000 of a permitted 360 000 square feet so that 65% of their office space could be within 15 feet of a window.

After the United Nations Complex New York's next attempt at a planned open space – as distinct from one simply left over between the slabs – was developed from 1962–66 within the Lincoln Center for the Performing Arts. Once again the co-ordinating Architect was Wallace K. Harrison. His model, clearly, was Michelangelo's Campidoglio in Rome in that three of the major buildings, the New York State Theatre (Philip Johnson and Richard Foster), the Metropolitan Opera House (Harrison himself) and the Avery Fisher (Concert) Hall (Max Abramovitz) are grouped around a plaza open eastwards to Broadway. All three buildings have all-glass façades shaded – rather like Niemeyer's in Brazilia – by open colonnades. Since the Met provides the axial focus to the plaza its columns support vast semicircular arches. The plaza is rather well proportioned but since the columns are backed by glass, rather than solid walls, they have a rather cardboard quality.

The Met and the Avery Fisher help contain a second plaza with a pool reflecting the inevitable Henry Moore. The other two sides of this second plaza are formed by the Vivian Beaumont Theatre (Eero Saarinen) and, linked by an extension of the plaza over 66th Street, the Julliard School of Music (Pietro Belluschi, Catalano and Westerman). These are genuine urban spaces but their location, in what used to be one of the toughest neighbourhoods in New York, means that they are only alive when people stream into the auditoria and out again when the performances are over.

The Lincoln Center Buildings are abstractions of Classical architecture and much criticized for that in the days when simple, geometric abstraction was the rule. There were indeed many variations on that geometric theme including Saarinen's CBS Building of 1965, Skidmore, Owings and Merrill's Marine Midland of 1967, their 1 Liberty Plaza and Emery Roth's 55 Water Street (1973). Saarinen's CBS had a certain abstract elegance with its V-shaped granite piers alternating with vertical strip windows whilst Roth's was a vast lump of a building, the largest private office block in the world containing 3 200 000 square feet.

Whilst some of Skidmore's buildings were merely dull, others were actively damaging to the street. Their Nine West 57th Street for instance and their 1114 Avenue of the Americas, both 1972, exploit the set-back laws by curving back, in section, from the building line to the front of their 25% slab thus destroying *any* sense of enclosure at street level.

But above all, as we have seen New York is an *electric* city, not only in

Fig. 3.13 Johnson and Burgee (1978). A T & T Building, Madison Avenue (top left) with, right of it IBM and behind it the Trump Tower. Bottom left on Park Avenue is Lever House and right of that the former Seagram Building.

Fig. 3.14 Park Avenue, New York after the oil crisis (1973) (author's photograph).

the sense that it is exciting, or even in the more literal sense that in Broadway and Times Square it has – or had in the 1930s – the highest concentrations of neon light-scapes in the world. It is electric in the sense that neither the city itself, nor any of the tall buildings which comprise it, could have taken the forms they do without the steady supply of electricity in very large quantities.

Without electricity to drive their elevators, those buildings could not have been so tall. Without electricity to drive their ceiling lighting, not to mention their air-conditioning, they could not have been so deep in plan, nor have so much glass in their façades.

Nor could the hundreds of thousands who commute to them every day from the distant suburbs actually do so without first the Elevated Railway – electrically driven from 1900 – and the subway. It simply would not have been feasible for such numbers to come in by private transport, nor indeed by streetcars and other forms of public transport at surface level.

This was demonstrated very clearly on those two extraordinary occasions, in November 1965 and July 1977 when the electricity supply failed completely (Rosenthal and Gelb, 1965).

The electric city: blackouts

Curiously enough New York's blackouts occurred at a moment of transition when many were beginning to realize that the Modern Movement by no means solved all their problems.

As a *New York Times* Editorial put it after the second occasion:

> New York is an Electric City. A massive power outrage might handicap Chicago or Los Angeles but it would not have so paralysing an impact.
>
> People outside New York might lose their radio alarms in the morning, but they would not be so dependent on electric pumps to bring them wash water, electric elevators to get them out of their homes, electric trains to take them to work, nor on electric nervous systems of such giant industries as securities, banking and communications to give them jobs.

Whilst some 30 million people were affected, one way or another, by these power failures it is interesting to see exactly what of urban life *was* lost; this seems to have differed on the two occasions. Each time there were no railways, no elevators, no lights, no air-conditioning (Rosenthal and Gelb, 1965).

The *New York Times* reports that during the first failure from 5.27 p.m. on Thursday 9 November 1965 to 7.00 a.m. on the morning of 10 November some 800 000 people were stranded for up to 12 hours; some 60 of them all night, indeed for 14 hours in a BMT subway. Hundreds of others tried to sleep on the stationary escalators, in the railway stations, hotel lobbies and even the Armories which had been opened for them.

The Secretary General of the United Nations, U. Thant was stranded in an elevator for 5 hours. Others were stuck for even longer periods in the 13 failed elevators of the Empire State, the six of Pan Am, the RCA Building and elsewhere whilst their rescuers hacked through the concrete elevator shafts.

Opportunists bought candles and sold them for twice the price they paid; bars and restaurants made the most of the situation and so did taxi drivers. In many office buildings, food and drink were to be found only in executive suites. Since their refrigerators were failing, the more generous employers made 'crab-meat and graham crackers' available to their office staffs, not to mention comfortable couches, which may indeed have contributed to the somewhat increased birth-rate observed in and around New York some nine months later.

On the whole, though, the blackout of 1965 seems to have engendered an all-in-this-together spirit of the kind which brought London through the Blitz. Even so, next morning, as the *New York Times* reports, people were 'hungry, thirsty and unwashed. . . . The fun had gone out of the thing . . . crankiness replaced good humor'.

Despite the precautions which supposedly had been taken, much of this was repeated in the blackout of 13 July 1977. As the *New York Times* reported on 14 July: 'It was a morning without water, without elevators, without subways, without banks and even, for a while, without a good hot cup of coffee to make it all bearable. . . .'

But there were differences, in particular the incidence of crime was so much higher in 1977 that State Troopers had to be sent in. The *New York Times* reports shattering glass, wailing sirens, the metallic clash of trash cans.

Circumstances of course were different in three major ways: since this was the second such failure people, including criminals, could move into action much faster. In July also New York is notoriously hot and sultry; tempers flare; there had been a vast increase in unemployment. So liquor stores were looted, as were clothing stores, dry-cleaning establishments and outlets for electrical and other appliances. There were 2700 arrests.

There are those who suggest that whatever else they may have done these power failures forced New Yorkers to return to more human values. And there is something in these claims as shown, for instance, by the birth rate increases!

The atrium

By this time, however, new urban forms were emerging. John Portman of Atlanta had decided that if the downtown areas were dangerous then it might be prudent to build small-scale urban spaces contained and protected by buildings.

Hence a resurgence of interest in indoor urban-scale spaces to which end Portman revived, one cannot say invented, the atrium in a series of spectacular hotels such as the Hyatt Regency in Atlanta, Georgia (1967) and, more spectacularly still, San Francisco (1974). These brought cathedral-scale spaces into downtown areas where people can sit and watch the world go by, into areas of cities where formerly it had even been dangerous to walk.

New York's first example was the Citicorp Center (1977) on Lexington Avenue at 53rd and 54th Streets, designed by Hugh Stubbins with Emery Roth. This rises to 915 feet over a large glazed atrium on four massive, 127 foot *piloti*.

The Citicorp atrium includes a shopping mall, a subway entrance, and even Saint Peter's (Lutheran) Church. The cladding is perfectly smooth, with a horizontal bands of brushed aluminium alternating with (slightly bluish) glass. The top slopes to the south, at 45 degrees, as a gesture to the Zoning Laws and Stubbins intended that it should be covered with solar collectors. Such collectors proved too heavy for the structure but at least, after 40 years, New York had a new contribution to its skyline; a roof that was other than flat.

Further contributions were to follow in the battle against stark Functionalism which was joined early in the 1960s. Hans Hollein for instance produced a joke photomontage of Downtown New York showing a skyscraper for Wall Street formed like a Rolls-Royce radiator. Johnson and Burgee obviously had this in mind, if only in their collective unconscious, when in 1977 they were designing the AT&T on Madison Avenue (at 53rd and 54th Streets). It has been called the Chippendale Skyscraper because of its pedimented top but there is more to it than that.

Johnson and Burgee themselves work from 375 Park Avenue, the former Seagram Building, and therefore are aware of its many faults. What is more their clients, The American Telephone and Telegraph Company, specified an energy-conserving building and one in which their executive could work in comfort with their visual display units. Which meant individual rooms with walls and small windows. These clearly give better thermal – and glare – control than curtain-walled buildings ever did. What is more they are set deep within the walls between granite ribs which naturally gave a strong vertical emphasis to the façades.

Just as Sullivan's office shafts needed proper termination at top and bottom, so did Johnson and Burgee's. Hence the broken pediment at the top of AT&T, not to mention the arcading at street level. The building rises sheer from Madison Avenue, over the sidewalk, and the entrance is marked by a large Alberti- or Brunelleschi-like arches, flanked by two smaller ones.

So rather than destroying the street-line, as Skidmore's did at West 52nd and on the Avenue of the Americas, Johnson and Burgee strengthen it whilst providing usable amenities; their arcades and their shopping mall, rather than a windswept Seagram-like plaza.

Next to the AT&T Edward Larrabee Barnes built the 43-storey IBM five sided in plan and sheathed with extremely smooth slabs of grey-green granite. Its most notable feature, however, is a glazed, four-storey plaza; the apotheosis of the conservatory and open to the public. And next to IBM the Trump Tower by Der Scutt of Swanke, Hayden and Connell is a 52-storey saw-toothed, diagonal tower rising, by a complex system of set-backs out of a rectangular base. The tower is clad in golden glass whilst the internal entrance mall – or atrium – is a lavish confection indeed of marble terraces and fountains.

These three buildings all have urban spaces within them but there has been no attempt to make urban spaces between them.

Since most of New York has been built over there are fewer opportunities there of building in this incoherent way. Indeed given the pattern of land-ownership in New York it is increasingly difficult to assemble sufficient lots, or even blocks, to plan further groups of buildings with *designed* urban spaces between them. Which has not prevented Donald Trump from trying. For more recent demonstrations of the forces which formed New York: greed, opportunism, the exploitation of invention, we ought to look at places such as Houston, as indeed we shall in Chapter 13.

The crucial point about our three paradigms, however, is that they resulted from different ways of thinking. In the case of the Piazza, successive architects used their senses to assess what was there already and to design for complementary sensory delight. We shall argue that such designing ought to be called 'empirical'. Héré certainly used his senses but his chief preoccupation was with geometric order of a kind which is rooted in 'rationalist' philosophy, whilst New York simply grew by *ad hoc*, trial-and-error events of a kind we shall call 'pragmatic'.

PART TWO

PHILOSOPHIES AND THEORIES

4
Philosophical bases

These historic modes of planning and our paradigms clearly embody different ways of thinking about the city and its design. The Greeks and Romans used mystic ceremonies to determine where their cities should be founded, consulting the oracles, the augurs and so on. And having decided on a site they would lay out their city as a gridiron of streets. Thus their actual planning was based on simple geometric systems, as indeed were the Spanish cities built according to the Laws of the Indies.

But the Greeks, the Romans and the Spanish also knew that geometry alone is not enough. Hippocrates, Vitruvius, not to mention the drafters of the Spanish Laws were equally concerned with aspect, prospect, the need for water, the sun path as it related to the city, the need for shade, the direction of the prevailing winds and many other factors which affected the comfort, the convenience, the well-being, not to mention the pleasure of those who were to live in the city. The planners, in other words, were concerned with what would be seen within the city, what would be heard, with temperatures and air movements as they would be felt on the skin, the smells of noxious processes such as tanning, and so on. In the cities of Islam, of course, the primary generator of the built forms was visual protection of the women.

Nor could any city builder ignore the exigencies of the site, whether it was flat, sloping or formed of rocky outcrops. The Greeks, for instance, faced with a steeply sloping site for their City of Priene built it as a stepped gridiron. But neither they, the Romans nor the Spanish built much on such difficult terrains as those chosen, for defensive purposes, by the founders of many cities in Medieval Europe.

These three basic ways of thinking: (1) starting – and sometimes finishing – with pure geometric layouts, (2) starting with concern for what the human senses would experience and (3) finding out by trial-and-error what could be made to stand up of course were known and distinguished from each other by the ancient Greeks.

In the *Timaeus* for instance Plato stated his belief that the structure of the Universe itself is based on simple, geometric forms. He is also known too to have 'inveighed with great indignation' against those who tried to solve geometric problems by trial-and-error methods using 'mechanical devices' (Broadbent, 1973). Aristotle showed far more respect for the human senses in the *Physics* and the *Metaphysics*.

These three basic ways of thinking were developed, over the centuries, into coherent – and rival – philosophies: Empiricism, which puts its trust in the human senses; Rationalism which does not, preferring to work in logical steps from first principles and Pragmatism which prefers things which are known to work in practice.

Empiricism

Bacon

In 1620, for instance, Sir Francis Bacon argued that everything we know about the world around us has been gained by experience as received by our senses. We build our ideas by processes of induction, although not the crude induction which Karl Popper and others have attempted to demolish (1959, 1963). In Bacon's induction, one collects examples of some phenomenon or other – such as heat – and prepares a Table of Essences and Presences. One then tries to find for each example a contrary one which enables him to form a Table of Deviation or of Absence.

In the case of heat, for instance, he finds many examples of its presence in, for instance, fire, the sun's rays, pepper, fresh horse-dung and so on. But then for each of these he finds a contrary example, an absence of heat. The sun's rays are hot but the moon's are not and so on. Then starting with his Table of . . . Absences – eliminating the things which are *not* hot that Bacon finally comes to his conclusions as to what heat actually comprises.

Popper suggests (1963) that any Conjecture can be destroyed by a single Refutation. Brought up in the Northern Hemisphere one could deduce – or, rather, induce – that all swans are white; a Conjecture which would be Refuted by a single sighting of an Australian black swan. Bacon would have tried to find examples of swans of many colours before concluding that all swans are white or black!

Other British philosophers, such as Locke, Berkeley and Hume followed Bacon, in their explanations of how we gain all our knowledge by experience gained by our senses; from which they extracted their entire philosophy of empiricism.

Locke, Berkeley, Hume

The first of the true Empiricists was John Locke (1632–1704) whose chief work in his *Essay Concerning Human Understanding* written in 1687 and published in 1690.

According to Locke, all our ideas are based on sensation – receiving information by means of our senses – and on reflection, that is contemplating later what the senses have told us. A child at birth may have sensations of hunger and thirst, warmth, cold and possibly pain. But there cannot be any knowledge; at birth. Knowledge can only be built up by experience over the years.

By which we build up such ideas as: yellow, white, heat, cold, soft, hard, bitter, sweet, and so on. We perceive an object with such qualities, learn that the object has a name and recognize other, similar objects because they have similar qualities.

Once we have built up our ideas in this way, we can operate on them by such processes as thinking, doubting, believing, reasoning, knowing and willing on which basis is founded our understanding.

The trouble is that the qualities we can perceive by means of our senses are all, as it were, on the surface: colour, shape, taste, sound and so on. But these, for Locke, are only secondary qualities whereas objects in themselves have primary qualities such as solidity, figure, motion, rest, number and so on which we cannot always perceive. Since the earth rotates, so do all the objects on its surface, but we cannot perceive *their* rotation.

Locke's distinction, of primary and secondary qualities, raised a number of questions, not to mention nagging doubts. Later Empiricists, such as Bishop Berkeley (1685–1753) and David Hume (1711–76), examined these questions in much detail. If all we can perceive are Locke's secondary qualities, then how do we suppose that the primary qualities actually exist? And if we are so unsure about their qualities, how can we suppose that the objects themselves exist?

Berkeley argued from this (1709) to an extreme conclusion: that objects themselves simply cannot exist outside the mind of a perceiver.

David Hume subscribed to Berkeley's sceptical view and developed his own explanations in the *Treatise on Human Nature* of 1739–40.

For Hume the real world crumbles into a series of mere sensory impressions. Nothing exists at all unless someone is there, to see, hear, touch or otherwise experience it.

Hume also developed much further Locke's ideas of associations. There are, he says, three ways in which different ideas become associated in the mind. First of all the one may call to mind the other because of a certain resemblance. The one thing is like or otherwise seems like the other so the mind runs freely between them. Secondly, he says, they may be associated by contiguity. Having experienced two ideas together, at the same time or in the same place we shall always associate them. And thirdly there are relations of cause and effect. We perceive that one event seems to cause another (there is no smoke without a fire) so whenever we perceive one of them this causes us to recall the other, to presume the existence of the other.

What is more, as Ayer says (1956), Hume raised the fundamental problem of induction in such a way that it still remains much as he left it.

All the Empiricist can do is to accept, directly, the evidence of his senses, comparing new sensations, as they occur, with the residues of past experiences as recorded in his brain. We have learned from experience, so far, that the sun has risen every day – at least everywhere between the Arctic and the Antarctic circles. That is our personal induction.

We might try to deny the existence of induction, as Popper does, but that would make it quite impossible to live our everyday lives. We should have to work out, from first principles, everything we did each day. Whether to get up or not, to bathe, to get dressed, to eat and so on. Design also would be quite impossible. No engineer, for instance, could assume that, because a certain column has stood for many years, another one, of the same design, can be trusted to stand up at all!

Hume presents the splendid example of a river. We may have learned from our lifetimes of experience that a shallow river, moving fast, over stones which we can see through the transparent water is safe to cross, even by walking. We may have learned also that a slow-moving, muddy river may be deep and turbulent indeed. Hume, of course, would test the depth of such a river before deciding if and how to cross it. But the Popperian, refusing to learn by experience, would simply go blundering in and, possibly, drown. If one denies the existence of induction there may be no good *logical* reason for pausing at the bank but some extremely good *psycho*logical ones of a kind which, literally, help us to survive!

Rationalism: Descartes

The Empiricist position was much disputed by Renée Descartes (1597–1650) who argued that, since our senses can be confused by optical or other illusions, our brains, of their own volition, generate dreams and nightmares, delusions and even hallucinations; we really cannot trust the evidence of our senses and must search, instead, for universal truths which, like Plato, he believed could be reached by logical thinking. The philosophy of Descartes and his followers is known as Rationalism.

In a sense Descartes was trying to apply the scientific models of Galileo and Newton, especially their mathematical methods, to more general issues in philosophy.

Descartes meditated on the processes of thinking itself and in the *Discours del la Méthode* (1637) he set out his conclusions as to how we can distinguish the true from the false.

Curiously enough his thoughts turned first to meditations on architecture. He says, of those thoughts:

> . . . one of the first that came to my mind was that there is often less perfection in what has been put together bit by bit, and by different masters, than in the work of a single hand. Thus we see how a building, the construction of which has been undertaken and completed by a single architect, is usually superior to those that many have tried to restore by making use of old walls which have been built for other purposes.

Clearly Descartes had little respect for picturesque irregularity! He goes on:

> So too, those old places which, beginning as villages, have developed in the course of time into great towns, are generally so ill-proportioned in comparison with those an engineer can design at will in an orderly fashion that, even though the buildings, taken severally, often display as much art as in other places, or even more, yet the disorder is such with a large house here and a small one there, and the streets all tortuous and uneven, that the whole place seems to be the product of chance rather than the design of men who use their reason.

So it was that in urban design Descartes preferred the new, fortified towns which had or were being built in France, such as Nancy (1588) and Charleville (1605). He saw these as conceived in the mind of a single engineer and thought them far superior to older, medieval towns with their narrow, winding streets and their various buildings: evidence of growth and change over the centuries.

We must be clear, of course, that the Nancy Descartes had in mind was the star-shaped fortress, built shortly before he was there and *not* the Nancy of the Place Stanislas which Henri de Corny was to design some 115 years later.

But the crucial part of Descartes, for us, is his attitude to the senses. In the *Meditations* (1641) Descartes describes the methodology of doubt against which he tried to test all his former opinions. 'Now truth', he says, 'seems to have come to me hitherto, either directly or indirectly, from my senses' – just as the Empiricists said it did. 'But', according to Descartes: 'the senses, in my experience, are sometimes deceptive; and it is but prudent not to trust entirely to those who have once deceived me'.

Which, of course, is true. As Descartes put it:

> How often has it happened to me to dream at night that I was here, in this place, dressed and seated by the fire, when all the time I was lying naked in my bed . . . and when I reflect upon the matter more closely, I see clearly that there are no conclusive signs

by which to distinguish between our waking and our sleeping moments, that I am dumbfounded, and my confusion is such that I can almost believe myself at this moment.

Whether he was asleep or awake, however, the objects which Descartes seemed to be perceiving were identical anyway. Real parts of his body, such as his eyes, his hands, his head or whatever had a true, physical existence and so did those same parts even when he was dreaming of them. The illusions he saw in his sleep were accurate, coloured representations of the real things. They could not be formed in any other way.

A colour would be the same whether it was real or illusory so, for Descartes, a colour is a universal entity. So is anything else which takes concrete, physical form, which has 'corporeal nature and its extension'. So the shapes and figures of things extended in space, their quantity, magnitude and number, the spaces in which they exist, the time through which they endure, and so on are all universal entities.

Sciences such as arithmetic and geometry deal with relations between objects, rather than with the objects themselves. Thus they possess certain manifest truths:

> For, whether I be asleep awake or asleep, two and three always make five, and a square always has four sides; nor does it seem possible that such manifest truths should ever incur the least suspicion of falsehood.

Such things are universal, indubitable and immutable. So Descartes goes on to say:

> . . . when, for example, I imagine a triangle, although perhaps there is not, and never has been, any place in which it can exist outside my mind, yet this triangle possesses a nature, or form, or essence, which is immutable and eternal, which I have not invented, and which in no way depends on my mind. This follows from the fact that it is possible to demonstrate various properties of the triangle, and that its three angles are equal to two right angles . . . even though, when I first imagined this triangle, I had no thought of these properties, which cannot therefore have been invented by me.

As Descartes says, the idea of a triangle might have reached him through his senses. He has, after all, seen triangles, or bodies which were triangular in shape. He dismisses such an explanation.

> The fact is that I can conceive a mass of other figures, about which there can never be any suspicion that they have come under the observation of my senses, but of which I can demonstrate various properties touching their essence as I can in the case of the triangles.

Knowing of three-sided figures (triangles) and four-sided figures (squares) he can then conceive of other figures with five sides (pentagons), six sides (hexagons) and so on. And if he can conceive of such objects with such properties such things must also be true for anything which he knows, 'clearly and distinctly', to be true.

But suppose this is all a great illusion? Descartes contemplates the possibility with horror and concludes that he must find *something* of which he can be certain. He finds it by starting to suppose that everything is false, that nothing has ever existed: body, figure, extension, movement, place – suppose that these are all fictions! Ostensibly there is nothing to confirm that they exist except for one thing; that he, personally, is thinking about them so, evidently, he exists. If he did not, how could he think!

His conclusion, of course, is usually presented in the original Latin: *cogito, ergo sum:* I think, therefore I am. Which statement, he insists, must be true every time he utters it.

So the essence of Rationalism is this: things can exist without the benefit of anyone's ever experiencing them. And these include such concepts from arithmetic and geometry as number, shape, three-dimensional form and so on.

According to Rationalism, we can know such forms without ever having had any sensory experience of them. Which of course is the fundamental difference between Rationalism and Empiricism; the philosophy that, above all, depends on the senses. So it is hardly surprising that Rationalists of every epoch should have attached fundamental importance to these things. The Rationalist, by definition, is more concerned with purity of form, two-dimensional, three-dimensional or whatever, than with the ways in which his designs might affect the senses of the users.

Pragmatism

As for the Pragmatist position, that we understand objects by thinking of their practical consequences: this was the work of Charles Sanders Peirce (1839–1914), of William James (1842–1910) and of John Dewey (1859–1952).

Their philosophies grew out of American conditions, for as new technologies were applied in industry – and in building – it seemed that poverty, crime, disease and ugliness should have diminished but, far from doing so, they all flourished as they never had before. And, what is more, since technology – which had been so successful – was based on the sciences of chemistry and physics these sciences, literally, must be true. So, by extension, other sciences such as astronomy and biology must also be true. But if these were true then religion manifestly must be false. There could be no spiritual truth, no God, no soul, no immortality, no reasons for aspiring to honesty and justice, to goodness, truth and beauty. If technology were indeed true, then these intangible things must be mere by-products of chemical and physical forces acting within the brain, the very forces on which technology was based.

If traditional philosophy and religion had failed these in human day-to-day affairs then new ways must be found of helping modern man at least to understand his condition. And if he began to understand it then there might be some hope of his working to improve it. First of all man would have to learn; to think straight about the nature of thinking itself, about systems of belief and how they had been lost; about the world as it was and why it was by no means the world that it could be. He should think these things through from first principles so he needed to know how thinking itself could be guided in the setting and achievement of goals.

There were precedents for the kind of thinking that needed to be done in Empiricism, and there were precedents too in Charles Darwin's – then – recent demonstration of Empirical Method in *The Origin of Species* (1859). According to Darwin man had survived, as a member of the animal kingdom, by using his mind, observing his environment and then, by applying his intellect, deciding what to do to make it serve his needs even better.

Thus Peirce was the first to apply the methods of science and technology to thinking in general. He called his way of thinking – after Kant – *Pragmatism* (1902).

Peirce (1878) first defined Pragmatism in an article on: 'How to make our Ideas Clear' in which, among many other things, he said: 'Consider what effects that might conceivably have practical bearings we conceive the object of our contemplation to have. Then, our conception of these effects is the whole of our conception of the object.'

If he had really wanted to make his ideas clear he might have said something more like this: 'Think of a certain object, now think of all the effects that object might conceivably have. Now think further about the practical results of those effects. If you think of the results in this way then the thoughts they arouse within you will contain your whole conception of the object.'

Peirce shows how by questioning what concepts such as hardness, weight, and so on actually mean. Certain text books on mechanics, for instance, claim that we do not even know what such words as force really mean. But as Peirce points out (p. 94):

> The idea which the word force excites in our minds has no other function than to affect our actions, and these actions can have no reference to force otherwise than through its effects.
> Consequently, if we know what the effects of forces are, we are acquainted with every fact which is implied in saying that a force exists, and there is nothing more to know.

It is hardly surprising, given the complexity of his language, that Peirce was largely misunderstood. He complained of this (1905) and John Dewey went on to explain for him some of the more common misconceptions about Pragmatism in his essay on *The Development of American Pragmatism* (1931). As he said:

> It is often said of pragmatism that it makes action the end of life
> . . . subordinates thought and rational activity to (the) particular ends of interest and profit.

But Peirce himself was opposed to any idea that reason itself should be reduced to acting merely as servant to monetary interests.

Not that Pragmatism, as Peirce first articulated it, was an instant success. On the contrary, as William James said (1907), it lay dormant for twenty years until he, James, presented a paper on the subject, at the University of California (1896).

James's writing is very much clearer than Peirce's and he starts his definition of Pragmatism with a telling example concerning a human witness who was trying to get sight of a squirrel which kept on moving around a tree. However fast the witness moved, the squirrel moved at exactly the same speed in the opposite direction, thus keeping the tree between himself and the witness. So the point at issue was this: Does the man move round the squirrel or the squirrel round the man?

Asked to arbitrate in this ferocious metaphysical dispute James pointed out that in Pragmatic terms, since both sides described the same situation in perfectly intelligible practical terms, they could both be right and, literally, there was nothing to choose between them.

So: 'Given ideas of any kind, one simply submits them to the simple test of asking what their concrete consequences would be'.

James sees Pragmatism as an extension of Empiricism, one which makes it less objectionable. He is indeed scathing of Rationalism, which he thinks a mere pretension. As he puts it (p. 54): 'Pragmatism is uncomfortable away from facts. Rationalism is comfortable only in the presence of abstraction.'

The Pragmatist talks about truths in the plural, about their utility, their practicality, the ways in which they work. Which suggests to the Rationalist – the intellectualist mind – a sort of coarse, lame, second-rate makeshift article of truth.

For the Rationalist, objective truth must be non-utilitarian, haughty, refined, remote, august, exalted . . . an absolute correspondence of our thoughts with an equally absolute reality.

One would expect that, holding such views, James would dismiss religion as mere, metaphysical speculation. He does indeed dismiss the idea of an Absolute Mind but if belief in God has positive effects on the way that people behave in practical terms, then, true Pragmatist that he is, James is prepared to accept it. As he says (p. 57):

> If theological ideas prove to have a value for concrete life, they will be true, for pragmatism, in the sense of being good for so much. For how much more they are true, will depend entirely on their relations to the other truths that also have to be acknowledged.

Such as the truths of science!

Indeed, for Dewey (1908, p. 279), Pragmatism's finest achievement was its: 'reconciliation of the scientific view of the universe with the claims of the moral life'. By Pragmatism he meant (p. 276): 'the doctrine that reality possesses practical character and that this character is most efficaciously expressed in the function of intelligence'. Which, he believes, enables us to solve a basic question (p. 279): 'Are judgements in terms of the redistribution of matter in motion (or some other closed formula) alone valid? Or are accounts of the universe in terms of possibility and desirability, of initiative and responsibility, also valid?'

His own predilections are embraced by the second of these views; scientific judgements, he says, 'are to be assimilated in(to) the moral'.

For Dewey, then: 'action and opportunity justify themselves only to the degree in which they render life more reasonable and increase its value'.

As far as designing is concerned, each of these three philosophies has its latter-day adherents. The latter-day Rationalists actually think of themselves as, and indeed call themselves such. Latter-day Empiricists form nothing like such a coherent group yet nevertheless they exist. As for latter-day Pragmatists, there are plenty of them around and we shall be looking at two kinds; those who still develop cities by the suck-it-and-see methods which formed, for instance, New York, and those who have been looking more closely at the practical effects of actually living in cities.

5

Philosophies into practice

The Rationalists

Laugier

Once the philosophy of Rationalism had been developed, it is hardly surprising that before long aestheticians should try to translate it into design principles. One of the first to do so was an Abbé of the French Church, Marc-Antoine Laugier whose *Essai sur l'Architecture* was first published in 1753. Just like Descartes, Laugier claims to have drawn on the methods of the Natural Sciences and especially the ideas of Isaac Newton.

His aim was to establish the true principles of architecture which, in his view, could be drawn from Vitruvius or, rather, from one of the examples which Vitruvius cites as possible origins for architecture: the so-called primitive hut of posts, beams and a pedimented roof (Fig. 5.1). (See Rykwert (1976) for a splendid history.) Such archaeological evidence as we have suggests that Laugier was quite wrong; architecture started in other ways such as piles of stones, pallisades, lean-to's in the mouths of caves, nests in the ground covered with woven branches which in turn were covered with turf, and so on.

But even if Laugier had known about those things it is unlikely that he would have changed his views. Such Empirical evidence would be quite irrelevant; as a Rationalist, obviously he was more concerned to think things through from first principles which he does with a very seductive story. He says:

> Let us consider man in his first origin with nothing to help him, nothing to guide him but the natural instincts of his needs. He needs a place to rest. He notices, beside a tranquil stream, a bank, its newly sprouting grass is pleasing to his eyes, its tender down inviting; he goes and stretches himself out, indolently on this enamelled carpet; he dreams of nothing but toying, at peace, with the gifts of nature: he wants for nothing, there is nothing he desires.

But then the heat of the sun forces him to look for shade which he finds, of course, beneath the trees. But:

> Meanwhile a thousand vapours rise, swirling around and growing ever denser; thick clouds cover the skies, a frightful rain pours down like a torrent on this delightful forest. The man is hardly protected by the shelter of the leaves, they do nothing to spare him from the uncomfortable dampness that penetrates everywhere.

Fig. 5.1 Marc Antoine Laugier (1785): the Primitive Hut (from Laugier, 1753).

So he shelters in a cave. But it is dark, the air is foul so he decides to correct the faults of nature by making a shelter:

> The proper materials for his design are some branches fallen in the forest. He chooses four of the strongest, raises them upright and arranges them in a square. He places four others across the tops of them; and onto these he raises others which incline, coming together from both sides to the highest point.

In other words it has a ridge with sloping roofs. He covers the roof with leaves 'so packed that neither sun, nor rain, can penetrate'. And thus man is housed.

Of course the sides of his hut are open so he feels the cold and the heat of the sun but he can fill in the spaces between the columns and thus feel himself secure.

On which basis Laugier deduces that the essence of architecture consists of columns, beams and pedimented roofs. There is, as he says (p. 12) 'no vault, no arch, no pedestals, no attic, not even a door or window'.

He develops such ideas in considerable detail, concluding that, of all known historical forms, the Greek Temple – especially the Doric Temple, came nearest in form to the essential architecture he was seeking.

But he wanted to go somewhat further, towards: 'something new, something from history which, at the same time, is uncommon'. Which, as he suggests, can be achieved:

> with the help of all the regular geometric figures; from the circle to the most elongated ellipse, from the triangle to the ultimate polygon.

Given these, one can 'make up forms from straight lines and curves' which means it will be easy: 'to vary the plans almost infinitely, giving to each a form which is nothing like the others and yet which is always regular'.

It is hardly surprising that a Rationalist should advocate the use of pure geometric forms nor that those who implemented his theories should actually design in that way. Having considered individual buildings in very considerable depth, Laugier goes on to discuss 'the Embellishment of Towns'.

Whilst as we have seen the planning of cities is described in ancient literature: Laugier's really is the first modern prescription for city planning. At the heart of his approach there are his descriptions of town and forest to one or other of which most current theories of urban design still adhere.

Laugier did not think much of Paris as it was in his time. Indeed he says (p. 121):

> Most of our towns have remained in a state of neglect, of confusion and of disorder . . . by the ignorance and rusticity of our forebears. New houses have been built but nothing has been changed of the evil distribution of the streets nor the inelegant deformity of random decoration. . . . Our towns remain as they were, an agglomeration of houses heaped together pell-mell without system, planning or design. Nowhere is this disorder more noticeable and more shocking than in Paris. The centre of this capital has hardly changed for three hundred years; one sees

still the same number of small streets, narrow and tortuous, which smell of nothing but uncleanliness and filth, where the encounter of carriages causes constant obstruction. . . . Paris, on the whole, is far from being a beautiful town.

So he starts by assuming the planning of a walled town, as Paris was in his day, approached by wide avenues and penetrated by city gates. The entries to the town must be free and unobstructed, numerous in proportion to the circumference of the wall and sufficiently ornate. The avenues which approach them should be as wide as possible and beyond the city gates there should be squares from which wide streets fanned out *en patte d'oie* that is in the form of a goose's foot. The gates would take the form of triumphal arches, not the miserable toll-houses which were found in Laugier's time and which Nicholas Claude Ledoux was to replace – following Laugier's precepts – some 30 years later.

As for the actual planning within the walls, it is this which Laugier describes in term of a forest (p. 128):

> One must look at the town as a forest. The streets of the one are the roads on the other; and must be cut through in the same way. That which forms the essential beauty of a park is the multiplicity of roads, their width and their alignment.

Actually he seems to be thinking in terms of a great landscaped park of the kind which Le Nôtre had designed (Jeannel, 1985). Laugier goes on to say:

> But that is by no means enough: it needs a Le Nôtre to design the plan, that he applies taste and intelligence, that one finds there at one and the same time order and whimsicality, symmetry and variety, that here one perceives (roads in the pattern of) a star, there in that of a *patte d'oie*, this side the roads in a featherlike arrangement, the other side roads in a fan, further away, parallel roads and everywhere *crossings of different design and form.*

He sees variety as essential, for:

> The more variety, abundance, contrast and even disorder in this composition, the more piquant and delicious the beauties of the park . . . everything which is susceptible to beauty, demands invention and design is proper for the exercise of imagination, the fire, the verve of genius. The picturesque can be found in the embroidering of a parterre as much as in the composition of a painting.

The uninspired, of course, can design a town with perfectly aligned streets but their boring accuracy and cold uniformity actually cause one to miss the disorder of towns like Paris which have no kind of alignment at all. In the too-regular town: a large parallelogram traversed lengthwise and crosswise by lines at right angles:

> One sees nothing but a boring repetition of the same objects, and all quarters look so much alike that one becomes mistaken and gets lost. A park which is nothing but a great assemblage of isolated and uniform squares and of which all the roads differ only in number would be something wearisome and dull.

So:

> Above all, let us avoid excess of regularity and symmetry. When
> one dwells too long on deadens it. Whoever does not vary our
> pleasures will never get to the bottom of pleasing us.

For Laugier therefore the art of planning a town consists of dividing
the whole into an infinite number of beautiful, entirely different
details. One should hardly ever meet the same kind of object twice
and, as one wanders from end to end of the city so one comes in every
quarter across something new, unique, startling. Within a particular
order which also produces a certain kind of confusion. Everything will
be within a basic alignment and of course there will be regularities of
urban form, building form and so on. But this multitude of regular
parts brings with it a certain impression of irregularity and disorder,
disorder of the kind which suits great cities so well.

Paris, according to Laugier, provided ideal conditions for planning
of this kind consisting, as it did, of a plain and a hill, separated by a
great river and covered with a great forest. The river branched and
reconnected to form islands of various kinds.

Supposing, he suggests, that an artist were invited to slice and carve
this landscape as he pleased: 'What happy thoughts, ingenious tricks,
variety of expression, abundance of ideas, whimsical connections,
spiritual contrasts, what fire, what boldness (he could achieve) what a
hell of a composition!'

As for the problems of realizing such a plan, Laugier suggests that
since lesser cities already had achieved their lesser plans, such a plan
would be perfectly feasible for Paris, given time, if only there were the
will.

Quatremère

Quatremère de Quincy made his contributions to architectural theory
in his great Essay on *La Nature, le But et les Moyens de l'Imitation dans les
Beaux Arts* (The Nature, the Aims and the Means of Imitation in the
Fine Arts) of 1823 and also in the various entries he wrote for
Panckouke's *Encyclopaedie Méthodique* of 1788, reprinted separately in
1832.

It is indeed his entries in the *Encylopaedie* and especially his Essay on
Type that have attracted the attention of later theorists and especially
those, such as Aldo Rossi, who call themselves Rationalists.

Type, says Quatremère, is a word with many nuances; it can be used
to mean: model, matrix, imprint, mould, figure in relief or bas-relief.
So he tries to make it more specific. He says:

> The word *type* presents an image of a thing to copy or to imitate
> completely, than the idea of an element which itself ought to serve
> as a rule or a model. Thus one never says (or at least one should
> not say) that a statue or the composition of a complete and
> finished painting has served as a *type* for the copy one has made
> (for that, in Quatremère's terms would be a *model*). But when a
> fragment, a sketch, the thought of a master, or a more or less
> vague description, has given birth to a work in the imagination of
> an artist, one can say that the *type* has given him this or that idea,
> this or that motif, this or that intention.

> The model, as understood in practical execution by an artist is an object that should be repeated as it is; the *type* on the contrary is an object after which each (artist) can conceive works which may not be much like each other.

And:

> All is precise and more or less given in the model, all is more or less vague in the *type*.

So, says Quatremère, the mere imitation of a model is a matter of sentiment. We draw nothing of the spirit of the original nor anything that helps us fight ignorance and prejudice. That, in his view, is how things were in the architecture of his time.

He goes on to clarify what he means by *type*:

> One still applies the word *type* in architecture to certain general forms and character istics of the building to which they have been applied. This application fits perfectly into the intentions and the spirit of the preceding theory. As for the rest, one can still, if one wishes, invest it with many uses proper to certain mechanical arts, which are able to serve as examples. No one can ignore the many pieces of furniture, utensils, seats and clothes which have their necessary *type* in the uses one makes of them and the natural uses for which they were destined. Each of these things really does not have its model, but its *type* in our needs and our nature. Notwithstanding that the bizarre spirit of industry seeks to make innovations in these objects, and to contradict even the simplest instincts, who, for instance does not prefer a circular vase to a polygonal one. Who does not believe that the form of the human back must be the *type* for the back of a chair? that a rounded form is not the only reasonable *type* for hair styling?

So it is for architecture. There have been, he says, a great number of edifices in architecture:

> No one can deny that some of them owe their constant and characteristic form to the primitive *type* that gave birth to them. We have proved this with regard to tombs and sepulchres, under the words 'pyramid' and 'tumulus' (see these words elsewhere in the Encyclopaedia).

One cannot help feeling that despite the lengths to which he went in trying to present it, Quatremère left the notion of 'type' very confused. He and his later disciples might have clarified things a good deal more if they had admitted to drawing on Plato's notion of ideal forms.

Ideal forms: Plato

Plato's notion of ideal forms is developed in *The Republic* (Book XXXV) where Socrates, as usual, is in discussion with a group of friends. We like to think, he says, that when a craftsman is making a table, a chair or a bed, he will have in mind the ideal form of the one or the other.

The problem, for Socrates, is knowing where that ideal form exists. For whoever comprehended ideal tables, chairs or beds would also have to know, not only their forms, and those of any kind of artificial thing; he would also have to know the ideal forms of 'all the plants and animals, himself included, and earth and sky and gods and the heavenly bodies and all the things under the earth in Hades'.

Only one kind of craftsman could know all that, which is to say God. One could give the illusion of making all these things simply by taking a mirror and flashing it around in all directions, by which means, 'In a very short time you could produce sun and stars and earth and yourself (not to mention) all the other animals and plants and lifeless objects which we mentioned just now'.

His listeners, of course, object to such creations on the grounds that whilst he may have produced the appearances of all these things he has by no means produced their substances.

To which Socrates, naturally, has a ready answer. A painter, obviously, produces the illusion of a bed. One cannot sleep on *his* bed but it is real enough as the *painting* of a bed.

But just as the painter's bed is unreal in relation to the carpenter's bed, so the carpenter's bed is unreal in relation to the ideal form of bed. He makes as it were 'a particular bed, not what we call the Form or essential nature of Bed'.

It is one of many craftsmen's beds each of which is like the ideal in certain respects but is, in itself, by no means *the* ideal.

Which leads Socrates to his crucial conclusion:

> We have here three sorts of bed: one which exists in the nature of things and which, I imagine, we could only describe as a product of divine workmanship; another, made by the carpenter; and a third by the painter. So the three kinds of bed belong respectively, to the domains of the painter, the carpenter, and god.

What is more for every living thing, not to mention every artificial thing, there can, by definition, only be a single ideal: 'the god made only one ideal or essential Bed . . . two were not created, nor could they possibly come into being'.

Later writers such as Quatremère – and Aldo Rossi – have attached great importance to the notion of 'type' but as we have seen from the way that Quatremère uses it, his notion of type is a rather fuzzy version of Plato's ideal form.

Boullée and Ledoux

A number of architects tried to work out in practice the theoretical ideas which Laugier had presented. These included, in particular, Nicholas Claude Ledoux (1736–1806) and Etienne-Louis Boullée (1728–99). Both of them worked out architectures of exceedingly pure geometry and, indeed, Ledoux built a great deal, including some 40 toll gates for the new City Wall of Paris (c. 1782) which actually triggered the French Revolution (Fig. 5.2), and a number of private houses, for Mme Guimard and others.

Boullée built less but some of his propositions were even grander than Laugier's. These included his vast King's Library which, after the French Revolution, became a National Library or a Library for a Great Nation.

But he, more than anyone else, defended the use of pure geometry in architecture. In his *Architecture: Essai sur l'art*, for instance, he

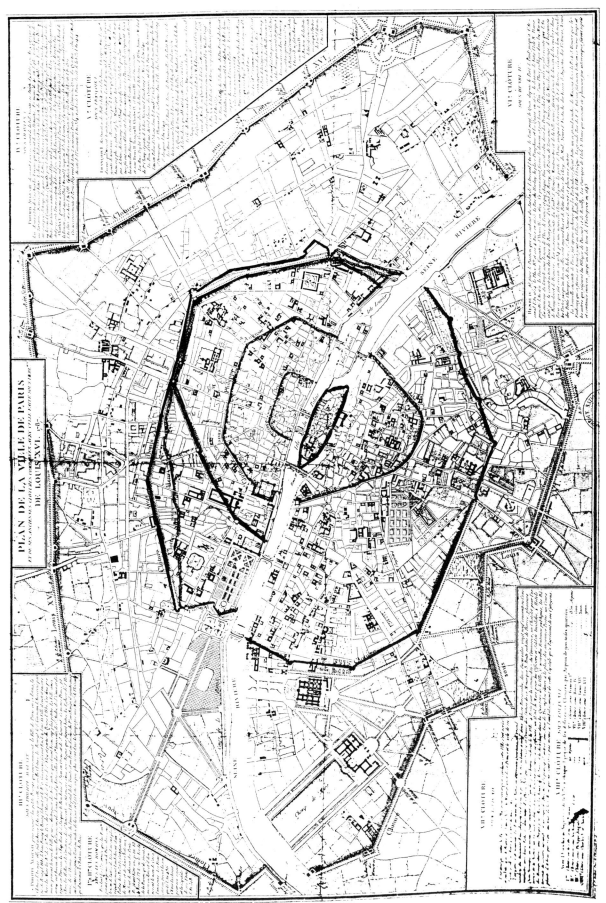

Fig. 5.2 Tardieu (1787) Plan of Paris showing successive clôtures by Medieval and later walls culminating in the eighth, built for Louis XVI's Farmers-General with some 40 barrières (toll gates) by Ledoux. (Bibliothèque Nationale: Cartes Ge C 3694; from Rice, 1976).

extolled the virtues of the pure sphere. Having asked why regular figures take precedence over irregular ones he says (p. 474):

> Because their forms are simple, their faces are regular and repeat themselves . . . their regularity and symmetry are the very image or order and this image is self-evident within them. Given these observations, the result is that man is unable to have clear ideas of the forms of bodies other than after having had this of regularity.
>
> After having remarked thus that regularity, symmetry and variety constitute the forms of regular bodies, I have seen that, in these properties collectively lies proportion.
>
> By the proportion of a body I mean an effect which is born in regularity, symmetry and in variety. Regularity produces in objects beauty of forms; symmetry their order and their beautiful harmony; variety faces which themselves are diversified to our eyes. So, by the bringing together and agreement resulting from all these properties, is born the harmony of the figure.
>
> For example, the sphere may be taken as bringing together all the properties of such figures. All the points of its surface are equally distant from the centre. From this unique advantage, the result is that from all the aspects that we can contemplate the figure, any effect of optics is unable to change the magnificent beauty of its form which always offers itself perfect to our contemplation.

So for Boullée the sphere is the very image of perfection. It brings together perfect symmetry, perfect regularity and the largest possible variety. It has the greatest development of any figure yet its form is the simplest.

In fact it made a certain kind of sense when Boullée applied the perfection of the sphere to his design of a Cenotaph for Sir Isaac Newton in 1784 (Fig. 5.3).

Boullée's comments on the Cenotaph were addressed to Newton himself:

> Sublime spirit! Vast genius and profound! Divine being! Please design to accept the homage of my feeble talents! Ah!

Fig. 5.3 Boullée (1784). Cenotaph for Sir Isaac Newton (from Rosenau, 1976).

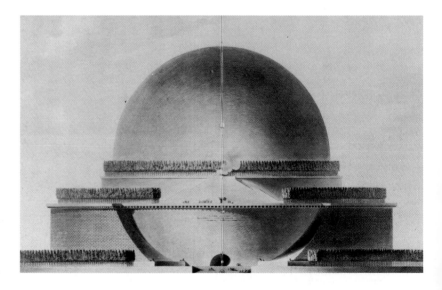

Boullée goes on to suggest that he has conceived the project of enveloping Newton with his own discoveries. So in serving Newton's divine spirit he has formed a sepulchral lamp to light his tomb, and in the process of doing it he himself, Boullée, was rendered sublime!

As far as one can tell by scaling from the human figures on Boullée's section the sphere would have been some 120 metres in diameter. Its upper parts were to have been pierced to let in points of light arranged as the stars may be seen in the night sky – an early planetarium in fact – and at its centre there was to have been an armillary sphere with the sun, the earth, its moon and the other planets represented, presumably, by candles, mounted on a series of interlinked rotating rings. Boullée shows Newton's sarcophagus on a low stepped pyramid at ground level with ten visitors or so standing around it. So in this case the spherical form, far from conflicting with the function of the Cenotaph, actually *was* its function.

Which cannot be said of Ledoux's essay in the same genre; a *House for Forest Guardians* which consists of an equally perfect sphere, some nine metres in diameter divided vertically and horizontally into thirds, with steps on all four sides up to the first floor which, of course, provided the only habitable space! (Fig. 5.4).

Some of Ledoux's Gates for Paris were almost as pure in their geometry (Ledoux, 1804). Of the four which remain, for instance, the Barrière de la Vilette is a perfect cylinder supported on a perfect square with porticos on each of its four sides. The porticos are in an extraordinary squared-off Greek Doric: a perfect amalgam of pure geometry with the Greek orders that one might expect from a true disciple of Laugier (Fig. 5.5).

Of all the 18th century French Rationalist designs, however, that which has had the greatest influence on latter-day theorists has been Boullée's Library for the King (1785) for Paris (Fig. 5.6). It was designed for a site, on the Rue de Richelieu, and Boullée would have roofed what was a courtyard between two existing buildings.

He says of it (Boullée, 1785):

> Profoundly struck, as I was, by the sublime conception of
> Raphael's School of Athens (in the Vatican) I sought to realise it;
> and undoubtedly I owe whatever success I have achieved to
> this. . . .

The 'givens' in this situation were the existing buildings and, as Boullée says, he found it extremely difficult to fit in with these whilst, at the same time, designing a noble and imposing structure.

Fig. 5.4 Ledoux (n.d.) Maison des Gardes Agricoles, Maupertuis showing, in section, how 'pure' Rationalist geometry produces a thoroughly incommodious architecture of sensory deprivation (from Avril, 1987).

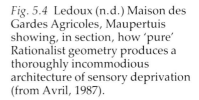

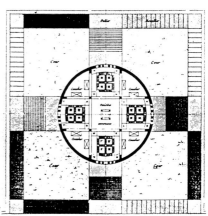

His solution was to line the walls of the Library or, rather, the buildings which enclosed it, with terraces, each containing book-shelves to the height that a librarian could reach. So when the King came to his Library and demanded a book, they could scuttle along the terraces and grab the chosen volume very quickly.

Above these terraces there are colonnades, which mask the existing buildings and over the whole a vast, semi-circular vault; exactly half a cylinder with coffering. Thus Boullée's design, like so many others of his contemporaries, represented a most amazing fusion between absolutely pure geometry: half a cylinder over a simple rectangular prismic space; and Greek orders where they were needed for architectural expression.

The Empiricists

Addison, Burke, Alison

Whatever the merits or demerits of Empiricism as a philosophy, it had profound effects, not only on aesthetic theory but also on the practice of design in 18th century England. The first translation from philosophy into aesthetic theory was effected by a series of writers starting with Joseph Addison (1672–1719) who wrote a series of essays for *The Spectator* – at that time a daily broadsheet – *On the Pleasures of the Imagination*, which were published between 21 June and 3 July 1713.

Addison starts with the sense of seeing, on the grounds that this is the most perfect of the senses. He draws very clearly on Locke to suggest that seeing gives us two kinds of pleasures: firstly those provided directly by objects as we see them which he calls the primary pleasures, and secondly those we still enjoy when the objects which gave us pleasure are no longer there giving us their enjoyment directly. We then have the pleasures of thinking about them, the pleasures of contemplation which he calls secondary pleasures.

To enjoy these secondary pleasures properly, however, we have to know how to be idle, something which, he says, the vulgar do not begin to understand. They are far too busy with other things such, presumably, as trying to scratch a living! Addison clearly anticipates W. H. Davies' sentiment (n.d.):

Fig. 5.5 Ledoux (1776) Barrière de la Villette; pure Rationalist geometry and the Greek Doric Order combined to form a toll-gate in the Farmers-Generals' wall (author's photograph).

What is this life if full of care,
We have no time to stand and stare?

Indeed Addison put it rather less succinctly when he said:

We might add that the pleasures of the fancy are more conducive
to health than those of the understanding, which are worked out
by dint of thinking, and attended with too violent a labour of the
brain.

If we take time to stand and stare, however, we shall find that three
kinds of things induce in us the pleasures of the imagination. Addison
calls them the Great, the Uncommon and the Beautiful.

Greatness, for him, is by no means a matter of size or bulk within a
single object. He sees it, rather, in amplitude and generosity of view
such as we find in open countryside, in vast deserts, huge mountains,
rock pinnacles, precipices and wide expanses of water. The imagination, according to Addison, loves to be filled, to be thrilled by things
such as these which are simply too vast for it to comprehend. Which is
precisely the effect that such stupendous works of nature have on us.

As for the Uncommon, that delights us too 'because it fills the Soul
with agreeable Surprise, gratifies the Curiosity, and gives it an Idea of
which it was not before possest'. The Uncommon thus diverts the
mind, serves to refresh it, staves off boredom and satiety. As Addison
says:

It is this that recommends variety, where the mind is every instant
called off to something new, and the attention not suffered to
dwell too long and waste itself on any particular object.

Which is why we enjoy fields and meadows in the spring, when
everything is verdant, fresh and green. It is why we find water so
fascinating, because it is in constant motion, and so on.

Fig. 5.6 Boullée (1785) Library for the
King of France later to be known as the
Library for a Great Nation (from
Pérouse, 1969).

As for Beauty, that is a different matter again. Beauty passes directly to the soul, permeating it with complacency and secret satisfactions. For Addison, Beauty lies firmly in the eye of the beholder; there are no universal standards. Beauty is a function of Nature herself and of things we have learned by experience. The most beautiful of men (and, presumably, women), birds, animals or whatever are those which conform most closely to the recognized and observable standards of their kind. Our delight in the Great, the Uncommon and the Beautiful resides, ultimately, in the way that 'the Supreme author of our being' has fashioned our very souls. We *will* delight in the Great and Uncommon, they inspire us in the pursuit of knowledge. As for the Beautiful, that delights us for the very simple reason that, like all other living creatures, it encourages us to reproduce our kind.

Compared to Nature herself, according to Addison, Art is a second-rate pursuit. He says:

> The prettiest landscape I ever saw was one drawn on the walls of a dark room, which stood opposite on one side to a navigable river, and on the other to a park. The experiment is very common in optics. Here you might discover the waves and fluctuations of the water, in strong and proper colours, with the picture of a ship entering at one end and sailing by degrees through the whole piece.

Clearly he is writing about a camera obscura but who can doubt that, given his love of the Uncommon, Addison would have delighted in cinema, television, any kind of art that moves?

Curiously enough, in view of the effects his thinking was to have on the future of landscape gardening, Addison preferred formal, French or Italian gardens to informal English gardens although he thought the Continentals went too far when they resorted to the clipped precision of topiary work.

Addison raises a curious point which was to perplex most of those who explored in directions which he had pointed out. As he says, ugliness and suffering, by their nature, are thoroughly repellent. Yet when we see them in painting, sculpture, even the theatre at second-hand they can give us the most enormous pleasure, albeit secondary pleasure. Pictures themselves may be pleasant enough when they simply present 'the nicer and more accurate productions of art'. But they can give us much greater pleasure if they encompass the grandeur and the wildness of real Nature.

So with Addison's Essays the seeds were sown of an interest which was to preoccupy several generations of English gentlemen of leisure for the rest of the 18th century, on and into the 19th: their inquiry into what it is we find most pleasing, pleasurable, in buildings, landscapes, paintings and other forms of art.

Hipple's exceedingly thorough account (1957) traces the many complex strands in these aesthetic studies undertaken by philosophers, painters and aestheticians such as Hutcheson, Hume, Hogarth, Gerrard, Burkem, Lord Kames, Sir Joshua Reynolds and others. Clearly there is no need here to repeat Hipple's splendid account but some of the ideas are of crucial importance for what followed, and continues to follow. The debate raged furiously at times and various contributions make highly entertaining reading.

Edmund Burke for instance published *A Philosophical Enquiry into the Origin of our Ideas of the Sublime and the Beautiful* in 1757. He makes rather clearer distinctions between Addison's three categories suggesting, for instance, that the Uncommon, or Novel, is different in kind from the other two, that the attractions which objects hold for us depend on other qualities. These are bound up with our passions, some of which themselves are founded in our instinct for self-preservation. He says:

> Whatever is fitted in any sort to excite the ideas of pain and danger, that is to say, whatever is in any sort terrible, or is conversant about terrible objects or operates in a manner analogous to terror, is a source of the *sublime*; that is, it is productive of the strongest emotion which the mind is capable of feeling.

Beauty, on the other hand, has the special function of directing sexual feeling towards particular individuals. It is not a matter of proportion, or of fitness for purpose – a hog's snout, after all, is well-adapted to its office – it is a matter, rather, of certain qualities in bodies 'acting mechanically on the human mind by the intervention of the senses'.

These qualities which make for Beauty are, in Burke's view, smallness, smoothness, gradual variation, delicacy, variety of colours from those low in saturation to those of high brilliance (quoted Hipple, 1957).

One would have expected Burke to explain these characteristics, quite simply, by drawing on the association of ideas as described by Locke, Hume and others. But he does nothing of the kind. Association, for him, is a snare and a delusion: as he says, it is 'to little purpose to look for the cause of our passions in association, until we fail of it in the natural properties of things'.

In other words, he looks to the physiology of the nervous system for a deeper-seated explanation and finds it in a very curious place. It is, he says, all a matter of stretching and relaxing the nerves! Pain and fear produce an unnatural tension in the nerves and, conversely, if the nerves are stretched mechanically, then feelings like pain and terror will be induced. Since that sounds like torture, surely, the pain and terror will be rather real!

Conversely and as one might expect for Burke Beauty relaxes the nerves and tends to enervate the beholder. What we need, therefore, is to maintain our nerves 'in proper order' that is neither too taut not too relaxed. To achieve this, he says, 'they must be shaken and worked to a proper degree', hence the pleasures of mild exercise!

In contrast to all this, Archibald Alison (1790, 1815) takes a firmly Empiricist line, drawing directly on the Associationism of Locke and Hume although Alison thought he was drawing directly on Plato! His *Essays on the Nature and Principles of Taste* first appeared in 1790 and, as far as Hipple is concerned: they 'exhibited an originality, complexity and logical coherence unmatched in British aesthetics'.

Alison criticized his predecessors on two grounds: firstly that the artists among them believed that our emotions were determined by original laws of our nature, so that certain of our senses are appropriated for the perception of Beauty or Sublimity. And secondly, the philosophers among them tried to reduce taste into some more general law of our mental constitution (Hipple, 1957).

There were, according to Alison, fallacies common to both these views; both groups perceived the emotions of taste in far too simple a minded fashion whilst, in reality, they are extremely complex.

Alison himself analysed this complexity, concluding that the emotions of taste are felt 'when the imagination is employed in the perception of a regular train of ideas of emotion'. It is this regularity of ideas, associated with some particular emotion, that distinguishes such a train from other trains of ordinary thought within which each idea is merely *connected* to the next one.

When an object is capable of generating such a connected train of thoughts, Alison labels it Picturesque, and its effect might well be as follows:

> . . . when we feel either the beauty or (the) sublimity of natural scenery – the gay lustre of a morning in spring, or the mild radiance of a summer evening, the savage majesty of a wintry storm, or the wild magnificence of a tempestuous ocean – we are conscious of a variety of images in our minds, very different from those which the objects themselves can present to the eye. Trains of pleasing or of solemn thought arise spontaneously within our minds; our hearts swell with emotion, of which the objects before us seem to afford no adequate cause; and are never so much satiated with delight as when, in recalling our attention, we are unable to trace either the progress or the connection of those thoughts, which have passed with so much rapidity through our imagination.

The object, in other words, gives rise to emotions which, at first sight, have no obvious connections with it. But these emotions depend on the observer's state of mind for 'reasons of care, of grief, or of business', can diminish our aesthetic responses.

And so, says Allison, can too much exercise of the critical faculty. 'The mind', he says, 'in such an employment, instead of being at liberty to follow wherever trains of imagery the composition before it can excite, is fettered in the consideration of some of its minute and solitary parts. . . . In these operations, accordingly, the emotion, whether of beauty or sublimity, is lost. . . .' So, according to his state of mind, the observer will have different aesthetic reactions to the same object, and permanent differences of character will certainly produce differences of sensibility in different people.

The problem, therefore is to decide how objects made of physical materials can produce aesthetic feelings, even though the materials themselves are inherently incapable of arousing any emotions at all. Alison believes that the qualities of materials themselves become 'either from nature, from experience, or from accident' signs for some quality which is capable of producing emotion. Having written extensively of signs elsewhere (1977, 1981b, 1987) I have every reason to agree. Let us also agree with Alison that:

> . . . it appears necessarily to follow, that the Beauty and Sublimity of such objects is to be ascribed not to the material qualities themselves, but to the qualities they signify; and of consequence, that the qualities of matter are not to be considered as sublime or beautiful in themselves, but as being the Sign or Expression of such qualities, as, by the constitution of our nature, are fitted to produce pleasing or interesting reaction.

He finds, for instance, that the sound of thunder gives rise to sublime emotions, but when the same sound turns out to have been the rumble of a passing cart, it loses all such emotional overtones. One wonders what he would have made of *Concorde*?

Beauty, too, can be reduced to the same simple principle, which subsumes all considerations of proportion, line and even utility; that principle is association. In the matter of proportion, for instance, 'The common proportion is generally conceived to be the fittest, and is therefore considered the most beautiful'.

Alison devotes some fifty pages of his second Essay to the subject of proportion in architecture. He finds, for instance, that the proportions of rooms depend on three kinds of fitness; fitness to carry the superimposed loads, fitness for the emotional character of the room, and fitness for the purpose to which it is destined. The two first expressions, he says, 'constitute the *permanent* Beauty, and the third the *accidental* Beauty of an apartment. Fitness for weight and fitness of character must be united in any beautiful apartment whilst fitness for weight and fitness for purpose will unite in any (merely) convenient apartment'. So, he concludes:

> The most perfect Beauty that the Proportions of an apartment can exhibit will be when all these Expressions unite; or when the same relations of dimension which are productive of the expression of sufficiency, agree also in the preservation of Character, and in the indication of Use.

Hussey (1927) believes that Alison 'denied absolutely the existence of objective quantities inherent in objects, accounting for all emotions by the association of ideas aroused in the mind of the spectator. Anything might be beautiful if it aroused pleasant and therefore beautiful ideas'.

Hussey then goes on to suggest that: 'The truth of Alison's theory cannot be denied. Its gradual abandonment has been caused, not by any fallacy, but by its devastating effect on every standard of beauty. According to it, every man's taste is as good another's'.

Others too have opposed the principle of Associationism because it seems to deny the idea of absolute beauty. If there is no such thing as absolute beauty, there can be no general rules in aesthetics either.

Hipple defends Alison against this charge on the grounds that, at one point, he observes that philosophical criticism is necessary, so that the artist can judge whether or not his work is 'adapted to the accidental prejudices of his Age, or to the uniform constitution of the human Mind'. Elsewhere he suggests that: 'Form will be most universally and most permanently beautiful, in which the Expression of Utility is most fully preserved'. Of course this raises the central problem of aesthetics as to whether, or not, there can be absolute standards.

Rationalists have always assumed that there can, but the great value of the Empiricist tradition is the way it demonstrates that there need not be.

Gilpin and Price

Alison's psychology may have been suspect, and Burke's physiology most certainly was but still they have much to offer design theory. Their immediate successors – also Empiricist aestheticians – had even more to offer. They include William Gilpin, Sir Uvedale Price, Humphrey Repton and Richard Payne-Knight.

Gilpin was a parson who travelled extensively to study the landscape and the ways in which it could be represented in drawings, paintings and prints. He also wrote extensively on the subject (1748, 1768, 1794, 1808). It seemed to Gilpin, as it did to many others, that certain subjects lent themselves particularly well to representation in these different media whilst others did not. He called those which did so lend themselves Picturesque; a highly appropriate term. The origins of the word itself seem to be rather uncertain and the 18th century writers used it in various forms. Hipple, for instance finds: 'pittoresk, pittoresque, picturesque, pikturesk' and so on. He suggests that they may all have been derived from a 17th century Dutch word: *shildeachtig*.

Gilpin above all made it the key term in a new aesthtic attitude and certainly his original definition that which is suitable to pictorial representation is as clear and succinct as any. It comes from his *Dialogue at Stowe* of 1748 and in a later essay, *On Picturesque Beauty* (1762) Gilpin distinguishes between the Beauty of a real object and the (picturesque) Beauty of a picture:

> *roughness* forms the most essential difference between the *beautiful*, and the *picturesque*; as it seems to be that particular quality which makes objects chiefly pleasing in painting. – I use the general term *roughness*; but properly speaking roughness relates only to the surfaces of bodies: when we speak of their delineation, we use the word *ruggedness* (Figs 5.7a and b).

These days we might speak of texture in both contexts. Gilpin

Fig. 5.7 William Gilpin: *(a)* 'Beautiful' but dull landscape of soft curves. *(b)* 'Picturesque' landscape of rugged outlines (both from Gilpin, 1762).

(a)

(b)

supports his view by suggesting that the painter, invariably, will prefer ruins to perfect architecture, an overgrown track to a finished garden, an aged face to the smooth face of youth, a human figure in motion to one in repose, and a cart-horse to a polished Arabian (steed) (Hipple, 1957). Sidney Smith put it more succinctly when he suggested: 'The Vicar's horse is beautiful, the Curate's picturesque'.

There are obvious reasons as to why the painter should prefer rough, shaggy textures to smooth and polished ones. Given the nature of painting, which is built up from separate brush strokes, the nature of the medium itself makes such things easier to represent. Rough subjects invite virtuosity in the handling of paint in terms of light, shadow, massing, colour and so on.

Having thought along these lines for some time, however, Gilpin concluded that whilst the medium of art naturally affected the kind of picture that could be made it should only be allowed up to a point to define the properties of nature herself which were worthy of our contemplation. Once those properties have been defined however one's taste can become increasingly refined by contemplating nature directly, undistorted by translation into art. And as one's tastes develop in this way works of art in themselves will come to be seen increasingly as insipid (Gilpin, *On Picturesque Travel*, 1782).

Sir Uvedale Price took an opposite view to Gilpin's in his *An Essay on the Picturesque* (1794). There and in subsequent writings he extolled the virtues of studying pictures for the purpose of improving the real landscape. It was not, he suggested, that landscape designers should study paintings for the purpose, literally of copying them in the real landscape, although that certainly happened. He intended, rather, that landscape architects should study paintings to derive from them principles of composition, of grouping, harmony, breadth, effects of light and shade, and so on.

It was important, he believed, to formulate standards of judgement for forms and colours. They could be derived from studies of natural scenery and the various known styles of man-made gardens, supplemented by studies of painting. But the art of landscape improvement – of actually designing the landscape – was so new that studying that alone was by no means enough. Being new it had no real history, no examples, so far, which had stood the test of time long enough for them to be recognized as the best of their kind. And certainly no one had emerged so far of such transcendent genius that he was recognized, universally, as the finest of landscape gardners.

Paintings, by contrast, had a long and distinguished history and there had been many painters of acknowledged genius. What is more canons of excellence had been established in painting and standards of judgement also were well established. These could be studied with profit and then translated, by analogy, into the design of the landscape. As Price (1794) put it:

> It is not necessary to model a gravel walk, or drive, after a sheep
> track or a cart rut, though very useful hints may be taken from
> them both; and without having water-docks or thistles before
> one's door, their effect in a painter's foreground may be
> reproduced by plants that are considered as ornamental.

Price drew on Burke for his basic ideas, nerve-stretching and all. But there is also a nod towards Hume's Associationism in Price's writings. He believed that distinctions between the Beautiful and the Picturesque were based on the associations with human feelings that they evoked. Beauty, for instance, depends on: 'those which are in a high degree expressive of youth, health and vigour, whether in animal or vegetable life; the chief of which qualities are smoothness and softness in the surface; fulness and undulation in the outline; symmetry in the parts, and clearness and freshness in the colour'.

Conversely, of course: 'the Picturesque is associated with old age and decay; it is a matter of roughness and sudden variation, of irregularity and, decidedly, asymmetry'.

Price's catalogue of Picturesque subjects includes Gothic cathedrals and old mills, gnarled oaks and shaggy goats, decayed cart-horses and wandering gypsies. These all display roughness of surface texture and this is important because as he points out the perception of roughness depends on associations between the sense of seeing and the sense of touch.

As a further clarification of the differences between the Beautiful and the Picturesque, Price invents a new category: the Ugly. This, he says:

> . . . does not arise from any sudden variation; but, rather, from
> *want* of form, that unshapen, lumpish appearance which,
> perhaps, no one word can exactly express; a quality (if what is
> negative may be so called) which never can be mistaken for
> beauty, never can adorn it, and which is equally unconnected
> with the sublime and the Picturesque.

Yet again it depends on associations – or lack of them – with norms for the species in question. Ugliness, alone, is disagreeable; when deformity is added it becomes hideous.

Price has much to say about architectural design. A country house, for instance, will be connected with scenery rather than with other buildings, so it *ought* to be Picturesque. Ruins, especially ruins of once-beautiful, are by far the most Picturesque buildings of all. But one can hardly design and build a ruin for live human beings to inhabit.

Indeed one should bear in mind their sensory needs, so, one makes a building Picturesque, by turning its windows to face the best views, framing them, where possible, by trees. Later writers, practitioners such as Voysey developed a comprehensive prescription out of this whereby one walks on to the site, locates the main rooms to face the best views, and 'turns' the windows, as Price suggests, to frame them. If one does so, then of course, the house is bound to be irregular on plan, the windows too will be irregular and so will the roofs and chimneys. Such thinking, of course, is at the very heart of Picturesque design.

Of course if one is searching for the Sublime one's approach will have to be different. Price believed one could achieve Sublimity by drawing visual analogies with Sublime forms in nature. He says: 'the effects of art are never so well illustrated as by similar effects in nature: and, therefore, the best illustration of buildings, is by what has most analogy to them – the forms and characters of rocks . . .'. Presumably he would have approved Gaudi's Casa Milà (1906–10) which is known to this day in Barcelona as La Pedrera – the Quarry.

Clearly architecture cannot derive quite so directly from nature as painting can. Architecture has to function and the serpentine line which, for aestheticians and painters such as Hogarth characterizes beauty in so many natural forms, cannot usually fit to function. Beauty in buildings involves straight lines, (right) angles and symmetry.

Price devotes considerable space to the use of architecture by painters in their landscapes and historical scenes. He concludes from all this that certain painters have developed principles which can be translated directly into architecture. In particular he commends the

Dutch and Flemish masters for their village scenes. Yet even these will not translate directly into architecture. There may well be occasions when, to improve the view from his house for Picturesque effect the landowner wants to reduce the houses of his villagers to half-ruins. In such cases, however, he should be swayed by humanitarian principles; the gentleman must forgo his aesthetic pleasures and exercise social responsibility instead.

Payne Knight

Price himself, of course, was a gentleman of leisure and so, for that matter, was his contemporary – and adversary – Richard Payne Knight. Knight's *Analytical Enquiry into the Principles of Taste* (1806) was perhaps the most sophisticated study of any in Empiricist aesthetics. Knight is usually dismissed these days as a pernickety stamp collector – a numismatist – a failed antiquarian whose greatest blunder was to dismiss Elgin's Marbles as mere copies dating from the time of Hadrian, and a pornographer whose most notorious works were *Two Essays on the Worship of Priapus* (1786). (1865 edition consulted, London, privately printed!)

His *Enquiry* however is sufficient compensation for these various transgressions. It is divided into three major parts: the first of which is a study of the senses or, as he says, Sensation. Then he has a section on the Association of Ideas and again, not surprisingly, he concludes with section on The Passions.

Taste according to Knight is a matter of feeling. The only kind of feeling that all men have in common is rather generalized. But each generation rejects its parents' values so there cannot be any kind of general rules.

As far as the senses are concerned, Knight starts with what he calls the simpler ones: taste and smell. Then he considers touch, sight and hearing, developing these last because as he says:

> the proper object of taste is in the more general sense of the word, as used to distinguish a general discriminate faculty arising from just feeling and correct judgement implanted in the mind of man by his Creator, and is improved by exercise, study and meditation.

Knight's analysis of sensation follows Burke's to some extent, but not the latter's naïve physiology. Starting with taste and smell, leads Knight to the conclusion that sensations are irritations of the sense organs. The normal processes of living maintain the organs at certain levels of irritation which particular impressions from the world around us may enhance or diminish. Such impressions give us more than mere sensations – simple irritations of our sense-organs – and result in true perceptions in our minds.

Knight quite rejects the view that Beauty is nothing more than smoothness. This view, he suggests, confuses a mere sensual sympathy with a more general principle.

The pleasures of touch *do* arise from irritation of sensors within the skin and the pleasures of seeing too depend on irritation of the sensors within the eye. This irritation is a function of light and colour alone and we learn by association the crucial connections between these irritations and relationships in space of distance and magnitude. Ultimately:

> Visible beauty consists in harmonious, but yet brilliant and

contrasted combinations of light, shade and colours; blended, but not confused, and broken, but not cut, into masses: and it is not peculiarly (particularly) in straight or curve, taper or spiral, long or short, little or great objects, that we are to seek there; but in such as display to the eye intricacy of parts and variety of tint and surface.

These are of course the distinguishing features of those objects which look good in paintings and Knight, like Gilpin and Price, calls them Picturesque. If we concentrate on such things, we can separate out from any object those qualities which are pleasing to the eye, and dissociate them from other qualities which might well displease the other senses. So an object which in real life *could* be offensive – Rembrandt's meat carcases perhaps – can be attractive in a painting.

As far as association is concerned, Knight suggests that in its simplest form, this is merely a matter of improved perception. We *learn* to deduce distance from changes in light and colour in the landscape. For Knight too this principle of improved perception extends to such subtle and complex skills as wine-tasting. Indeed wine-tasting might be taken as the paradigm of how we learn taste in other fields.

Even the novice will recognize white or red and may well prefer sweet to dry. Indeed the novice may dislike the finest of wines on first acquaintance; the palate has to be educated. Which can only be acheived by systematic tasting, learning how to use the senses in the specific order of seeing – the bottle shape, the colour of the wine, the label; hearing – the pop of the cork, the pouring of the wine and the tinkling of the glasses; seeing again, to assess in greater detail the colour, depth and clarity of the wine, especially its intensity at the rim which is the best indicator of age; smell – to assess the bouquet; touch, in the mouth, to detect weight and prickliness; taste, by rolling it around the different sensors at the tip, along the upper edges, the back and the sides of the tongue which detect, in that sequence, sweetness, sourness, bitterness and saltiness (M. Broadbent, 1973). By all of which, of course, we can form associations with our previous experiences of tasting wine and identify the grape, the region from which it comes, the producer, its age, and so on. It is hardly surprising that something of such complexity has to be *learned*.

As Payne Knight goes on to say, once we have built up such associations, 'the mind requires that these properties, the ideas of which it has been invariably habituated to associate, should be associated in reality, otherwise the combinations will appear un-natural, incoherent or absurd'.

Like Repton, Knight requires a formal garden immediately around the house, although if the house is a ruin, then the paths too should appear neglected. His own house, Downton Castle near Ledbury, is a mixture of styles: with a Grecian interior and a Gothic exterior. In his writings, too, Knight seeks to dissolve the notion of stereotyped styles; for him there is only one general rule: congruity with the situation and purpose of the building.

So whilst a Greek temple may be supremely beautiful on the hills of Agrigentum, a stereotype copy in an English park will be quite unsatisfactory in so far as 'the extent of its exactitude (as a copy) will become that of its incongruity'. The error of imitations, in fact, is that they:

> . . . servilely copy the defects, which they see produced, instead
> of studying and adopting the principles, which guided the
> original artist in producing them; therefore they disregard all

those local, temporary or accidental circumstances, upon which their propriety or impropriety – their congruity or incongruity – wholly depend: for principles in art are no other than the traces of ideas which arise in the mind of the artist out of a just and adequate consideration of all such circumstances. . . .

So the real authority of style lies in the trained vision of the great painter and for Knight, the greatest of them all is Claude Lorraine (1600–82) whose landscapes, together with those of Nicolas Poussin (1594–1665), provide the finest conceivable style for Picturesque houses and landscapes.

But Knight has no intention of setting up general rules for art, having denounced repeatedly every kind of rigid system or attempt to codify:

. . . in all matters of taste and criticism, general rules appear to me to be, like all general theories in government and politics, never safe but where they are useless; that is, in cases proved by (previous) experience.

Knight castigates particular examples of systems and systemizers:

. . . without some mixture of passion, sentiment or affection, beneficence itself is but a cold virtue; and philosophers and divines, who have laboured to subject them all to the domination of reason, or sink them in the more brilliant illuminations of faith, have only succeeded in suppressing the mild and seductive, together with some few of the sordid and the selfish passions; while all those of a sour and sanguinary cast have acquired additional force and acrimony from that pride and confidence, which the triumph over the others naturally inspired. The censor Cato, the saint Bernard, and the reformer Calvin, were equally insensible to the blandishments of love, and the allurements of pleasure, and the verity of wealth; and so, likewise, were the monsters Marat and Robespierre; but all equally sacrificed every generous and finer feeling of humanity, which none are naturally without, to an abstract principle or opinion; which, by narrowing their understandings, hardened their hearts, and left them under the unrestrained guidance of all the atrocious and sanguinary passions, which party violence could stimulate or excite.

Certain matters depend entirely on sentiment, and cannot be directed by logic; they are too subtle for that. There is no test of aesthetic excellence but feeling, and it is possible to discriminate between the various modes and causes of feeling. But they are by no means universal, they depend on individual states of the human mind, and on the different states of culture; variations are induced by custom. And any attempt to formalize them is bound to result in sterility. As Knight says:

the whole history of literature obliges us to acknowledge that, in proportion as criticism has become systematic, and critics numerous, the powers of composition and purity of taste have in all ages and countries, gradually decayed.

So instead of formal rules, we must use our judgement, which: 'is commonly used to signify the talent of deciding justly and accurately in matters that do not admit of mathematical demonstration'.

Knight's analysis of associative reasoning, according to Hipple, is too simple to serve in logic – he fails to distinguish proof from probability – but he is searching for an *artistic* probability which, by its very nature, cannot be susceptible to mathematical analysis.

Knight's analysis of the Passions is concerned largely with literature and drama; he concludes that literature is by no means an instrument of moral reform, but an object of aesthetic appreciation. And finally Knight reiterates Addison's plea for novelty:

> Change and variety are . . . necessary to the enjoyment of all pleasure; whether sensual or intellectual; and powerful is this principle, that all change, not so violent as to produce . . . painful (irritation) is pleasing; and preferable to any uniform and unvaried gratification.

There are limits, however, to the desirability of change. Novelty causes a progressive improvement in taste as long as it is confined to generalized imitation. But as soon as novelty calls on invention to usurp the place of imitation, it begins to produce extravagance of manner. And inordinate gratification of the taste for novelty leads to aesthetic and moral evil – the Marquis de Sade, after all, was forever searching for new modes of gratification. Such a search clearly reduces one's powers of sensibility, so, as Knight says:

> The end of morality is to restrain and subdue all the irregularities of passion and affection; and to subject the conduct of life to the dominance of abstract reason, and the uniformity of abstract rule.

Ultimately, however, the end is happiness and:

> The source and principle of it is, therefore, *novelty*, the attainment of new ideas; the formation of new trains of thought the renewal and extension of affection . . . and above all the unlimited power of fancy in multiplying and varying objects, the results, and the gratification of our pursuits beyond the bounds of reality, or the probable duration of existence. A state of abstract perfection would, according to our present weak and inadequate notion of things, be a state of perfect misery. . . .

Repton

Eighteenth century England was indeed a rich seed-bed for the new aesthetics, based on Empirical philosophy, to grow. In addition to the theorizing however much was achieved in the way of practical design.

There were of course the great landscape gardens, such as Stowe (from 1734), Rousham (*c.* 1739) and Stourhead (from 1741) (Fig. 5.8). Indeed for many people, and I am one of them, Stourhead is in Reyner Banham's memorable words (1962) 'a total and authoritative master-work' (Banham, 1962). Since this is a book on *urban* design, however, this is hardly the place to discuss it. Suffice is to say that a Y-shaped, artificial lake is surrounded by well-wooded landscape within which Classical temples – somewhat in the manner of Claude – a rocky grotto and other features are grouped along a clearly defined route around the lake. The owner, Henry Hoare, saw parallels between his own life and Aeneas's travails in Virgil's *Aeneid*. So each temple and every other building in the original scheme, represents an incident in the *Aeneid* and therefore, metaphorically, in Hoare's own life. To understand the garden fully, one has to have learned what they mean. Not to mention the kind of knowledge which enables one to see, as one progresses round the lake, three-dimensional likenesses, built into the real landscape, of paintings by Claude Lorraine.

So Stourhead is the most glorious of the practical results of converting Empiricist philosophy into a theory of landscape. And for lesser mortals too a century of aesthetic speculation was reduced to a series of practical prescriptions for designing landscapes by Humphrey Repton in his *Sketches and Hints for Landscape Gardening* (1794) – and many other writings (edited by Loudon, 1840).

Repton's *Sketches and Hints* with Loudon's additions – including extracts from 37 of Repton's amazing *Red Books* in which he showed potential patrons before and after views of what he was proposing for their landscapes – provided a practical manual for other landscape gardeners to follow. Yet in the long run Repton asked to be judged on his writings, rather than: 'the partial and imperfect manner in which my plans have sometimes been executed'. Many architect-theorists, one suspects, would ask for a similar indulgence!

Unlike many of his contemporaries, Repton has no profound excursions into metaphysics, nor, for that matter much theory. He is concerned, rather, with practical applications, so his writings include innumerable check-lists: rules for achieving the Picturesque both in landscape design and architecture. Repton's *Sources of Pleasure for Landscape Gardening* (in Loudon, 1840) include, for instance: Congruity in the adaptation of the parts to the whole, Utility, that is fitness for purpose; Convenience; Order; Symmetry – these clearly derive from the grand tradition of architectural theory going back to Vitruvius; Picturesque effect – in terms of light and shade, the forms of groups, outlines, colouring, balance of composition, the occasional advantages of roughness and decay, the effects of time and age on materials; Intricacy, which is: 'the disposition of objects, which, by a partial and uncertain concealment, excite and nourish curiosity': Simplicity; Variety; Novelty, Contrast; Continuity; Association of ideas, historical or personal; Grandeur; Appropriation, which means displaying the extent of the owner's estate; Animation – of water, vegetation, animals; Changes due to the seasons and times of day.

The first three of these, he says: Utility, Convenience and Comfort, are by no means conducive to Picturesque beauty. They include

Fig. 5.8 Henry Hoare and others (from 1748) garden at Stourhead, Wiltshire (author's photograph).

everything that conduces to the purpose of habitation with elegance but not, be it noted, Profitability. Repton, in fact, opposes in principle any idea that the landscape can be both ornamental and profitable; Shenstone's ornamental farm, the *ferme-ornée* is not for Repton. Convenience is a matter of such things as using gravel paths to keep the owner's shoes dry, a south-east aspect to catch the most favourable weather and so on. Utility may be connected with aesthetic excellence but only by association. If a house is situated in an exposed position, he says, it may hurt the eye because it calls to mind half-conscious notions of unpleasant rain and cold (Hipple, 1957).

So, starting for our purposes at the scale of buildings, Repton, naturally, has rules for siting them. His check-list amounts to four considerations:

1. the aspect
2. the levels of the surrounding ground
3. objects of convenience, such as water supply, space for offices (in the 18th century sense), accessibility to roads and towns
4. the view from the house

Of these, he says, only the last has any real aesthetic connotations. The other three are matters of convenience and utility.

As for the forms the buildings should take, first of all he states the choices available in his time:

> The two characters of architecture might, perhaps, be distinguished by merely calling the one Gothic, or *of old date*, and the other Grecian, or *modern*.

Of these he advocated Gothic, whilst advising a certain amount of caution in its application:

> . . . the prevailing taste for the Gothic style must often be complied with; and, after all, there is no more absurdity in making a house look like a castle, or convent, than like the portico of a Grecian temple . . . so great is the difference of opinion betwixt the admirers of Grecian and those of Gothic architecture, that an artist must adopt either, according to the wishes of the individual by whom he is consulted; happy if he can avoid a mixture of both in the same building; since there are few who possess sufficient taste to distinguish what is perfectly correct, and what is spurious in the two different styles.

Indeed Repton claims to have discovered the fundamental fact that Greek architecture consists, predominantly, of horizontal lines whilst Gothic consists of vertical. It is this difference, he says, which leads to incongruity when the two are mixed. The distinction between them, he says, depends on habits of vision acquired by association. He also had views on the *kind* of Gothic that should be used: it ought, he said to be Queen Elizabeth's Gothic rather than castle or abbey Gothic.

Repton chose Gothic for the highly practical reason that in non-ruinous architecture – and he agrees with Price on this – Picturesque effect can only be achieved by irregularity, and the most irregular architecture he knew, of course, was Gothic. He prescribes four rules for achieving Picturesque irregularity:

> The . . . great principle on which the picturesque effect of all Gothic edifices must depend . . . is irregularity of outline: first, at

the top by towers and pinnacles, or chimneys; secondly, in the outlines of the faces, or elevations, by projections and recesses; thirdly, in the outlines of the apertures, by breaking the horizontal lines with windows of different forms and heights and, lastly, in the outline of the base, by the building being placed in ground of different levels.

As for the landscape around the house, Repton distinguishes three distances, those of the Garden, the Park and the Forest. The Garden, immediately around the house, should be fairly formal. Or it might consist of several small gardens with the most formal close to the house. Beyond these, the Park should be landscaped in a much more natural way and beyond that again, the Forest should be left to its own wild devices. He says:

> . . . in forest scenery we trace the sketches of Salvator and Ridinger; in park scenery, we may realise the landscapes of Claude and Poussin: but, in garden scenery, we delight in the rich embellishments, the blended graces of Watteau, where nature is dressed, but not disfigured, by art; and where the artificial decorations of architecture and sculpture are softened down by natural accompaniments of vegetation.

As for roads and paths within the Park, Repton naturally has ideas on how these should be designed. Whilst of course he is concerned with landscape he, like Laugier, might well have drawn the relevant analogies between landscape and urban design. He says:

> The degree of curve in a walk, or road . . . will depend on its width; thus looking along (a) narrow line of walk, you will not see (a) second bend; but in the same curve, if the road be broader, we should naturally wish to make the curve bolder by breaking from it. . . .

Repton also had ideas as to how roads and paths should meet:

> When two walks separate from each other, it is always desirable to have them diverge in different directions . . . rather than give the idea of a reuniting. . . .

And:

> When two walks join each other, it is generally better that they should meet at right angles . . . than to leave (a) sharp point, as (with an) acute angle.

So of course whilst his ideas were meant to serve the purposes of landscape design they can be applied, with equal felicity, to the design of streets lined by buildings.

As for his overall strategies, it is often enough, according to Repton, to present the *appearance* of Utility rather than pursue some kind of illusory functionalism. As he says 'the highest perfection of landscape gardening, is to imitate nature so judiciously, that the interference of art shall never be detected'. Elsewhere Repton elaborates on the ways in which this may be achieved. He says:

> The perfection of *Landscape Gardening* consists in the four following requisites: First it must display the natural beauties, and

hide the natural defects, of every situation. Secondly, it should give the appearance of extent and freedom, by carefully distinguishing or hiding the boundary. Thirdly, it must studiously conceal every interference of art . . . making the whole appear the production of nature only; and, Fourthly, all objects of mere convenience or comfort, if incapable of being made ornamental, or of becoming proper parts of the general scenery, must be removed or concealed. . . .

Concerned as he is with aesthetic effect Repton dislikes in principle the idea that landscape design and architecture should be subservient to painting. He makes his point with simple humour by suggesting that 'if the principle is applicable in these instances, it ought to be extended to others', suggesting that:

> In our markets, for instance, instead of that formal trim custom of displaying poultry, fish, and fruit, for sale at different stalls, why should we not rather copy the picturesque jumble of Schnyders and Rubens? Our kitchen may be furnished after designs of Teniers and Ostade, our stables after Woovermanns, and we may learn to dance from Watteau or Zuccarelli. . . .

In any case, for Repton, there are substantial differences between landscape and painting. The painter's point of view is fixed, whereas the gardener's moves about; in painting, the field of vision is restricted; there is no way in painting, for instance, of representing the view down a hill: the lighting too is fixed at an instant in a painting – one thinks of Monet's many versions of Haystacks, Rouen Cathedral and so on – whereas in a real scene the light shifts during the course of a day and each part may be illuminated in turn. The painting too is framed, and has a foreground whereas frame or foreground appear only very rarely in the real landscape.

So, Repton suggests, the best thing might be for painter and landscape architect to work together – the former to conceive a plan, and the latter to put it into practice. The painter sees things as they are, the landscape designer as he believes they can be.

Repton's Picturesque architecture, in many ways, is close to Price's and for him in particular association is one of the main sources of aesthetic delight. Indeed he set down a most touching account of association in these terms:

> Association is one of the most impressive sources of delight; whether excited by local accident, as the spot on which some public character performed his part; by the remains of antiquity, as the ruin of a cloister or castle; but more particularly by that personal attachment to long known objects: a favourite seat, the tree, the walk, or the spot endeared by the remembrance of past events . . . such partialities should be respected and indulged, since true taste, which is generally attended by great sensibility, ought to be the guardian of it in others.

Repton, of course, was a gardener and most of the Picturesque theory which was built up in England during the 18th and early 19th centuries was concerned with the landscape natural or artificial. Where architecture was mentioned and, as we have seen, it was, quite frequently the buildings under discussion were usually *in* the landscape. Nevertheless, much of the theory was translatable into an urban context as it was in many articles on Townscape published by the

Architectural Review throughout the late 1940s and the 1950s. Indeed the major authors, Ian Nairn and Gordon Cullen, both published books derived from these (Nairn, 1955 and 1957; Cullen, 1959).

Just as paintings by Claude could be analysed to provide principles for landscape design so paintings by, for instance, Canaletto, could have been used for urban design.

But the owners of the great landscape estates tended to spend more time there than ever they did in the city. They might go to London, or Bath, for The Season at which time they would occupy their large terrace house in a Georgian square, circus or crescent. So it was not until the end of the 19th century that architects such as Camillo Sitte began to turn their attention to the development of picturesque principles for urban design. We shall be looking at their work in Chapters 6 and 9.

6

Later planning theories and practices

Public Health Acts

So far we have been looking at 'pure' expressions of Rationalism and Empiricism in designs for kings, princes and aristocrats or, at least, for very rich land owners. But the so-called working classes of the newly industrialized cities had to make do as best they could with the appalling houses built for them by factory owners, private speculators and so on (Tarn, 1973).

There were rumours of incipient working-class revolt but upper-class interest in their welfare waxed and waned, as might be expected, as cholera and other urban diseases waxed and waned. Since cholera was no respecter of persons – Prince Albert himself was to die of the disease in 1861 – it is hardly surprising that a few brave spirits, most notably Edwin Chadwick, should be doing what they could to improve sanitation, and indeed living conditions generally, for the poor urban masses.

As Secretary of the Poor Law Board, he was responsible, in 1842, for a Report on the condition of the working-classes and this, more than any other document, was responsible for the various Public Health Acts of 1848 and subsequent years, culminating in the most comprehensive of them all, the Act of 1875.

These Acts successively prescribed minimum standards for urban living resulting in what we know now as Bye-Law Housing. If modes of planning are to be changed – and certainly they needed to be, then an Act of Parliament, clearly, is the most effective means of ensuring that the necessary changes will be made (Fig. 6.1).

The Act of 1848 required that local authorities formulate, and enforce, regulations to do with the provision of sanitary facilities and drainage, at adequate standards in all new houses. It also empowered the authorities to build water-supply systems, drains and sewers. But empowering is by no means the same as requiring so most of them, at the time, demurred on grounds of the cost.

The Act of 1875 was a good deal more specific about such things as the actual construction of dwellings. In addition to the enforcement of adequate sanitary facilities, local authorities also were required to formulate Bye-Laws covering such things as the levels, widths and construction of new streets, their drainage and so on.

One key section, 157, required Bye-Laws to be written on the following:

1. with respect to the level, width and construction of new streets and provision for the sewerage thereof

2. with respect to the structure of walls, foundations, roofs and chimneys for securing stability and the prevention of fires and for the purposes of health
3. with respect to the sufficiency of space about buildings, to secure a free circulation of air, with respect to the ventilation of buildings
4. with respect to the drainage of buildings, from water closets, earth closets, privies, ashpits, and cesspools in connection with buildings, and to the closing of buildings, or parts of buildings, unfit for human habitation and to prohibit their use for such habitation

The Act recommended that carriageways should be 36 feet wide and all other streets no less than 24 feet; that each dwelling should have a clear, open space in the front of at least 24 feet, a back yard of at least 150 square feet, and so on.

It is interesting to see how many of these requirements are equivalent to those enshrined in the various Costituti of Medieval Siena; for just as they prescribed the forms which the city would take, and which can be seen to this day, so did those which the British Government enacted; their effects too can be seen in the English cities! Mutthesius presents (1982) a particularly sympathetic survey of *The English Terrace House* from this – and several other eras.

Attention was drawn to the appalling conditions in which the urban working classes were living by novelists such as Charles Dickens in *Oliver Twist* (1838), *Bleak House* (1853) and *Hard Times* (1854); by political theorists such as Frederick Engels in *The Condition of the Working Classes* (1845) and, with Karl Marx *The Communist Manifesto* (1848), not to mention William Morris, *News from Nowhere* (1891), almost all of which were well preceded by a Report for the Poor Law Board in London by Chadwick *et al.* (1842). Something clearly had to be done. A massive

Fig. 6.1 Successive improvements in 19th century houses in Birmingham planned according to changing Bye-Laws (from Hiorns, 1956).

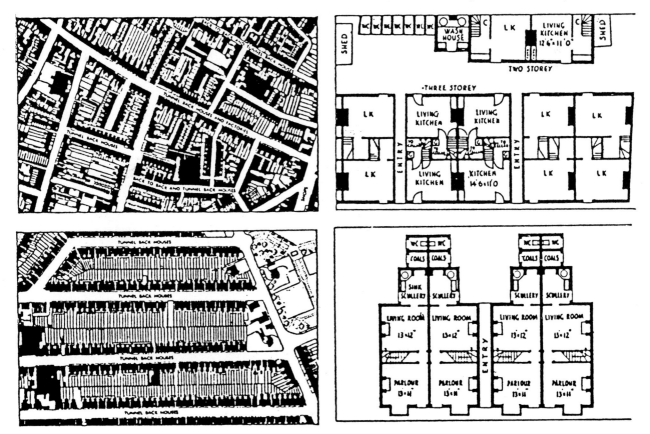

change was needed in public opinion and that occurred following the multi-pronged attack. Prince Albert himself, after all, had commissioned Henry Roberts to design Model Houses for families to be shown at the Great Exhibition of 1851 (Tarn, 1973) now re-erected on Clapham Common.

Remote from each other as they seem, Repton's ideals and Chadwick's had certain crucial points in common. Repton, obviously, was thinking of, and designing for, a very rich cultured élite. And what he designed for them was a multitude of sensory delights. Chadwick was not so much concerned with providing delight as with providing the minimum acceptable level of daylight, fresh air, sanitation and so on for the urban underprivileged. Yet at their very different levels both of them were concerned with the effects on the human senses – and sensibilities – of the physical environment!

Haussmann's Boulevards

Chadwick's approach, of course, was informed with the finest theoretical knowledge available to him at the time, concerning public health, preventative medicine, and so on. Baron Haussmann's work in Paris (c. 1855–69) had no such theoretical underpinning. It was a straight, pragmatic solution to a highly practical problem, which Louis Napoleon put to him; of how to redevelop Paris, after the Revolution of 1848, in such a way that never again could the angry mob build barricades in the streets and lob missiles at the police from behind them.

Saalman (1971) tends to play down this aspect of Haussmann's programme. He concentrates instead on Haussmann's formidable skills of organization pointing out also that behind Haussmann's Plan there was the clear intention of focusing 'visually and functionally' on the great monuments of Paris: the National Assembly, the Bourse, the Church of the Madeleine, the Panthéon, the Cathedral of Notre Dame, the enlarged Hôtel du Ville, the Arc de Triomphe, Garnier's new Opera House, the old Monastery of St-Germain-des-Prés and so on. And since the new railway stations of Paris were so peripheral these too were to be connected to make for more efficient transport between them and into the city. As Saalman points out, there were precedents

Fig. 6.2 Haussmann: Parisian Boulevard (author's photograph).

for such planning in the era of the Baroque. He cites Wren's Plan for rebuilding London after the Great Fire of 1666 and he might have included also Sixtus V's Plan for Rome. Sixtus, after all, had similar reasons for linking the major monuments in *his* city to speed up the flow of (pilgrim) traffic between them.

So Haussmann's Boulevards (Fig. 6.2) by no means were designed for any kind of instrinsic beauty. They did indeed give long perspective views towards the major monuments, and, with the various *rond-points* in front of or around they also speeded up the flow of traffic between them. But they also afforded the longest feasible sight-lines for Louis Napoleon's troops. As for the trees which seemed to humanize the boulevards it was they, above all, together with the great width of the boulevards themselves, that made barricade-building difficult.

Benevolo (1960) describes Haussmann's planning as neo-conservative, not to say neo-Fascist, a view which no doubt would have been shared by those dispossessed of their homes as the boulevards were pushed through. But as he also says, boulevard planning became the norm towards which most great European cities were developed, or redeveloped in the 1870s. He cites some 20 of them, including the Ensanche with which Cerda extended Barcelona from 1859, Forster's Ringstrasses plan for Vienna, destroying the medieval walls (1858–72), and even colonial examples such as Pretoria (1855) and Saigon (1865). And the biggest Boulevard of them all, no doubt, is the Avenida 5 de Julio in Buenos Aires.

Sitte's artistic planning

Like any such powerful set of ideas, of course, Haussmann's boulevard approach soon had its opponents, those who felt the whole thing too grandiose, too formal and too monumental. The most influential was Camillo Sitte whose *City Planning According to Artistic Principles* (1889) was above all a plea for irregularity in planning. In a sense he was formalizing the kind of planning which Picturesque architects, such as Repton or Nash, had achieved rather more spontaneously. Just as the Picturesque theorists had attempted to abstract principles for landscape design from the analysis of landscape painting, so Sitte attempted to abstract principles for the designs of plazas, streets and public squares from the analysis of historic examples, with particular reference to the medieval Italian city (Fig. 6.3). As Sitte put it in writing of recent planning:

> . . . one can observe a widespread satisfaction with that which has been so well accomplished along technical lines – in respect to traffic, the advantageous use of building sites and, especially, hygienic improvements. In contrast there is almost as prevalent a condemnation of the artistic shortcomings of modern city planning, even scorn and contempt. That is quite justified; it is a fact that much has been accomplished in technical matters, whilst artistically we have achieved almost nothing. Modern majestic and monumental buildings being usually seen against the most awkward of public squares and the most badly divided lots.

> It seemed appropriate, then, to examine a number of lovely old plazas and whole urban layouts – seeking out the bases of their beauty, in the hope that if properly understood these would comprise a sum total of principles which, when followed, would

lead to similar admirable effects . . . the present work is to be neither a history of town planning nor a polemical tract, but instead will offer study materials and theoretical deductions for the expert.

Sitte, in fact, expressed a certain guarded admiration for Forster's Vienna, whilst suggesting his own detailed improvements to make it more artistic. But in general he disliked intensely the boulevard approach which had been so fundamental to Haussmann-like planning. As he said:

> The melancholic city dweller suffers from a partly imaginary, partly real sickness . . . a longing, a nostalgia for unfettered nature. . . . This ailment . . . is . . . to be cured . . . only by the sight of greenery, by the presence of beloved Mother Nature. . . . However, the mere suggestion the mere sight of green foliage is in itself sufficient even if it be only a single tree reaching over a garden wall.

> The *Motif of the single tree* . . . has been almost totally ignored in modern town planning.

> The exact contrary of the motif of the individual tree is that of the Allée. . . . All the tree lined streets are tedious (and in) modern geometric city planning . . . disproportionately wide ring boulevards and avenues have been planted on both sides with unbroken alleys of trees. . . . These poor trees are always sick . . . with root rot . . . because their leaves are forever covered with dust . . . because on one side of the street they stand constantly in the shade of tall town houses.

Sitte calculated that the allées or boulevards of a single city such as Vienna, Cologne or Paris would contain enough trees to form an entire forest which in his view would be far better deployed as two or three parks – 'far more effective as regards the health, recreation, peace; air and shade that city dwellers seek'.

Sitte conceives the picturesque as an urban stage-set and catalogues its idiosyncrasies (109):

> . . . stronger architectural projections, more frequent interruptions of the building line, zig-zag and winding streets, uneven street widths, different heights of houses, flights of stairs, loggias, balconies, gables . . .

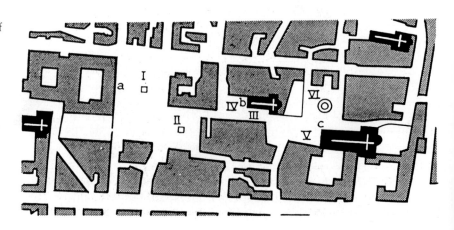

Fig. 6.3 Camillo Sitte (1889): plan of Lucca (from Collins, 1986).

concluding that these, and 'whatever else make up the picturesque trappings of stage architecture would in the end be no misfortune in the modern city'. Of these, the most important for Sitte are those which we associate normally with the interiors of buildings but transfer, for this purpose, to the exterior. As he says: 'It is precisely *the external use of interior architectural elements* (staircases, galleries, etc.) that is a most essential ingredient in the charm of ancient and medieval designs'. Yet other features which have obvious visual attractions cannot be translated into new constructions, these include:

> . . . that large class of picturesque details whose charms derive from their unfinished or ruined character . . . that which is falling apart or even dirty, which has touches of bright colour or varied stone textures. (These) may look effective in paintings (but) the reality is totally different.

Picturesque decay may look attractive but in real life we need the benefits of modern sanitation, standards of comfort and transport systems.

These new demands must be satisfied whilst making the city as splendid and pictorial as possible. The fundamental question for Sitte, of course, is whether those new demands *can* be reconciled with the delights and irregularities of the true picturesque. He says:

> In order to produce the effects of the old masters, their colours as well must form part of our palette. Sundry curves, twisted streets and irregularities would have to be included artificially in the plan; an affected artlessness, a purposeful unintentionalness. But can the accidents of history over the centuries be invented and constructed *ex novo* in plan? Could one truly and sincerely enjoy such prefabricated ingenuousness, such a studied naturalness?

He answers:

> Certainly not . . . spontaneous gaiety is denied at any cultural level which constructs its plans intellectually at the drawing board rather than building at apparent random from day to day. Nor can this whole course of events be reversed, thus in large part most picturesque beauties we have mentioned probably will be lost irretrievably to contemporary planning. Modern living and modern building techniques no longer permit the faithful imitation of old townscapes; we cannot overlook this fact without falling prey to barren fantasies.

So what could one do about it? Neither the gridiron system on which so many American cities from Washington onwards had been planned, nor the Boulevards of Paris, nor Vienna, displayed the artistic treatment which Sitte thought proper. Haussmann's Boulevards, of course, were cut through Paris with scant regard for the parts of Paris which were being cut through. In other words, those accidental conjunctions which Sitte so liked were simply papered over with late 19th century façades. It was simply not in the spirit of Haussmann's planning that picturesque effects be *allowed* to happen. And so with Förster's Vienna Ring. It follows the line of the 13th century city wall which, after the Zabian Siege of 1529, was given the ramparts and moats which, with the *glaas* of open land, some 600 paces wide, were derived from the latest Italian developments in the technology of fortification. The fortifications themselves enclosed truly picturesque

Old Vienna (now the First District) and the picturesque nature of which could have been enhanced, rather than destroyed, if the existing Medieval streets, and parts, at least, of the old fortifications had been allowed to play their part in Sitte-like conjunctions of buildings from different times. But all that was swept away to make way for a 57 metre highway, lined with a succession of monuments, from Baumann's Government Buildings (Regierungs Gebäude) at the north-eastern end to Hansen's Stock Exchange (Börse) to the north-west, with great, incoherent open spaces around Semper's incomplete part of the Hofburg (Imperial Palace). But whilst there was no way of starting again, Sitte felt that the Ring at least could be retrieved in part by the more extensive use of urban spaces. He showed, with many variations, how such spaces could be fitted into gridiron plans. And whilst, in general, he approved the Place which Semper had designed on the Ringstrasse, between his Museums of Art and Natural History, Sitte felt that similar spaces should be built elsewhere along the Ring: in front of Hansen's Palace of Justice (now the Parliament House), between Schmidt's Rathaus and Semper's Burg Theatre, in front of Förster's University and in front of Förster's Votif Church, thus breaking the linear form of the Ring and forming instead a string of linked urban spaces.

As one might expect, Sitte's urban spaces display that regularity, indeed that formality, which was all that in his view *could* be designed self-consciously. The Votive Kirche is off-centre, opposite a Y-shaped junction, yet he planned for it a symmetrical urban space, a simple rectangle with its far corners somewhat splayed. The irregularities of its relationship to the plan of Vienna were to be absorbed by the buildings by which it was enclosed from the streets. The Rathaus and the Burg Theatre, whilst different in architectural style – Gothic and Baroque revivals respectively – are symmetrical about the same axis, so he simply separated them by a screen of buildings – with an axial opening – to form another rectangular urban space, with splayed corners, enclosing the Rathaus.

Julien Gaudet

Cammillo Sitte loved the picturesque hill towns of Northern Italy but felt that, since their forms resulted from developments over the centuries, they could not, and should not, be emulated by any particular designer working at a single moment in time.

Support for Sitte's views came from a most unexpected source: Julien Gaudet, Director of the Ecole des Beaux Arts in Paris who wrote in his *Eléments et Théories d'Architecture* (1902) the classic description of the Beaux Arts Course and Method surprisingly says: 'I adore the Picturesque and certainly, (when) a stranger . . . arrives in a town (it is) the Picturesque that seizes him most'. 'But', Sitte-like, he continues: 'one cannot compose the Picturesque. It alone composes itself by the work of that greatest of artists: Time'. In Paris, for instance, in the 'Palais de Justice, seven centuries have worked and left their imprint, so who dare flatter himself that he could do that on his own in a single day?'

An artist of genius may compose a (regular) Place de la Concorde but one does not, cannot, compose an irregular Piazza di San Marco, a Florentine Piazza de la Signoria or a Sienese Campo.

So, Gaudet says:

you want the Picturesque? Then don't go looking for it. That is the only way you will get it. In having to complete the great edifices of the past, past centuries did not think themselves bound to the (original) obsolete styles. They continued the Palais de Justice without doing it in the manner of the XIIIth century and the Palais de Justice is Picturesque. At Notre Dame, and in many churches you find a succession of styles from the XIIth to the XVth centuries, and Notre Dame is Picturesque . . . what kills the Picturesque is archaeological anachronism.

So what *is* the Picturesque? In a word it is, for Gaudet, variety, which architects, therefore, can and must ensure. For variety is nothing but character which, for Gaudet, is: 'identity between the architectural imprint and the moral imprint of the programme'.
Yet regularity too has its dangers. As Gaudet says:

Regularity is only justified when it constitutes a coup d'oeil, as at the Place Vendôme. One easily senses the composition there; one is, in fact, within a monument. The site does not exceed what the eye can encompass whereas at Lyons, for example, the immensity of the Place Bellecou does not allow one to appreciate the symmetry of the opposing forms – otherwise lacking artistic value – there (is) no valid reason to impose on these buildings the constraint of useless regularity.

Of course there is intrinsic beauty in architecture itself:

. . . we admire the splendid remains of monuments the purpose of which is otherwise unknown. But beauty is by no means a banal quality, in the pursuit of which we have no right to make an abstraction of character. The magnificent forms of a palace applied to a prison would be ridiculous; they would be equally out of place applied to a school or a factory.

As far as urban design is concerned, Gaudet sees planning for traffic as one of the major challenges. Indeed he sees the absence of highway regulation in the past as a key factor in the growth of the Picturesque. Given a city which has grown over time by: 'the precious collaboration of chance and time. . . . The needs of circulation impose, as an afterthought, the slow labour of rebuilding, of alignments, needs against which it would be childish to recriminate, but which often inflict on the artist many well-founded regrets and occasional protestations'.
But times change; we move on. Road planning is based entirely on utility but there are times when this has to be compromised:

at best we must bend or deviate (from) its brutality to conserve some precious monument as an ornament . . . such scruples (are rare); almost all of Philibert de l'Orme's work in Paris has perished because of (road) alignments. Road planning has been conceived for a very long time as inflexible necessity, mowing down all obstacles. The great Church of Cluny was demolished (in 1798) because, if due deference had been paid, a road would have been a (mere) 200 metres longer.

So, Gaudet insists: 'road works can and must be artistic'.
Given his position as Director of the Ecole des Beaux Arts it is hardly surprising that Gaudet should have his views on Classical architecture. As he says (p. 83):

Classicism: That is everything which remains virtuous in the
eternal struggles of art; everything which remains in possession of
a universally proclaimed admiration. And all its heritage
proclaims, in tracing the infinite variety of combinations and
forms, the same invariable principles: reason, logic, method.

The City Beautiful

Few heeded Sitte or Gaudet at the time and indeed the next
distinguishable form of city planning – the American City Beautiful –
was almost diametrically opposed in principle. Devised as it was from
Haussmann's Paris and its successors, the City Beautiful proper seems
to have originated in the World's Columbian Exposition held at
Chicago in 1893.

Chicago had been developing through the 19th century as a great
commercial centre and, following the disastrous fire of 1871, its more
progressive architects, as we have seen, concentrated their energies on
the development of fire-resisting construction for the office and
warehouse buildings which were essential for its commercial success.

Historians such as Giedion (1941) therefore have seen it as a
tremendously retrograde step that Daniel Burnham (who, with J. W.
Root, had been responsible for such pioneering buildings as the Rand
McNally building of (1888) should be responsible, with Frederick Law
Olmsted and others, for the design of an Exposition which far from
expressing further progress *looked* like reproduction Baroque. Yet the
Exposition itself was sponsored by those same business men who,
having demonstrated their commercial skills, now wanted to buy
cultural respectability. They wanted Chicago to be known, not only as
the commercial centre of America, but also as its cultural capital.

Olmsted was responsible for the layout, Burnham for choosing the
architects, sculptors, painters and others who between them would
develop a three-dimensional realization of their sponsors' aspirations.
Hunt, Saint-Gaudens, McKim, Millet and others worked out, with
Burnham, certain ways of achieving architectural unity throughout the
Exposition by agreeing a common architectural language, with uniform cornice lines. McKim and Saint-Gaudens in particular had been
overwhelmed by the splendours of French Classicism during a trip to
Europe; they also turned to Classical examples for their architecture
because, like Jefferson, they believed that such forms 'had the
approbation of thousands of years'. As Hugo van Brunt put it, they
wanted 'a uniform and ceremonious style – a style evolved from and
expressive of the highest civilisation in history' rather than the current
'mediaeval or any other form of romantic, archaeological (*sic*) or
picturesque art'.

Burnham himself described his ideas of unity in the following terms:

There are two sorts of architectural beauty, first, that of an
individual building; and second, that of an orderly and fitting
arrangement of many buildings; the relationship of all the
buildings is more important than anything else.

Designed thus as it was in the Classical manner, the Exposition
naturally encouraged all those who (in America and elsewhere) had
been looking for a revival of that grand approach to city planning
exemplified by Penn's Philadelphia (1681), Jefferson's University of
Virginia (1814–18), L'Enfant's Washington (1791–2) and so on. So it is
hardly surprising that when, in the 1890s, a number of American states

decided that they would build new capitals, the Exposition's architects should find themselves in considerable demand.

Burnham, McKim, Saint-Gaudens and Olmsted themselves were asked (1901) to revive L'Enfant's great plan for Washington. They toured Europe to study those cities which had been replanned in the Haussmann manner and then returned to prepare their recommendations, after which most great American cities, including Boston, Massachusetts; Kansas City; St Louis, Missouri; and so on were 'beautiful' in a similar way. But Burnham's greatest concern was for the city of Chicago itself. Already in 1897 he had told the Merchants' Club 'that the time had come for Chicago to make herself attractive', but nothing was to come of his proposals for another ten years or so. Then in 1906 the Commercial Club of Chicago commissioned from him a comprehensive plan for the development of the city.

He and his staff looked well beyond the confines of the city to the region beyond, concerning themselves, not just with buildings, but with railways, roads and parks, playgrounds, forests and bathing beaches. At the same time, of course, they wanted to perpetuate the kind of architectural philosophy which had permeated their design for the 1893 Exposition. Burnham wished to dramatize the relationships between his buildings, surrounding the City Hall with lower buildings and stepping up to the centre so that its dome would dominate higher building again at the periphery.

Unfortunately, as Tunnard and Pushkarew (1963) suggest, the Classical monumentality of Burnham's Civic Center – the heart of his City Beautiful – soon gave way to the squalors of the City Efficient; nor could his ingenious transportation system ever have coped with the demands which would have been put on to it by thousands, if not millions of commuters. The roads and motorways which had to be provided for them soon began to dominate the reality of built Chicago. Yet Burnham's Plan for Chicago was by far the most complete and thoroughly worked out that had ever been attempted for any city. Burnham's practical methods had many parallels with those which were to be formulated later by that pioneer Scottish ecologist, Patrick Geddes, who generalized all planning processes into matters of 'survey, analysis and plan' (1949).

The City Beautiful Movement, of course, had its derivatives in Britain ranging in time from the City Hall and Law Courts at Cardiff by Lanchester and Rickards (1897–1906) with additions by Vincent Harris in the 1930s, to Barry Webber's Civic Centre in Southampton (1929–39). More than anything, of course, these are vast public expressions of civic pride and it may be that the last gasp of such thinking is to be found in the Civic Offices at Portsmouth, by Teggin and Taylor (1973), in which an L-shape in bronze glass curtain-walling reflects, literally, William Hill's white stone Guildhall of 1886–90.

Howard's Garden City

The next great set of planning conventions, those of the Garden City movement, for obvious reasons, had hardly any effect on the internal planning of existing cities. They were indeed intended to free the pressures on such cities by decanting population to new and much smaller towns, built well outside the city in virgin countryside. The chief exponent of this particular approach of course, was Ebenezer Howard whose ideas were first published in *Tomorrow: A Peaceful Path to Real Reform* (1898) which, within four years, had been republished as *Garden Cities of Tomorrow*. Howard's major concern seems to have been to stem the drift of population from rural to urban areas, presenting the alternatives as town and country magnets, each of which has its attractions and corresponding disadvantages (Fig. 6.4). He characterizes the town, for instance, as closing out nature and catalogues many disadvantages such as the isolation of crowds, distances from work, high rents and prices, excessive hours of work, the army of unemployed, fogs and droughts, costly drainage, foul air, murky sky, slums and gin palaces. But he balances these with concomitant advantages: social opportunity, places of amusement, high wages, chances of employment, well-lit streets and palatial edifices. The country certainly has its advantages: the beauty of nature, wood, forest and meadow, fresh air, low rents, abundance of water, bright sunshine, but these too have their concomitant disadvantages: lack of society, lack of work, land lying idle, long hours, low wages, lack of drainage, lack of amusement, no public spirit, the need for reform, crowded dwellings and deserted villages.

His Garden City, of course, would combine the advantages of both whilst eschewing their disadvantages. Whilst he is careful to point out that any actual plan would have to be comprised against the form of the particular site, Howard's notional plans are based very firmly on the idea of a central park/garden of some five acres about which all of the city's main functions are grouped concentrically. Indeed, major components would all be segregated. The first ring around the central garden consisted of public buildings: the town hall, concert and lecture halls, a theatre, library, museum, picture-gallery and hospital. These were surrounded by a ring of parkland, cut through radially by the six principal boulevards and surrounded by the Crystal Palace – a wide glass arcade which 'in wet weather (is) one of the favourite resorts of the people', who also were tempted to use the park more often than otherwise they might have done, safe in the knowledge 'that its bright shelter is ever close at hand . . .'. It served a variety of purposes:

> Here manufactured goods are exposed for sale, and here most of that class of shopping which requires the joy of deliberation and selection is done. The space enclosed by the Crystal Palace is,

Fig. 6.4 Ebenezer Howard (1902): Garden City plan (from Howard, 1902).

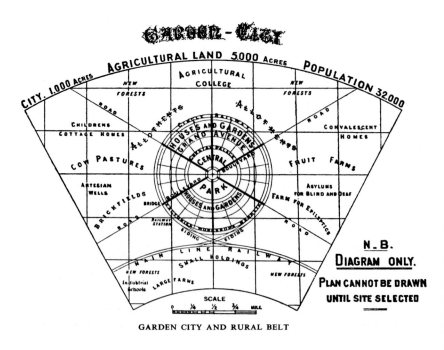

GARDEN CITY AND RURAL BELT

however, a good deal larger than those required for these purposes, and a considerable part of it is used as a Winter Garden – the whole forming a permanent exhibition of a most attractive character, whilst its circular form brings it near to every dweller in the town – the furthest removed inhabitant being within 600 yards.

The next ring outwards from this urban wonder, combining as it did in the one building all the functions of a Greek agora, a Roman forum and a 20th century fun palace, was a broad ring of houses 'each standing in its ample grounds' and conforming to Howard's general pattern.

> . . . that the houses are for the most part built either in concentric rings, facing the various avenues (as the circular roads are termed), or fronting the boulevards and roads which all converge to the centre of the town.

There were some 5500 building lots, averaging 130×20 feet, for a population of some 30 000 with a further 2000 housed on the agricultural estates around the town.

The houses themselves were greatly varied in character, some having common gardens and co-operative kitchens whilst 'general observance of the street line or harmonious departure from it are the chief points as to house building'. The municipality would encourage 'the fullest measure of individual taste and preference' in the actual designs, whilst exercising the strictest possible control over 'proper sanitary arrangements'.

The main ring of housing would be surrounded by a Grand Avenue, some 420 feet wide forming a 'belt of green' – an annular park, dividing the main part of the town into two concentric belts. The Avenue itself of course would be divided by the six radial boulevards into six segments, occupied by the public schools, their surrounding play-grounds and gardens, whilst other sites along the Avenue would be reserved for churches 'of such denominations as the religious beliefs of the people may determine.' The Avenue itself was to be bounded by inner and outer concentric roads, themselves lined by houses in looping crescents, thus ensuring 'a longer line of frontage on Grand Avenue'.

The outer regions of the town would be given over to 'factories, warehouses, dairy markets, coal yards, timber yards, etc.' – all with access to circular railway lines which, surrounding the town, enabled goods to be loaded or unloaded at any point for shunting to or from the main line. Beyond this again there would be a further range of uses – all agricultural – including 'large farms, small holdings, allotments, cow pastures, etc.' in whatever proportions proved most profitable to the town as a whole; thus,

> . . . it may prove advantageous to grow wheat in very large fields, involving united action under a capitalist farmer, or by a body of co-operators; while the cultivation of vegetables, fruits and flowers, requires closer and more personal care, . . . may possibly be best dealt with by individuals or by small groups. . . .

Whilst believing that in terms of day-to-day living his Garden City would have many advantages over both the great metropolis and the unspoilt countryside, Howard recognized that certain functions – he mentions theatres, picture galleries, libraries, universities and so on –

simply could not be sustained, at an adequate metropolitan level, by his city of 32 000. So he postulated the idea of a Central City – planned much like his Garden City, but with a population of 58 000 – connected to a ring of Garden Cities by a railway-based rapid transit system. Thus everyone, in each of Howard's Garden Cities, would have access to such central facilities within a very few minutes.

Howard himself, of course, initiated the building of two Garden Cities, Letchworth and Welwyn, as living exemplars of what his city should be like whilst his ideas were taken up and expanded by others such as Sir Patrick Geddes, who, as Jane Jacobs says (1962)

> . . . saw the Garden City idea not as a fortuitous way to absorb population growth otherwise destined for a great city but as the starting point of a much grander and more encompassing pattern . . . the planning of whole regions. Under regional planning, garden cities would be rationally distributed throughout large territories, dovetailing into natural resources, balanced against agriculture and woodland, forming one far-flung logical (she might have said 'ecological') whole.

This view in turn influenced Lewis Mumford, Clarence Stein, Henry Wright and Catherine Bauer, a group which Bauer herself called the Decentrists. They endorsed enthusiastically Howard's view that cities should be thinned-out and their populations dispersed into smaller towns, whilst at the level of detailed planning they believed the street itself to be inherently 'bad' – 'houses should be turned away from it and faced inwards, towards sheltered greens'. Mumford himself believed the great city to be 'Megalopolis, Tyrranopolis, Nekropolis; a monstrosity, a tyranny, a living death'.

Stein's neighbourhood

Clarence Perry developed the idea of the neighbourhood unit by analysing the things he found good – including gardening and community participation – about living in a Long Island suburb named Forest Hills Gardens. The neighbourhood was focused on a community centre, a place for debate and discussion, not to mention co-operative action on issues which would affect the community politically. Crucial to Perry's concept was the idea that all day-to-day facilities: shops, schools, playgrounds and so on should be within walking distance of every house. This in itself determined the overall size of a neighbourhood, whilst heavy traffic was to be kept out, confined to arterial roads which skirted around the neighbourhood. Perry thus estimated the optimum size for a neighbourhood to be around 5000 people; large enough to provide for most people's day-to-day needs, yet small enough for a sense of community to develop. In Perry's view, however, the neighbourhood itself would not be an impermeable unit, indeed he envisaged a rich interaction with other neighbourhoods and with the rest of the city.

Henry Wright analysed the problem of urban growth in New York State for the Commission for Housing and Regional Planning (1920–26). He suggested that the continued metropolitan growth of New York and Buffalo in particular would exacerbate their already massive disabilities, whilst the new kinds of urban diffusion which he, Clarence Stein and others had developed, would enable growing populations to be accommodated in what they saw as a much more humane manner.

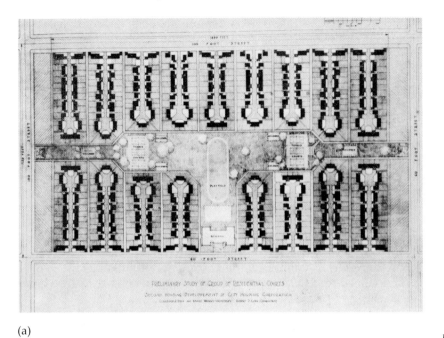

(a)

(b)

Fig. 6.5(a) Emerich and others (1928) Theoretical Study of Residential Courts. *(b)* Application to Radburn, New Jersey (both from Stein, 1957).

Wright and Stein themselves demonstrated a variety of ways in which Perry's ideals could be realized – on to a gridiron system of streets (Sunnyside Gardens, 1926), on to rolling agricultural land (Radburn, 1928) and even on to a hillside (Chatham Village, 1930). Two particular features were developed out of these: the separation of through-traffic from the neighbourhood roads and streets, and the neighbourhood park, which may take the form of a complete green belt surrounding the town, as in many English examples, or an internal band of greenery within an individual neighbourhood. The best known example of the latter, of course, is Radburn, New Jersey, in which particular attention was paid to the segregation of pedestrian from vehicular traffic in various ways (Fig. 6.5a and b). These included the use of underpasses and overpasses, which had been pioneered by Olmsted in New York's Central Park. Stein (1957) summarizes the chief elements of the Radburn Plan as:

1. the superblock – in place of the narrow, rectangular block
2. specialized roads planned and built (each) for one use instead of for all uses
3. complete separation of pedestrians and automobiles
4. houses turned around; living and sleeping rooms facing towards gardens and parks, service rooms towards access roads
5. park as backbone of the neighbourhood.

Thus they used cul-de-sacs for vehicular access to the fronts of the houses, leaving fingers of traffic-free land behind where children could play in safety – the continuous strip parks in the Olmsted manner. Also they separated the neighbourhood access roads from major traffic arteries, used the school and the swimming pool, set in a park, as the focus of neighbourhood activities. But the housing itself was sub-urban–conventional, which somewhat compromised Radburn's 'revolutionary' claims whilst the 1930s depression prevented its development into a fully developed green-belt town.

Neither Howard himself nor his dispersionist followers expected their ideas to have much effect within the city itself, but dispersion of the kind they advocated did take place extensively, in such post World War II new towns as Stevenage (1946), Crawley, Hemel Hempstead and Harlow (all 1947), Basildon (1949) and so on.

On a much larger scale, the Town and Country Planning Association were influential in seeing that decentrist ideas in general were adopted in the planning of the English New Towns.

Le Corbusier: Ville Radieuse

At first sight, the greatest opponent of dispersionist planning was Le Corbusier, with his vast glass and concrete tower blocks, apartment slabs and so on. Yet as Jane Jacobs points out (1961), he too tried to get 'all this anti-city planning right into the citadels of iniquity themselves' by converting the city into a park within which the actual buildings – even at its very centre – would occupy only some five per cent of the land. In the surrounding residential suburbs slabs of luxury housing – each dwelling with its balcony – would occupy some fifteen per cent of the land, leaving the rest for open green courtyards. Although it seemed diametrically opposed to Howard's notion of the small-town Garden City, Le Corbusier's vision had grown out of Howard's. As Le Corbusier put it:

The garden city is a will-o'-the-wisp. Nature melts under the invasion of roads and houses and the promised seclusion becomes a crowded settlement. . . . The solution will be found in the vertical garden city. . . .

Like Howard, Le Corbusier described the city in a very tendentious way, with a certain exaggeration of its worst features.

Le Corbusier on the street

Here, for instance, are his views on 'the street' (1925b, 1929):

The definition of a street which has held good up to the present day is a roadway that is usually bordered by pavements, narrow or wide.. . . . Rising straight up from it are walls of houses, which, when seen against the sky-line present a grotesquely jagged silhouette of gables, attics and zinc chimneys. At the very bottom of this scenic railway lies the street, plunged in eternal twilight. The sky is a remote hope, far above it (Fig. 6.6).

So, for Le Corbusier:

The street is no more than a trench, a deep cleft, a narrow passage. And although we have been accustomed to it for more than a thousand years, our hearts are always oppressed by the constriction of the enclosing walls.

Not only that:

The street is always full of people; one must take care where one goes. For several years now it has been full of rapidly moving vehicles as well: death threatens us at every step between the twin kerb-stones. But we have been trained to face the peril of being crushed between them.

Having thus described the evils of the street as he perceived them, Le Corbusier then goes on to prescribe the city as he thinks it should be without conventional streets:

I should like to draw a picture of 'the street' as it would appear in a truly up-to-date city. So I shall ask my readers to imagine they are walking in this new city, and have begun to acclimatise themselves to its untraditional advantages.

Then follows his lyrical description which, probably more than any of his other writings, persuaded architects and planners, world wide, to adopt his outrageous model:

The air is clear and pure; there is hardly any noise. What, you cannot see where the buildings are? Look through the charmingly dispersed arabesques of branches out into the sky towards those widely-spaced crystal towers which soar higher than any pinnacle on earth. These transluscent prisms that seem to float in the air without anchorage to the ground – flashing in the summer sunshine, softly gleaming under grey winter skies, magically glittering at nightfall – are huge office blocks.

Fig. 6.6 Barcelona: street in the Barrio Chino. Historic centre (author's photograph).

Beneath each is a vast underground station (which gives the measure of the interval between them). Since the city has three or four times the density of existing cities, the distances to be traversed . . . (as also the resultant fatigue) are three or four times less. For only 5–10 per cent of the surface area of its business centre is built over. That is why you find yourselves walking among spacious parks remote from the busy hum of the *autostrada*.

Le Corbusier's ideas for a Contemporary City, the City for 3 Million Inhabitants were first displayed as drawings and models at the Salon d'Automne in November 1922. Instead of being a city *with* gardens of the kind which Howard had proposed, this was to be a City *in* a garden based on four fundamental principles: freeing the centre from traffic congestion, enhancing the overall densities, enhancing the means of circulation and augmenting the area of planting.

His aim, described three years later in *L'Esprit Nouveau* no. 28 (and later still in *Urbanisme* (1924)), was 'not to overcome the existing state of things but *by constructing a theoretically water-tight formula* (my emphasis) to arrive at the fundamental principles of modern town planning'. The solution, he said, was a rough one. There were no notes to accompany his plans; he was simply presenting a – fairly abstract – concept of what cities *ought* to be like.

The abstract nature of his thinking is clarified in various articles published in *L'Esprit Nouveau* including his essays on: *The Pack-Donkey's Way and Man's Way* (1922) (no. 17) and *Order* (1922) (no. 18). As one might expect, these are much concerned with geometric order, indeed the first of the two essays is a kind of homage to the straight line. He says:

Man walks in a straight line because he has a goal and knows where he is going; he has made up his mind to reach some particular place and he goes straight to it.

The pack-donkey meanders along, meditates a little in his scatter-brained and distracted way, he zigzags in order to avoid the larger stones, or to ease the climb, or to gain a little shade; he takes the line of least resistance.

Corbusean man, clearly, would hack away the stones, scrambling upwards in a straight line, whatever the gradient whilst eschewing any shade to lighten his physical labours!

If the first of these essays is an homage to the straight line, the second is an homage to the right-angle:

The laws of gravity seem to resolve for us the conflict of forces and to maintain the universe in equilibrium; as a result of this we have the vertical. The horizon gives us the horizontal, the line of the transcendental plane of immobility.

Whatever that may be!

The right angle is, as it were, the sum of forces which keep the world in equilibrium. The right angle, therefore, has superior rights over other angles; it is unique and constant. The right angle is, it may be said, the essential and sufficient instrument of action because it enables us to determine space with an absolute exactness.

Le Corbusier first published his ideas on *Urbanisme* in *L'Esprit Nouveau*, and then an augmented collection of these writings as *Urbanisme* (1925), *The Present State of Architecture and Urbanism* (1930), *The Radiant City* (1935) and *Propos d'Urbanisme* (1946). These contain variations on a series of themes; on the city as a park with (individual) buildings standing within it, on the use of a rectilinear (he calls it Cartesian) grid as the basis for city planning, on the city designed around a transport interchange. These were to be connected to the centre by fast motor tracks for as Le Corbusier says (1925): 'A city built for speed is built for success'.

It is hardly surprising, given his views on the right-angle, that Le Corbusier's City is rigorously Cartesian. It *is* drawn within a strict, rectangular grid – although, like Washington, it also has major diagonals! Each section within the grid is some 400 yards square, surrounding the central area. These reflect another of his preoccupations at the time: the need for designing cities so that traffic could move fast.

As he says, 'all modern motor vehicles are built for speed. But given the actual state of our streets . . . the highest speed obtainable . . . in the city . . . is about ten miles an hour! . . . the street is no longer a track for cattle, *but a machine for traffic, an apparatus for its circulation*'.

New forms of street must be designed so that traffic can flow freely at optimum speed, or, at least, at 60 miles an hour. Le Corbusier's Plan therefore includes elevated motorways, each some 120 feet wide, running north–south and east–west.

This City was centred on a railway station, with an airport, or at least a landing-platform for air-taxis – which were supposed to thread their ways through his office towers – on top. And of course there would also be a large, central intersection there of his motorways (Figs 6.7 and 6.8).

The centre itself was to be surrounded by a park, some 2400 by 1500 metres within which 24, 60-storey skyscrapers would be located, spaced some 250 metres apart. These would be office buildings and at their feet, between them, there would be buildings of two or three storeys in the form of stepped terraces containing restaurants, cafés, luxury shops. There would also be theatres, concert halls and other urban facilities not to mention parking both at ground level, open to the sky and in multi-storey parks.

There would be large public buildings to one side of the centre such as the town hall, museums and other public facilities and beyond them again, a picturesque *jardin anglais*! Warehouses, industrial zones and

Fig. 6.7 Le Corbusier (1924) Centre of the Ville Radieuse with transport interchange (from Le Corbusier, 1929).

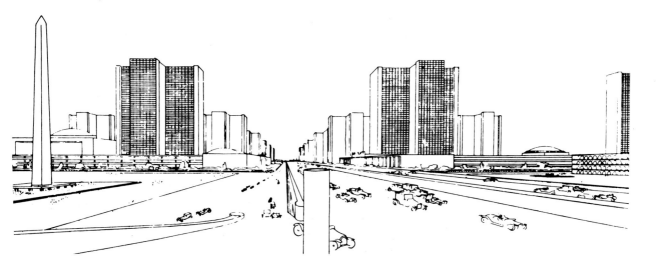

goods yards would be built underneath the motorways and the City would be surrounded, in turn, by a service zone, forest and grass land. Beyond these again there would be a large belt of houses with gardens.

The skyscrapers of the central business district, which, because of their strict, rectilinear geometry he also called Cartesian, were to be cross-shaped in plan and 60 storeys high or more. There would be terraces between them, with cafés, theatres, public halls and so on.

Le Corbusier was quite clear that his 40-storey, steel and glass towers, would *not* be suitable for family life. He proposed two kinds of housing immediately around the City Centre: terraces and apartment blocks.

The terraces would consist of six-storey maisonettes crossing the parkland in rectilinier ribbons and beyond these there would be his apartment blocks: *immeubles-villas* in his familiar form of maisonettes with adjoining balconies hollowed, cave-like, into the façades of his blocks.

Le Corbusier's higher-density housing was to be built of two-storey maisonettes, each with its two-storey balcony flanking a two-storey living room with a smaller balcony at the back which was to carry single-storey bathrooms and bedrooms over the kitchen and dining area, much in the manner of the typical Parisian artist's studio (Fig.

Fig. 6.8(a) Beijing, China (1960s). *(b)* Portsmouth, England (1970s): two of many attempts world-wide to realize Le Corbusier's vision in built reality (author's photographs).

(a)

(b)

Fig. 6.9 Le Corbusier (1924). Each apartment was to have its private balcony for outdoor living, open to 'Sun, Space and Greenery' (from Le Corbusier, 1929).

6.9). The whole arrangement was intended to open up day-to-day living to sunlight, fresh air and greenery in a way which was quite impossible in the narrow streets of the medieval city, or even the wider streets of the 19th century city. For there, even if the sun could penetrate at certain times of day, the houses faced into each other and there could be no privacy.

But Le Corbusier's apartment slabs were to be wide-spaced in his parkland; and this, not to mention the trees, would afford sufficient privacy for one to pursue the exercises which Paul Winter promoted so vigorously in *L'Esprit Nouveau* on one's open balcony, at the mouth of one's cave, as it were, in the cliff-face of maisonettes, free from the prying eyes of (distant) neighbours.

Le Corbusier's lower-rise set-back housing would also consist of two-storey maisonettes varying, it seems, from six to 12 storeys high. They would meander across the parkland in a Cartesian arrangement of open, U-shaped courtyards with connecting blocks. Among other things he gave considerable thought to the separation of his fast motor tracks, slower access roads and pedestrian routes.

Le Corbusier's plans and perspectives, captured the imagination of architects and planners worldwide. In the 1960s particularly, a remarkable number of them were enabled to make their own cities – or large segments of them – look remarkably like Le Corbusier's perspectives with their motorways slashing between their skyscrapers.

Le Corbusier on New York

More than any other theorist, it was Le Corbusier who persuaded the world that New York offered prototypes for the city of the 20th century. Given all the thought which Le Corbusier had put into such things already, it is hardly surprising that when he first went there – at the age of 52 – he arrived with certain preconceptions. And the city most certainly made its impact on him. As he said in the book in which he describes his journey of 1937: *Quand les Cathédrales étaint Blanches* (1946a, p. 34):

> . . . when my ship stopped at Quarantine, I saw a fantastic, almost mystic city rising up in the mist.

And again (p. 39) he recalled: 'The city's violent silhouette . . . like a fever chart at the foot of a patient's bed. . . .' (Fig. 6.10).

But as his ship came in closer, all was by no means as it had seemed (p. 34):

> . . . the apparition is transformed into an image of incredible brutality and savagery. . . . This brutality and this savagery do not displease me. It is thus that great enterprises begin, by strength.

For of all the cities in the world (p. 34), New York alone made it possible for: 'the city of modern times, the happy city, the radiant city to be born'.

Once arrived within the streets of Manhattan, as he says (p. 55):

> One sees canyons surging up, deep and violent fissures, streets such as no one had ever seen before. Not ugly either! I will even say: a very strong architectural sensation which is equal to that experienced in the narrow streets of Rouen and Toulon, with, in this case, the enthronement of a grandeur and intensity well calculated to inspire courage.

So New York represented a beginning for Le Corbusier but it did not go nearly far enough. As the *New York Herald Tribune* proclaimed on his arrival (quoted p. 51):

Fig. 6.10 New York: Skyline in the 1930s with a cluster of skyscrapers along Wall Street, another Mid-town and a 'Valley' between them (from Korn, 1953).

Skyscrapers not big enough
Says Le Corbusier at first sight
Thinks they should be huge and a lot further apart.

In other words he wanted them to be like those he had visualized already. Indeed he wanted to see New York rebuilt according to his own visions of the City for 3 Million Inhabitants (1922), the Radiant City (1935) and so on.

New York, for him, was a vertical city but by no means vertical enough (p. 36). But still (p. 40) a proper plan 'can make New York the city *par excellence* of modern times'. For (p. 42):

> It is the first time that men have projected all their strength and labour into the sky – a whole city in the free air of the sky. . . . What perfection already, what promises! What unity in a . . . gridiron street plan, office on top of office, clear crystallization. It is sublime and atrocious, and nothing succeeds any longer. There is nothing to do except to see clearly, think, conceive, begin over again.

But the basis of a city was there for him all right. As he says (p. 47):

> In length it is laid out in nine parallel avenues; across, in nearly two hundred streets parallel to each other and at right angles to the avenues. . . . Everything is determined with a Euclidean clearness.

Given such a layout, of course, you can pinpoint your position exactly wherever you are and your destination, know exactly how many streets you will need to traverse north or south, how many avenues east or west and so on.

Contrast this, he says, with the romantic city (p. 49):

> One man sowed that foolish idea. He was an intelligent and sensitive Viennese; Camillo Sitte, who, quite simply posed the problem badly. In travels of discovery through Italy . . . he was won over by an art which so exactly adjusted house to house and palace to church, each stone of each city (endowing it with) a living and subtle plastic character, a spectacle of quality.

Loving such cities as he did, Sitte compared them to their 19th century, Cartesian counterparts and came to his fundamental conclusion: 'Confusion is beautiful and rectitude is base . . . the beautiful was curved and . . . (thus) . . . large cities should be contorted'.

New York already had Le Corbusier's basic Cartesian Plan, not to mention his skyscrapers.

Indeed Le Corbusier was thrilled by many of their features: the sheer efficiency of their elevators, with their self-opening doors. He also admired, as did so many Europeans, American plumbing, not to mention the teams of specialist designers whose careful co-ordination ensured that each building would have a 'perfect and faultless life'. Above all Le Corbusier believed that the elevator would revolutionize the form of the city.

He was thrilled too by the experience of space as he looked out from Wallace K. Harrison's office 820 feet up in the Rockefeller Center, the extensive views across the city and the sense of freedom that he felt. Le

Corbusier indeed loved height for, as he said, referring to the title of his book (p. 68): 'When the cathedrals were white, no one thought that height was the sign of a degeneration of spirit'.

Not that the American skyscrapers were perfect by any means. Obviously for him they should have taken the Cartesian form he had described in 1931: a thousand feet high, or at least the 720 feet which 60 storeys would require. They should be steel-framed, sound proofed and given the 'extraordinary perfection' that American services seemed to allow in terms of electric lighting, precisely conditioned air, and the 'demonstrated efficiency' of elevators.

Unlike the New York skyscrapers, which had to conform to the Zoning Laws with their set-backs, Le Corbusier's Cartesian skyscraper would be 'plumb vertical' from top to bottom; it would be a 'light radiator' – presumably he means by night.

The overall form would be determined according to the sun path and there would be no offices on the north side. Wind resistance also would be taken into account whilst the detailed planning would be derived from an appropriate hierarchy of locations for the elevators, the corridors and the offices themselves. No office wall would be deprived of light and the depth of the offices too would be proportionate to the heights of the windows.

His drawings show cross-shaped skyscrapers. In later versions, such as those in the *Plan Voisin* for Paris (1925) the arms themselves have cross bars giving projections and recesses to ensure the maximum possible area of external window. Construction, of course, would be steel frame, with 'a skeleton woven like filigree in the sky' nor would there be any substantial external walls. The ends of the arms were to be covered in thin stone slabs whilst their sides were to be covered in glass. Indeed as Le Corbusier says these façades would be made from 'films of glass: that is to say skins of glass'.

Thrilling as he found the New York skyscrapers by day, Le Corbusier was even more entranced by the sight of New York at night. As he says (p. 90):

> The night was dark, the air dry and cold. The whole city was lighted up. If you have not seen it, you cannot know or imagine what it is like. You must have had it sweep over you. . . . The sky is decked out. It is a Milky Way come down to earth: you are in it. Each window, each person, is a light in the sky. At the same time, a perspective is established by the arrangement of the thousand lights of each skyscraper. It forms itself more in your mind than in the darkness, perforated by illimitable fires. The stars are part of it also – the real stars – but sparkling quietly in the distance.
> Splendour, scintillations, promise, proof, act of faith, etc. Feeling comes into play; the action of the heart is realised; crescendo, allegro, fortissimo.

Le Corbusier actually was looking at New York by night from the roof of J. J. Sweeney's apartment, some sixteen floors up, between the East River and Central Park.

So several things about New York thrilled Le Corbusier as they have thrilled many others: the skyline of Manhattan, the skyscrapers themselves (although he had his reservations), the canyon-like streets between them (although again he had his reservations), views down and into the city from the skyscrapers themselves and, above all, his views of the city by night.

Taken as a whole, these presented an experience unique to the 20th century. No city ever before had looked, or could have looked, as New York did in the 1930s.

7

Urban realities

Jane Jacobs

For Le Corbusier, the lower-scale developments between the sky-scrapers of Wall Street and those of Midtown Manhattan were too mundane, too ordinary to be of any interest. Yet for many people these days they represent the essence of what makes life worth living in New York. For they contain, among other things, Little India, Greenwich Village, the Ukrainian East Village, SoHo (*South of Houston*), Little Italy, Chinatown and other ethnic districts which, whilst generally small in scale, are immensely diversified in character. For in addition to those which gained their names from certain ethnic groups there are areas too where writers, traditionally, have congregated (Greenwich Village), and, more recently, artists (in SoHo), not to mention the galleries where their work is displayed. Indeed the cast-iron buildings of Bogardus and others, with their great open loft spaces, have proved eminently suitable for their use. And as SoHo and The Village became too expensive for another generation of artists, they colonized that area of the Lower East Side, which, for their purposes, they call TriBeCa – the *Tri*angle *be*low *Ca*nal Street.

It was Greenwich Village, however, that was drawn to the world's attention by Jane Jacobs as one kind of ideal environment for urban living. She lived on Hudson Street, not far from the river, and wrote of its many qualities in her book on *The Death and Life of Great American Cities*. When this was first published, in 1961, it infuriated those whose lives had been devoted to the design, planning and building of brave new worlds based on Le Corbusier's vision of the Radiant City.

For Jane Jacobs, indeed, the streets and squares of the Village were the very stuff of which real urban fabrics are made. For as she says (p. 39): 'Think of a city and what comes to mind? Its streets. If the city's streets look interesting, the city looks interesting; if they look dull, the city looks dull.'

Unlike suburban or even small town streets, city streets are full and lively with people. Many of them may be strangers, indeed they, above all, give the city streets the vitality they should have. But strangers, of course, can be menacing, so the bedrock attitude of a truly urban city street is that people feel safe and secure even among all those strangers.

No one feels really secure within the canyons of Wall Street or of Midtown Manhattan. Nor does anyone feel secure within – or between – the slab-blocks and towers of the Corbusean City. Such areas have to be policed, regularly, otherwise they simply are not safe for those who are obliged to be there. In a *real* city street – the kind which Jane Jacobs approves, such policing is quite redundant, for, according to her:

the public peace – the sidewalk and street peace . . . is not kept primarily by the police, necessary as the police are. It is kept primarily by an intricate, almost unconscious, network of voluntary controls and standards among the people themselves, and enforced by the people themselves.

Nor can such controls be achieved by simply spreading building to low densities, whether in suburban estates, or in high-rise slab-blocks in parkland. They need a certain minimum density of people, of buildings and of building use. A well-used street is also likely to be a safe street.

In writing of the street in this way, Jacobs was drawing on her personal experience of many streets in many places, especially in the North End of Boston and of course in Greenwich Village. But as she points out, certain parts of Uptown Manhattan also have the qualities she seeks. These include some of the grander Avenues such as Lexington and Madison. These, with their shops and galleries, have the requisite vitality needed for lively – and therefore safe – street life. Fifth Avenue has this too, as it passes through Midtown Manhattan where it is lined with some of the finest shops in the world. But Uptown, as it passes Central Park, is no longer safe nor, in this area, is Park Avenue itself. For here they are largely residential; there is no longer that mix of uses which is needed for liveliness and therefore for safety.

Jacobs goes on to analyse the things which give a street that liveliness. She suggests there are three main conditions:

1. Firstly, if a street is to be safe, there must be a clear demarcation between public space and private space, between the territory which belongs to a particular house, a particular household, a particular shop or whatever and that which 'belongs' to all. Oscar Newman elaborates on this point in his *Defensible Space* (1972), since when, Alice Coleman has brought even more statistical evidence to bear on it in her *Utopia on Trial* (1985).
2. Secondly, a constant watch must be kept; the eyes of those whom Jane Jacobs calls: 'the natural proprietors of the street' must be scanning it all the time. Their scanning will be all the easier if the buildings which line the street are orientated towards it, planned with projections and recesses, bay windows, balconies, stoops, steps and so on. All of which will make it easier for the 'proprietors' to see up and down the street thus maintaining their constant vigil.
3. Thirdly, the street itself and the sidewalks in particular must be in constant use. The street must actually go from one place where people want to be to another, and there must be enough attractions along the street itself for them to want to linger there. An empty street has nothing much to offer but those who love their fellow human beings find it fascinating, not to say hugely entertaining, simply to watch the world go by. Quite simply we enjoy 'people watching' and if that is made easy for them then the 'proprietors' of the street will spend large amounts of their time doing it.

So the street will gain and maintain a reputation for being interesting, lively and secure. People will enjoy going there to see and to be seen. The street will take on a life of its own.

Any street which lacks these basic conditions may be perceived as insecure, hostile and indeed actively dangerous. Given such a street then according to Jacobs people will try to cope in various ways. They may simply stay away, thus leaving the street exclusively to those who have no option but to use it. Innocent or not they will be stuck with all the problems that this may raise. Secondly, they may think of the street as something like a safari-park, full of wild animals, in which one leaves one's car at one's peril. Thirdly, the younger residents in particular may form gangs, stake out 'their' particular 'turf' or territory and defend it from unwelcome intruders. Indeed Leonard Bernstein's *West Side Story* (1956) – set in the Upper West Side of Manhattan – depicted such behaviour on the part of the Jets and the Sharks.

But teenage gangs are by no means the only urban groups to stake out their 'turfs' in this way. Jacobs describes, for instance, those fenced or walled suburban enclaves where certain of the more prosperous middle classes languish, protected by their security guards. She might just as well have mentioned those exclusive apartment blocks – some of them on the Upper West Side – where affluent New Yorkers take their refuge equally well protected by their guards.

Jacobs sees such segregation – whichever kind of 'gang' has chosen its 'turf' – as sterile and destructive of proper urban life. Jacobs likes to see the people of her natural street: 'loitering on busy corners, hanging around candy stores or bars, drinking soda-pop on the steps'. She also loves the places where people do these things; the candy stores themselves, the bars, the bodegas and the restaurants for it is these above all which provide for such behaviour.

Such things – mixed in with housing – are too messy for the planner who, in addition to planning their physical environment, also wants to plan the lives of those who will live within it. So he plans his meeting rooms for them, his craft rooms, his art rooms, his games rooms, his pedestrian malls with their outdoor benches and those neat globular lights which make all planned urban schemes everywhere look the same.

Jacobs dislikes such things intensely and finds them no substitute for her natural street. Not only are they planned according to the planner's concept of what people should do in their spare time, the very names they attach to the rooms they have planned: meeting room, craft room, and so on imply the things that people must be planned to do, implying that they will not do them unless their leisure time is planned and supervised.

Which of course is anathema to Jacobs for in her view, the fundamental point about urban life – as distinct from certain other kinds of life – is that people must be free to come and go as *they* please with no outside interference or constraint.

People must be given choices and the kind of diversity which Jacobs has in mind is offered by such things (p. 163) as grocery stores, pottery schools, movie houses, candy stores, florists, art shows, immigrants' clubs, hardware stores, eating places of many kinds, and so on. Every natural street needs things of this kind and each street too should have its own specific amenities: a Gallery for African Sculpture, a Drama School, a Romanian Tea House and other such exotica. The street which has such things becomes special, and people go there for those special things. One would not expect to see them everywhere.

Jacobs points out that Wall Street – which Le Corbusier admired so much – is entirely lacking in such things. When Jacobs was writing (late 1950s) all told, some 400 000 people commuted into the Financial District each day and a vast, undetermined number, came to visit them in their offices. Yet in terms of the amenities and services which such people needed every day, this extremely rich district was thoroughly impoverished. One would not look, necessarily, for a drama school or even a tea house but Wall Street was lacking – in anything like adequate numbers – such basic things as bars and restaurants. It had indeed been rich in such amenities at one time. There had been food-stores, hardware-stores and so on, the kinds of places in which busy people might do a little essential shopping at lunch time. But these had been forced out by economic pressures, escalations in property values, the lack of a resident population, and so on.

The requisite variety of urban choices can only be sustained by a large resident population and in an area such as Wall Street, there simply is no room for such a population. Despite that it could be enlivened a little if it became a tourist attraction. Tourists tend to come, not only in the working day, but also in the evenings and at weekends. Tourists demand amenities and once tourists insist on having them, they will become available for the working population.

So for Jacobs the essence of urban life lies in exuberant diversity, in the making available to anyone, at any time, a vast range of choices of things to do. That diversity can be generated by the form of the street itself. Indeed one can design for it by observing four basic rules. They are (p. 166):

1. That the district as a whole serve at least two, and preferably more, primary functions: living, working, shopping, eating and so on. These should be so varied in kind that different kinds of people come and go at different times, working to different schedules, come to the same place, the same street for different purposes, using the same facilities at different times and in different ways.
2. That no block along the street exceed a certain length, which Jacobs then goes on to specify. She finds the 900 feet or so between certain of Manhattan's Avenues far too long and prefers to see it crossed by several short streets thus making access easier between the east–west streets and giving many corner sites.
3. That buildings of different ages co-exist in what she calls a 'close-grained' mingling. There should be quite a high proportion of old buildings because of their importance to the *economy* of the street.
4. That there be a high concentration of people in the street, including that essential nucleus of those who live there, work there, and act as its 'proprietors'.

Jacobs is quite clear that these four conditions form the very heart of her thesis, the core of her book, and she goes on to expand on each of them.

Her plea for mixed uses, of course, contradicts directly and absolutely the argument for zoning on which so much post-Corbusean planning had been based. There was a certain logic to segregation where industry – such as steel-making – was large in scale, noisy, polluting, a great generator of traffic and so on. But in the age of electronics when so much can be done at small scale, where the factory itself may be a small, clean, quiet, neat and tidy place that argument has lost its force. Increasing sophistication obviously makes it increasingly possible for larger and larger numbers to live – as they did in medieval times – literally over the shop.

As far as small blocks were concerned, Jacobs made some clear and even obvious points. The north–south Avenues of Manhattan change in character from Downtown to Uptown. West of Central Park, for instance, Amsterdam, Columbus and Central Park West are some 800 feet apart. If one finds oneself, say, on West 88th Street, halfway between Columbus and Central Park West, aiming for an equivalent address on 87th Street one has to walk along 88th to one of the

Avenues, turn south, walk a 200 foot block, turn into 87th and walk to one's destination, a total of 1000 feet.

At Rockefeller Center, however, where the Avenues are just as far apart, intermediate roads, and the Rockefeller Plaza, reduce the distance of the equivalent walk to 400, 300 or even 200 feet. In Jacobs territory, the Village, there are two north–south roads between each pair of Avenues, offering a choice of routes and reducing walking distances whilst at the same time increasing the number of sites available for corner shops.

As far as aging buildings are concerned, of course they are the essence of the city, enshrining its memory in the way that Rossi (1966) describes (see p. 00). They give scale by their overall forms and their detail and having been built over the years they are inherently varied. But above all, as Jacobs points out, they have crucial economic roles to play. Clearly demolition and new building incur high costs, and these costs are passed on to building users. Only two kinds of enterprise can use new buildings: the highly profitable and the heavily subsidized.

Thus chain stores, chain restaurants, and banks will move in whilst neighbourhood bars, specialist restaurants and specialist shops will be forced out. Supermarkets may move in, not to mention chain book, record, shoe shops and so on. But specialist book shops, record shops, shoe shops, private art galleries, artist studios and so on will simply have to move out because, by their nature, such enterprises cannot be highly profitable.

An orchestra, an opera company – clearly she was thinking of the Lincoln Center – or an art museum may move into heavily subsidized premises but the users of such facilities need considerable back-up services: galleries, studios, suppliers of artists' materials, musical instruments, specialized books and records. The new and subsidized building simply cannot be used to maximum advantage *unless* it is surrounded by old and therefore cheaper buildings.

Those who offer these specialized services will by no means be concerned with making the maximum profit. They will love their stock-in-trade, as their customers do; indeed that is why they will attract their customers. They will want to talk about these things, discuss them, compare notes, seek advice, all time-consuming activities which will make it quite impossible for these specialist services to compete very vigorously in the market place. They can never be very profitable, hence their need for low-rental accommodation.

As for the concentration of people; as Jacobs points out, there are subtle but compelling differences between crowding and density. For if a given area contains enough buildings, of the right kind, then very considerable densities can be achieved without any one's feeling over-crowded.

Of course this depends on location. In the outer suburbs, for instance, it may be perfectly possible to build houses at a density of, say, six to the acre. Each will have a generous garden but such gardens, and indeed such densities, are simply not feasible in the city. Apart from the cost of land, which prohibits such densities anyway, they, by their very nature, are simply not urban.

Of course suburbs may be built at, say, 10 dwellings to the acre but as they approach 20, so urban values begin to taker over. At six to the acre, all the neighbours know each other; or at least they know who is who even though they may keep themselves to themselves. But at 20 dwellings to the acre quite close neighbours may be strangers to each other and once such estrangement manifests itself then they might as well accept *real* strangers to the city.

Urban vitality starts for Jacobs at 100 dwellings to the acre; a density which allows for great variety of dwelling form. In Greenwich Village, for instance, densities range from 125 to 200 or more dwellings to the acre. These are achieved by the mixing of dwelling types; including single family (row) houses, houses with flats over them, tenement blocks, apartment houses with flats, 'elevator apartments' and so on. Between the streets themselves, some 60 to 70% of the land is covered with building and the remainder is left open as small courts and yards. Such land-use ratios are high indeed but they have the advantage, for Jacobs, that they force people out of their dwellings and into the streets whilst ensuring, at the same time, that the courts and back yards are perceived as private space.

Above such densities, however, dwellings have to be packed so closely together – especially if there are generous open-spaces between – that a certain uniformity is bound to creep in. And uniformity of architectural form, for Jacobs, spells, inevitably, social uniformity.

Christopher Alexander

As Christopher Alexander says (1965) he drew on Jane Jacobs when he was writing his extremely elegant essay entitled *A City is not a Tree*. But whilst he thought her a brilliant critic he found her proposals for new building somewhat less enchanting, describing them, indeed, as 'a sort of mixture between Greenwich Village and some Italian hill town'. Yet he agreed that there was a difference, indeed many differences, between what he called natural cities such as Siena, Liverpool, Kyoto, Manhattan, and what he called artificial cities such as Levittown, Chandigarh and the British New Towns. He liked certain British ideas, however, not only those described as anti-Outrage by Gordon Cullen and others in the *Architectural Review* (1959) but also the village housing realized by Llewelyn Davies and Weekes at Rushbrook in Suffolk (1955–64). Without naming them he discusses also the notions of *Megastructure* as described by Reyner Banham in his book of that name (1981).

At this time, however, in the '60s, Alexander thought it important not so much to look for examples of good form as to search for underlying principles. And at that time too he thought that principles could best be expressed, not in pictures (as Gordon Cullen had done), in words (as Jacobs had done) or even in built examples (as Llewelyn-Davies and Weekes had done) but in terms of more abstract relations. Hence the Tree of his title is not 'green . . . with leaves'; it is an abstract pattern of thought from Set Theory.

As he says: 'A set is a collection of elements which for some reason we think of as belonging together'. Thus we might think of sets of people, blades of grass, cars, bricks . . . houses, gardens and so on. When the elements of a set belong together, because they work together or co-operate in some way then Alexander calls the set a 'system'. He gives an example:

> in Berkeley at the corner of Hearst and Euclid, there is a drug store, and outside the drug store a traffic light. In the entrance to the drug store there is a newsrack where the day's papers are displayed. When the light is red, people who are waiting to cross the street stand idly by the light; and since they have nothing to do, they look at the papers displayed on the newsrack which they can see from where they stand. Some of them just read the headlines, others actually buy a paper while they wait.

All this, for Alexander, is a system because:

> This effect makes the newsrack and the traffic light interdependent; the newsrack, the newspapers on it, the money going from people's pockets to the dime slot, the people who stop at the lights and read the papers, the traffic light, the electric impulses which make the lights change, and the sidewalk which the people stand on form a system – they all work together.

In this system, the newsrack, the traffic light and the sidewalk are all fixed parts of the system; product, as it were, of design, whilst the people, their money, the newspapers and the impulses which drive the traffic light are all things over which the designer has much less control.

So to start with he has two categories: the fixed parts of his system and the changing parts. Each part can be numbered, of course. People might be [12345] their money [678910] and so on. The people, too can be categorized: males [123] and females [456] and one could, as he shows, plot these into a hierarchy: 1: a single male; [123] all the males; 4: a single female, [456] all the females, and so on. So the full set of humans, standing on the corner, would amount to [123456].

Such a structure Alexander calls a tree and as I have shown elsewhere (1973) he shows it both in plan (as a Venn diagram) and in section as a graph, branching downwards from the top (Fig. 7.1a and b).

This is his tree of which he says:

> A collection of sets forms a tree if and only if, for any two sets that belong to the collection, either one is wholly contained in the other, or else they are wholly disjoint.

One can on the whole sort humans biologically into male or female thus forming wholly disjoint subsets.

But the humans may be sorted in other ways: as teachers or students; as university or non-university people and so on. Each can belong to many different subsets. Alexander also draws such more complex relationships in plan and section and his section in this case is a semi-lattice. As he says:

> A collection of sets forms a semi-lattice if and only if, when two overlapping sets belong to the collection, then the set of elements common to both also belongs to the collection.

Thus whilst the males might be [123] and the females [456] the university people might be [145], the non-university people [236] and so on.

The whole point, of course, is that whilst tree-like structures lead to rigid separations, semi-lattices contain very complex overlappings, mergings and fusings together. As Alexander puts it: 'a tree based on 20 elements can contain at most 19 further subsets of the 20 whilst a semi-lattice based on the same 20 elements can contain more than 1 000 000 different subsets'.

So clearly a city which is zoned, say, into working, residential and service areas forms a tree in Alexander's sense whilst a mélange of houses, shops and so on of the kind which Jane Jacobs describes is, in his terms a semi-lattice.

(a)

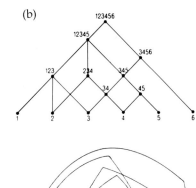

(b)

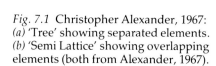

Fig. 7.1 Christopher Alexander, 1967: (a) 'Tree' showing separated elements. (b) 'Semi Lattice' showing overlapping elements (both from Alexander, 1967).

Having thus defined his terms, Alexander goes on to analyse a number of city plans in tree/semi-lattice terms, including Abercrombie's Greater London, Tange's Tokyo, Soleri's Mesa City, Le Corbusier's Chandigarh, Costa's Brazilia, and so on taking as the most extreme example of a tree-like plan that described by Hilbersheimer in *The Nature of Cities* (1964). And in the second part of his paper, Alexander goes on to show that whenever a city is thought out by planners it is bound to have a tree-like structure. Natural cities grow over time but they are the most appropriate containers for the complex, semi-lattice forms of our complex social relationships.

Nicholas Taylor

In his book on *The Village in the City* (1973) Nicholas Taylor does for the suburbs of London what Jane Jacobs had done for the streets of Manhattan. He traces a history of the English town and the English house up to and including the tower blocks. As he says he learned much about housing when he was canvassing for the Labour Party from the base which he and his wife had set up for their family in the south-east London suburb of Lee. As he says (p. 79):

> it was increasingly borne in on me by commonsense and by personal observation that this kind of house did in fact satisfy not just myself and my own family but an extraordinarily wide range of ages and income groups. These quite anonymous little houses, built by Victorian speculative builders, were in fact marvels of sophisticated design, based not so much on self-conscious artistic decision-making as on gradual evolution over centuries of ordinary family life, which is itself, anthropologically, something very sophisticated.

As Taylor went on to point out, the architects themselves who at the time were building high-rise flats for other people increasingly were living in houses of this kind, or updated versions of them by Eric Lyons. They simply failed to relate 'what was good for their own families to what was good enough for other people's'.

Taylor extols the virtues of the front door which opens directly on to the street with its associate private space defined by its threshold and two or three steps. He points out also the virtues of the traditional back yard: 'with its effortless ability to absorb on equal terms the baby's pram, the toddler's toys, the housewife's washing lines and the dog's kennel, every-one of them closely overlooked from the kitchen'. And he also extols the virtues of the small front garden as an encouragement to self-expression 'with its semi-public display of roses, rocks and gnomes', not to mention the back garden, 'with its semi-private sand-pits, shrubs and sheds'.

Such things are quite impossible in the high-rise flats with their useless public space between the blocks, their common entrance halls, their lift halls on each floor. They offer no chance at all for self-expression, no chance, even, for informal outdoor living in the summer. For it is of such things, according to Taylor, that freedom is made: 'blossoming literally in the private gardens and psychologically in the well-rooted growth of family life'.

Taylor's street, of course, encourages that sense of neighbourly responsibility, proprietorship, which Jane Jacobs found in her Greenwich Village Street. But Taylor's neighbours are quieter. They do not favour 'the kind of clattery hothouse Naples-in-the suburbs' which Jacobs – or even her Hampstead equivalents – view with such romantic affection: he favours quieter human relationships.

Its first ingredient for Taylor is neighbourliness which flourishes best, for him, when each family has its sense of identity engendered by the feeling that the house, and the small plot on which it stands, is 'mine, all mine'. He can stand on his steps as proprietor and nod, if nothing more towards those neighbours who are also exercising their proprietorial rights. He knows all of them by sight but in terms of relationships they will shade from close personal friends to others who quite literally are nodding acquaintances.

Taylor's house, of course, was built about the time the motor car was being invented (1886). As he points out, a street like his can accommodate the cars of those who live there, actually outside their own front doors, where the cars themselves contribute to self-expression, and therefore to their owners' sense of identity, as do their front gardens and, indeed, the fronts of their houses themselves. But parked in the street a car is unprotected, from the weather, or even from vandals; not that vandalism seems to be much of a problem in Taylor's London street. But as he points out (p. 104) the lower densities of Hampstead Garden Suburb, permitting detached and semi-detached houses as they do, also made it possible – as cars began to be fashionable, around 1911 or so – for car-ports and even for garages to be added.

Faced with the problems of building new at high densities whilst accommodating the car, Taylor advocated courtyard housing of the kind which Richard McCormack actually built for the London Borough of Merton at Pollard's Hill. In this case the garages are located around the periphery of the development in short access streets.

March and Trace

It is no coincidence that in the design of Pollard's Hill McCormack had drawn on the work of researchers in Land Use and Built Form Studies (now the Martin Centre) at Cambridge University. For McCormack had been a student at Cambridge where various permutations of Martin, March and Trace had been researching into the nature of efficient land use. In 1968, for instance, March and Trace had published *The Land Use Performance of Selected Arrays of Built Forms*. They started from Le Corbusier's basic premiss: that dwellings should be so planned that, even on the worst day of the year, the winter solstice, sunlight – in the absence of clouds – should penetrate for a minimum of two hours into each living room.

Le Corbusier, Geopius and others had used this to argue that, given the same sun-angle the slab-blocks of the Modern Movement, wide spaced in park land, were more efficient users of the land than two-storey, three-storey, or other terrace-forms might be.

Given access to computers which the pioneers had never had, March and Trace were able to test a wide range of building forms against the criterion of sun-penetration: terrace housing at various heights, blocks, slabs, T-shaped, X-shaped and other kinds of tower, concluding that of all possible built forms, the most efficient of all in terms of land-use would be four-storey courtyards (Fig. 7.2).

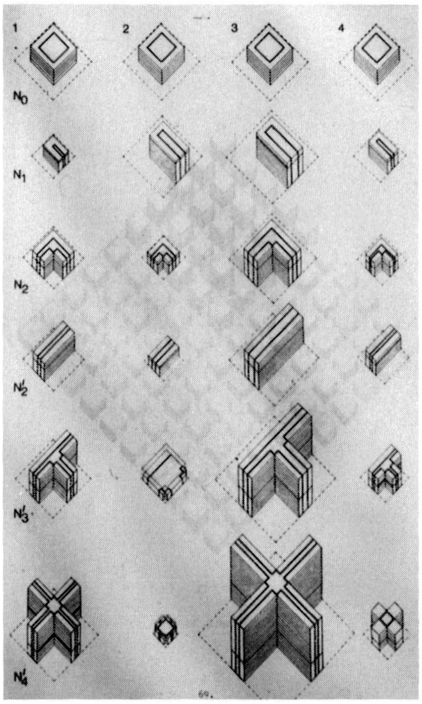

Fig. 7.2 March and Trace (1962) 'Selected array of built forms' showing courtyard housing as the most efficient way of covering the ground (from March and Trace, 1962).

It is hardly surprising that, working in Cambridge as they were at the time, March and Trace should be aware of the court – or the Oxford quad – in terms of its social advantages, but their analysis of sun-penetration was thoroughly objective and remains one of the most significant pieces of research ever to have been undertaken on urban built form. What is extraordinary is that, with the honourable exception of McCormack, until recently so few architects should have seized the opportunities which March and Trace had provided for building such urban forms.

Especially since the founding father himself, Le Corbusier, had, quite intuitively, come to similar conclusions concerning land use, which he demonstrated in the Maisons Jaoul of 1955?

He built these two houses in an L-shape – obviously the corner of a courtyard – on a concrete platform raised half a storey out of the ground. There was parking underneath and the houses themselves were built in that assemblage of masonry – in these cases brick – with shallow vaults in concrete of the kind which, mistakenly, Le Corbusier thought to be Catalan.

The houses themselves represent a thorough recantation by the Master himself of the position he had taken up in the 1920s. Their thick wall, thick vault, small window construction, with its excellent thermal capacity, avoidance of solar heat gain, admission of daylight to give sparkle where required, sound insulation properties, and so on, was a direct, highly personal refutation of his *Five Points for a New Architecture* of 1927.

Those are architectural matters but in the Jaoul Houses also, Le Corbusier attempted, very clearly, to refute his planning ideals of the 1920s. Here the towers and slabs have been abandoned; so have the motorways. Instead we have a human-scale environment; the houses themselves are nowhere more than three storeys high, on their half-storey plinth. What is more the car is stored where it should be, underneath, thus allowing human scale to prevail at ground level.

Peter Cowan

March and Trace were dealing with the spaces *between* buildings but the spaces *within* buildings clearly are related to these. The (small) Georgian square came close to their optimum, of four-storey housing around courtyards, and, curiously enough, the interiors of houses around such squares have some rather special properties. For they were built for The Season in London, Bath or wherever, so they had reception rooms, for The Family facing the square, with smaller rooms for the servants behind them and over them too in the attics.

This mix of rooms means that even now these urban Georgian Houses can be used for many purposes: as houses, still for grand families, as embassies, consulates and so on. They can be divided into apartments; converted, with very little change, into schools – the Architectural Association in Bedford Square, London, occupies three such houses – nursing homes, offices – especially for publishers – and so on.

This flexibility depends, in particular, on the rooms built originally for servants. For often these are of the size which Peter Cowan showed (1964) to be highly significant. He measured room-sizes, first of all in designs for new hospitals, and found that some 30% of them were around 150 square feet in area (13 square metres). He found that also in other building types and he then asked a rather different question.

Cowan plotted a wide range of activities starting, as he says, with the 'five senses and ranging up to large group activities such as dances and conferences'. He then plotted these activities on to a chart showing room sizes from about four square feet (0.370 square metres) to 10 000 square feet (920 square metres) against the number of activity-types which each room could contain.

The smallest room, he thought, might accommodate some 10 activities and as room size increased, so did the number of activities. Indeed it rose very steeply, up to about 200 square feet (18.5 square metres) after which it levelled off abruptly. Beyond this point, indeed, quite large increases in floor area made very little difference to the number of additional activities that could be housed.

Since Georgian houses were planned to contain quite a lot of rooms of, or around, this significant size, and since also Georgian window-spacings enable larger rooms to be subdivided into rooms more or less of this size, it is hardly surprising that the basic Georgian form has proved so eminently usable for so many purposes.

Jane Jacobs, Nicholas Taylor, March and Trace, Peter Cowan – not to mention Le Corbusier himself – all presented evidence against the tower and slabs of Modern Movement housing. Oscar Newman and Alice Coleman were equally critical and they presented evidence of rather different kinds.

Oscar Newman

Oscar Newman suggests (1973) that Jane Jacobs's view on urbanity represents unsupported hypotheses. As he points out (p. 112), the presence of commercial or institutional facilities in a project does not necessarily lead to that kind of proprietorial surveillance which Jacobs suggests it would. On the contrary, he says, the New York City Housing Authority Police found that projects adjacent to commercial streets suffered proportionately higher crime rates. As the victim of a mugging in south-side Chicago, I can testify to that although State Street at that point was under constant surveillance, I was simply perceived as a hostile stranger of the wrong colour!

Unlike Jacobs, Newman supports his contentions with statistical analyses. He finds correlations, for instance, between project size and building height with the mean number of crimes per thousand of population which, summarized, are as given in Table 7.1.

He finds double-loaded corridors particularly dangerous, that is corridors lined with apartments on both sides for which reason no-one can watch them from outside. He also finds (p. 112) more crime in the spaces between housing blocks than in the public streets which border them. The latter, indeed, sound rather like Jane Jacobs's streets whereas no one feels responsible for the spaces between the blocks. They create indeed a kind of no man's land which, in Newman's view, could be made much safer, not to say usable, if *someone* felt responsible for them.

Table 7.1 Crimes per thousand according to project size and building height

Project size	Building height 6 storeys or less	Higher than 6 storeys
1000 units or less	47	51
More than 1000 units	45	67

It is on these grounds that Newman developed his concept of Defensible Space, that is space controlled by the residents in such a way that any potential criminal is recognized, and dealt with as an intruder. So, as Newman says (p. 3):

> Defensible space is a surrogate term for the range of mechanisms – real and symbolic barriers, strongly defined areas of influence, and improved opportunities for surveillance – that combine to bring an environment under the control of its residents.

So:

> A defensible space is a living residential environment which can be employed by the inhabitants for the enhancement of their lives, while providing security for their families, neighbours and friends.

So in Newman's view there should be a hierarchy of space-types from the most public: the street to the most private: the inside of the dwelling. Between these extremes there would be semi-public space, clearly reserved for those who live, or are visiting the dwellings for legitimate purposes, and semi-private space, that is space which clearly belongs to a single dwelling even though it is open to public access.

Thus new projects should be designed, and old projects modified, to incorporate these hierarchies of spaces (Fig. 7.3). In one of the various cases Newman analyses the objectives were (p. 167):

1. to intensify tenant surveillance of the grounds
2. to reduce public areas by unambiguous differentiation between grounds and paths; thus creating a hierarchy of public, semi-public, and private areas and paths
3. to increase the sense of proprietorship felt by residents
4. to reduce the stigma of public housing and (to) allow residents to relate better to the surrounding community
5. to reduce inter-generational conflict among residents within the project

Fig. 7.3 Brownsville Housing, New York with a triangular 'buffer zone' easily observed from the apartment windows, used for play, sitting and parking (from Newman, 1972).

6. to intensify the use of semi-public ground within the project in predictable and socially beneficial ways, and to encourage and extend the areas for which tenants feel responsible.

There were those such as Bill Hillier (1973) who saw this as a rather wicked plot to provide social manipulators with a set of tools for controlling the urban masses. It was based, Hillier said, on a dangerous misconception, that of territoriality as described by Konrad Lorenz (1952), Robert Ardrey (1967, 1969) and Desmond Morris (1967, 1969). But contrary to what these ethnologists have to say – or so Hillier argues – man is not by nature an aggressive animal, intent on defining and defending his personal territory, or, worse still, his private property.

Hillier argues that, on the contrary, the archaeological and anthropological evidence available to us: 'almost universally supports the social view of man – that he is man because he is social'. Society is *not* a mechanism for restraining man from his natural excesses: 'All our basic cultural facts – languages, production systems, cities above all – confirm this interpretation'.

Of course it is wrong to draw evidence from the behaviour of seagulls – as the ethnologists did – that man is an aggressive, territorial animal. But it may be equally wrong to draw evidence from the behaviour of Trobriand Islanders, as Hillier does, that man is essentially a co-operating social animal. Or, at least that he is wherever he has been allowed to develop naturally. Since the Trobrianders do not build cities, we can only speculate as to how they might behave if they did!

As we saw in Chapter 1 the whole concept of the Muslim city was that each house should have its clear, unambiguous and defined private territory even though Islam also requires a profound sense of social responsibility of its adherents. One cannot brush aside hundreds, and indeed, thousands of years of cultural diversification – in some of which territoriality is absolutely fundamental – to say that because the first men seemed to be highly social all men ever since have been, but of course one can believe that they *should* have been!

Hillier, nevertheless, has a point and his reworking of Newman's statistics is helpful in suggesting that the physical form of dwellings is one thing, and the social status of those who live there quite another. For of course the deprived, the underprivileged, the poor, the unemployed, the desperate, are more likely to turn to crime, wherever they live, than the affluent and contented who among other privileges have been able to buy privacy and protection!

Alice Coleman

Alice Coleman builds on Oscar Newman's work in her *Utopia on Trial* (1985). She and her colleagues at King's College, London extended very much further the kind of statistical work that Newman and his team had done. They measured the frequencies with which various kinds of anti-social behaviour occurred in different kinds of estates: from single-family houses through houses divided into flats to purpose-built, low-rise blocks of flats and, most particularly, high-rise blocks of flats of the kind which Newman and his team had found so alienating.

Coleman's team mapped the occurrence of such behaviour in no less than 4099 blocks of flats containing, between them, 106 520 individual

Table 7.2 Percentage abuse levels by dwelling type

	Single-family houses (1800)	Converted houses (200)	Purpose-built flats (4099)
Litter	19.8	37.0	86.1
Dirty and decayed litter	4.0	16.5	45.7
Graffiti	1.2	0.5	76.2
Damage	1.9	2.5	38.8
Urine	0.0	0.0	22.9
Faeces	0.1	0.0	7.5

dwellings thus accommodating, collectively, some quarter of a million people. They also mapped the same range of behaviour in and around 4172 individual houses.

The behaviour itself extended, in ascending order of social disturbance, from the more-or-less casual dropping of litter, through the deliberate spraying of graffiti, damage by deliberate vandalism, the number of children in care, the deposit of urine and even faeces in entrances, corridors, lifts and so on.

In one study, for instance, they compared the percentage incidence of these things in single-family houses, houses converted into flats and purpose-built flats with the results given in Table 7.2.

With one very obvious anomaly – and that seems to have been caused by the presence of a horse and its manure – there are clear increases of Coleman's anti-social behaviour as one moves from single-family flats to flats in converted houses to purpose-built blocks of flats.

Then she analyses in much more detail than Newman ever did the features of high-rise flats which seem to correlate most strongly with anti-social behaviour. She finds that for 15 blocks of flats, containing between them, 4099 dwellings her anti-social behaviour patterns

Table 7.3 Relative influence of design variables

Variables to do with size:	
Number of dwellings served by same entrance	57.7
Number of dwellings in the block	46.7
Number of storeys to the block	41.1
Number of storeys in each dwelling:	
i.e. flats, maisonettes etc.	13.8
Variables to do with circulation routes:	
Number of overhead walkways between blocks	32.6
Number of connected lifts, staircases etc.	26.7
Number of interconnected exits	22.4
Corridor type (single or double loaded)	20.6
Features of the grounds and the layout:	
Spatial organization: public, semi-private, ambiguous, etc.	31.2
Number of access points from street into site	24.6
Number of blocks sharing site	18.3
Number of play areas	7.1
Characteristics of entrances:	
Type: communal or separate for each flat	9.8
Access: from street, internal court etc.	8.5
Between stilts and/or garages	6.6

seemed to be related – in percentages – to the design features given in Table 7.3 (combined from Coleman's Tables 7 and 9).

In each case where numbers are concerned: number of dwellings, number of blocks, number of storeys to each, number of walkways connecting them, number of escape routes and so on, more seems to mean, invariably, worse. Even children in large numbers seem to overwhelm, for as Coleman says, multi-storey layouts with large schools, rather public playgrounds and so on mean that children tend to spend their time together, rather than with adults, including their parents, and thus they have less chance to *learn* what good behaviour is supposed to be.

Like Newman she has her strategies for discouraging anti-social behaviour. Like him she suggests they be applied to new designs and used to retro-fit existing designs. They include, for houses, the provision of gardens, fences and gates; car spaces, and provision for making one's personal mark. And for flats she suggests a number of principles; first, and most important, the removal of overhead walk-ways then the clear demarcation of individual blocks to give each of them an obvious autonomy; reducing the number of access and escape routes and therefore the anonymity of blocks; the improvement of entrances and streetscapes so that public entrances, for instance, actually face into the street rather than into some internal court.

Unlike Newman, however, she anticipates – and answers – her critics. She finds that size alone is by no means bad in itself, nor is the age of the building. Nor is density in itself, indeed in some cases she advocates increases rather than reductions in density. But she does find that much anti-social behaviour is related to the density of children.

Above all she maintains that poverty, unemployment, the concentration of problem families in certain blocks, do *not* correlate with anti-social behaviour. Indeed she points out that however bad these things may have been in the 1980s, they were even worse in the '30s. But most people then lived in houses, in streets with all the advantages that Jane Jacobs describes. Except that, curiously enough. Coleman finds that far from being beneficial effects, the presence of shops, places of recreation, entertainment and so on can bring anti-social behaviour if they are located *within* a housing estate.

Despite her anticipating what they might say, Coleman of course has had her critics. Brian Anson, for instance (1986), springs to the defence of those who offend against 'civilised standards'. He sees the petrol bomber, the graffiti artist and the vandal lumped together with the mugger, the rapist and the child molester as criminals. Yet their protest may be just what society needs for in his view, none of what Coleman and others have to say 'explains the general malaise manifested by the 1981 riots or the widespread drug abuse which goes far beyond the system-built estates; nor the deepening despondency, which ultimately tends to show itself in apathy towards the environment, in areas of endemic unemployment'. In his view these are all caused by despair, a despair which has far less to do with the quality of the built environment than with unemployment, and therefore, money.

Lacking money the once house-proud mother deteriorates into 'a slovenly person who seems not to care anymore'. And after the mother: 'the street, then the neighbourhood and even the whole town. But the child (the new, informed generation) perhaps turns from despair to anger and ends up throwing a petrol bomb'. Then of course he is branded as a criminal.

Like Hiller before him Anson sees the demolition of overhead walkways, and other of Coleman's proposals, as simply a further set of confidence tricks to be played on the poor and disadvantaged. In his view there are reasons for writing graffiti, and even for throwing petrol bombs.

As he says, 'in Belfast they shoot the graffiti man', whereas 'What we really should be doing is taking the trouble to read what he writes'. In that way we might begin to understand the nature of the real urban problems of our age.

PART THREE

THEORIES INTO PRACTICE

8
Neo-Rationalists

Tendenza 1

The Tendenza towards a neo-Rationalism emerged in the pages of *Casabella*, the glossy Italian magazine, during the 1950s and 60s. Its Editor, Ernesto Rogers, had gathered together a group of young architectural theorists including Vittorio Gregotti, Mario Zenuso and, most particularly, Aldo Rossi. They began to explore the nature of architecture itself and, of course, to develop their own philosophies. Rossi forms a personal link with the next most important bastion of the Tendenza, the Institute of the History at the School of Architecture in Venice of which Manfredo Tafuri became Chairman in 1968. His colleagues included Carlo Aymonimo with whom Rossi was to collaborate.

The Tendenza first sprang to international attention in 1973 with their Exhibition of Architettura Razionale at the Milan Triennale. The organizers included Ezio Bonfanti, Rossaldo Bonicalzi, Massimo Scolari, Daniele Vitale and, of course, Aldo Rossi. In addition to their own designs, they included the work of pioneer Rationalists from the 1930s and the work of Rationalists from other countries – such as the Krier Brother from Luxembourg and the self-styled New York Five.

These neo-Rationalists worked with an architecture of abstract, geometric purity derived, as they said, from the work of the French 18th century Rationalists such as Laugier, Ledoux and, especially, Boullée. Most of the Tendenza claimed to be Marxists – largely of the kind which Charles Jencks described as Lamborghini Marxists – and some still advocate communal living which makes them *Communists*.

Of course one can understand why those who came to maturity during the Fascist dictatorships of the 1930s and 40s should insist that *their* political sympathies lie far to the left; this has been especially true in Italy and the Latin world in general. But others elsewhere still use Marxist as a shorthand term for 'Not Fascist'!

Rossi himself rebelled, not so much against the Tendenza's 'Marxist' declarations as against the interminable political debate which it engendered. For the Lamborghini Marxists architecture itself was hardly worth discussing, and certainly designing until *they* had decided how to put the world to rights.

Manfredo Tafuri

So the Tendenza can be comprehended only against this rather bourgeois Marxism, the fullest, if not the clearest, statements of which are contained in Manfredo Tafuri's voluminous writings, including his Essay: *Per una critica dell' ideologia architectonica* (1969), modified and expanded as *Progetto e Utopia* (1973) and translated into English as *Ideology and Utopia* (1976). Llorens's Review (1981) is a splendid archaeological excavation through the book down to Tafuri's original Essay! Despite execrable translation, this book, above all, introduced most English-only readers to the stance of the Tendenza.

There is, of course, a long history of writings about Utopia starting with Plato's *Republic* – although some would see that as rather totalitarian. More's *Utopia* (1534) of course is central to the literature but utopias have had many exponents since (Choay, 1965; Tod and Wheeler, 1978).

That stance is best understood in the context of another Tafuri Essay: *L'Architecture dans le Boudoir* (1974) in which he argues that the large, multi-national corporations can, by their size and power, override city planners everywhere. Which city could resist their blandishments given the vast revenues their very presence brings in, their promises of employment for large numbers of people, the purchasing power of those employees and so on? How could *any* city refuse them permission to build even on land zoned already for something else?

For Tafuri, the very existence of multi-nationals makes socially responsible planning impossible. And whilst in previous centuries, architects and other visionaries had imagined Utopias, Capitalism has destroyed the very concept. If they cannot even conceive of Utopias, they have no hope of achieving anything like them. Nor will they ever again whilst Capitalism retains its grip on human affairs. So Tafuri looks for:

> . . . the emergence of an architecture which aims to redistribute the capitalistic (*sic*) division of labour, which moves towards an understanding of the technician's role in building – that is, as a responsible partner in the economic dynamics and as an organizer directly involved in the production cycle.

There are marxist planners of course who would argue that, whatever Tafuri says, Castells's *The Urban Question* of 1972 is rather more relevant to the real and serious issues of planning. So before exploring Tafuri further we ought to look at the theoretical background from which the Tendenza's ideas emerged.

Ideologies

Marxism

Like Marx and Engels before them the Rationalists saw the large industrial city as profoundly alienating.

First of all the city alienates man from nature and, since everything in the factory is geared to the rhythms of the machines, human beings are reduced to the status of mere 'hands' operating those machines. The machines themselves are laid out for most efficient production and the 'hands' are organized around them, spatially, as if they were mere appendages of the machines. Their spatial distribution around the factory, not to mention the noise, precludes any kind of social interaction.

The 'hands' of course are there to see that the machines are running properly, prompting them, with numbing regularity, by pushing buttons, pulling levers or whatever. Worst of all the 'hand' never sees the finished product; never has the craftsman's satisfaction of making something, anything, in which he can take a personal pride. So the factory worker is alienated in several ways; from nature, from his fellow human beings, from the products he plays a small part in making. And each, most profoundly, is alienated from himself.

So the Rationalists envisage a return to (idealized) medieval conditions in which the craftsman worked in his own shop, made things with pleasure and enjoyed personal transactions in selling them to others, had an active social life within the street and lived literally over the shop.

Of course they accepted Marx's view that throughout history there have always been two classes, the exploiters and the exploited and if one accepts this primitive two-class division – which Marx abandoned on his deathbed (Marx, 1883) – then most of what qualifies as Architecture – as distinct from the Vernacular – in the standard histories was designed, literally, to express the power of some political, social, economic, religious or other élite.

Frederick Engels

Tafuri (1973) and other Rationalists cite the views of Marx's colleague, Frederick Engels, on the city. In 1845, for instance, Engels wrote of London and other Great Towns. He admired, in a way, this 'colossal centralization . . . the giant docks . . . the thousands of vessels . . . the masses of buildings'.

But for Engels the cost had been too great:

> After roaming the streets (for) a day or two, making headway with difficulty through the human turmoil . . . one realizes . . . that these Londoners have been forced to sacrifice the best qualities of their human nature . . . that a hundred powers which slumbered within them have remained inactive . . . been suppressed (so) that a few might be developed more fully. . . . The very turmoil of the streets has something repulsive . . . against which human nature rebels.

The millions crowding past each other actually were *human* beings, with the same qualities, the same potentials, the same interest in being happy:

> And still they crowd (past) one another as though they had nothing in common, nothing to do with one another . . . their only agreement is . . . that each keep to his own side of the pavement.

Indeed:

> The brutal indifference, the unfeeling isolation of each in his private interest becomes the more repellent and offensive, the more these individuals are crowded together . . . this isolation of the individual, this narrow self-seeking . . . is nowhere so shamelessly barefaced . . . as . . . here in the crowding of the great city.

For Walter Benjamin (1955) the charm of Engels's description lies 'in the intersecting of unshakeable critical integrity with an old-fashioned attitude', suggesting that Engels found the crowd so distressing because he: 'came from a Germany that was still provincial (where) he may never have faced the temptation to lose himself in a stream of people'. He contrasts this view with Charles Baudelaire's, a contrast which, as we shall see, Tafuri finds telling.

Fig. 8.1 Gustave Doré (1872): *A City Thoroughfare* (from Doré, 1872).

In the year that he wrote *The Condition . . .* (1845) Engels also started writing *The German Ideology* with his colleague Karl Marx. They described their vision of the perfect Communist society in which everyone would live in collaborative harmony with everyone else. No one would specialize in anything and above all there would be no 'division of labour'. As they said:

> . . . as soon as the division of labour comes into being, each man has a particular, exclusive sphere of activity, which is forced upon him and from which he cannot escape. He is a hunter, a fisherman, a shepherd, or a critical critic, and must remain so if he does not want to lose his means of livelihood; whereas in a communist society nobody has one exclusive field of activity, but each can become accomplished in any branch he wishes, society regulates the general production and thus makes it possible for me to do one thing today and another tomorrow, to hunt in the morning, fish in the afternoon, rear cattle in the evening, criticise after dinner, just as I have a mind, without ever becoming hunter, fisherman, shepherd or critic.

This would be fine, of course, if the animals came along to be hunted in the morning and the fish in the afternoon. But suppose no one felt like milking the cattle that day? Indeed Marx and Engels go on to say:

> with a communist organization of society, there disappears the subordination of the artist . . . to some definite art, making him exclusively a painter, sculptor, etc., the very name . . . expresses . . . his dependence on the division of labour. In a communist society there are no painters but only people who engage in painting among other activities.

Nor of course could there be architects, planners, philosophers or indeed political theorists like Marx and Engels themselves!

Nor could there be any cities. Marx and Engels went on to state in their *Communist Manifesto* (1848) that agriculture would be combined with manufacturing industry so that there would be a: 'gradual abolition of the distinction between town and country, be a more equable distribution of the population over the country'.

No Communist true to the *Manifesto* therefore can be an urbanist, of any kind.

At least early Marx and Engels were consistent for as we saw in Chapter 1 the first cities were founded in the very distinctions between town and countryside they deplore, in the production of food by regulated irrigation and, most specifically, the division of labour. Of course they were quite wrong in seeing this as an evil specific to the Industrial Revolution. It was rather, the root from which civilization itself had started to grow some 8000 years earlier! For the specialized crafts of the earliest cities were the first divisions of labour.

No one, certainly not Marx himself, has ever been able to reconcile his bucolic vision of the ideal Commune, where everyone lives in collaborative harmony, with our – and his – liking for things such as books which can only be produced in quantity by highly specialized divisions of – mostly machine-based – labour into author, editors, printers, distributors, retailers and so on. That paradox of course underlies much neo-Rationalist polemic as to what human beings ought to be, how our societies should be formed, how cities should be planned to shape societies in those ways and so on!

Charles Baudelaire

Baudelaire's views on the city were quite different. He set them out in an essay on *The Painter of Modern Life* (1863) where he describes the *flâneur*, which Charvet translates (1972) as the Dandy.

> The crowd is his domain, just as the air is the bird's, and water that of the fish. His passion and his profession is to merge with the crowd. For the perfect idler, for the passionate observer, it becomes an immense source of enjoyment to establish his dwelling in the throng, in the ebb and flow, the bustle, the fleeting and the infinite. To be away from home and yet to feel at home anywhere; to see the world, to be at the very centre of the world, and yet to be unseen. . . . The observer is a prince enjoying his incognito wherever he goes.

In absolute contrast to Engels, the *flâneur* is:

> . . . the lover of universal life (who) moves into the crowd as though into an enormous reservoir of electricity. He . . . may . . . be compared to a mirror as vast as this crowd . . . a kaleidescope endowed with consciousness . . . every one of its movements present(ing) a pattern of life, in all its multiplicity . . . the flowing grace of all the elements that go to compose life.

As Reff points out (1983) the city where Baudelaire's *flâneur* strolled with such ease was the Paris of Haussmann's new boulevards (Fig. 8.2).

Tafuri detests the *flâneur*, seeing the arcades of Paris, the department stores, the exhibitions and other events in which he had his being as the spatial and visual means by which the proletarian masses were brain-washed into understanding their positions within the system, the:

> . . . ideology of the city as a productive unity in the proper sense of the term and, simultaneously, as an instrument of coordination in the production–distribution–consumption cycle.

Fig. 8.2 Eduard Manet (1862). Concert in the Tuileries Garden. A scene from 'Modern Life' of the kind which Baudelaire's flâneur enjoyed (from the National Gallery, London).

Tafuri is particularly scathing of Georg Simmel who, in his Essay on *The Metropolis and Mental Life* (1903) compared a 'metropolitan type of individual' with what he called 'small town man'.

His metropolitan man seeks constant stimulation whereas his small town man prefers: 'impressions which take a regular and habitual course'. The latter lives his life in rhythm with the seasons, the day-to-day needs of his animals. The rhythm of his life 'flows more slowly, more habitually, and more evenly' than that of metropolitan man.

Metropolitan man by contrast, flourishes on deadlines. He likes a constant stream of appointments, dashes constantly from place to place. Which means that he keeps time with exact precision; precision is the key to his life. If he wants goods or services he does not wish to argue for them, or even to discuss them. He wants to go and get what he requires, pay for it and move on quickly to something else. He flourishes in the money economy. He tries to keep his relationships impersonal too since, given the number and range of his contacts, he simply could not cope with knowing all of them well.

In Simmel's small town life by contrast: 'self-preservation . . . requires the establishment of strict boundaries . . .'. People know each other suffocatingly well, and everyone's activities are monitored. No-one can have any private life and any kind of unusual or eccentric behaviour is seen as threatening to the group. No one *can* develop as an individual.

Nor are new ideas accepted. Everything has to be done in the time-honoured way: '. . . small town life in Antiquity and the Middle Ages set barriers against movement and relations of the individual toward the outside . . . set up barriers against individual independence and differentiation within the individual. . . . These barriers were such that under them modern man could not have breathed'.

Even now, metropolitan man feels stifled whenever he has to live a small town life, since: '. . . the smaller the circle . . . the more (it) guards the achievements, the conduct of life, and the outlook of the individual'.

Simmel's originality lay in his view that metropolitan and small town life are *both* possible, and indeed *necessary* ways of being human. Small town life may be gentle, uncomplicated, free of stress – and relatively long – but metropolitan life engenders 'a heightened awareness and a predominance of intelligence'. And, what is more, the sheer concentration of men and their things in the city stimulates the nervous system, literally, to its highest achievements. Throughout history, human achievement has reached its peaks in the Metropolis.

And life in the Metropolis grants to the individual the kind and amount of personal freedom which he cannot find elsewhere. So metropolitan man is free in a 'spiritualised and refined sense' of the 'pettiness and prejudices which hem in the small town man'. The Metropolis, in other words, is the true: 'locale of freedom'.

Most of us, certainly, in the English-reading world, have been brought up to understand from Jane Austen, Anthony Trollope, Thomas Hardy and others that English village or small town life is inherently better than life in the throbbing city. Indeed the novel *set* in the city, by for instance, Charles Dickens, reinforces the view that cities are dangerous cess-pits of iniquity!

Thus literature teaches us that rural life is richer, fuller, more honest and more fulfilling than life in the city can be. But, as Simmel points out, rural life also has its problems including a close-minded, profound conservatism, a desire to know everyone else's business and to comment, however hurtfully, on what other people do, an urge to bring dissidents into line. There are formidable barriers in Simmel's rural life not only to the movement of people but, more particularly, to the movement of ideas engendered by small-minded, mean-spirited desires of small town people to maintain the petty routines of their lives.

The true metropolitan – Baudelaire's *flâneur* – feels thoroughly stifled by all this. He misses the freedom to do as he wishes, with no constraints, no gossip. He enjoys the privacy to get lost in the crowd which is possible only within the anonymity afforded by Simmel's metropolitan life.

Whilst Tafuri is extremely hostile to Simmel, and to Baudelaire's *flâneur*, he nowhere extolls, specifically, the virtues of small town life.

But like Marx before him Tafuri makes the basic error of believing that metropolitan man emerged first of all in the great industrial city. No doubt Çatal Huyuk, Jericho, Babylon and Memphis had their *flâneurs*: Athens, Rome, Florence and Venice most certainly did, as we know from writers of the time. Indeed Baudelaire himself cites Caesar, Carilina, Alcibiades and Chateaubriand as brilliant examples!

Architecture and Utopia

Such were the philosophical, political and social backgrounds to the Tendenza, and Tafuri dealt with – I will not say articulated – them most fully.

As far as I understand them his propositions seem to be that according to the philosophers of the Enlightenment, architects should express, in built form, the ideologies of society. Thus they should envisage and develop social utopias for which their task, then, is to find appropriate three-dimensional built forms.

But the architects of the Enlightenment concentrated instead on designing buildable forms. Thus the 'gigantic architectural fantasies' of Boullée, Ledoux, Lequeue and others were 'not so much unrealizable dreams, as experimental models of a new method of architectural creation'. And things got even worse with the rise of Capitalism. Architects, quite simply, became functionaries of the bourgeousie. Thus it was they designed building after building, and even city after city, in ways which encourage, even if they do not force, the proletariat to accept their places in society, each a cog in the industrial machine. Which seems to be what Tafuri means when he asks for:

> . . . the precise identification of those tasks which capitalist development has taken away from architecture. That is to say it has been taken away in general from ideological prefiguration.

That being at the heart of Tafuri's argument, how does he actually argue it? That is by no means clear but one can extract a series of disconnected thoughts – most of them embedded, randomly, in Chapter 5 of *Architecture and Utopia*, to form a – reasonably – coherent argument. Its various steps might include:

1. It is the first task of any artist, including any architect, to focus attention on the condition of society and to encourage the development of authentic – by which, of course, he means Marxist – values (ch. 4);
2. Capitalism, self-evidently, is an evil system. Therefore it is the task

Fig. 8.3 Gerritt Rietveld (1924): Schroder House, Utrecht: Architecture reduced to the geometric abstractions of de Stijl (author's photograph).

of any artist to promote correct, that is proletarian values, whilst at the same time doing what he can to discredit bourgeoise values (Tafuri (1974) *L'Architecture dans la Boudoir*);

3. The Capitalist city itself is structured objectively. It is, thus, 'structured like a machine for the extraction of surplus value . . . (it) reproduces the reality of the ways of industrial production' (p. 81) (also ch. 5, p. 107);

4. The result of this, as Simmel says, is a blasé attitude; a blurring of distinctions, (reification) in which things appear 'in an evenly flat grey tone; no one object deserves preference over any others' (p. 86);

5. Some bourgeoise artists, ranging in Tafuri's view from Piranesi to Picasso and the Dadaists, tried to counter the greyness by shock tactics, thus proving themselves to be just as anti-nature as the bourgeoisie themselves (p. 90);

6. Others, such as the *de Stijl* artists including Mondrian, and the Constructivists, such as Tatlin, sought, in their work, to reconcile man with the mechanistic values of the industrial city by idealizing pure – or mechanistic – forms (p. 92);

7. The bourgeoisie accept this because they, above all, want to minimize the conflict between capital and labour (ch. 3) and thus to contrive a reconciliation of these opposing stances in art (ch. 4) in which the chaos of Dada, and the existing city, is seen as a datum on to which the order of Constructivism and de Stijl can be superimposed (p. 95);

8. This particular reconciliation was effected by the Bauhaus which 'fulfilled the historic task of selecting from all the contributions of the avant-garde by testing them in terms of the needs of productive reality' (p. 98);

9. Art and design, including architecture, thus lost any aspiration to social criticism and, above all, they opted out of that responsibility – determined for them by the Enlightenment – of developing utopias. They simply accepted the reality of Capitalism, including the mechanistic city which Capitalism produced, and agreed to serve its purposes as efficiently as they could.

So what is to be done? Curiously enough, and having dismissed Aldo Rossi's reasoning towards it as sheer poetry Tafuri adopts his solution and praises him for having achieved it:

> . . . one is led almost automatically to the discovery of what may well be the drama of architecture today: that is, to see architecture obliged to return to *pure architecture*, to form without utopia; (and) in the best cases, to sublime uselessness.

So Tafuri prefers the sincerity of those who pursue a silent and outdated purity to those who try to give architecture some ideological dress. He seems to be looking for an architectural equivalent of what Roland Barthes (1953) called *Writing Degree Zero*; the simple, objective truth with no expression of the writer's personality. How can one explain this apparent contradiction?

The answer, I believe, lies in Marx's concept of alienation or, rather, his reification. This is a particular case of alienation in which human beings, with their properties, relations and actions are thought of as thing-like beings – automatons who behave, not in any human way, but according to the laws of the thing-world (Bottomore, 1983). It is, in other words, a matter of regarding people as abstractions; units to be housed and so on.

Fig. 8.4 Le Corbusier (1924): Maison la Roche, Paris. Architecture reduced to the forms of shipbuilding as a 'machine à habiter' (author's photograph).

Which of course is what Tafuri does, as a Utopian, especially a frustrated one. For Utopians are great reifiers. They envisage perfect, that is reified societies which can only be set up by perfect, reified people. And those perfect, reified people, of course, will need perfect, reified architecture.

Tafuri himself offers no prescriptions as to what architects and planners ought to do in their search for his Utopia. But he does approve of those who opted for an architecture of 'silent and outdated' purity. These ranged from Tafuri's colleagues in Venice, such as Rossi and Aymonimo to the Krier Brothers, from Luxembourg, and above all the self-styled New York Five: Eisenmann, Graves, Gwathmey, Hejduk and Meier.

Their work had been shown in the Exhibition which launched the Tendenza in 1973 but before we discuss what was displayed there we ought to look at the text which, more than any other, gave the Tendenza a certain coherence: Aldo Rossi's *The Architecture of the City* (1966).

Aldo Rossi

Tafuri believed that given the impossibility, under Capitalism, of making ideological statements through architecture, architecture would have to be reduced to a state of sublime uselessness, preferably in terms of pure geometry. Aldo Rossi had shown what he could do on these lines with his very first buildings such as the small – anti-Fascist – Monument to the Partisans at Segrate which he designed in 1965 although the Monument itself is only a partial realization of Rossi's aims for the Civic Piazza as a whole (Fig. 8.5).

Its geometry is extremely simple consisting, as it does, of a rather massive cylinder supporting a triangular pediment, perfectly isosceles in section, its back end supported by two parallel concrete walls enclosing, between them, a flight of stairs up to a landing, or viewing platform, immediately behind the pediment. Here, indeed, is an architecture of sublime uselessness.

Whilst he was designing this, Rossi was also working on his first major text: *L'Architectura della Città* published in Italy in 1966. It is a measure of the time lag between two cultures that the English Translation: *The Architecture of the City* only came out in 1982.

In the book Rossi crystallized arguments he had been developing over the years in *Casabella*. He sees the book itself (p. 27) as divided into four parts: In the first he defines his terms, considering problems of description and clarification which leads him, inevitably, to a discussion of Typology in the Quatremère/Plato sense. In the second he looks at the structure of the city as a whole and in terms of its different elements; in the third he looks at the architecture of the city and the locus, the actual site on which the city is imprinted; and in the fourth, he looks at problems of urban dynamics which lead him, as one might expect, to discuss the politics of choice.

Rossi's concern throughout the book is to study architecture for its own sake without reference to outside disciplines such as sociology and other sciences, nor even, he says (p. 22) to the history of architecture although the use of historical examples is fundamental to his method. So Rossi deals, he says, with urban facts, as they are in themselves, the actual physical objects of which cities are made, with their individuality and their evolution. The English translator calls them artefacts, thus missing many resonances of the Italian *fatti*, which are facts, actions, deeds . . . achievements etc.

Rossi looks at the elements of which cities are composed and the ways in which these are grouped together to form neighbourhoods, in, for instance, Howard's Garden City, Le Corbusier's Ville Radieuse and so on.

Architecture, for Rossi, is the physical expression of certain thoughts and the architect's task, therefore, is to explain those thoughts and convert them into built reality. So he says at the outset (p. 21):

> The city, which is the subject of this book, is to be understood here as architecture. By architecture, I mean not only the visible image of the city and the sum of its different architectures, but architecture as construction, the construction of the city over time.

One need hardly add that 'construction' for Rossi is by no means the physical structure of the city's buildings. For Rossi the word construct means to act on the basis of reason'; a thoroughly Rationalist position.

As Rossi says:

> As the first men built houses to provide more favourable surroundings for their lives, fashioning artificial climates for themselves, so they built with aesthetic intention. Architecture came into being along with the first traces of the city; it is deeply rooted in the formation of civilization and is a permanent, universal, and necessary artefact.

Rossi, therefore, is concerned with how reason produces results in the construction of architecture and how architecture, in its turn, results in the construction of the city.

So Rossi describes the elements of which cities are made, that is to say the different building Types. Type for Rossi, as for Quatremère, is that which remains constant and unchanging behind and underlying all the particular built examples.

He hopes to identify the Types by choosing different kinds of building: houses, churches, schools and so on as expressed in the

Fig. 8.5 Aldo Rossi (1965) Monument to the Partisans in Segrate (from *A + U*, 1976/5).

forms of actual built examples – specific 'architectural facts' and analysing them in ways which reveal whatever fundamental structure underlies *all* the buildings of a specific Type. In this way he hopes to find the essences of the Types. So Rossi sees 'the study of building typology' – in relation to the city – as 'the fundamental hypothesis of the book'.

Ideally Rossi would have to examine every building of the Type ever constructed, which is by no means the same thing as tracing its development over time, as a historian would. But only by analysing every single one could he be sure that he *had* penetrated to the essence of the Type. Architects, indeed, should work as botanists did – examining every kind of plant they could find before establishing the classification of *their* types.

Having established his basic types, Rossi hopes to determine the laws by which each Type was constructed – within his special meaning of that word – and once he has established the laws for constructing the various Types Rossi then hopes to establish the further laws by which building Types are grouped – constructed – together to form that much more complex entity, the city itself.

Within the lifetime of the city as a whole, of course, there will be constant changes to the corpus of buildings it contains, the architectural 'facts' of which it is composed. Each building will have been designed, built, used for a while and then, perhaps, demolished. But the city itself will continue to exist through all these changes and our concept of it as a particular city will be founded in our memories (Fig. 8.6).

Our memories will depend in particular on the presence of certain monuments; particular architectural 'facts' which, because of their sheer quality, have withstood the ravages of time. A true monument, for Rossi, adds far more to the city than its mere physical, atmospheric and visual presence. It actually gives meaning to the city thus acting, in a sense, as a locus of the city's memory.

So-called functionalist critics, of course, decry the monument as individualistic and rhetorical. They want to see the monuments torn down, to be replaced by neutral, commonplace buildings designed to

Fig. 8.6 Arles: Roman Amphitheatre. Engraving of 1686 showing the Amphitheatre as man-made 'site' for a Medieval village (from Rossi, 1966).

meet their specific, so-called functional programmes. But Rossi sees monuments as essential to retaining the very concept of city.

Rossi's aim, therefore, is to use the idea of type to establish the basic continuity that underlies the apparent diversity of the individual urban 'facts'. Indeed it extends beyond the individual 'facts' to whole sectors of the city, not to mention the city itself which of course is a combination of such things.

Architectural Types are revealed, above all, ·in plans, in the relationships of the various spaces to each other within the building. But the urban spaces between the buildings also have their Types. These too are legible in plan as indeed are other urban Types at the scale of the city as a whole.

Rossi quotes Levi-Strauss to the effect that 'space possesses its own values; just as sound and perfume have their own feeling'. Rossi calls a single spatial fact of this kind a 'place'. So: 'place is that which allows a particular architectural 'fact' to acquire its condition of being'.

But place itself is far more than any mere physical environment. Place encompasses both that physical reality *and* its history. No-one builds in a particular place, at a particular time, unless they have particular reasons for doing so.

Yet there is still a difference between architecture, in its fullest sense, and any mere urban 'fact':

> . . . architecture becomes a determining factor in the constitution
> of urban facts when it is able to subsume the entire civil and
> political dimensions of an era; when it is highly rational,
> comprehensible and transmissible. In other words, when it can be
> judged as style.

Obviously one can identify 'a certain environment of space/time with discreet precision in the Gothic city, in the Baroque city, in the neo-Classic city', and so on.

So style becomes the major determinant of urban form. For style, as Rossi puts it, is a way of thinking which:

> . . . contradicts the belief which many hold that pre-ordained
> functions can give the necessary directions to facts and that the
> problem consists (merely) in giving form to certain functions; in
> reality, the forms themselves, in their materialization, seperate the
> functions; they are stated in the city itself.

As Rossi rightly points out, the great historic buildings, the monuments which have remained from ancient times in various cities are often used now for purposes which were quite unknown to those who originally built them. He shows the Arena at Nimes for instance which, having been built for murderous Roman spectacles, formed a man-made landscape into which a medieval village was built. These days, in its restored form, it might be used for anything from a bull-fight to an Ice Show or an Opera. In such a building, clearly, function literally follows form.

Whilst Rossi's declared aim was to analyse architecture in itself, quite free of any social, political or economic pressures, his Marxist views naturally led him to a study of the economic components which determine certain aspects, at least, in the development of urban facts. He draws on the analysis by Halbwachs (1909) of the forces which determined the growth of Paris concluding, naturally, that the growth of industry had destroyed the physical and political homogeneity which, previously, characterized Paris.

As we have seen (p. 26) the medieval craftsman, literally, lived over (or behind) the shop so the first signs of change he says:

> . . . can be discerned in the destruction of the fundamental structure of the medieval city, (which had been) based on absolute identity between dwelling and workplace within the same building.

During the Industrial Revolution, of course, the workers moved in ever larger numbers to the factories so, says Rossi, the second, decisive stage of destruction began, 'with progressive industrialization provoking the definitive split between residence and work and destroying the relationships of the neighbourhood' (Fig. 8.7). And of course the divisions became even greater in the third phase which, according to Rossi, 'starts with the beginning of individual means of transportation', especially the motor car.

But, Rossi asks, 'if the architecture of urban facts is the construction of the city, how can we leave out (the) construction which gives it decisive moment – politics?' The city, of course develops in the way it does because certain *political* choices are made. 'The city realises, in itself, its own ideas of a city when it materializes in stone'. And, of course, that materialization depends almost entirely on political decisions. So whilst the individual urban 'fact' – the work of architecture – can be studied in purely architectural terms, the decision to place a building of that type at that locus within the city cannot. That is a political decision.

Rossi sees the city as a continuous mass into which large-scale elements – often simple in their geometry – can be inserted. These insertions, of course, will conform to the types which have been derived from the study of historical precedents: centralized blocks, courtyard forms, linear blocks and so on. He sees these as planted into the city as foreign bodies with an intentional exaggeration of the discontinuities which occur between the existing fabric of the city and these insertions.

So for Rossi, the function of architectural theory is to examine those

Fig. 8.7 Preston: an Industrial Revolution City with back-to-back housing 'for' the workers grouped around the cotton mills (from Hiorns, 1956).

laws which actually make construction possible. The simplest architectural laws, obviously, are those which determine how one achieves an actual form with a given set of elements and he finds the clearest demonstration of such laws, and their application – not surprisingly – in 18th century neo-Classicism. In discussing Boullée's *Library for a Great Nation* (Fig. 8.8) for instance he says (1967):

> . . . at the beginning he (Boullée) sees his library as the physical site (place) for the spiritual heritage of great men, of the culture of the past; it is they and their works that constitute the library. We must notice that these works, the books, remain throughout the development of the project as the primary data, organised material for the project . . . as in the case of the national palace, the material of architecture will be constituted by constitutional laws.
>
> Moneo (n.d.)

But architecturally the building Type *library* already possesses certain features: centralized light, accessibility to the books, intelligible arrangement, and so on. As an architectural 'fact', therefore, it can be constructed within this established Type. It will be generated as a form which can then be analysed in structural and technical terms. After which it can be realized, full size in three dimensions, as an architectural 'fact'.

It so happens, says Rossi, that because of its timing in the course of human development, (and its relationship to the Industrial Revolution) the neo-Classical period witnessed the development of many new architectural Types: museums, banks, office buildings, and so on, all 'in the service of a civil vision of history'. By their very nature these Types were quite different from the original Classical Types, the temple, the arena and so on, which naturally led to distortions and misuses of the Classical orders.

The new types required that the orders be assembled in quite new dimensions, at quite new scales and in new formal relationships with each other. That is because the orders themselves remained so closely bound to the types of 'primary constructed reality'. Neo-Classicism

Fig. 8.8 Etienne Louis Boullée (1785) the King's Library, known after the Revolution (1789) as the Library for a Great Nation (from Pérouse de Montclos, 1969).

solved this problem, as Moneo (n.d.) puts it in writing of Rossi's work, 'by a logical development of architectural form, by a will to rational expression which is perhaps the most pronounced characteristic, a differentiated feature of style'.

So Rossi finds the answer to his problem of how – having established the Type of his building – to realize it as a three-dimensional fact. It lay, for him, in neo-Classicism, or, more specifically, in the Rationalism of the architecture of Enlightenment, the adventure of a new formal world in which 'History, the collective memory of a certain past, is poured into the architectural object to make it intelligible, thus receiving its nature'.

The Rationalists of the Enlightenment were, for Rossi, the first architects in history to make an autonomous discipline out of Architecture itself. They alone discovered the principles which allow for architectural construction in Rossi's particular sense and this led to an 'objectification' of various elements within the building, of buildings within the city, and so on.

Canaletto demonstrates such an objectification when, for instance, he takes a number of Palladio's Venetian buildings and repositions them where he (Canaletto) thinks they should be. He makes collage-like juxtapositions of Palladio's architectural facts, buildings, which are quite different from the relationships of Palladio's as, and where, they are placed in the City of Venice and the Veneto.

But the question still remains as to how, having established the actual Type of a building one then realizes it as a three-dimensional architectural fact. The answers are to be found not only in Rossi's enthusiasm for Boullée's buildings – with their pure Enlightenment geometry – but also in Rossi's own buildings, at least in those from the early part of his career, the Monument at Segrate (1965), his Apartments at the Gallaratese in Milan (1969–73), his School at Broni (1969–70), his Cemetery at Modena (designed 1971) and his School at Fagano Olona (1972) are all realized in an architecture of simple, geometric forms: perfect circles, perfect squares, perfect triangles, all projected, as necessary, into the third dimension to form perfect cubes, perfect cylinders, perfect prisms.

Aymonimo

Whilst Rossi was reviving the idea of Typology – as described by Quatremère – Carlo Aymonimo was preparing a thoroughly worked example (1973). He analysed social housing, as described at Conferences of CIAM (Congrès d'Architecture Moderne) at Frankfurt in 1929 and Brussels in 1930. He also presented built examples from Frankfurt, Berlin and elsewhere submitting them to thorough Typological analysis (Fig. 8.9). His results were published in 1973 as *L'Abitazione Razionale: Atti dei Congressi CIAM 1929–30*.

Aymonimo reprinted papers by Giedion, May, Gropius, Le Corbusier and Bourgeois from CIAM 1929, and Giedion, Böhm and Kaufmann, Gropius, Le Corbusier, Neutra and Tiege from CIAM 1930. But, rather more to our particular point, he showed almost 100 model plans of apartments from most European capitals, not to mention Basel, Rotterdam, Utrecht, Dessau, Frankfurt, Celle, Turin, Lodz, Breslau, Karlsruhe, Hamburg, Wiesbaden, Zurich, Stuttgart, Mailand, together with special solutions from Moscow and the USA.

His primary concern, of course, was the *Existenzminium* dwelling which had been such a feature of European, and especially German, social housing in the 1920s. It had been pursued with particular vigour

FRANKFURT A.M.

FRANKFURT A.M.

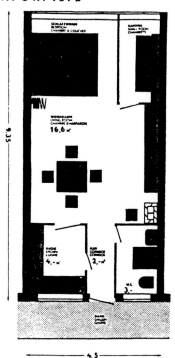

FRANKFURT A. M.

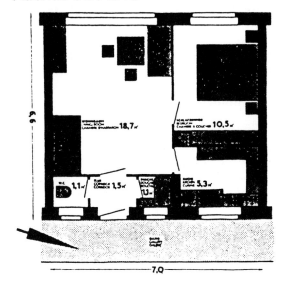

FRANKFURT A. M.

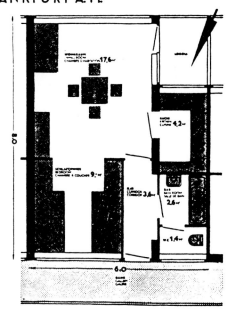

Fig. 8.9 Carlo Aymonimo: Rational Housing apartment types from Frankfurt (from Aymonimo, 1973).

in Frankfurt where Ernst May had been appointed City Architect in 1924 (Miller-Lane, 1968; Rodriguez-Lores and Uhlig, 1971; Bullock, 1978).

The work of the Architect's Department was publicized from 1924 to 1934 in a Journal, *Das Neue Frankfurt*, edited by May and Wichert, in which May himself argued, among many other things, that where possible, people should be housed in single-family houses each with an outdoor garden 'room', that the city should be ringed by housing developments, each housing from 10 to 20 000 people, separated from the city centre, and from each other, by green open spaces 'right up to the core of the City'.

Indeed two of May's erstwhile colleagues, Böhm and Kaufmann, made a spirited defence of Frankfurt's low-rise developments in general, and individual houses in particular, at the CIAM meeting of 1929–30 – which was held in Frankfurt – against Gropius's attempt to bulldoze through his idea of high rise as correct CIAM policy!

May and his colleagues designed no less than 18 housing estates around Frankfurt including Westhausen, Praunheim, Romerstadt and so on. Given this amount of building, May and his colleagues could experiment, as most certainly they did, with housing layout, orientation, aspect, sun-penetration, room size, methods of construction, including prefabricated construction, and so on.

Their work included the first large-scale experiments anywhere – 900 dwellings – in large-panel concrete construction and Frankfurt is remembered also for Grette Schütte-Lihotsky's *Frankfurter Küche* (1927) (Fig. 8.10). Christine Frederick already had applied to Household Engineering in general the methods of work study developed by F. W. Taylor (1911) for analysing such things as the productivity of bricklayers and Schütte-Lihotsky applied them specifically to kitchen design. So the smallest Frankfurt kitchen – on the Praunheim Estate – was no more than 1.87 metres by 3.44 but with everything prefabricated and built in, from the ironing board to the various food containers.

Whilst the kitchen seems to have been analysed more thoroughly than most, *all* the rooms in the house – or apartment – were subject to this kind of analysis so it is hardly surprising that Aymonimo included several examples from Frankfurt in his study.

Fig. 8.10 The (ergonomically efficient) Frankfurter Küche (from Schütte-Lihotsky, 1927).

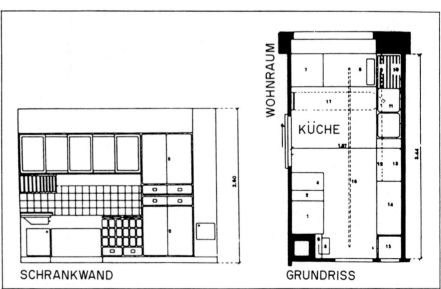

SCHRANKWAND

WOHNRAUM

KÜCHE

GRUNDRISS

He also showed historic layouts such as linear housing, courtyard housing, and so on from Vienna, Berlin, the Soviet Union, Frankfurt and Brussels, also more recent layouts from Letchworth, Rotterdam, Amsterdam, Abo in Finland, Zurich, Mailand, Plessis-Robinson in France, Frankfurt, Warsaw, Paris, Budapest, Brussels, Amsterdam, Berlin, and Karlsrühe most of which were designed with parallel rows of the 'sunlight, fresh air and greenery' housing of the kind which CIAM was promoting at the time.

In a very real sense, therefore, Aymonimo's *L'Abitazione Razionale* was a study of Typology of the kind which Rossi advocated at the level of the individual dwelling. The only other aspect of urban design to be given equivalent treatment so far is at the scale of *Urban Space* in the work of Robert Krier (1975). Before we consider that, however, we ought to look at the stocktaking which the Tendenza undertook at the Milan Triennale of 1973.

Tendenza 2

Tafuri and Rossi between them, not to mention other contributors to *Casabella*, set out the background from which the Tendenza towards neo-Rationalism emerged. Their explorations were theoretical and practical. Not only did they design projects to explore and demonstrate their ideas, they also won competitions which enabled them to build.

Urban facts

Like his Monument for Segrate, Rossi's project for the City Hall at Scandicci (1968) was assembled from equally pure geometric elements; such as a perfect hemisphere and various rectangular blocks grouped symmetrically along, or across, a central axis. His project for the City Hall at Muggio (1972) had a central truncated cone with side wings, each enclosing three open courtyards, reflecting each other diagonally across the central axis (1972). His School at Fagano Olona, near Varese (1972–76), has a cylindrical central hall with a conical roof within a courtyard enclosed by rectangular blocks at right angles to the main axis which continues beyond the court to be marked by a chimney and an open pergola.

And from 1967 to 1970 Rossi collaborated with Aymonimo on the design of speculative housing, the Gallaratese outside Milan. Aymonimo designed a complete urban complex with three housing blocks hinged as it were in an arrow formation about an open amphitheatre. Rossi's single block runs behind and parallel to Aymonimo's central one.

Aymonimo's housing, naturally, is based on the *Existenzminimum* Types he had analysed so assiduously in his *Vivienda Razionale* (1973). He packs apartments of different sizes, for different kinds of household, with some ingenuity into stepped sections with access balconies on alternate sides every two floors or so. The upper floors are given over to various penthouse forms: duplexes, apartments with open courtyards and so on.

These, together with Aymonimo's exposed circular lift-shafts, give the roof line a rich articulation and the elevations too are articulated with Corbusier-like panels of glass brick and pierced concrete balconies. Aymonimo clearly draws his references from the Le Corbusier of the Marseilles Unité and Chandigarh. Aymonimo too applies a coherent colour-coding: with, against wall surfaces which generally are a dark reddish-brown, orange window mullions, a yellow footbridge, blue corridors, and, in the 'undercroft' orange between yellow Corbusean *pilotis*!

Rossi's Gallaratese II was completed in 1974 and we shall examine it on p. 185.

The Krier Brothers 1

By the early 1970s other people in other places were thinking of urban space very much on Rationalist lines. These included, most particularly, the Brothers Krier, Leon and Robert of Luxembourg.

Both had started thinking in quite un-Rationalist ways. Rob Krier's earliest built project, for instance, the Siemer House (1968–70) was white-walled but rather more complex in its geometry than a true neo-Rationalist would have made it. There are indeed some amazing geometric analyses of the human figure from which Krier actually selected the proportional system for his House which steps down a hill under a vast 30 degree roof. Rationalist as, say, the windows may seem to be, certain excrescences, such as the glazed staircase turret, can only be described as art deco (*Architecture and Urbanism*, 1977:06).

But then in 1970, Rob Krier began to work out his urban ideas in and around Stuttgart which he took as it stood, inserting streets and squares where appropriate within the existing context. The horseshoe of his Osterreichisser Platz clearly is derived from Taut's Berlin Britz but the most ambitious of his studies is that for Leinfelden, a rather amorphous suburb which he sought to unify by inserting a Megastructure; some 1200 metres long between an Assembly Hall with a U-shaped Plaza by way of a shopping street, an open courtyard, a covered Galleria, another courtyard, another shopping street, and an open Market to a garden beside an existing Church. The Galleria was to be a multi-layered interchange between the metro, car parking, buses at ground level, shops, offices, housing and so on, grouped under and around a glass-vaulted Arcade with aisles (Fig. 8.11).

So, in quite a literal sense, Krier's Leinfelden represents a study of

Fig. 8.11 Rob Krier (1971): project for Stuttgart Leinfelden: a linear suburb with shopping malls, open squares, transport interchanges etc. (from Bonfanti *et al.*, 1973).

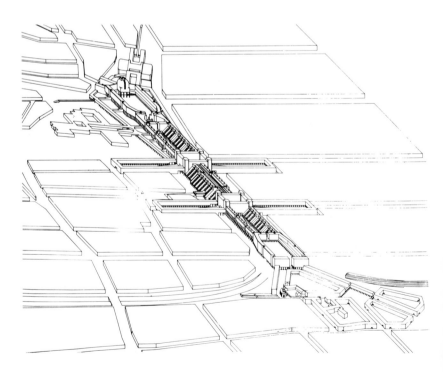

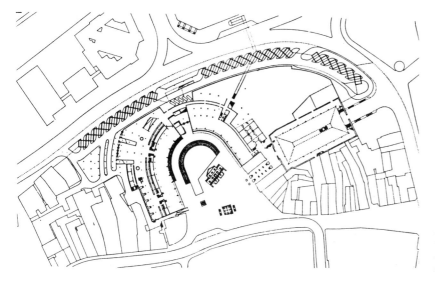

Fig. 8.12 Stirling (1971) Project for Derby Civic Centre with a U-shaped, glazed Galleria and the façade of the old Derby Assembly Rooms rebuilt at an angle of 45 degrees (from Bonfanti *et al.*, 1973).

urban Types – especially of sections as one progresses on the drawings – along his Plaza his shopping streets, his open courtyards, his covered Galleria, his open Market and so on. As we shall see, he was to extend this kind of thinking to other aspects of urban space.

Leon Krier's early work was by no means Rationalist in form or content. He admits that as a schoolboy he was a fervent admirer of Le Corbusier and himself given to planning grandiose schemes for Luxembourg that would make 'the Obus-Plan for Algiers look like

Fig. 8.13 Leon Krier (1970): Echternacht: extensions to the Lycée Classique, a covered arcade, a boulevard etc. (from Bonfanti *et al.*, 1973).

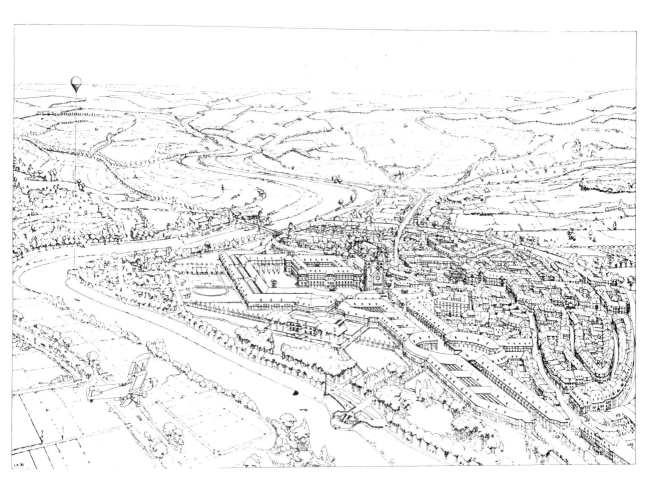

timid stuff' (L. Krier, 1985a). He had even envisaged a national grid of immensely powerful lights suspended above all the inhabited areas of his native country at 100 metres height (1985b and 1985c). (A&D Sept 85 Washington A&D Dec 85).

And what is more his earliest professional – as distinct from student – schemes were Hi-Tech too, including a scheme for the University of Bielefeld (1968) and several equally Hi-Tech projects on which he worked with James Stirling: for Siemens A. G. in Munich (1969) and Housing in Runcorn (1969–70). What is more the urban design scheme in which he assisted Stirling, for Derby Civic Centre (1971), is equally 'hi' in its 'tech' consisting as it does of a glazed barrel-vaulted Galleria curling in a U-shape around the façade of the neo-Classical Assembly Rooms, carefully reconstructed, sloping backwards at an angle of 45 degrees. The façade of Galleria itself splays at 45 degrees into the U-shaped space it encloses (Fig. 8.12).

Much of Krier's own scheme for Echternacht (1970) also seems to be Hi-Tech. The scheme was generated from the Baroque Abbey including extensions to the adjacent Lycée Classique. Krier surrounds the three sides of the Lycée with identical buildings with a gap covered by an arcade between them (Fig. 8.13). He also presents sketches of some rather vernacular porches and porticos for the Abbey, the axis of which is extended South Eastwards by means of a colonnaded street with a circus half way along it and the axis is extended further to become a Haussmann-like Boulevard.

The whole project cuts across the edge of the medieval Echternacht, separating it from its landscaped river frontage to which Krier adds, significantly, a Monument to the Russian Constructivist Ivan Leonidov. Indeed in 1971–72 Krier was to design two Leonidov-like Tower Blocks for the Lewishamsrtrasse in Berlin!

Tendenza Exhibition

Aware of such work by their architectural cousins, Rossi and his colleagues believed that the time was ripe for their neo-Rationalism to be launched as a more-or-less coherent Movement at the Milan Triennale of 1973. So we ought to look now at what they chose to exhibit.

Fig. 8.14 Oud (1927): Housing at the Weissenhoffsiedlung, Stuttgart (author's photograph).

Much of the material, but by no means all, was published in the book: *Architectura Razionale* – also 1973 – by Bonfanti, Bonicalzi, Rossi, Scolari and Vitale. The works contained therein can be grouped under a number of headings. There is, first of all, the work of those whom the neo-Rationalists saw as their ancestors: the architects of the white-walled International Style of the 1920s including Loos's pioneering Goldmann and Salasch Shop in Vienna, Oud's little terraces at the Hook of Holland and the Weissenhofsiedlung in Stuttgart (Fig. 8.14). There was Mies's own slab of housing at Weissenhof and his glass-faced slabs for the Alexanderplatz in Berlin. There were Hans Schmidt houses from Basle.

In reviewing the Exhibition for *Casabella*'s rival, *Domus*, Joseph Rykert (1974) saw Schmidt as a new cultural hero, one of the founders of the Existenzminimum, 'that odious concept which is now being excavated from the libraries' – by, among others, Aymonimo!

There were Constructivist projects such as Hannes Meyer's Peterschule, also for Basle, Leonidov's Commissariat for Industry project, Ginsberg's Narkomfin collective housing in Moscow and Samona's latter-day Constructivist competition entry for the Chamber of Deputies in Rome.

Then of course there was work by the Rationalists of the 1930s, as the Italian representatives of the International Style called themselves, such as Banfi, Belgiojoso, Peresutti and Rogers' Colonia Elioterapica at Legnano, Terragni's Novocomum (1928) and his Casa del Fascio (1936) both at Como.

Le Corbusier, surprisingly, was represented at the Triennale by his monastery of La Tourrette which, being thoroughly Brutalist, surely has nothing much to do with Rationalism? There was the smoothed-down Brutalism of Matthias Ungers's Niebl Housing in Cologne and Max Bill's Hochschule für Gestaltung at Ulm. But the building which was covered most completely was Harvey Court, Gonville and Caius College, Cambridge, by Sir Leslie Martin and Associates, with no less than four photographs and two plans (Fig. 8.15).

All of these were shown as parts of the context out of which the Tendenza had emerged but they seem different in kind from the rather eclectic work of other 'ancestors' whom the Tendenza also claimed. These included Ridolfi's INA Housing in Rome, with exposed beams and columns forming a graph paper grid across the façade, surmoun-

Fig. 8.15 Leslie Martin and Colin St J. Wilson with Patrick Hodgkinson. Harvey Court, Gonville and Caius College, Cambridge, with the 'short-walls-as-columns' which Rossi was to call 'septa' (author's photograph; plans etc. from Martin, 1983).

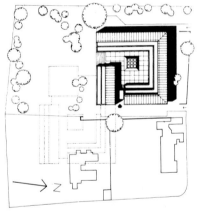

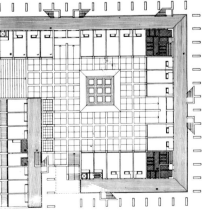

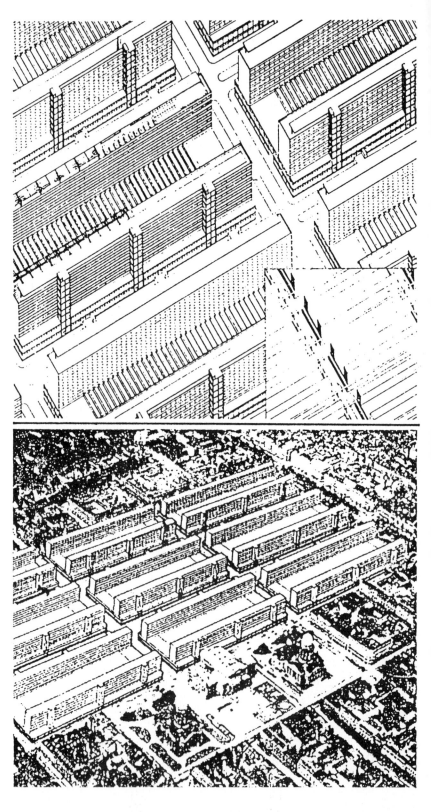

Fig. 8.16 Ludwig Hilbersheimer (1964) Theoretical City layouts (from Bonfanti *et al.*, 1973).

ted by a curious hipped roof; Figini and Pollini's similar but flat-roofed Housing on the via Harrar in Milan; Gardella's vernacular Palazzo on the Zattere in Venice and BBPR's almost Gothic Torre Velasco in Milan.

But whilst the Tendenza claimed a wide range of architectural 'ancestors' there was a frightening, not to say frightful, consistency of urban 'ancestors' on display. These ranged from Tony Garnier's Cité

Industrielle, by way of Le Corbusier's City for Three Million Inhabitants to Bruno Taut's Berlin Britz, the EUR designed by Piacentini and others for Mussolini's Third Rome.

Even bleaker, perhaps, were several of Hilbersheimer's theoretical housing-slab layouts (Fig. 8.16), Bottoni's QT 8, Housing, the Milano Verde Project of Albini, Gardella, Pagano and others and, more frightening than these because it had been built, the Halle Collective's Neustadt, and the mile-long Karl-Marx Allee (1952) in East Berlin, designed by Joseph Kaiser, his Collective and others (Schultz and Gräbner, 1987) but based, quite clearly on the monumental Axis through Berlin which Albert Speer had designed for Adolph Hitler.

Karl-Marx Allee is lined with six sixteen-storey, largely neo-Classical buildings but all the other projects in this group take the form of extremely bleak, mechanistic, sterile and thoroughly inhuman forms: serried ranks of rectangular housing slabs, stamped with machine-like precision across the fabric of whatever city their designers were trying to desecrate. If Tafuri looked for evidence that the 20th century city was forcing people into mechanistic lives he could have found it here. But none of these were Capitalist buildings. They were, rather, designed and even built for Marxist regimes by Marxist architects.

As Rykwert says, Bottoni's QT 8 had been singled out by Le Corbusier himself as being quite exceptionally bad. As for Hilbersheimer, Rykwert calls him:

> the inflator of Mies who makes the master's Chicago manner really unacceptable by multiplying the scale of everything by 100 and showing it up for the inhuman, monstrous composition it is. And indeed the catalogue . . . holds up for our admiration a quite revolting Hilbersheimerian concoction, the East German housing by the Halle-Neustadt-collective.

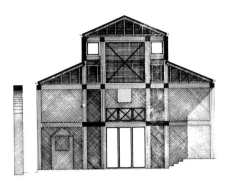

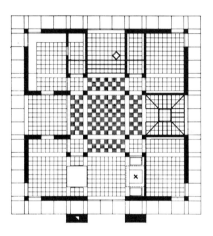

Fig. 8.17 Reinhart and Reichlin (1973) Villa Tonini, Lugano. Plan and section (from Bonfanti *et al.*, 1973).

Having thus set the – rather bleak – scene, the Tendenza were ready to show their own work, including Reichlin and Reinhardt's Kahn-like Villa Tonini (four square pavilions around a central square with a pyramidal roof) (Fig. 8.17), Rossi's School at Fagano Olona (Fig. 8.18); his projects for Segrate and the Gallaratese (Fig. 8.19), Aymonimo's Plan for the Gallaratese and his reconstruction for the Teatro Paganini in Parma, with a surrounding housing development; Grassi's project for the Castello di Abbiategrasso in Milan (Fig. 8.20) and projects by Schnebli, Monteiro, Gisel and Bisogni.

Fig. 8.18 Aldo Rossi (1972) School at Fagano Olona (Varese) (from Bonfanti *et al.* 1973).

As for the work of the Tendenza's cousins this included Ludwig Leo's Pumping Station on the Jandwehrkanal in Berlin, Takefumi Aida's Annihilation House, Leon Krier's scheme for Echternach, Stirling and Krier's scheme for Derby, Robert Krier's project for Leinfelden and his Casa Siemer, Sawade's project for Housing on the Kurfustendam in Berlin, Natalini, with Superstudio's Monumento Continuo for New York City and Samona's late Constructivist Chamber of Deputies scheme for Rome.

But above all the Tendenza saw affinities with the New York Five who at that time, of course (1973), were all working in the white-walled manner of the International Style and, especially, Le Corbusier's villas of the 1920s. So they showed one house by each of the Five: Peter Eisenman's House I, Charles Gwathmey's Steel Residence, Michael Graves's Hanselman House, John Hejduk's Bernstein House, and Richard Meier's Salzman House.

Indeed despite their Marxist predilections American architecture was important for the Tendenza; their catalogue contains an Essay by Colin Rowe on its relationships with the Modern Movement.

There was a section by Bonfanti, on Building for Historic Centres which, in addition to Piacentini's (1916) Plan for Rome, included various Marxist rebuildings of Gdansk, East Berlin, and Bologna.

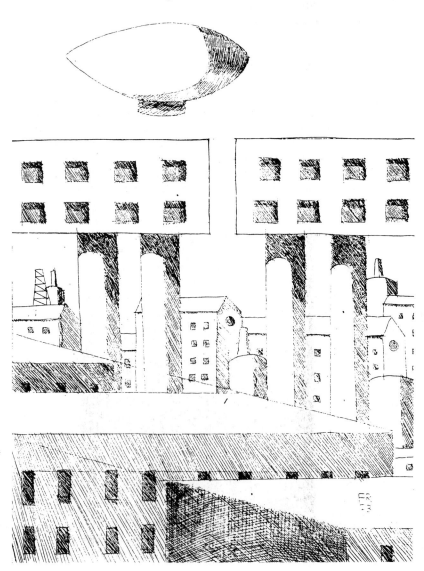

Fig. 8.19 Aldo Rossi (1967–69) Conceptual sketch of the building 'type' housing which he was to develop for the Gallaratese in Milan (from Bonfanti *et al.*, 1973).

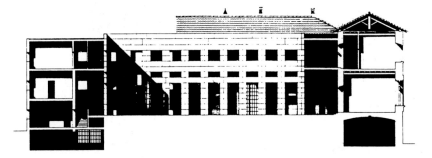

Fig. 8.20 Georgio Grassi (1973) Restoration of the Castello di Abblategrasso Milan (from Bonfanti *et al.*, 1973).

There were projects too from Schools of Architecture in Pescara, Rome, Naples, Berlin, where Grönahl and Rothe had been tutored by Matthias Ungers, Zurich, where Roze, Cantoni, Serena and Bosshard had been tutored by Aldo Rossi, Milan, where Bonicalzi, Braghieri, Scolari and others had also been tutored by Rossi.

Having given such attention to the New York Five – from the bastion of Capitalism itself – the Tendenza felt they had to restate their Marxist position by ending their book with two unequivocally Marxist images, of Ehn's Karl Marx Hof in Vienna and the very final drawing (1946) of the design by Iofan, Schuko and Gel'freich which had won the (1931–36) Competition for the Palace of the Soviets in Moscow!

Alan Colquhoun

Having analysed Triennale designs exhibited in London in 1975 Alan Colquhoun clarified a number of tendencies which the Rationalists displayed in their various designs. As he said, unlike adherents of the Modern Movement, who wanted to sweep everything away and start again, the Rationalists always assumed the existence of the city into which they would make their interventions. He saw two main scales of intervention; one of which, the 'insertion' was simply that – a new building to be inserted somewhere into the fabric of the existing city.

The other was more ambitious: a whole complex of buildings, such as a school or a university campus, self-contained in its geometric unity and often symmetrical, laid into, or across the fabric of the city. He called groupings of this kind 'organisms'. As Colquhoun says:

> In nearly all the schemes, the city is considered a continuous mass, in which are inserted (these) large-scale elements of simple geometric form, belonging to the typology of the historical city; centralised blocks forming enclosed courtyards . . . or linear blocks forming routes from one part of the city to another . . . and so on.

And, what was crucially important:

> The elements are planted in the city like foreign bodies in an organism, exaggerating the discontinuity between the old and the new, texture and structure, ground and figure, context and meaning.

So it is that by these contrasts the historical city is seen as the essential context which 'gives meaning to the new structures'.

Sometimes the clashes were exaggerated where, for instance, the new organism was skewed at some strange angle to the regular grid of the city; or there may even be a 'fault line' at which two systems, each regular in itself, collided.

Clearly Aymonimo had been looking for strange angles, and 'fault lines' at the Gallaratese and, since that part of Milan had nothing much to offer in the way of context had embodied them within his own scheme!

It seems to Colquhoun that the 'organism's' designer was less concerned with the existing city and its fabric than with creating a new element 'with its own self-contained, self-sufficient dynamism and unity'. He saw this exemplified in certain schemes such as Leon Krier's for Echternach, Luxembourg (1970), in which long axes are flanked by facades – sometimes frankly historicist – and Rob Krier's scheme for Leinfelden with such neo-Classical planning devices as squares and quadrants quite indifferent to their surroundings.

As for individual 'insertions', Colquhoun sees these as rather less damaging to the city. He says of them:

> although they consist of strong figures against the ground, (they) allow the empirical irregularities of the city to modify these figures, or their relationships to each other.

Fig. 8.21 Carlo Aymonimo (1967–69): plan of the Gallaratese housing in Milan. Aymonimo's blocks are labelled A1, A2, B and C; Rossi's is labelled D (from Nicolin, 1974).

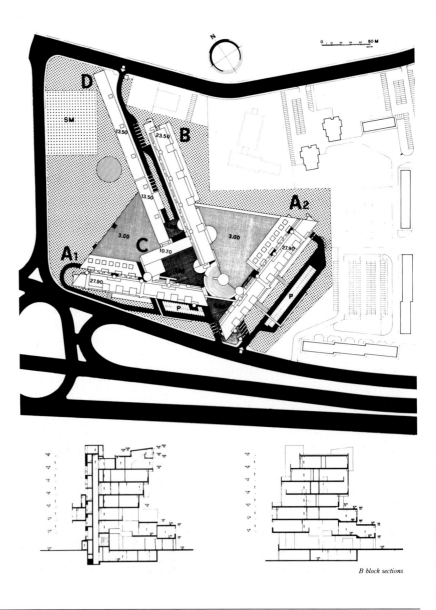

B block sections

Fig. 8.22 Aymonimo block A2 and theatre (author's photograph).

Colquhoun suggests that these 'insertions' were derived from typical Baroque or neo-Classical plans, such as Sixtus's Plan for Rome, or Le Notre's for Paris, in which avenues, piazzas and churches 'punctuate, but do not radically alter, the anonymous medieval grain'. So it is that they respect existing institutions and show a desire 'to overlay them with additional meanings' so that the city still remains continuous in time and space.

Rossi

Gallaratese

Rossi's Housing at the Gallaratese was presented in rather sketchy fashion at the Tendenza Exhibition (Figs 8.19, 8.23 and 8.24). There was an Engraving showing the junction between his two blocks: of cylindrical columns some four storeys high carrying, each side of the gap between them, two storeys of very white, very horizontal housing with absolutely square windows. Another version of the same gap showed two-storey cylindrical columns, and two-storey septa –

Fig. 8.23 Rossi block D, left. Aymonimo block, right.

wall-columns – supporting again, two storeys of housing with square windows opening obviously on to access decks.

Rossi's single block as completed in 1974 is stark and white, much in the manner of Le Corbusier in the 1920s. Except that Le Corbusier had nothing quite so big to build at that time! Of course it represents Rossi's building Type Housing. It is indeed an architectural 'fact', a constructed version of the very many sketches by which, Rossi had shown what, for him, is the essence of architecture (Conforti, 1981).

So there are two, long, thin, rectangular slabs meeting at a 'fault line' – or expansion gap! One contains three storeys of apartments, reducing, near the 'fault', to two. The other has two storeys throughout its length and both have single-loaded access galleries. Needless to say the galleries have perfectly square, blank window openings and so do the upper apartment floors. The blocks themselves are supported, over undercrofts, by 'septa' like those which Sir Leslie Martin used at Harvey Court.

Where the longer block meets the shorter at the 'fault' the 'septa' are replaced, Segrate-like, by four perfect cylinders-as-columns. So Rossi's Block for the Gallaratese represents a paradigm for neo-Rationalism almost as potent as Laugier's Primitive Hut was for the Rationalism of the 1750s!

Fig. 8.24 Rossi block D showing wear and weathering (author's photograph).

Shortly before completion Rossi's was occupied by squatters who, as Nicolin says (1977), were: 'surprised and puzzled' by it. They were struck, so Nicolin says, by the: 'emblems of community life'. They simply could not understand 'why tenants (concentrated) casually in these buildings were supposed to carry on particular social relations'.

They preferred 'the concept of a much larger quartier and social relations on the job'. Thus they found Rossi's corridors too wide, the undercroft between Rossi's 'septa' to be a complete waste of space especially since the apartments seemed to them too tight and the finishes too carelessly executed. Eventually the squatters were evicted; Milan City Council bought the Gallaratese and reserved the apartments for city employees (Fig. 8.24).

Modena Cemetery

But Rossi's Rationalist scheme, *par excellence*, of course, is the Cemetery of San Cataldo for Modena (1976) (Moneo, 1976, Johnson, 1982). Rossi won the Competition in 1971 for an extension to Costa's 18th century

Fig. 8.25 Aldo Rossi (1976): Cemetery of San Cataldo, Modena: plan (from *A + U*, 5: 1976; Moschini, 1979).

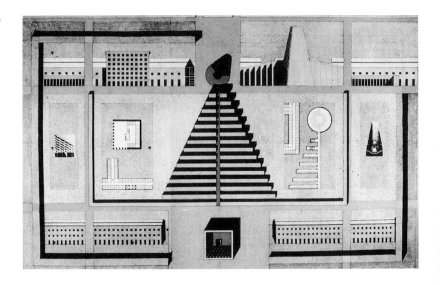

Fig. 8.26 Modena Cemetery: House of the Dead (author's photograph).

Cemetery at Modena (Fig. 8.25). Like many Italian cemeteries, Costa's was a large elongated courtyard – long, that is from east to west – surrounded by (rather heavy) brick neo-Classical ossuaries with wide, top lit, corridors lined, on both sides, by five storeys of niches each large enough to take a coffin with room also for flower vases and memorial lamps. The central courtyard of Costa's Cemetery is a sea of more or less conventional tombs.

Rossi set up a new axis west of Costa's courtyard, parallel to its shorter sides, grouped a Jewish Cemetery and central services symmetrically about this axis and then planned his own, rather larger, courtyard (almost) balancing Costa's beyond the central axis.

Having thus linked old and new on plan, Rossi then separates them visually by building a very linear spine immediately west of his central group with a very narrow gap between this and the eastern side of his courtyard. This is raised, Gallaratese-like on two-storey septa with a single-storey ossuary above. Like Rossi's Gallaratese also this has absolutely square windows but it is painted a light pink, with a light blue metal roof pitched to almost, but not quite, an equilateral section.

Like Costa's original, Rossi's Cemetery is surrounded by ossuaries three storeys high, like his spine but with external walls for their full height, pierced on the upper two floors by square windows and by similar windows elongated down to ground level in the lower storey.

Fig. 8.27 Modena Cemetery: Spine and Ossuary (author's photograph).

Naturally Rossi intended his Cemetery to demonstrate his concept of Type. As he says (1976), 'The cemetery, when considered in terms of building, is a house for the dead' (Fig. 8.26). So, initially, 'no distinction was made between the typology of the house and that of the tomb. The typology of the tomb and of the sepulchral structures overlaps the typology of the house; rectilinear corridors, a central space, earth and stone materials'.

Except that in the most house-like of all tomb-types, the Egyptian *mastaba*, there were no corridors, simply solid walls containing rooms quite unconnected by door or other openings. The dead had no need of such things; they could simply pass through solid material if they needed to!

But clearly Rossi's perimeter buildings are idealized, abstracted, geometricized versions of the (Italian) cemetery-type as represented by Costa's. For Rossi, however, the ossuary walls with their rows of niches represent a fundamental Type of storage thus inviting gloomy meditations as to what, in this case, actually is being stored! (Figs 8.27 and 8.28).

The buildings within his courtyard are a different matter. They are symmetrical about a central axis along which are strung, to the north a steep but truncated red Cone and to the south a large red Cube. Between them, symmetrical about the axis, is a series of 14 parallel, rather slender, buildings which start high and narrow at the Cone, stepping down to a triangular section towards the Cube whilst at the same time lengthening – either side of the axis – to a triangular plan.

As Rossi says: 'The longest element is therefore the lowest while the shortest element is the tallest . . . thus a shape analogous to the vertebrae of some osteological formation results'. The last of these narrow buildings extends much further east and west than the others, turning north at both ends to frame the triangle and, almost, the Cone in a wide, squared-off U-formation.

The fourteen parallel buildings form the galleries of a complex ossuary but instead of being double-loaded – as Costa's and Rossi's perimeter ossuaries are – these have vaults or niches only on one side so they open, north and south, towards each other across the spaces they enclose.

The number of storeys available in each naturally depends on its height within the triangular system or, as Rossi says: 'When the section

Fig. 8.28 Modena Cemetery: Interior of Ossuary (author's photograph).

allows, the same structure is repeated in the upper part of the building'.

The geometry of this ossuary, of course, leads to strange distortions in perspective. It is, Rossi says: 'an understood and assimilated labyrinth in which the creation of architectonic form is presented as a problem of distance and proportion'. This confusion of our senses in time and space suggests, so Rossi says, a timeless journey.

There is a bridge along the central axis giving access to the paved roofs of the lower ossuaries and access into a gallery within Rossi's Cone. The Cone is a Communal Grave; as he says, it is 'like a smoke stack' – an enlarged and widened version of his chimney at Fagano Olona! – intended 'for the remains of those who fell in the war'. If one enters at ground level then, as Rossi says:

> From the pavement of entry, a series of (concentric) steps
> descends toward the funerary stone which covers the communal
> grave . . . (where) . . . the remains of the abandoned dead are
> found; dead whose links with the temporal world have
> disappeared, generally people coming out of madhouses,
> hospitals and jails – desperate or forgotten lives. To these
> oppressed ones the city builds a monument higher than any
> other.

As for Rossi's Cube, this.is his Sanctuary and, quite specifically, his House for the Dead. As he says, it:

> . . . has the appearance of a house with no floors and no roof. The
> windows, which cut directly into the wall, have no frames or
> panes: this is the house of the dead and, in terms of architecture, it
> is unfinished and abandoned and therefore analogous to death
> . . . one of the four walls is solid. On the other three are windows
> of one-metre-by-one-metre which aligned with the gates at
> ground level. . . . The sanctuary is a collective monument where
> funeral, civil, or religious ceremonies take place . . . the sanctuary
> belongs to the whole community.

Inside it has bright metal balconies and staircases of the kind which Rossi proposed for his Student Housing at Trieste. Here they give access to burial niches.

The crucial point about the House for the Dead is suggested by Moneo (n.d.) (when he says: 'The house is inhabited by people (who) no longer need protection from the cold: it is occupied by the living (only) as they remember their dead.') Which makes it the quintessential neo-Rationalist building. The dead need no roof to protect them from the rain, no windows to keep in the heat, everything will be open, as Rossi puts it (1976) to: *The Blue of the Sky*.

For the dead no longer have senses; they do not feel the heat, the cold, or other physical stimuli. Which of course makes them perfect clients for an architect whose preoccupations are with pure, abstract, geometric perfection. Which of course is what renders Rationalism, at this extreme, quite unsuitable for the living.

The Krier Brothers 2

At the time of the Tendenza Exhibition the Krier brothers were both engaged in schemes for London (1973–74) in the projects for what

Robert calls Tower Bridge Housing (R. Krier, 1973) and Leon the Royal Mint Square (L. Krier, 1974).

Tower Bridge Housing is quite modest in scale but interesting, nevertheless, in the light of Krier's future work. It took a form he was to develop in Berlin of placing an urban square in the centre of a rectangular block and connecting it to the perimeter by streets running north, south, east and west. There is housing around the perimeter of the block just as for Leinfelden which seems to be almost a catalogue of Krier's elevational Types.

Leon Krier's scheme for Royal Mint Square (1974) is very different. The site is surrounded by perimeter housing, and he also has a central Square but this is placed diagonally, halfway along a diagonal street which runs from corner to corner of the site. Detailed drawings (in Rational: Architecture: Rationelle) show that this scheme too was to be Hi-Tech in construction with three-storey colonnades (cylindrical columns) fronting what looks like curtain-walling and supporting a projecting upper storey which also is clad in prefabricated panels.

Robert Krier

Urban space

Robert Krier's Leinfelden and his Tower Bridge housing both represent worked examples of a study which he had been undertaking into Urban Typology.

Fig. 8.29 Rob Krier (1975): Square urban spaces (from Krier, 1975).

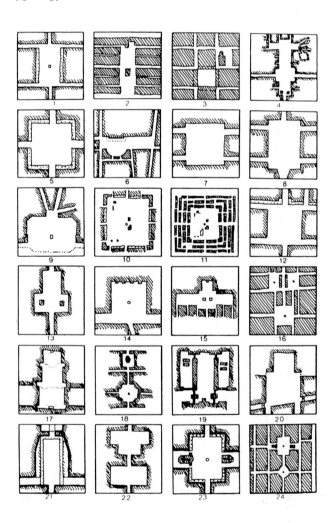

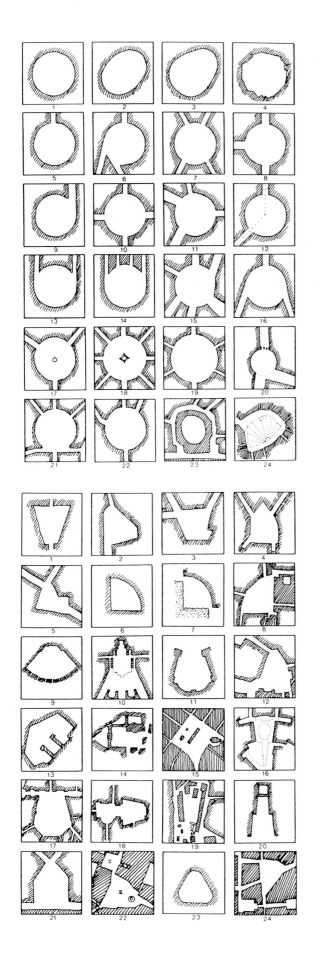

Fig. 8.30 Circular urban spaces (from Krier, 1975).

Fig. 8.31 Triangular urban spaces (from Krier, 1975).

191

His *Stadtsraum in Theorie und Praxis* (1975) was translated into English as *Urban Space* in 1979. It includes a massive analysis – some 350 examples in plan alone – of significant urban spaces in different cities of Europe.

Krier defines urban space as openly as he can as 'comprising all types of space between buildings in towns and their localities'. These range from the courtyard within an individual building by way of contained urban space, such as the Piazza Navonna in Rome, to the wide open spaces of, say, a Chandigarh where such containment as there is seems to be provided by the landscape – the mountains beyond – rather than by any group of buildings!

So it is hardly surprising that Krier's analysis is followed by a history – with particular reference to Le Corbusier – of how there has been an 'erosion of urban space in 20th century town planning'.

Fig. 8.32 Typologies of urban spaces (from Krier, 1975).

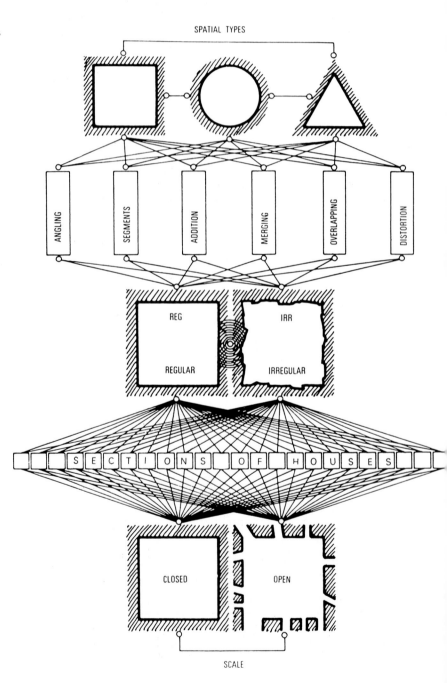

Krier suggests, with due modesty, that a pedantic reader might notice that some of his spatial Types may not be in their proper places within his morphological analysis. He attributes this to that fact that he 'did not have the patience necessary to reach this pinnacle of perfection' and nurses the silent hope that some dedicated expert will try to complete a perfect, definitive encyclopaedia of Urban Spaces. He describes this as a monstrous undertaking but his splendid analysis, as it stands, supplies more than enough material to draw our attention, at least, to the concept of 'urban space'.

Krier sees the city itself as formed essentially of urban spaces in the form of streets, squares and other open spaces. Or, rather, urban spaces in various forms, essentially square, circular or triangular. The urban tissue itself is formed of such elements either pure or in various combinations. In Krier's analysis he shows that the urban spaces of Europe generally fall, pure or compromised, into three main forms: square, circular or triangular (Figs 8.29–8.31). Each of these occurs on its own or compromised against others. Each may be twisted, divided, added to others, penetrated, overlapped or alienated (Fig. 8.32).

Each can be regular – a precise piece of geometry in itself – or irregular: compromised against the site or whatever. They can be closed, by walls, arcades or colonnades from the streets around them, or they can be open to their environment.

Of course the streets and squares of the city are lined by buildings; literally they are framed by façades. What is more the façades themselves can take many forms from solid, unrelieved masonry, to masonry with openings of various kinds: windows, doors, arcades, colonnades, to façades which are entirely glazed. What is more these facades have sections: from the absolutely vertical, with a pitched roof

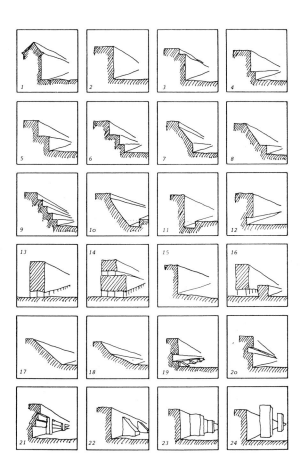

Fig. 8.33 Typologies of sections (from Krier, 1975).

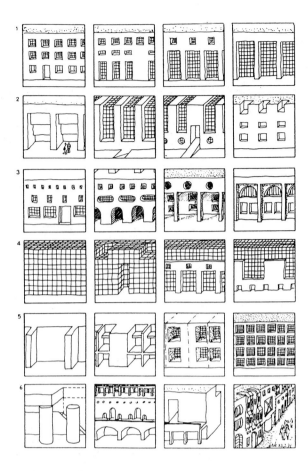

Fig. 8.34 Typologies of elevations
(from Krier, 1975).

or a flat roof, to the stepped section, with various gradations of
stepping, to diagonal sections, the sections on *pilotis*, the sections with
buttresses and so on (Figs 8.33 and 8.34).

This survey of Types seems quite exhaustive. Krier, in other words,
gets closer with his plans of urban spaces, his elevations and his
sections to the concept of Type than anyone else at *any* scale of design
from that, say, of the doorknob as a Type to that of the city as a whole.

The physical form of the city is determined by relationships between
the streets and the open spaces, the elevations and sections which
enclose them. Krier shows a vast range of possibilities, including the
great historical set pieces of Europe: the Forum at Pompeii, the Piazza
di San Marco, the Circus and the Crescent at Bath.

Krier demonstrates his Typologies in use with various applications
to Stuttgart, especially his own large project for Leinfelden (see p. 176).

Leon Krier

Luxembourg

By 1973 Leon Krier had started moving further in Rationalist directions
as he prepared an Appeal to the citizens of Luxembourg to rehabilitate
their city. He said (Architectural Design 1/1979):

> If shoemakers decided one day to make shoes in the shape of
> bananas, if cabinet makers started to make tables in the shape of a
> toboggan, if greengrocers one day sold you pebbles . . . (for) . . .
> apples, I think there would be a revolution.. . . . However for
> twenty years now . . . architects have been selling you houses and

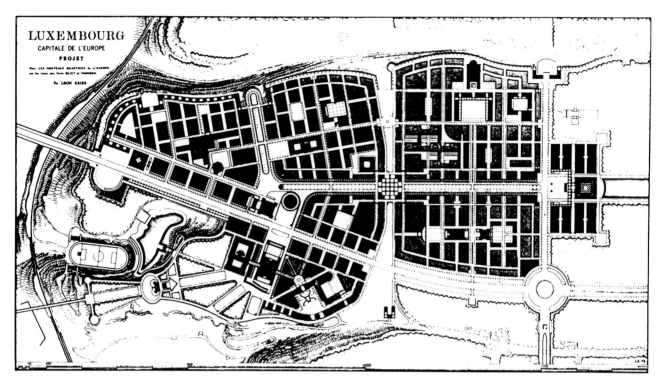

Fig. 8.35 Leon Krier (1973–78) Luxembourg, capital of Europe: proposed new Quartiers (from *Architectural Design*, **49** (1), 1979).

palaces in the shape of aquariums, aeroplanes and tin cans while trying to convince you that what you thought to be the issues of architecture, the city, a house, a palace, streets and squares; have finally been resolved – but that resolution was beyond the comprehension of non-specialists.

But after the 'crimes committed against the cities and landscapes of Europe over the past twenty years' it was time to take stock, to realize that the city and its public places: 'can only be built in the form of

Fig. 8.36 Luxembourg: Krier's new Parliament Building with, to the left, the existing Administration Tower to which Krier has added a pediment (from *Architectural Design*, **49** (1), 1979).

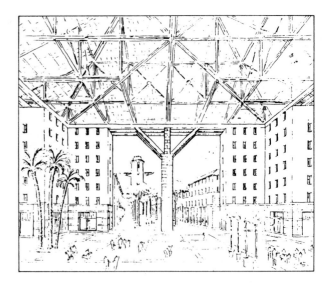

Fig. 8.37 Luxembourg: the first of Krier's covered squares (from *Architectural Design*, **49** (1) 1979).

Fig. 8.38 Leon Krier (1976) Urban Quartiers for La Villette in North East Paris. Perspective of the whole area (from *Architecture d'Aujourd'hui*, No. 187, 1976; *Lotus International*, **13**, 1976; *Archives d'Architecture Moderne*, No. 9, 1976; *Architectural Design*, **47**, 3, 1977; *A + U*, No. 11, 1977; *Architectural Design* (7/8), 1976; Delevoy *et al.*, 1978).

streets, squares and quartiers of familiar dimensions and character', based on local and European traditions.

The most destructive force, he argued, had been the zoning of cities into areas of different functions: sleeping, working, consumption. The only way to restore the social, economic and cultural health of the city would be to revive the Quartier – an area up to 33 hectares within which there would be *all* urban functions (Fig. 8.35). It is, he says the size of a pre-industrial urban community 'based on the human figure. It is a size of territory which a man can cross in less than ten minutes'. Such an area could house, comfortably, some '10 000 to 15 000 people, including work and culture'. The crucial point was that each would be

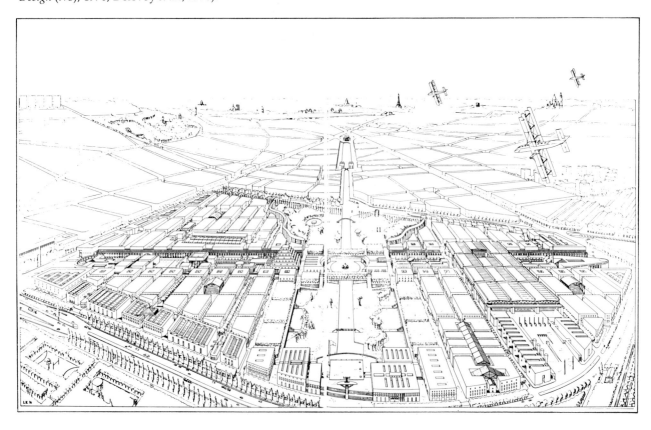

autonomous on the functional as well as the cultural level. So he divides Luxembourg into 23 such Quartiers.

He was ready now to abandon Hi-Tech, on the grounds that the industrialization of construction: 'has not brought forward any serious technical improvements, has not reduced the cost of construction, has not shortened the time of construction'. Nor has it improved the condition of the workers, on the contrary it has destroyed 'an ancient and accomplished artisan culture'. So, he suggests: 'A new architectural culture must, necessarily, be based on a highly developed and professional manual and material culture'.

Krier, in other words was moving towards 'small is beautiful' ideas of self-sustaining communities; Quartiers to be formed by adding, where necessary, new streets and squares and also by forming urban

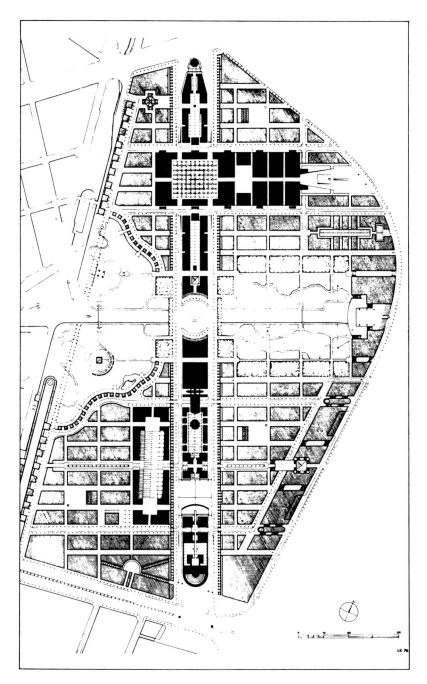

Fig. 8.39 La Villette: Plan (from *Architectural Design*, **3**, 1977; Delevoy *et al.*, 1978).

Monuments either by monumentalizing existing buildings or building new ones. His most dramatic transformation, for instance, concerned the Administration Tower of the European Parliament: curtain-walled and cigar-shaped on plan. Krier proposed stone cladding with individual windows and a pedimented top – an interesting precursor of Philip Johnson's AT & T (Fig. 8.36).

There was to be an Asplund-like new Parliament Building; a cylinder over a square base, a cylindrical, domed Library, as ziggurat-like Grand Hotel and – the first of many of Krier's designs – a Covered Square of which he says: 'The most spectacular element . . . will be a vast wooden roof (65 m × 65 m) which – at a height of 30 m – will protect the terraces of the social centre'. The roof was to be supported, literally, by L-shaped buildings wrapping around the four corners of the square and large stone piers between them as intermediate supports (Fig. 8.37). Krier's drawings confirm his growing interest in the building crafts with a truly pragmatic attention to the bonding of his stonework, the jointing of his timbers and so on.

La Villette

Many of the ideas which Krier developed for Luxembourg recur in his large scheme for *La Villette* in Paris (L. Krier, 1976) which again he plans as two Quartiers. At first glance his site Plan, with a south-west/north-east axis, some 2500 metres long, with two cross-axes each of 1000 metres or so seems like *une folie de grandeur*, the very pinnacle of Rationalist megalomania (Fig. 8.38).

But Krier's long axis is the Canal Ourcq, his tilted cross-axis the smaller Canal St Denis. They meet at the Bassin de la Villette. Krier's own axis, at right angles to the Ourcq, links his two Quartiers (Fig. 8.39). Much of the northern one was taken up already by the frame of a vast new Abattoir under construction to replace Les Halles whilst the southern one contains a large, cast iron Cattle Market by Baltard.

Krier's Quartiers of course are intended to form a new city within the City of Paris, where: 'industry, leisure, living, all urban activities are gathered in an area of adequate size where the car as a means of transport is no more a necessity but at best a luxury'.

He planned a hierarchy of streets including his Grand North/South Boulevard, avenues, streets and passages according to the public or private nature of the access they afforded. The Boulevard has, at its northern end a Hotel, and a Street Market. It then passes through the Abattoir construction, converted into a Conference Centre, and Exhibition Halls, opening, as it passes through, into a Covered Square south of which is another Street Market, Public Baths, a Casino, another Hotel, an Enclosed Market, and, at the southern end, a Mairie and a Cultural Centre (Fig. 8.40).

Either side of the Boulevard are north/south strips of department stores, offices, schools, more offices, hotels and department stores. The old Cattle Market, somewhat reduced in size, is given over to craftsmen, and elsewhere, in the eastern perimeter road are offices, shops, a hospital, museums, and industry.

Almost the whole of Krier's Boulevard is lined with two-storey colonnades of Martin/Rossi-like septa and many of the buildings beyond are Gallaratese-like in the purity of their forms (Fig. 8.41). In most of them, of course, he would have tried to crystallize a Type, *the* Grand Hotel, *the* Cultural Centre, *the* Mairie and so on. His Grand Hotel, for instance, would be planned as a ziggurat around a large open atrium – somewhat in the manner of John Portman!

DISTRIBUTION OF FUNCTIONS

A	Local centre (club, foyer)
B	Town hall
C	Library
D	Museum
E	Conference centre and exhibitions
F	Hotels
G	Public bath
H	Casino
I	Department stores
J	Bazar
K	Commerce
L	Craftsmen
M	Industry
N	Offices
O	Schools
P	Crèche
Q	Maison du Peuple
R	Hospital

Fig. 8.40 La Villette urban functions along the main axis (from *Architectural Design*, **3**, 1977).

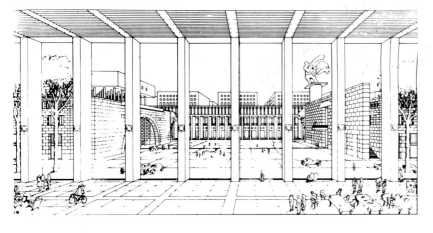

Fig. 8.41 La Villette: the Main Square (from *Architectural Design*, **3**, 1977; Delevoy *et al.*, 1978).

Halfway down the Boulevard Krier planned a Central Square open east and west to public gardens. The Garden to the east is fairly formal whilst that to the west, open to Canal St Denis, has freer-form edge, towards the Boulevard.

From which it is screened by towers or, rather, buildings-as-columns. They form, indeed, a linear version of Krier's Covered Square in that they support a continuous roof which takes the sinuous form of the screen itself. Like the Covered Square's, this roof has exposed roof trusses whilst the columns themselves contain artists' studios, with two floors of living space below. The studios have hoists so that a sculptor, for instance, could haul up a block of stone, work on it, then lower it to the paving between his column and the next, leaving it there for sale, protected by the continuous roof! Indeed Krier sees the whole screen as rather like the Loggia di Lanzi in Florence, cluttered with sculpture (Fig. 8.42).

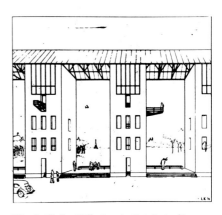

Fig. 8.42 La Villette: Artists' studios – the building as column (from *Architectural Design*, **3**, 1977; Delevoy *et al.*, 1978).

St Quentin en Yvellines

Krier's School for St Quentin en Yvellines (1977–79) represents a departure from his previous schemes in that even though it has a central axis, a series of linked places with two gate-houses, a library, an

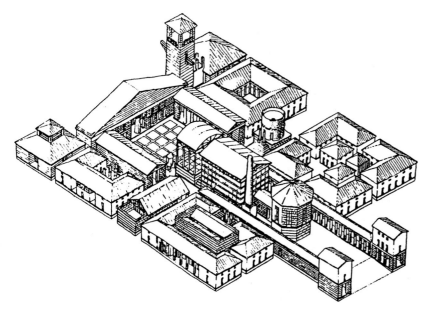

Fig. 8.43 Leon Krier: (1977–79) School for St Quentin en Yvellines, perspective (from *AMM*, **19**, 1980).

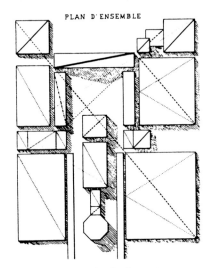

PLAN D'ENSEMBLE

Fig. 8.44 School for St Quentin en Yvellines: Plan (from *AMM*, **19**, 1980).

Fig. 8.45 School for St Quentin en Yvellines, details (from *AMM*, **19**, 1980).

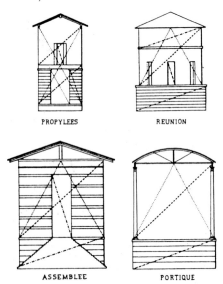

PROPYLEES   REUNION

ASSEMBLEE   PORTIQUE

assembly hall, a portico, a public square and two restaurants, these are all disposed symmetrically about it, the rest of the accommodation, containing a nursery school, a primary school, buildings for leisure activities, with their ancillary spaces, is arranged more informally around private open spaces (Figs 8.43 and 8.44). As Krier says, it is designed like a town with a series of elements which could be arranged in many ways. Most of his variations have some kind of axial grouping of library – an octagonal tower – assembly hall, a classical temple, and the restaurants; two slender buildings disposed across the axis rather like the arms of a 'T' but joined by a huge pediment connecting them across the axis and acting as a firm termination to it (Fig. 8.45). This huge-pediment idea, of course, spanning the long axis of the building, has antecedents in the Walow House by McKim, Mead and White (1887); in the Vanna Venturi House which Robert Venturis built for his mother in Philadelphia (1961) and a notable successor in the Mississauga City Hall by Jones and Kirkland (1987).

Krier's other buildings at St Quentin are more or less Classical in form; some of them are linked by open colonnades. There are many permutations from small, square buildings with (low) pyramidal roofs, a U-shape, a C-shape or even a series of L-shapes enclosing courtyards, with pitched roofs following their forms.

In one variation, for an imaginary site, Krier has one side of the school peeling away from the central axis in a gentle curve so the various (square) formations of buildings, rather than being parallel, begin to touch each other at rather acute angles thus introducing a greater informality than merely having mismatches across his axis.

Rational: Architecture: Rationelle

The collection of essays – and images – entitled *Rational: Architecture: Rationelle* was published in 1978 and intended, as Delevoy says in his Introduction, to put forward a *theory* of architecture (*AAM*, 1978). The lack of such a theory, so he says, had been cruelly felt since the 1930s. A new form of *practice* also was needed to fill the gap created by such city planning as Brazilia (1960).

Delevoy's theory, of course, will be based on the idea of Type and he cites a whole range of Italian, British and American authors who had resorted to the idea suggesting, of course, that one should go back to Quatremère's original definition (see Chapter 5). Delevoy also appeals to the first principles laid down by Laugier as to the nature of architecture itself, based on the Primitive Hut and of the Park as designed by Le Nôtre; the model for how cities should be planned.

But whilst Rossi, the Kriers and many others *had* gone back to Quatremère for their notions of building Type Antony Vidler, in this

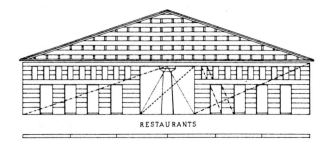

RESTAURANTS

collection, takes rather a different approach. He looks for Types which permeate the whole of architecture, rather than certain building Types, suggesting that since the middle of the 18th century, two Typologies have: 'served to legitimise the production of architecture'.

The first of these is Laugier's: 'The small rustic hut (as) the model upon which all the wonders of architecture have been conceived'. Strange that Vidler should write of model rather than type when Quatremère, Rossi and the others had been so careful with their distinctions! But the point, for Vidler, of this Model is that Nature herself presented a fundamental kind of order based on the primitive rusticity of the hut. But she presented also another kind of order; the ideal of perfect geometry which, according to Newton, was the guiding principle in physics.

Vidler's second Typology came, not from Nature but from the Industrial Revolution. Which meant that architecture was assimilated into the world of machine production. The basic metaphor in this case – not, apparently Type or Model – was not the Primitive Hut but the Engine.

The building was seen as a machine and, in its most extreme form, as a machine from processing unruly human users. The Prison, the Hospital and the Poor House, apparently, were paradigmatic examples of this kind even though they had all been established long before the Industrial Revolution!

Vidler suggests that this Second Typology developed in several phases. Towards the end of the 19th century, for instance, buildings were being made from prefabricated components, as products of factory production, and their industrial origins were displayed by the building itself. Then early in the 20th century Le Corbusier urged that the house become a machine for living. As cities grew, they became larger-scale and more efficient machines, more efficient because Taylor's methods of Work Study (see Chapter 8) were used in their design. The city as machine *forced* people to live more hygienic and productive lives!

For Vidler, however, this Second Typology contained within itself the seeds of its own destruction. Which is why, he says, the Third Typology of Rationalism was needed.

Vidler's first two Typologies of course were drawn into architecture from Models or Metaphors outside it – from Nature and the Industrial Revolution. But his Third Typology is drawn out of architecture itself. What is more it is drawn at every scale, from that of an individual column, to a house or even a city as a whole. It sees the city *whole* in all its historic continuity and the actual Types are derived from analyses of the city, manifest in its physical structure, the urban facts, including buildings and the spaces between them, as they have survived from the past. Thus it draws on three levels of meaning which Vidler identifies as follows:

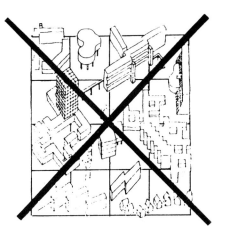

Fig. 8.46 Leo Krier (1978): Crossing out buildings which do not make urban spaces (from Delevoy *et al.*, 1978).

1. The first, he says, is 'inherited from the ascribed means of the past existence of the forms'; perhaps he means the meanings which have been ascribed to them in the past;
2. The second is derived 'from the specific fragment and its boundaries'; presumably the example we are analysing quite separated from anything else;
3. And the third is 'proposed by a recomposition of these fragments in a new context'. One juxtaposes the fragments in new relationships.

Vidler sees this Third Typology as denying all the 'social Utopian and progressively positivist' concepts against which architecture has been understood and developed over the last 200 years, on the grounds that all considerations of function, and even of social mores are quite eliminated.

But if one looks at Types in the Quatremèrian sense then surely they contain within themselves indications of social norms? The Types obviously have developed around patterns of human use and in potentials for using them, in the old but also in quite new ways embedded within them? Take the case of 'house' for instance. If one makes a Rossian survey of the House as a Type going back into history, and even into pre-history, one will find, as Ashcraft and Scheflin did (1976), that the same room sizes can be found in Babylonian, Egyptian, Greek, Roman, medieval and other housing up to, but not including, the late 19th century. That size, they say, was the medieval rood but worker-housing in the 19th century naturally was built to lesser standards and so, most certainly, was the *Existenzminimum* housing which Aymonimo recorded so assiduously!

The crucial point, of course, is that such simple things as room sizes have profound effects on the social, and other lives, which people can live in them. There is no way in which 'all considerations of function, of social mores' *could* be eliminated!

Which in no way denies the power of Typology if it is considered in a full historical perspective. Aymonimo's analysis of housing was impossibly limited in scope. He took one of the meanest modes ever of house design, the *Existenzminimum* of the 1920s and tried to extract housing types from that. But if he had gone back to Babylon – as Ashcraft and Scheflin did (1976) – then he might well have established the essence of House-as-Type with all that this implies for social and psychological relationships, embedded in the work of many centuries, which might well contain, in their *architectural* forms, certain truths about the human condition, and indeed about the living *human* Type.

Such a concept of Type clearly applies to all building forms: churches, schools, theatres or whatever. So concentrating, as he does, on Types the Rationalist, however unwittingly, *is* facing up to three basic problems of the human condition *and* its relationships to architecture.

So whatever their intentions Rationalists cannot deal with the city in terms which Vidler suggests, of: 'the city itself, emptied of specific social content from any particular time and allowed to speak only of its own formal conditions'. And why would he want to, anyway?

Of course such a Rationalist attack is directed against a 'one to one reading of (form and) function' and especially against the Positivist idea that any one-to-one analysis of function will lead to a perfect fit of form *to* function. One agrees that this is rarely so, at least in architecture, and one agrees also – with Rossi – that forms available from the past do not come 'deprived of their original and practical social meaning'. The meanings they carry already may provide keys to their newly invented meanings. But the forms which the Rationalists want to use based, as they are, on 18th century Enlightenment originals *do* carry with them connotations. Boullée's Library was designed for a King before it became the Library for a Great Nation, Ledoux's pure form Toll Gates were made for the extraction of taxes, which incited the French Revolution, and so on.

Rodrigo Pérez d'Arce

The 'insertions', and 'organisms' which Alan Colquhoun described of course were meant to be placed into the city replacing, probably, buildings which were there already. But neo-Rationalism could be applied also to filling in the empty spaces between the self-contained blocks, the individual pavilions, of the Modern Movement.

Of these one of the more ingenious applications was presented by Rodrigo Pérez d'Arce. Like Leon Krier and other neo-Rationalists he was worried by the way in which the Corbusean vision had destroyed any sense of being in the city of streets and squares, by the vast emptinesses of such Corbusean cities as Brazilia and Chandigarh, not to mention Louis Kahn's Dacca. He had taken these worries to their logical conclusions by designing re-urbanizations of the latter two.

These were parts of a larger project in which he was concerned with *Urban Transformations*. He suggested (Pérez d'Arce, 1978a) that the ways in which towns may be expanded, renovated and updated generally fall into three basic types:

1. Urban growth by extension – characterized by the urbanization of new areas which are incorporated into the town.
2. Growth by substitution – which occurs whenever new urban elements replace the pre-existing ones, (involving) demolition and reconstruction.
3. Growth by additive transformation – in which an original nucleus is transformed by the sedimentary and incremental process of (adding) new parts.

He sees this as largely neglected and shows it worked historically: in the case of various Roman buildings: Temples, Triumphal Arches, Amphitheatres; in various historic settings such as Diocletian's Palace at Spalato and the Incan Cuzco, in Santa Maria Maggiore, in Sitte's proposals for Vienna.

He analyses Leon Krier's proposals for Amiens, Echternach and La Villette; Stirling's for Dusseldorf and Berlin; the transformation of housing estates before presenting his own proposals for Le Corbusier's Government Sector in Chandigarh and Louis Kahn's for Dacca.

In the case of Chandigarh he suggests that major elements: the National Assembly, the High Court and the Secretariat stand in isolation from each other or, at most, form a very loose grouping.

Taking his cue from Nolli's Plan of Rome, then, he points out that if the general urban texture were removed, leaving only the monuments, there would be no possibility of urban order. So, he suggests, 'If the

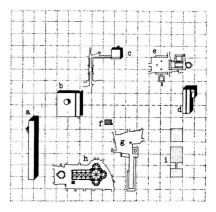

Fig. 8.47 Pérez d'Arce: Le Corbusier's Capital Group at Chandigarh compared with other large urban spaces in Florence (from *Lotus*, **19**, 1978; *Architectural Design*, **49**, 1978).

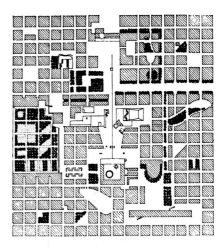

Fig. 8.48 Pérez d'Arce: Le Corbusier's Capital Group at Chandigarh urbanized (from *Lotus*, **19**, 1978; *Architectural Design*, **49**, 1978).

Fig. 8.49 Pérez d'Arce: Le Corbusier's Secretariat along one of his new avenues (from *Lotus*, **19**, 1978; *Architectural Design*, **49**, 1978).

Fig. 8.50 Bofill and the Taller de Arquitectura (1973): La Muralla Roja, Calpe (author's photograph).

monumental centre of Chandigarh were re-urbanized in much the same way as (during its history) Diocletian's Palace (had been) but basing this action on a plan of re-urbanization developed in relation to Le Corbusier's layout, a surprisingly effective result could be achieved.' (Figs 8.47–8.49).

Pérez d'Arce plans his new streets on a 50 metre grid relating appropriate urban spaces to Le Corbusier's monumental buildings including a Grand Boulevard running towards the Secretariat.

As he says (Pérez d'Arce, 1978b): 'Monuments and fabric are inter-dependent elements in . . . urban composition. . . . In reversing the process of analytical decomposition we have elaborated a system which could . . . be applied (not only) to Chandigarh and Dacca. . . .' He sees it as a model for re-urbanizing the empty spaces in so many cities which resulted from applying the principles of the Athens Charter.

Fig. 8.51 Bofill and the Taller (1974–75): project for Les Halles in Paris (from *Architectural Design*, 9/10, 1980).

Bofill

Whilst Rossi, Rob Krier and others have built individual Rationalist buildings they have had few opportunities to develop large-scale 'organisms' of the kind which Leo Krier, for instance, designed for La Villette. Rationalist thinking at urban scale has been applied, rather, by Ricardo Bofill and the Taller de Arquitectura of Barcelona in a series of large-scale projects, most of them in France.

Initially the Taller worked with complex geometric system, as in the Barrio Gaudi at Reus (1953) the Murulla Roja (1969) at Calpe (1973b) (Fig. 8.50) and Walden (1975) at San Justo d'Esvern an industrial suburb of Barcelona (Broadbent 1975a and b). Whilst the forms were intended for prefabrication the nature of the Construction Industry in Spain – as in most other countries – meant that this would have been hopelessly uneconomic.

That was not so in France, however, where Coignet and others had developed, and continued to use, prefabricated systems, based on room-height concrete panels which, however bleak architecturally, worked well, under French conditions, in economic terms.

Even so the Taller's first attempts to break into the French market were abortive with such projects as La Petite Cathédrale for Cergy

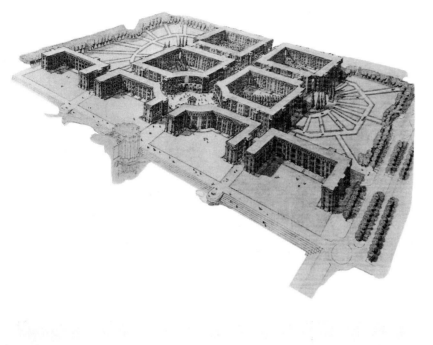

Fig. 8.52 Bofill and the Taller (1972–75): Les Arcades du Lac, St Quentin en Yvellines (courtesy Taller de Arquitectura).

Fig. 8.53 Les Arcades du Lac (1974): main axis (author's photograph).

Fig. 8.54 Les Arcades du Lac (1974): Le Viaduc (author's photograph).

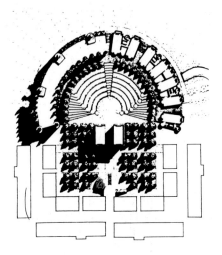

Fig. 8.55 Marne la Vallée: plan of Le Palais d'Abraxas (1979–83), Le Théâtre and L'Arc (1979–83) (from Norberg-Schultz, 1985, in Bofill, 1985).

Fig. 8.56 Le Palais d'Abraxas (author's photograph).

Pontoise – a vast Gothic Mall of shops, offices, apartments and so on (1971) – and a series of Baroque urban spaces, most of them surrounded by apartments, for the site of Les Halles in Paris (1974–78). Work had actually started on the fourth of these schemes (Fig. 8.51) when Jacques Chirac ordered its destruction to symbolize his power as the Mayor of Paris. But French prefabrication and Bofill's architecture finally came together in a series of projects which were built such as Les Arcades du Lac and Le Viaduc at St Quentin d'Yvellines, west of Paris (Fig. 8.52).

Les Arcades has a central axis with four-storey courtyards of housing either side and a Bath-like Circus contained by the last of these (Fig. 8.53) whilst Le Viaduc actually projects into the (artificial) lake in the manner of Chenonceaux (Fig. 8.54).

All this is constructed in the Dreux system which the Taller have humanized by their use of arcades lining the main axis, hints of classical pediments at strategic points in the parapets, the articulation of the façades in general by relief modelling, by contrasts of colour and texture in the surface-finishing of the panels.

I have argued elsewhere (1981a) that the general flavour is Romanesque rather than Classical, which is hardly surprising, given the Taller's concern for their Catalan heritage.

A further scheme for St Quentin has been built in the form of a Palladian Villa of apartments on the same axis as Les Arcades and Le Viaduc but at the far side of the artificial lake.

Les Arcades have much to be said in their favour. The four-storey courtyards reflect the urbanity of the London Squares, Cambridge Courts, Oxford Quads and so on. Indeed as Martin and March demonstrated (1972) four-storey courts are the most efficient way of covering the ground in terms of sun-penetration to each room. It also has social advantages in terms of easy access, clear distinctions between public space – in the streets and the circus, semi-private spaces within the courtyards and fully private spaces within the blocks themselves. What is more the whole of Les Arcades du Lac is built on a platform with parking spaces underneath which means that one fundamental problem has been solved: how to accommodate cars close to where people live without at the same time cluttering, or even destroying, the scale of the urban spaces.

But Les Arcades also has defects; some of them intrinsic to the Taller's approach. It is, very much, an urban scheme yet it is located in the suburbs of a New Town, some two kilometres even from the centre of that. There are no shops, no bars, no restaurants, none of the services which make for urban living apart from a school, not unfortunately by Leon Krier, on an adjacent site. Such things no doubt were developers' decisions but the Taller themselves are – to some extent – culpable over the internal planning.

Of course there have always been problems when planning – at the small-scale of individual rooms – has to be crucified against the components of large-panel concrete systems. To put it crudely, the units of the system are too big, by their nature, to allow the minute adjustments – to within a centimetre or so – which are needed in domestic planning.

When the essential awkwardnesses of the system itself are compounded by the geometry of a layout – as, for instance in the Circus of Les Arcades – it is hardly surprising that some of the apartments leave a great deal to be desired in terms of convenient internal planning.

The very strict division also between public space and private space, however desirable in Oscar Newman's terms, coupled with the fact that people can go directly from the underground parking up to their own apartments means that hardly anyone – except visitors – uses the public streets which thus take on a rather sinister, empty, di Chirico-like quality. Which of course could be relieved if some public services were provided, possibly in the Circus; such as corner shops, bars and so on.

Whatever its faults, Les Arcades was a worthwhile experiment and that can be said also of the Taller's larger scale developments at Marne la Vallée, a New Town to the east of Paris: Les Espaces d'Abraxas (1979). Here three buildings are grouped along a central axis but the scale is huge, the two outer ones being up to eighteen storeys high. They are Le Palais d'Abraxas and Le Théâtre with the 10 storey Arc (de Triomphe) between them (Figs 8.55–8.57). Le Palacio is built around a U-shaped courtyard some 40 bays wide with 14 bay wings. The planning is double-loaded but there are no hidden corridors inside, rather two concentric U-shaped blocks containing vast, full height spaces, crossed by bridges and staircases, thoroughly Piranesian in scale.

Elevationally Le Palacio is divided – Sullivan-like – into base, middle and top with, internally at least, a five-storey plinth, twelve-storey shafts and a three-storey entablature. The shafts in this case are provided with vast, precast, eleven-storey, fluted Classical columns with rudimentary bases and capitals (Fig. 8.56).

The ends of the wings are more complex in that they have flat pilasters in place of columns, surmounted by full-blooded entablatures and pediments, the whole being capped – as at Les Arcades – by pediment-like forms made by openings and mouldings in the parapet.

Fig. 8.57 Le Théâtre (author's photograph).

This is not Classical construction. It is, rather, the collage-like use of Classical devices to articulate what is, basically, flat-panel, precast concrete slab construction.

Which of course serves two distinct purposes. It gives what otherwise would be bleak, not to say hostile elevations, scale, intricacy and interest. It means that the joints between the panels can be incorporated into a system of architectural, as distinct from merely a structural articulation. And, since the joints are hidden – for architectural effect – they are also protected from the weather. Which means that as the buildings wear, the pattern of weathering itself will be controlled by the architectural forms. Thus they will be enhanced, thrown into relief rather than degraded by the streaking and staining which renders so much concrete construction drab and dismal.

Le Théâtre is even more dramatic (Fig. 8.57). Externally the articulation is a further variation of that used on the inner and outer façades of Le Palacio. But the internal curve is a different matter. Here there are ground-to-entablature columns but these are made of glass rather than precast concrete. They are surmounted by a vast double-entablature.

The columns provide bay-windows for each apartment which leads to certain awkwardnesses of the internal planning.

Le Théâtre – which is rather more than half a circle – encloses a system of concentric terraces stepping down towards L'Arc which is exactly what it says: a Triumphal Arch, quite Classical in form, containing apartments within its piers and over the arch.

Since Les Espaces d'Abraxas are close to the centre of Marne, are separated from the Métro only by a large shopping centre with multi-storey car park, they display more sense of urban life although it may extend in various cases to that kind of urban life which Alice Coleman found so unacceptable!

Clearly the Taller learned from these projects when they were designing Antigone in Montpellier (1979–83) (Fig. 8.58). This is the

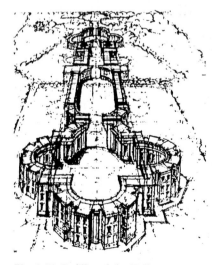

Fig. 8.58 Bofill and the Taller (1978–83): Antigone, Montpellier, perspective (from Norberg-Schultz 1985).

Fig. 8.59 Antigone (author's photograph).

largest of the Taller's Classical projects; smaller in scale than Les Espaces d'Abraxas but much more complex than Les Arcades. Again there is a central axis along which are placed a series of rather Baroque spaces; a Square with large hemicycles on each side, La Place d'Occitanie, an elongated Place which also terminates in hemicycles, a narrow space with semicircular places symmetrically either side of it and a triangular Place of three interlinked hemicycles. Behind the latter part of this progression are Arcade-like arrangements of courtyards.

Fig. 8.60 Bofill and the Taller (1979): Les Echelles du Baroque Paris, XIV Arrondissement (from Norberg-Schultz, 1985).

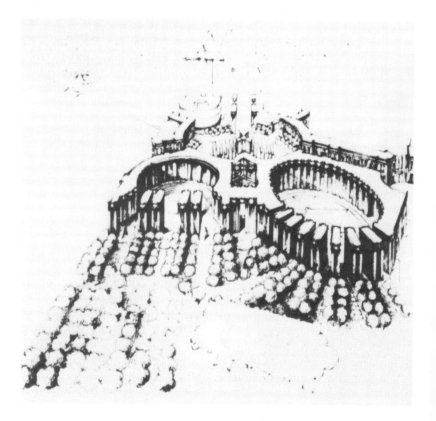

The detailing is more Classical, at least on the outer façades, with fully pedimented windows and a massive cornice which projects some 45 degrees over the two upper storeys affording them substantial shading from the sun (Fig. 8.59).

Antigone is near the centre of Montpellier and thus is truly urban. Indeed it was planned as a complete town centre with schools, health, cultural and social facilities. There is a social mix of housing types; it also contains shops and other services of a kind which should preclude the de Chirico-like emptiness of Les Arcades.

That is true also of Les Echelles du Baroque (1979–83) a smaller but equally urban – and equally Baroque – scheme for Montparnasse in the heart of Paris (1979) (Figs 8.60, 8.61(a) and (b)) and L'Amphithéâtre Vert at Cergy-Pontoise (1981–).

Les Echelles are planned around three urban spaces, one large and circular with housing around about half of it, one elliptical and almost contained by housing, and a D-shaped amphitheatre. Again there are permutations in the treatment of the elevations (Fig. 8.61(a) and (b)).

(a)

Fig. 8.61 Les Echelles du Baroque (author's photographs).

(b)

Some have precast columns which, rising as they do to four storeys, are a good deal smaller than those at Marne; others have pedimented windows between quite plain concrete panels; others again have pilasters and precast concrete balconies to the windows; others yet again have further permutations of these.

L'Ampithéâtre Vert is smaller still in scale, rising to a maximum of three storeys. It consists of two linked squares, each surrounded completely by housing, and a large hemicycle the diameter of which is equivalent to the squares and their link together.

As we shall see, the Classicism which Bofill began to embrace in the late 1970s was to be taken up with even greater enthusiasm, not to say accuracy, not only by the neo-Rationalists, but by the neo-Empiricists too.

9

Neo-Empiricists

Reventós, Folguera, Nogues and Utrillo

Pueblo Español

The possibilities for making a serious architecture on Empirical – Picturesque – lines were demonstrated by several of Sitte's disciples and, in particular, by the Barcelona architects Ramón Reventós and Fransesc Folguera working – and this is important – with the painters Xavier Nogues and Miguel Utrillo. Collectively they designed the Pueblo Español – a Spanish Village – for the Barcelona Exposition of 1929. Although they may be unaware, the Pueblo is, for most architects and planners, one of the most familiar images in the whole of 20th century architecture for it appears, top right, in the best-known photograph of the Pavilion which Mies van der Rohe designed for the same Exposition (Fig. 9.1). In the photograph one sees a Romanesque tower and a battlemented wall silhouetted against the sky. But behind the wall, there is a whole Pueblo with, running from east to west, a Plaza Mayor, a Plaza Aragonesa, a Plaza de la Fuente and a Romanesque Monastery of which the visible Tower is but one part.

The plazas are connected by a maze of streets (*calles*) with steps, arches, arcades and turnings-round-the-corner which, collectively, provide the kinds of urban surprise which Sitte, Gaudet and others found so enchanting (Fig. 9.2). The urban spaces themselves are formed between, as it were, built collages, assemblages of photographically exact – rather lavish – vernacular detail measured from originals in various parts of Spain. These details are assembled, in

Fig. 9.1 Barcelona Exposition 1929: Mies van der Rohe's German Pavilion with the Pueblo Español in the background (from Johnson 1947).

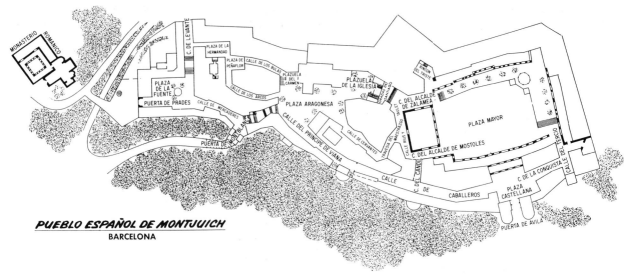

Fig. 9.2 Nogues, Reventós and Folguera (1939): plan of the Pueblo Español (from Voltes, 1971).

more or less formal compositions to make houses, shops, palaces, churches and other buildings.

One enters the Pueblo southwards through a Gateway reproduced from San Vincente de Avilla which opens directly on to a small Castillian Court. Streets open out to east and west and most of the Pueblo lies westwards. Ahead there is an Arcade reproduced, with arches at twice their original scale, from Sangüesa, Navarra opening directly on to the Plaza Mayor. This Plaza is an assemblage of elements from Valderrobres (the Consistery), Aragon, Guadalajara, Burgos, Soria, Huesca and so on. Elements from different provinces may be combined to form a single house; thus Number Two has Gothic Arches from the Monastery of Casbas surmounted by balconies from a house in Guadalajara.

The Plaza Aragonese lies westwards, along the Calle de Cervantes, and it forms a complete ensemble such as one might find in Aragon. This Plaza itself is dominated by a Church which has, as it were, an inbuilt history ranging from Mudéjar – the translation of Islamic forms by Christian craftsmen – to Catalan Gothic and even Baroque not to mention a sundial of 1777!

West of the Plaza between the Calle de las Bulas and the Calle de los Arcos there is a typical Andalucian section with the labyrinthine planning of Islamic Spain. And furthest of all to the west – actually outside the walls – the Monastery is an assemblage of details from Catalan Romanesque originals, such as Sant Sebastià de Montmajor (Barcelona), Santa Maria de Porqueres (Gerona), a belfry from Taradell (Barcelona), internal, and external, apses from Montmajor, wall paintings and cloisters from San Benet del Barges (Barcelona).

Throughout the Pueblo such reproductions extend to the streets and their furniture: fountains, well-heads, balconies, steps, handrails, street lamps and so on (Fig. 9.3). Each is traced to its origin in some specific model – or a collage of models from different parts of Spain in the admirable guides by Voltes (1971) and Castell (1985).

So what makes it all hang together? Carreras Candi was quite clear in 1929 when he wrote of the visitors:

They will see that everything that the centuries has been consecrating, within a natural development of . . . universal urban innovations, has been adapted to our customs, climate and soil, and has acquired that environment of naturalness and idiosyncrasy, peculiar to the feeling of each and every Spanish region.

How is that?

> It is because, thank God, nothing has been invented in the Spanish Village. Everything that has been erected here still lives somewhere in our Peninsula in the place where it was copied and from where it has been transported to the Barcelona Exhibition, in exact reproduction, having first taken the necessary patterns.

Where there were discords in the originals – Gothic arches built next to rounded ones – these too might be reproduced exactly as they were or they might be edited out. Inconsistencies of that kind occurred at Valderrobres in the model for the Consistery. But in this copy on the Plaza Mayor the ground floor was built entirely of rounded arches and the upper floors of Gothic ones!
As Carreras Candi put it:

> . . . exact reproduction is a more painstaking task than (letting) the imagination fly away with artistic ideal(s). . . . The whole which is attained by conscientious and well-executed reproduction, as in (this) case is the very reality itself.

Another commentator at the time, Bassegoda (1929), pointed out, much as Gaudet might have done:

> The streets and inclines are (still) those which we behold in all of our old Spanish towns. (Traditionally) they got over these difficulties with little study and (still) less work, giving them . . . tortuous form(s), presenting more or less troublesome (gradients) and when these (became) excessive they constructed stairs.

Painters and photographers, naturally, were attracted to such cities with such Picturesque streets and similar effects 'are being offered . . . to us at every turn in the Spanish Village'.
What is more they still are. For whilst Mies's Pavilion was dismantled at the end of the Exposition – and resurrected, by careful reproduction in 1985–86 – the Pueblo retained its original forms – and its original functions – uninterrupted over the decades. It still offers Spanish folklore and crafts: metalwork, ceramics, glassware, mosaics, furniture, (blown) glasswork, cork, shell-work, prints, printed and woven textiles, toys, lacework and crotchet, coats (and suits) of armour, ironmongery, not to mention records, food, drink, music and dancing, all in splendid reproduction vernacular settings.
These have delighted the uninitiated ever since 1929, uninitiated, that is in the view that to be *good*, buildings must be simple geometric abstractions.
Suppose Reventós, Folguera and their colleagues had taken that view instead of drawing on historic models; suppose also that in addition to distributing the Plaza Major, the Plaza Aragonese, the Plaza de la Fuente and the Monastery along a curving axis from east to west they had done so about a straight, linear axis as the Rationalists would have done.
Or, taking their cue from Héré, suppose they had taken a single house, possibly the Casa Consistorial – edited from the Valderrobres model and used that, elaborated, for the major buildings along their

Fig. 9.3 Pueblo Español, typical street (author's photograph).

axis *and* simplified – for the repetitive housing lining their streets and their minor urban spaces, they would, of course, have achieved a certain unity.

To which end, of course, they would have had to level a platform on Montjuich for contours are the enemy of symmetry!

Instead of that they chose, as Bassegoda points out, to respond to the accidents of the terrain, turning their streets here *with* the contours, thus making them curve, and *there* against them thus requiring steep slopes or even steps.

That process, by its nature, gave them basic, indeed fundamental, irregularities but these in themselves were not enough. For still the designers had to make detailed decisions as to which houses *should* be grouped together, where they should be grouped, how a church might be set within a plaza, and so on. Sometimes such decisions derived from reality as in the Plaza Arogonesa and the Calle de Cervantes where picturesque groupings, which *had* grown over the centuries, reproduced with all their accidents intact.

But of course, still, there was more to it than that! Someone, clearly, had to take decisions of a different kind; how to make collage-like juxtapositions of given architectural forms: the distance one can see along a curving street, the vista one glimpses through an archway; above all the way a campanile is glimpsed and lost then glimpsed again as a definitive urban marker. Which of course is the stuff of Picturesque composition.

Clough Williams-Ellis

Portmeirion

The Pueblo Español shows quite clearly that, given skill and sensitivity, it is possible to assemble fragments of architecture from many places and to combine them during a single period of designing into a coherent, if very complicated whole. But of course there are problems in such an approach and some of these are revealed at Portmeirion a fantasy village designed by Clough Williams-Ellis between 1925 and his death in 1978.

He and his wife, in 1924, had written a book *On the Pleasures of Architecture* (Williams-Ellis, 1924) in which, as they say, they:

> . . . aimed at winning as yet uninterested and uninformed popular support for architecture, planning, landscaping, the use of colour and indeed for design generally, by a gay, light-opera sort of approach, whereby the casual visitor . . . might be ensnared into taking a really intelligent interest in the things that give some of us fortunate ones such intense and abiding pleasures.

They suggested, among other things, that 'a fine building not only expresses its epoch . . . but also the character and quirks of a human being, an individual architect. . . . Not only façades, but house plans, practical or absurd, and the layout of a street or a park, were, we suggested, humanly expressive'.

Later in the 1920s Williams-Ellis began to think that he ought to 'try in actual building an example of what I meant'. So he started looking for a site at the same time making 'abortive sketches, plans and models'. He finally realized what he wanted to do during a holiday in Northern Italy.

Williams-Ellis found himself 'constantly but silently in my imagination realigning the elements of some little hill town – the campanile, the various squares and fountains . . . to see how they might fit some other site'. Above all he was taken by Portofino where, as he says:

> .. . . one evening in the autumn twilight we found ourselves by the sea, groping our way down a great flight of steps past the open doors of a church whence issued music, incense and a file of angelic nuns. Soon we were down on the quay of a little enclosed harbour, a full-rigged ship alongside, light reflected in the still water, the piled-up multi-coloured houses palely visible and one quay-side café still open. . . .

Next morning:

> . . . we awoke in brilliant sunshine to enchantment – bells ringing, the people just astir, fishing boats setting out, a pervading smell of fresh bread and delicious coffee, *and* a backcloth of simple, colourful, unaffected southern building . . . an almost perfect example of the man-made adornment and use of an exquisite site. . . .

Eventually, in 1925, an absentee uncle offered Williams-Ellis the Deudraeth Castle Estate near Portmadoc in North Wales. Williams-Ellis renamed it Portmeirion, and converted the 'pale mansion' at the water's edge, 'somewhat tentatively' into an unlicensed hotel. Primitive though conditions – and the food – seem to have been, Williams-Ellis soon found himself having to turn away such notable would-be guests as Arnold Bennett and George Bernard Shaw.

By the end of the first summer the response had persuaded Williams-Ellis that 'tentatively and step by step' he should proceed towards the realization of his dreams.

He thought it important to establish focal points such as 'a watch-house on the brink of its precipitous cliff, the presiding campanile crowning Battery Rock, the Chantry at the highest point of all'. Once these had been established 'it was only a matter of choosing amongst the many possibilities and determining scale relation, general character, materials, detailing and colour' (Figs 9.4 and 9.5).

Fig. 9.4 Clough Williams-Ellis (1926–78): Portmeirion (author's photograph).

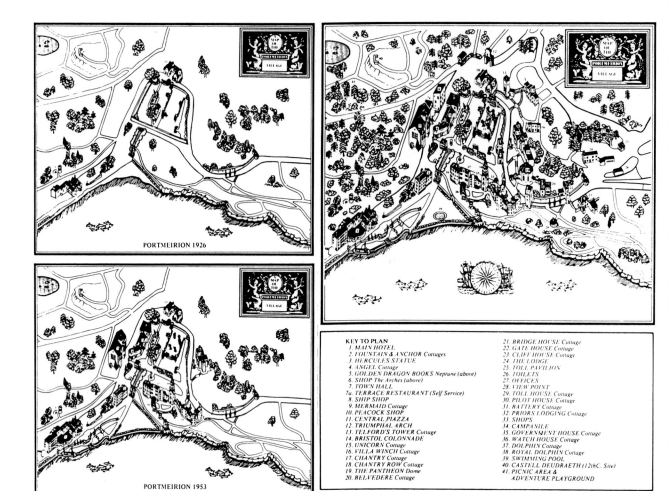

KEY TO PLAN
1. MAIN HOTEL
2. FOUNTAIN & ANCHOR Cottages
3. HERCULES STATUE
4. ANGEL Cottage
5. GOLDEN DRAGON BOOKS Neptune (above)
6. SHOP The Arches (above)
7. TOWN HALL
7a. TERRACE RESTAURANT (Self Service)
8. SHIP SHOP
9. MERMAID Cottage
10. PEACOCK SHOP
11. CENTRAL PIAZZA
12. TRIUMPHAL ARCH
13. TELFORD'S TOWER Cottage
14. BRISTOL COLONNADE
15. UNICORN Cottage
16. VILLA WINCH Cottage
17. CHANTRY Cottage
18. CHANTRY ROW Cottage
19. THE PANTHEON Dome
20. BELVEDERE Cottage
21. BRIDGE HOUSE Cottage
22. GATE HOUSE Cottage
23. CLIFF HOUSE Cottage
24. THE LODGE
25. TOLL PAVILION
26. TOILETS
27. OFFICES
28. VIEW POINT
29. TOLL HOUSE Cottage
30. PILOT HOUSE Cottage
31. BATTERY Cottage
32. PRIORS LODGING Cottage
33. SHOPS
34. CAMPANILE
35. GOVERNMENT HOUSE Cottage
36. WATCH HOUSE Cottage
37. DOLPHIN Cottage
38. ROYAL DOLPHIN Cottage
39. SWIMMING POOL
40. CASTELL DEUDRAETH (12thC. Site)
41. PICNIC AREA &
ADVENTURE PLAYGROUND

Fig. 9.5 Clough Williams-Ellis: Portmeirion plans (from Williams-Ellis, 1982).

In part, he says, he built 'a home for fallen buildings' of which the first was a Ballroom from the (Jacobean) Emral Hall which he bought in lots at auction; ceiling, leaded windows, oak architraves, cornices and, he says, very much more.

This became the nucleus of the Town Hall and having started to reuse old buildings in this way he bought the bits and pieces which form his Bristol Colonnade, a large Renaissance-Gothic fireplace by Norman Shaw for the façade for his Pantheon, an 18th century colonnade from Amos Court for his Piazza, a colonnade from Wyatt's Hooton Hall for his Gloriette – named after that at Schönbrunn, a Gothick Pavilion which fronts it from Nerquis Hall, in Flintshire, not to mention sundry statues, coats of arms, doorways, grilles and other architectural features.

Sometimes, as he says, his creativity got the better of him:

Thus would suddenly appear such non-utility items as the campanile, the dome, archways, gateways, belvederes, fountains, statues or whatever, whilst as time went on, honourable offerings for my 'home for fallen buildings', from far and near, could not always be resisted.

Apart from the major incidents there are various vernacular cottages enclosing urban, or at least village, spaces between them as they climb up the hill. Williams-Ellis saw Portmeirion as a community of buildings, albeit 'speaking', as they do, with 'different tongues'. Some of them quite frankly *are* sham; paper-thin façades stuck on the fronts of buildings but with their struts and stays exposed to show that there is no pretence.

Williams-Ellis reports with a certain glee a visit to Portmeirion by the redoubtable Frank Lloyd Wright:

> Understandably he approved my old mountain home. . . . But Portmeirion was quite another matter! Dare I let him loose on *that*? . . . to my profound astonishment, he took it all without a blink, seeming instantly to see the point of all my wilful pleasantries, the calculated naïveties, eyetraps, formed and faked perspectives, heretical constructions, unorthodox colour mixtures, general architectural levity, and all the rest of it.

He catalogues with even greater glee such puritans of the British architectural establishment as Lord Holford, Maxwell Fry and Sir Robert Matthew who, whilst foisting their abstract architecture, not to mention their prefabricated systems, on to others, chose Portmeirion for their own relaxation. Clearly they too, like Gaudet, adored the Picturesque but felt unable to show this in their own work.

Yet one can argue, with some justification, that Portmeirion is glib and superficial. Not so much in terms of its sham constructions – these are plain for everyone to see – nor, in principle, need stage set architecture arouse the moral problems by which Modernists seem to have been afflicted. Portmeirion's failures, for me, lie within its own terms of reference (Fig. 9.6).

They arise, largely, from Williams-Ellis's use of fallen buildings intermixed with new-build vernacular. For each fallen building has its scale and so, of course, do the new buildings. The Gloriette, for instance, is fronted by an exquisite, small-scale Ionic portico whilst behind it there is Telford's Tower – a vastly overblown dovecote and a cottage with a vernacular basilica-like façade. In each case the scale conflicts with the form and the three conflict with each other in any perspective view.

Faced with equivalent problems in the Pueblo Español Reventós and Folguera copied, say, the forms of the arcade from Sangüesa whilst doubling the arches in size.

Of course it would have been impossible for Williams-Ellis to have taken his fallen buildings as he found them and composed them at Portmeirion so that each, from every point of view, would have had correct perspectival relationships with its neighbours.

But still it seems ironic that the Pueblo Español designed by a team in a short space of time should actually prove to be more consistent than Portmeirion designed and built as it was *ad hoc* over some 50 years of 'growth and change'. Together, at least, they give the lie to the Sitte/Gaudet argument that the Picturesque can *only* grow over time!

Gordon Cullen

Gordon Cullen began to develop the idea of Townscape at the end of the war in 1945 when he joined *The Architectural Review* as an assistant editor. Cullen's beautifully illustrated essays of the subject were collected to form the book called *Townscape* (Cullen, 1961) and republished, in edited form, as *The Concise Townscape* (Cullen, 1971). Cullen argued that just as there is an art of architecture, so there is an art of relationship, in which all the elements which go to the making of

Fig. 9.6 Portmeirion: Gloriette and Telford's Tower (author's photograph).

Fig. 9.7 Gordon Cullen (1966): activities and spaces (reproduced from Cullen, G., *The Scanner*, 1966).

an environment, buildings, trees, nature, water, traffic, advertisements and so on are woven together in such a way that drama is released. This cannot be achieved by scientific research or by the technical half of the brain, although Cullen accepts the need for demographers, sociologists, engineers, traffic experts and so on. The result of their work according to Cullen is:

> . . . that a town could take one of several patterns and still operate with success. Here then we discover a pliability in the scientific solution and it is precisely in the *manipulation of this pliability* that the art of relationships is made possible . . . the aim is . . . simply to *manipulate within the tolerances*.

That manipulation, according to the Cullen of *Townscape*, will be a visual matter: 'for it is almost entirely through vision that the environment is apprehended'. He goes on:

> . . . vision is not only useful but it evokes our memories and experiences, those responsive emotions inside us which have the powers to disturb the mind when roused. It is this unlooked-for surplus. . . .

We are dealing, he says, with this unlooked-for surplus, which we appreciate in three ways. These are matters of:

1. Serial vision which is stimulated when, in addition to the view which is immediately present, the *existing view*, there are also hints of a different, *emerging view*. A long straight road or an open square can only give us the first of these whereas delight and interest are stimulated by contrasts, the 'drama' of juxtaposition.
2. Place – especially the sense of being *in* a particular place – a street or square – of being 'here' with the equally strong sense that around and outside *it* there are other places which we may think of as 'there'.

3. Content which is a matter of architectural style, scale, materials and layout. Cullen cites colour, texture, style, character, personality and uniqueness.

Given the hotchpotch nature of old towns, he says:

> . . . there exists at the back of our minds a feeling that could we only start again we could get rid of this hotchpotch and make all new and fine and perfect. We would create an orderly scene with straight roads and with buildings that conformed in height and style. Given a free hand that is what we might do . . . create symmetry, balance, perfection and conformity. After all, that is the popular conception of the purpose of town planning.

He draws an analogy with a party, which starts with the meeting of strangers, all observing the proprieties, making polite conversation in rather general terms so that no one reveals a personality. It is, he says, an exhibition of manners, of how one *ought* to behave, which also is very boring. But as the evening wears on, people relax and get to know each other. One is a good-natured wit, another is simply exuberant; each one acts as a foil for the others. People enjoy themselves hugely *because* they have agreed to differ, within certain recognized bounds. Cullen's view, of course, is that planning should be more like the latter stages of his party rather than the earlier, stiff and formal stranger.

Cullen's message was clear enough, and brilliantly presented, with his highly appealing sketches showing examples of his serial vision, ways of defining 'place', by means of enclaves, enclosures, focal points, precincts, outdoor rooms, hereness and thereness, closed vistas, deflections, projections and recessions, undulations, not to mention punctuations, the sense of possession, advantage and so on. He also looks at contexts: metropolitan, urban, arcadian, rural, industrial and so on; and at a whole range of details and devices by which we actually 'read' our environment. These include intimacy, propriety, bluntness, entanglement, nostalgia, exposure, illusion, metaphor, animal likenesses, relationships, scale, distortions, calligraphy, advertising and many more. He looks at the delights of the so-called 'functional' tradition: at iron and other bridges, at railings, fences and steps, at textures, lettering, bollards, cobblestones and so on, after which he analyses a wide range of environments, showing with his seductive sketches how they could be improved.

The result of all this, as Cullen says in the Introduction to his *Concise* edition (1971), was 'a superficial civic style of bollards and cobbles . . . traffic-free pedestrian precincts and . . . the rise of conservation'. But these, for Cullen, were merely the superficials; there had been no widespread understanding of what he was trying to do. In a very real sense, the deceptively easy nature of his presentation blinded people to the profundity of what he was trying to say. So it's hardly surprising that in comparison the Rationalists *look* more rigorous.

Yet between the two editions of his *Townscape* Cullen had been commissioned by Alcan Industries – producers of aluminium – to undertake various studies in planning, such as *Circuit Linear Town* and *A Town called Alcan*, as a platform for new ideas. One of these, *The Scanner* (Cullen, 1966) a 24-page brochure, is concerned specifically with the fabric of the town: the roads, the paths and the buildings. There, in some thirty drawings, a two-page chart and a 3000 word worked example, with 9 plans and 6 townscape comparisons, he gets closer to the heart of the matter than Sitte did in some 75 000 words and 115 plans. *The Scanner* itself is his two-page chart, the first page of

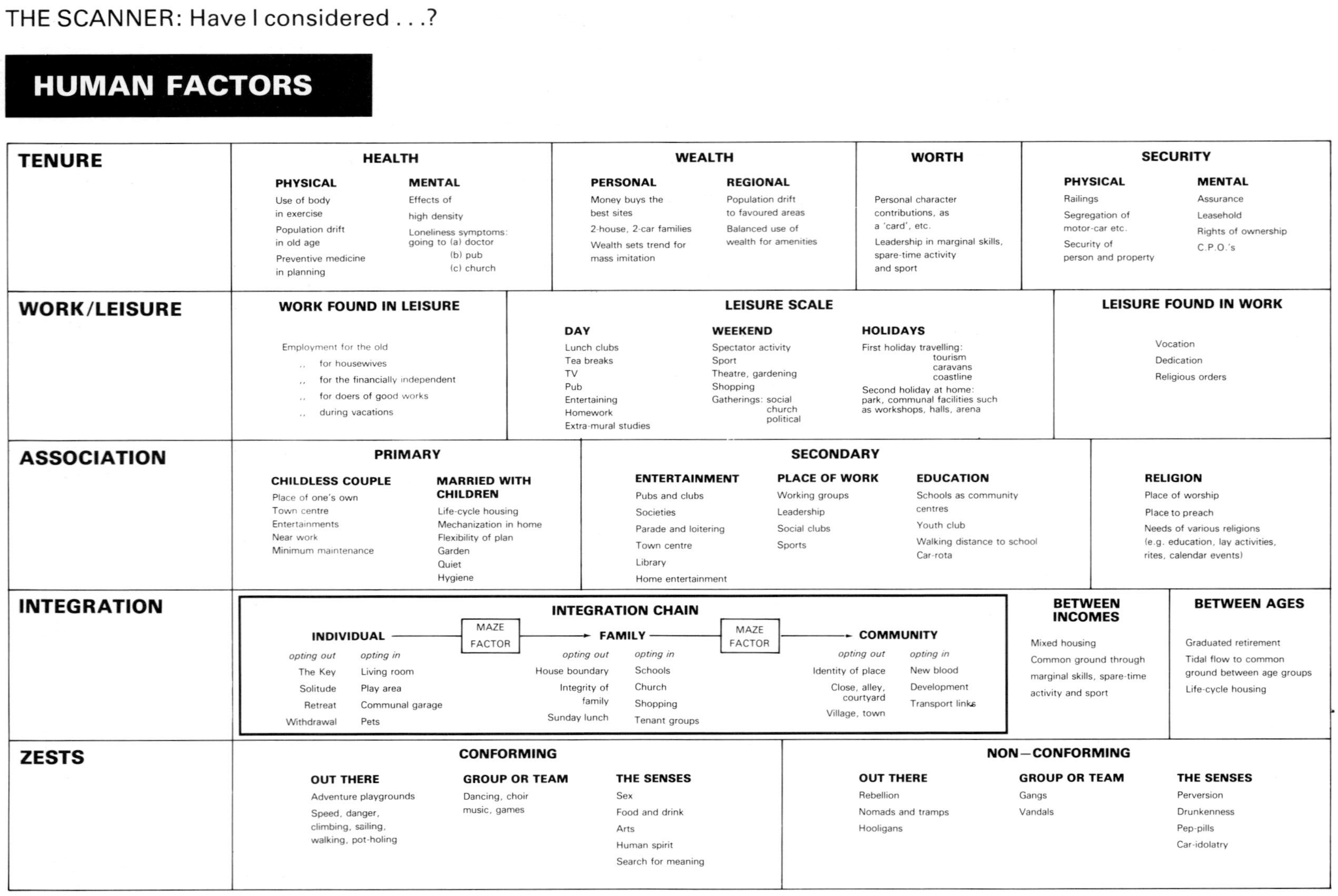

HUMAN FACTORS

TENURE

HEALTH

- **PHYSICAL**
  - Use of body in exercise
  - Population drift in old age
  - Preventive medicine in planning
- **MENTAL**
  - Effects of high density
  - Loneliness symptoms: going to (a) doctor (b) pub (c) church

WEALTH

- **PERSONAL**
  - Money buys the best sites
  - 2-house, 2-car families
  - Wealth sets trend for mass imitation
- **REGIONAL**
  - Population drift to favoured areas
  - Balanced use of wealth for amenities
- **WORTH**
  - Personal character contributions, as a 'card', etc.
  - Leadership in marginal skills, spare-time activity and sport

SECURITY

- **PHYSICAL**
  - Railings
  - Segregation of motor-car etc.
  - Security of person and property
- **MENTAL**
  - Assurance
  - Leasehold
  - Rights of ownership C.P.O.'s

WORK/LEISURE

WORK FOUND IN LEISURE

- Employment for the old
- .. for housewives
- .. for the financially independent
- .. for doers of good works
- .. during vacations

LEISURE SCALE

- **DAY**
  - Lunch clubs
  - Tea breaks
  - TV
  - Pub
  - Entertaining
  - Homework
  - Extra-mural studies
- **WEEKEND**
  - Spectator activity
  - Sport
  - Theatre, gardening
  - Shopping
  - Gatherings: social church political
- **HOLIDAYS**
  - First holiday travelling: tourism caravans coastline
  - Second holiday at home; park, communal facilities such as workshops, halls, arena

LEISURE FOUND IN WORK

- Vocation
- Dedication
- Religious orders

ASSOCIATION

PRIMARY

- **CHILDLESS COUPLE**
  - Place of one's own
  - Town centre
  - Entertainments
  - Near work
  - Minimum maintenance
- **MARRIED WITH CHILDREN**
  - Life-cycle housing
  - Mechanization in home
  - Flexibility of plan
  - Garden
  - Quiet
  - Hygiene

SECONDARY

- **ENTERTAINMENT**
  - Pubs and clubs
  - Societies
  - Parade and loitering
  - Town centre
  - Library
  - Home entertainment
- **PLACE OF WORK**
  - Working groups
  - Leadership
  - Social clubs
  - Sports
- **EDUCATION**
  - Schools as community centres
  - Youth club
  - Walking distance to school
  - Car-rota
- **RELIGION**
  - Place of worship
  - Place to preach
  - Needs of various religions (e.g. education, lay activities, rites, calendar events)

INTEGRATION

INTEGRATION CHAIN

INDIVIDUAL → FAMILY → [MAZE FACTOR] → COMMUNITY ... [MAZE FACTOR]

- **INDIVIDUAL**
  - *opting out:* The Key, Solitude, Retreat, Withdrawal
  - *opting in:* Living room, Play area, Communal garage, Pets
- **FAMILY**
  - *opting out:* House boundary, Integrity of family, Sunday lunch
  - *opting in:* Schools, Church, Shopping, Tenant groups
- **COMMUNITY**
  - *opting out:* Identity of place, Close, alley, courtyard, Village, town
  - *opting in:* New blood, Development, Transport links

BETWEEN INCOMES

- Mixed housing
- Common ground through marginal skills, spare-time activity and sport

BETWEEN AGES

- Graduated retirement
- Tidal flow to common ground between age groups
- Life-cycle housing

ZESTS

CONFORMING

- **OUT THERE**
  - Adventure playgrounds
  - Speed, danger, climbing, sailing, walking, pot-holing
- **GROUP OR TEAM**
  - Dancing, choir music, games
- **THE SENSES**
  - Sex
  - Food and drink
  - Arts
  - Human spirit
  - Search for meaning

NON-CONFORMING

- **OUT THERE**
  - Rebellion
  - Nomads and tramps
  - Hooligans
- **GROUP OR TEAM**
  - Gangs
  - Vandals
- **THE SENSES**
  - Perversion
  - Drunkenness
  - Pep-pills
  - Car-idolatry

Fig. 9.8 Gordon Cullen (1966): human factors (reproduced from Cullen, G., *The Scanner*, 1966).

THE SCANNER: Have I considered . . . ?

PHYSICAL FACTORS

COMMUNITY

SIZE
- Choice of climacteric sizes based on:
- Time cycle (e.g. weekly sufficiency)
- Growth of amenities
- Transport capacity

COMPOSITION
Balance of imbalance of:
- Ages
- Occupation
- Wealth

LOCATION
- The art of siting
- Catchment area
- Dominant or dependent
- Economic viability
- Communications

REGION
- Regional characteristics
- Seasonal fluctuations

GROWTH
- Projected growth
- Change of composition
- Self-limiting community

PATTERN

DENSITY

LOW
- Peace, tranquility, space, health, low land-use, random pattern, poor public transport, difficult for industrialized building, cash sale of houses, limited traffic segregation

MEDIUM
- Degree of privacy and space, medium land-use, possibility of corporate visual groups, viable for public transport, viable for industrialized building, mortgage, horizontal segregation (Radburn etc.)

HIGH
- Maximum need for amenity space, optimum land use, greater possibility of visual cohesion, public transport, optimum industrialized building, council rent, vertical traffic segregation

TRANSPORT

TRAFFIC TO PEOPLE
- Transport flow: motorway, clearway, amenity of traffic
- Problem of proximity: noise, smell, sight, nodal points, parking

PEOPLE TO TRAFFIC
- Exercise
- Peace of mind
- Environment
- Commuting
- Ease of contact or segregation

BY-LAWS
- Daylighting
- Road widths
- Sight angles
- Fire access

GIVEN PATTERNS

TRENDS
- Snob designs and colours
- Pop-art
- Layouts and gimmicks

INDUSTRIALIZED BUILDING
- Crane swing
- Unit weight
- Factory siting
- Production flow

LANDSCAPE

CATEGORIES
- Wild nature
- National park
- Uplands
- Coastline, estuary
- Arable land
- Industrial land
- Parkland
- Green Belt
- Rough Green Belt
- Twilight land
- Suburb
- City

CLIMATE
- Prevailing wind
- Local climate
- Artificial climate
- Population drift

NATURE
- Wild life
- Nature reserves
- Ecology
- Air pollution
- Industrial waste

AGRICULTURE & INDUSTRY
- New patterns of farming
- Factory farming
- Clean industry
- Automation
- Power/service grids

OPTICS

SPACE CHAIN

INTERNAL — MAZE FACTOR — EXTERNAL (BUILT) — MAZE FACTOR — EXTERNAL (NATURAL)

INTERNAL
- A room
- Sequence of rooms
- Flow of spaces
- Connection: stairs, ramps

EXTERNAL (BUILT)
- Courtyard
- Street
- Square
- Formal garden

EXTERNAL (NATURAL)
- Avenue
- Park and lake
- Hills and sea
- Horizon and sky
- Panorama

LIGHT
- Cubism
- Geometry
- Silhouette
- Texture
- Colour
- Artificial light
- Exploratory power of light

PERSPECTIVE
- Effects of foreshortening
- Division and organization of space
- Intrusion and excision by height
- The visual globe

SERIAL VISION
- Seeing in movement
- Development
- Joining and separating
- Growth of apparent size

IDENTITY OF PLACE

SITE SYMPATHY

AMBIENCE
- City
- Market town
- Suburb
- Quartier
- Village
- Genius loci

OBJECTS
- Character of building
- Historical appraisal
- Vitality
- Significant position

NATURE
- Levels
- Sky
- Water
- Trees and plants

COMBINATION

HOMOGENEITY
- Conformity
- Manners
- Heirarchy
- Enclosure

FOILS
- Scale
- Style
- Surprise
- Follies

Fig. 9.9 Gordon Cullen (1966): physical factors (reproduced from Cullen, G., *The Scanner*, 1966).

which is concerned with Human Factors and the second with Physical Factors:

> Human Factors . . . mean those conditions of happiness or sadness, fulfilment or despair, which arise from total human relationships.

> Physical Factors . . . mean the actual shape and arrangement of the urban environment, the mould into which mankind is poured.

Cullen sees these as a pair of interlinked chains: an Integration Chain of human activities and a Space Chain of the physical environments in which these activities take place (Figs 9.7–9.9).

The Integration Chain is based on those conditions of health, wealth, worth and security which he calls Tenure; on work/leisure and their interrelationships and on personal associations at various levels, from the family outwards, all motivated by certain Zests arising from the senses, from group or team relationships, from 'out there'. He sees some of these Zests as conforming and some as non-conforming. The Integration Chain therefore operates at various levels, from the individual, through the family, to the community. One can opt in or opt out at each of these levels, so at one extreme the individual will opt out in his search for solitude, retreat or withdrawal, whilst at the other he may opt in to some group activity within the community.

Cullen's Spatial Chain of physical factors literally is built by a community of a certain size, composition, in a certain location; it has a particular pattern of density, transport systems and so on and it is built within a given landscape with a particular climate, and a pattern of wild nature, agriculture and industry. Cullen sees the Space Chain as motivated – hopefully – by an identity of place which itself is based on sympathy for the site and the complex combination of those factors which make for homogeneity with those which offer foils. The Space Chain for Cullen is largely an optical matter in which light, perspective and serial vision all play their part and, like the Integration Chain, it operates at three levels: internal, external (built) and external (natural).

The individual links within Cullen's two chains are interlinked by what he calls a 'maze factor', a term which, as he suggests, may need clarification:

> The intention [he says] is to suggest that pleasant degree of complexity and choice which, although it is contained within a coherent framework, allows the individual to find his personal path. We feel that this degree of personal initiative, both socially and visually, helps to identify a person with his environment.

As Cullen saw it, the designer could take this (or his own) *Scanner* as a map of the design problem. It could even be used as a check list against which the designer could ask himself 'Have I considered . . .' or 'Is there provision for. . . .' In particular it would force him to draw out of the environment those things which were unique and particular to a certain place.

Of course, one can quibble with this, or any other mapping of the problem. I certainly should wish to see Cullen's Space Chain extended to include not merely Optical Factors but factors also concerned with the other senses, not to mention physical – anthropometric and ergonomic – relationships between the human body and the physical environment. Nor do I see room-high prefabricated panels as a necessary given pattern for house building, to be used right to the end of the century. But Cullen's idea of two interlinked chains, the one of human activities and the other of physical spaces in which they take place, seems to me an admirable one. So, too, is his view that the environment of a particular place should be allowed to give us clues as to how to design for that particular place.

But the proof of any such scheme obviously has to be found in the results. Cullen presents two worked examples in *The Scanner*: a hypothetical urban village for 2500 and an urban renewal scheme for the Borough of Rhondda Valley. The Village was designed for a hypothetical site and the main part of this proposal consists of Cullen's seductive sketches showing the various spaces of his Optic Chain populated by people participating in *their* Integration Chain. The Rhondda example naturally involves him more in some analysis of the existing environment, of Valley life in terms of tenure, work/leisure, association, integration and zests. He then contrasts photographs of the existing Rhondda environment, that is before any improvement, with Townscape sketches of what it could be like after. There is no attempt to show an Integration Chain of human activities taking place in the Optical Chain which he is thus proposing.

These two schemes are interesting enough but they are nothing like so comprehensive – or realistic – as Cullen's proposals for Maryculter, a new urban village near Aberdeen. This was prepared (1974) for Christian Salvesen (Properties) Ltd, with David Gosling as Planning Consultant and Kenneth Browne as co-Design Consultant. As we have seen, Cullen himself is perfectly clear that any design study should start with a proper scientific survey and the Maryculter study was a model of its kind, taking into account as it did location, land ownership, topography, landscape, existing development, services, geology and subsoil (Fig. 9.10). David Gosling's team then worked out on this basis their proposals for the village's overall form, circulation, population/employment/density, open space and recreation, community facilities, landscape, main drainage and phasing and it was within this framework that Cullen then presented his concept (Fig. 9.11). He saw this in terms of a Habitat for Houses, a Townscape Plan, and the Way to the Heart, followed by the detailed treatment of four neighbourhoods: East Park, Kaleyards, The Wynds and Burnside.

David Gosling had set the general flavour with sketches for the houses which in scale, form and materials were derived from the local vernacular within an overall philosophy which Cullen himself describes: 'the main purpose of this plan is to try to convert mass housing into an individual experience, to produce a sense of Identity, and Belonging'. The key question, as they saw it, was 'People live in houses, but where do houses live?'

The site itself formed a natural amphitheatre, which in itself suggested a U-shaped enclosure surrounding a park, open to the west with the main housing areas looking inwards on to parkland. This would establish immediately a sense of hereness within the village and thereness outside it. The main east–west axis formed by the open U would be cut about halfway along by a north–south axis, the High Street with a central market place and shops, whilst elsewhere in the scheme would be various markers or recognition points: a church steeple, a single tree closing the vista at the end of a street, a flagpole, a single red building in a street which was otherwise white and so on. These would be so placed as to form a network in which 'people quite understand where they are in the general context'. The edge of the village too would be marked by belts of trees forming a screen through which people would penetrate from the wild exterior to the domestic interior. Given the (relative) hostility of the climate, the house

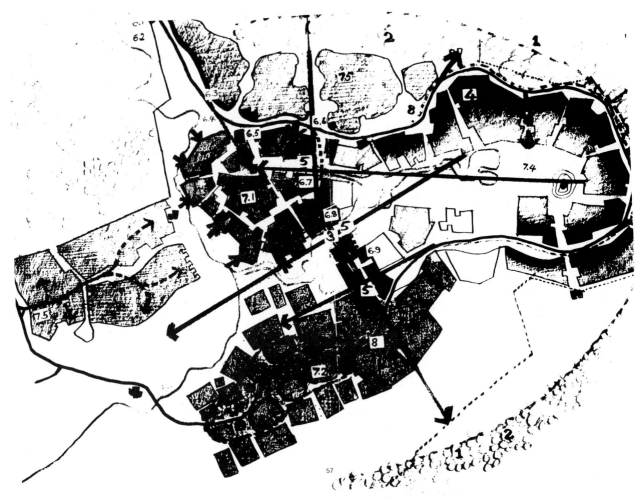

Fig. 9.10 Gosling, Cullen and
Donaghue (1974): New Town of
Maryculter: plan analysis (from
Gosling *et al.*, 1974).

groupings too would be protective, with walled enclosures in which
the wind was tempered so that 'what sun there is benefits the plants
and flowers'.

More than any other scheme Mayculter shows that far from being a
product *only* of time, picturesque effect *can* be generated from response
to a particular situation; a certain site with its contours, its climate and
other local conditions; views out, views in and other visual clues;
above all, a desire on the part of the designers to respond to a place
rather than imposing their own sterile geometry.

The Maryculter report, indeed, suggests a number of principles
which could be applied to other places wherever a sense of identity is
required. These (paraphrased) include:

1. fitting the development to the site
2. providing a central nucleus with the necessary authority, scale and
   incident
3. providing distinctive housing areas, each with its own identity,
   idosyncrasy and individuality
4. avoiding a vast, amorphous spread by separating the various
   developments so that each has recognizable edges or boundaries

Fig. 9.11 Maryculter: town centre perspective (from Gosling *et al.*, 1974).

5. encouraging a sense of individual places, not to mention aiding navigation, by providing a network of recognizable landmarks, each of which may act as a rallying point for some particular function or some particular zone
6. using the existing topography, and careful planting, to encourage a sense of drama, thus providing memorable situations
7. using carefully planned enclosures to provide a sense of locality and place (I am *here*)
8. leading people from one (enclosure) experience to another towards a climax, so that the unfolding drama itself will stick in the memory

As the Maryculter team say, these devices need not incur any extra cost; they can be achieved by simply reorganizing or regrouping the elements from which any development would have to have been made in any case.

Maryculter was never built, but the precepts which Cullen described certainly *could* be applied in any environment according to the clues that environment offers. Given the least evocative site, say, perfectly flat and with the most benign of climates, one can still think in terms of a nucleus – with recognizable landmarks – surrounded by areas of housing, each with its individual identity. And even the most benign of climates has certain suggestions to make about roof-form, wall density, the sizes and shapes of openings, whilst the laws, as it were, of the picturesque still have things to tell us about the visual – and climatic – advantages of curving streets, irregular places, colonnades, arcades and so on.

Kevin Lynch

One of the first coherent analysers of the urban scene in Empirical terms was Kevin Lynch in his *The Image of the City* (1960). Lynch had been working with Georgy Kepes at the Center for Urban and Regional Studies at the Massachusetts Institute of Technology and Kepes himself had edited a series of books (1965–6) to do with our perception of movement.

Lynch was concerned, above all, with The Image of the Environment for, as he says (p. 1) 'Every citizen has had long associations with some part of the city, and his image is soaked in memories and meanings'. As he also says: 'Moving elements in the city, and in particular the people and their activities, are as important as the stationary physical parts'.

Whilst he points out that 'Nearly every sense is in operation' as we perceive the city, Lynch's primary concern is with the visual quality of the (American) city, which he approaches 'by studying the mental images of (the) city which is held by its citizens'. In particular he looks for clarity and legibility in the cityscape, 'the ease with which its parts can be recognized and . . . ordered into a coherent pattern'. We read it, he says, by:

> the visual sensations of color, shape, motion, or polarization of light, as well as the other senses such as smell, sound, touch,

Fig. 9.12 Kevin Lynch (1960): Boston Images: verbal (from Lynch, 1960).

More than half the subjects expressed the following as part of their image of the Hill (in roughly descending order):

a sharp hill
narrow, pitching streets
the State House
Louisburg Square and its park
trees
handsome old houses
red brick
inset doorways

There were other frequent mentions of:

brick sidewalks
cobblestone streets
views of the river
a residential area
dirt and trash
social distinctions
corner stores on the back side
blocked or "curving" streets
the fence and statues, Louisburg Square
varied roof tops
signs on Charles Street
the gold dome of the State House
purple windows
some apartment houses in contrast

Still other comments are added by at least three people:

parked cars
bay windows
ironwork
houses packed together
old street lamps
a "European" flavor
the Charles River
the view to the Massachusetts General Hospital
children at play on the back side
black shutters
antique shops on Charles Street
three- and four-storey houses

kinaesthesia, sense of gravity, and perhaps of electric or magnetic fields.

In other words, his reading of the city is much like the reading of buildings which I described in my *Design in Architecture* (G. Broadbent, 1973).

Lynch is concerned with how we locate ourselves within the city, how we find our way around, and so on. He suggests, quite rightly, that this is easier in a regular, gridded city – such as Manhattan – given 'a structural understanding of (which) . . . one can order a substantial quantity of facts and fancies about the world we live in'.

As for the irregular city: '. . . let the mishap of disorientation once occur and the sense of anxiety and even terror that accompanies it reveals to us how closely it is linked to our sense of balance and well-being'. For Lynch, indeed, 'the very word "lost" . . . carries overtones of utter disaster'.

To know where we are within the city, therefore, we have to build up a workable image of each part and each of these images will comprise, first of all, identity – our recognition of its 'individuality or oneness' within the city as a whole – secondly our recognition of its spatial or pattern relationships to other parts of the city, also to ourselves and thirdly its particular meaning for each of us, 'whether practical or emotional'.

Lynch calls: 'that quality in a physical object which gives it a high, probability of evoking a strong image in any given observer' its imageability which in turn depends on 'that shape, color, or arrangement which facilitates the making of vividly identified, powerfully structured, highly useful mental images of the environment'.

Having conceived this notion of imageability Lynch then tested it by field studies in Boston, Massachusetts, Jersey City, New Jersey, and Los Angeles, California on which basis he concluded that several key elements come into play as we construct our images of the city, which he identified as paths, edges, districts, nodes and landmarks (Figs 9.12–9.15).

Lynch's definitions, paraphrased, are:

1. *Paths*, the channels of movement which people take, regularly, occasionally or may, potentially, take. They may include paths, streets, walkways, bus or tram lines, canals, railways and so on. As

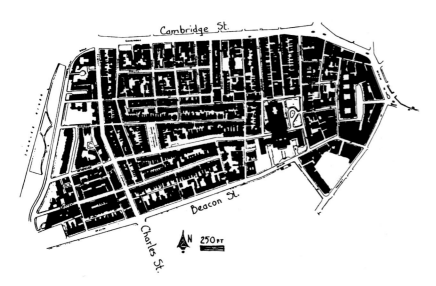

Fig. 9.13 Boston Images: maps (from Lynch, 1960).

Lynch says, we observe the city as we are moving through it and for many people, the paths themselves, and those elements of the city they perceive as they move along them predominate in their images of the city. They are, as Lynch put it 'coordinate axes';

2. *Edges* which for Lynch are linear elements which people do not use as paths. They perceive them, rather, as linear breaks or boundaries of some kind. They may be physical boundaries such as walls, railway cuttings, canals, shorelines, or they may simply be boundaries between adjacent developments. Whilst not so dominant as paths such boundaries are 'important organizing features' for many people especially when, in the form of, say, water or city wall they play the role of 'holding together generalised areas';

3. *Districts* which for Lynch are 'medium to large sections of the city which people visualize as having two-dimensional extent. Not only do they form districts on the map, they are also recognizable, especially from within, as having some common, identifying character, which indeed may be so strong that one has a distinct, mental impression of entering 'inside of'. This may be recognizable also from outside. Most people, according to Lynch, find this idea of district to be most important in building up their 'Image of the City'. Indeed, according to the city – and the individual perceiver – they may be more important than paths;

4. *Nodes* are strategic points within the city to or from which the observer travels. They may be crossings or convergences of paths, junctions, places where one changes from one mode of transport to

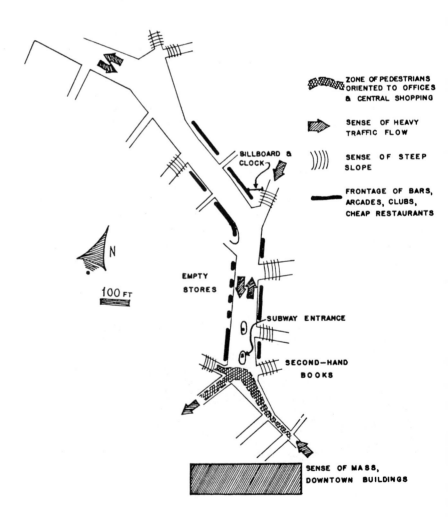

Fig. 9.14 Boston Images: elements (from Lynch, 1960).

another. Or they may be concentrations of some kind, which are important because of their physical form: such as urban squares, street corners. They may be condensers of particular uses. Some, nodes in fact, will be 'the focus and epitome of a district, over which their influence radiates and of which they stand as a symbol';

5. *Landmarks* too are reference-points but the observer does not actually use them. They consist, rather, of 'simply defined physical objects' such as a building, a sign, a store or even a mountain. A landmark in this sense will be a physical object which, because of its form, may be singled out from the surrounding environment. They may be large, man-made objects such as a tower, a spire or a dome, soaring over the rooftops and acting as a radial reference from many points within the city. They may be distant mountains which serve a similar purpose; the sun itself, even though it moves, may act as a landmark in this sense. Its movement, after all, is slow and its directions known.

6. *Landmarks* also occur at smaller scale; a tree within an urban square, a particular sign, a shop front, a door or even a doorknob. These, and other urban detail . . . fill in the image (for) most observers.

As Lynch suggests we make frequent use of such clues in our search for the identity of elements within the city and even for our understanding of urban structure. What is more we seem to rely on them more and more as our journey becomes increasingly familiar.

Having identified these elements as making the city imageable Lynch then goes on to describe their use during the process of design. Paths, for instance, should be planned so that each plays its part in the hierarchy of movement systems. The key lines, he says, should each be identified by some specific quality such as:

a concentration of some special kind of activity, along their margins, a characteristic spatial quality, a special texture of floor or façade, a particular lighting pattern, a unique set of smells or sounds, a typical detail or mode of planting.

Again he insists on perceivable clarity of direction since, he says, the 'human computer is disturbed by long successions of turnings, or by gradual, ambiguous curves which in the end produce major directional shifts'. But at the same time he recognizes the 'kinesthetic' qualities of paths, our sense of motion as we move along them; turning, rising, falling which, collectively, make deep impressions. If we are moving at high speed in, say, 'a great descending curve which approaches a city

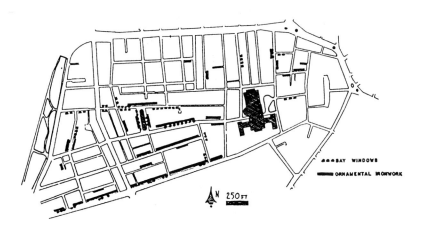

Fig. 9.15 Boston Images: visual form (from Lynch, 1960).

center' those impressions can be even deeper producing, as he says, 'an unforgettable image'.

And so Lynch describes applications for each of his major elements. It may, for instance, be difficult to design specific edges for, say a central business district although there are clues as to how this might be done in, say, 'the abrupt cessation of a medieval city at its wall, the fronting of skyscraper apartments on Central Park, the clear transition from water to land at a sea-front . . .'.

The inside–outside nature of a district may be reinforced by the use of contrasting materials, careful planting, by use of gradients, identifiable points placed at intervals along it, 'recognizable anchors' at the ends, and so on.

The most prominent nodes, he suggests, are those which occur at 'route decision points' which may not even have been designed consciously as such. Landmarks, on the other hand, will be designed specifically to serve that purpose although, as he reiterates, whilst a 'tower silhouetted over low roofs' may be an obvious landmark so may a doorknob also, if it is of the right kind in the right place.

Whilst Lynch's way of 'reading' the city has gained, perhaps, the widest currency, other effective systems of notation have been worked out by Thiel (1961, 1962, 1964, 1986); Appleyard *et al.* (1964); Halprin (1965, 1970) – whose method was based on methods of notation developed for ballet, and so on.

François Spoerry

Port Grimaud

There were indeed two notable attempts at Picturesque design in the 1960s; François Spoerry's Port Grimaud (from 1963) and Kresge College by Moore, Turnbull and Whitaker (1968).

Spoerry built his Port Grimaud on the Gulf of St Tropez on the Coast of Provence and within ten years, as Culot points out (1977), it had become the third most visited monument in France after the Eiffel Tower and Mont-Saint-Michel. These days, presumably, it takes fourth place to the Centre Pompidou in Paris which of course has a far larger catchment area.

Spoerry had known the site of Port Grimaud, a salt-marsh, since he had gone there bird-watching and sketching as a child. And later in his early 20s (1932–33) he had worked in the area with an architect who worked in the regional vernacular, Jacques Couelle.

Having survived, as a member of the Resistance, various Nazi concentration camps, Spoerry graduated from Ecole des Beaux Arts and opened a thoroughly commercial office in Mulhouse designing, among other things, the thirty-storey, curtain walled Tour de l'Europe whilst at the same time designing an electric car!

Culot describes him, at the time, as:

> . . . architect, builder, promoter, business man, man of politics, philanthropist, navigator, epicure, compulsive worker, and, at one and the same time, of burly professional dimensions linked to an entrepreneurial character.

Yet somehow Spoerry felt there was more to architecture than that and, at the age of 50, he started work on Port Grimaud. Other developers, looking for easy sites on the French Mediterranean Coast had thought the salt-marsh quite unsuitable for building but Spoerry made a careful survey, probing the subsoil, checking the flow of the river, the highest and lowest conditions of the tides, the impact of that most unpleasant of winds, the mistral. After which Spoerry bought the land cheaply because of its low agricultural – and potential for development – values.

Taking Ramatuelle and Aigues-Mortes as his models, Spoerry conceived the idea that concentric, if irregular rings of land could alternate with rings of water. Of course the rings would have to be broken – to allow boats to come in from the sea – and also connected by bridges so that pedestrians could cross the rings of water to reach the inner rings of land (Figs 9.16 and 9.17).

Thus broken, of course, the rings of land are more like fingers projecting into the water but Spoerry worried that the water between them might become stagnant, given the small Mediterranean tide (little more than 150 mm). So Spoerry toyed with the idea of windmill-driven pumps to keep the water swirling between the fingers.

But then he made a model of the fingers in which the tidal changes could be modelled. And he realized that if his fingers were to be cut where they joined the mainland, with bridges, the tiny swirl produced by tidal changes could indeed be quite adequate.

Having established the layout of his fingers at model scale. Spoerry could also model the houses which were to line them. For literally he had a Radburn layout with pedestrian routes between the houses along the fingers and vehicles – in this case boats – on the further sides of the houses on the main vehicular routes of Port Grimaud which of course are the rings of water. For Port Grimaud, like Portmeirion, is a pedestrian village with off-site parking for the cars.

Three whole years after presenting his scheme, Spoerry was permitted to go ahead. He had to develop the technology for building his fingers of land with retaining-walls lining the *quais* which he filled by dredging sand from his waterways and packing it behind the sheet-piles which outlined his various islands and fingers.

Having built his infrastructure of promontories, peninsulas, islands and isthmuses, Spoerry then planned his superstructure of houses which form, according to Williams-Ellis: 'an altogether captivating dress of endlessly variegated houses, terraces, shops, hotels, restaurants, offices and the rest . . . of all sorts and sizes and colours'.

In each case Spoerry started with initial concepts – doodles – which, with further elaboration, became his actual schemes. At which point Spoerry solved the fundamental problem over which Sitte, Gaudet and many others had anguished for so long.

He had small-scale, detailed wooden models made of each house and had them photographed – using a Modelscope – from every angle under different lighting conditions, often standing on reflective surfaces making, by pragmatic, trial-and-error processes, such alterations in form, detail, colour and so on to things which his Modelscope revealed.

Thus he transcended the Sitte/Gaudet problem of drawing things which look good as irregular plans but look too artful and contrived when translated into built, three-dimensional forms. Clough Williams-Ellis made a pertinent comment:

How much of this the creator of this knew . . . in his mind's eye
. . . I don't know, but I guess a good deal of it – for the unexpected
and always rewarding glimpses, framed between A and B of (a)
distant C are just the sort of views one would have invented for
oneself if they had not been ready made for one. If there is
anything wrong with building pictures, instead of planning them,
then M. Spoerry is a sinner indeed, and if condemned by the

Fig. 9.16 François Spoerry (1963) Port Grimaud: air view (from *AMM*, **12**, 1977).

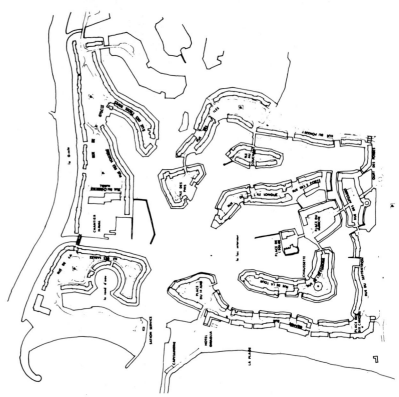

Fig. 9.17 Port Grimaud: Plan (from *AMM*, **12**, 1977).

architectural establishment to die, I should be proud to hang beside him.

As for the buildings themselves, much of their construction is of concrete, including party walls and roofs. The latter, indeed, are of waterproof concrete covered, over an air gap, with Provençal tiles. The movement of air between concrete and tiles helps keep the inner roofs, and therefore the bedrooms, cool in summer whilst firm fixing back of the tiles to the concrete means that, unlike traditional Provençal roofs, they are *not* blown off by the mistral at its worst.

Some of the external walls are, like traditional walls, of stone. Others – equally traditional – are of rough render painted in appropriate colours. Since they would not show Spoerry built them of the cheapest available material: concrete block.

There are wide variations in the size, shape and arrangement of the

Fig. 9.18 Port Grimaud: pedestrian finger (author's photograph).

Fig. 9.19 Port Grimaud: waterways (author's photograph).

windows and other openings, balconies, colonnades, arcades and so on, not to mention the external colour which varies from white to deepest red. All this is enhanced by skilful planting from tiny flowers in the patios to creepers up the walls, vine-covered trellises, shrubs and trees at strategic points.

The inner fingers of Port Grimaud radiate from an island on which are located the Market Place, with shops, linked to a smaller island which supports, among other things, a church with a bell tower – a Cullen/Lynch-like marker – which also provides a vantage point from which one can view the whole of Port Grimaud at least in its earlier phases. Williams-Ellis thought it should be higher for this purpose, and surmounted by a camera obscura but Spoerry felt that too Italian. His own house, with its defensive tower stands at the centre of Port Grimaud at the end of the longest of the fingers and from it he can survey the endless coming-and-going of every conceivable kind of personal sea-going craft.

Having provided at Port Grimaud basic, but highly varied 'shells', Spoerry encourages user-modifications, over the kind of time-scale which Sitte, Gaudet and others thought so vital to the achievement of Picturesque effect.

As one might expect, Williams-Ellis was enchanted by Port Grimaud and the way in which Spoerry had continued and developed the Picturesque tradition. For him, Port Grimaud actually provided 'a perfectly logical and viable town-planning exemplar for the almost tideless Mediterranean'. Whatever criteria one applies, efficiency of planning, economy of construction, response to climate and so on, Port Grimaud is serious architecture indeed. Much more serious, he says, than Portmeirion. If architecture of this quality, charm and sheer workability can be achieved by Picturesque methods, then why should we put up with anything else – or at least anything less?

Indeed Williams-Ellis called it (1978) 'The Miracle of Port Grimaud' and described it, probably, as 'the most hopeful and significant architectural and planning achievement of our time'.

Port Grimaud indeed *is* a success, commercially and in many other ways. It has been extended three times. Among many other things, Spoerry proves that one need not rely on contours for the basic Picturesque irregularity of street line, urban open space and so on. For nothing, clearly, could be flatter than a swamp! But by starting with his system of irregular rings – one thinks of Hiller's beady rings (pp. 21–3) – Spoerry sets up the basic possibility of that curvilinear planning which gives surprises round the corner wherever one goes. Unlike Reventós and Folguera in Barcelona, Spoerry at Port Grimaud does not use Provençal, or even Mediterranean models for direct copying. He works, rather, at the level of Mediterranean house types although the fragments from which they are composed: doors, windows, arcades, roof forms and so on are used at the level of models.

Alexander

Pattern language

In *A Pattern Language* (1977) Christopher Alexander and colleagues apply a thoroughly Empirical, perhaps even Pragmatic, approach to Towns, Buildings and Construction. Each Pattern consists of a fragment of the environment, at one or other three scales which, on the basis of their observations, is known to work.

There are 253 such Patterns each introduced by a photograph, an argument in favour of the Pattern, and supporting evidence, including, sometimes, further photographs and drawings amounting in each case to five pages or so.

The first 20 pages are concerned with scales – not to mention social strategies – much greater and more complex than those of urban space design including:

1. independent regions
2. the distribution of towns
3. city country fingers

4. agricultural valleys
5. lace of country streets

and so on, including:

8. mosaic of subcultures
10. magic of the city
12. community of 7000
15. neighbourhood boundary

But many of the Patterns are concerned with issues in urban space design; these include:

21. four storey limit: 'There is abundant evidence to show that high buildings make people crazy.' Which statement they support with Empirical evidence from Fanning (1967), Cappon (1971), Morville (1969), Newman (1972) and others. So, they conclude: In any urban area, no matter how dense, keep the majority of buildings four storeys . . . or less. It is possible that certain buildings should exceed this limit, but they should never be . . . for human habitation'
32. shopping street: 'Shopping centres depend on access. . . . However shoppers themselves . . . need quiet, comfort, and convenience, and access from pedestrian paths. . . .'
61. small public squares: 'A town needs public squares; they are the largest, most public rooms, that a town has. But when they are too large, they look and feel deserted'
69. public outdoor room: 'There are very few spots along the streets of modern towns . . . where people can hang out, comfortably, for hours at a time'
95. building complex: 'A building cannot be a human building unless it is a complex of still smaller buildings or smaller parts which manifest its own internal social facts'

Other Patterns are used to advocate:

97. shielded parking
100. pedestrian street
115. courtyards that live
119. arcades

and many other things which, at a small-is-beautiful, vernacular scale can indeed afford delight in the built environment.

Having presented their Patterns in these ways, Alexander and his colleagues then went on to produce design results (in *The Oregon Experiment* (1975)) and even built results: *The Linz Cafe* (1981). In practice, many of the Patterns ring true and they have been applied quite widely. Others must be taken with a pinch of salt nor can these, or any other Patterns, be applied in all cultures, all climates, all social conditions.

Venturi 1

Complexity and contradiction

Curiously enough, the two texts which, more than any others, have changed the course of architecture in the last quarter of the 20th century were both published in the same year: 1966. They are Aldo

Rossi's *Architectura della Città* and Robert Venturi's *Complexity and Contradiction in Architecture.*

Venturi starts with a quotation from T. S. Eliot on the nature of self-criticism in which he, Eliot, presents a view much like Popper's (1963) *Conjectures and Refutations.* Criticism, says Eliot (1932):

> . . . is of capital importance . . . in the work of creation itself. Probably, indeed, the larger part of the labour of sifting, combining, constructing, expunging, correcting, testing: this frightful toil is as much critical as creative. I maintain even that the criticism employed by a trained and skilled writer on his own work is the most vital, the highest kind of criticism. . . .

Venturi finds this critical faculty to be equally important in architectural design.

Eliot also insists on the 'presence of the past' in his work. He is careful to point out that as far as he is concerned, tradition by no means consists merely of 'following . . . in a blind or timid adherence . . . the ways of the immediate generation before us'.

It is, rather:

> . . . a matter of much wider significance. It cannot be inherited, and if you want it, you must obtain it by great labour. It involves, in the first place, the historical sense . . . nearly indispensable to anyone who would continue to be a poet beyond his twenty-fifth year; and the historical sense involves perception, not only of the pastness of the past, but of its presence; the historical sense compels a man to write . . . with a feeling that the whole . . . literature of Europe . . . has a simultaneous existence and composes a simultaneous order.

Venturi tries to be guided 'not by habit, but by a conscious sense of the past – by precedent, thoughtfully considered'. His other major literary source seems to have been Auguste Heckscher's (1962) book on *The Public Happiness.* Among other things Heckscher says:

> The movement from a view of life as essentially simple and orderly to a view of life as complex and ironic is what every individual passes through in becoming mature.

But, Heckscher goes on to say:

> Certain epochs encourage this development; in them the paradoxical or dramatic outlook colors the whole intellectual scene. . . . Amid simplicity and order rationalism is born, but rationalism proves inadequate in any period of upheaval. Then equilibrium must be created out of opposites. Such inner peace as men gain must represent a tension among contradictions and uncertainties. . . . A feeling for paradox allows seemingly dissimilar things to exist side by side, their very incongruity suggesting a kind of truth.

Venturi's intellectual roots, therefore, lie in the work of Eliot and Heckscher but he also agrees with Aldo van Eyck (1962) that those who, by stressing what is different about the 20th century, compared with other eras, have lost touch with those things which are essentially the same.

Nevertheless, as Venturi says, his primary concerns in writing the book were with 'the present, and the past in relation to the present'.

Given his particular historical interests, however, it is easy to see why Venturi should want to say such things as (p. 22): 'I like complexity and contradiction in architecture'; (p. 23) 'More is not less'; and (p. 25) 'Less is a bore'.

In the latter two of which, quite clearly, Venturi was attacking Mies van der Rohe, the architect who, more than any other in the early 1960s, seemed to be carrying all before him. He saw Mies's gnomic pronouncements, not to mention his actual buildings, to be gross over-simplifications.

As far as Venturi is concerned (p. 24) the architect who works in this way: 'can exclude important considerations only at the risk of separating architecture from the experience of life and the needs of society'. Venturi believes that these needs *can* be met only by an inclusive architecture which has room for: 'the fragment, for contradiction, for improvisation, and for the tensions these produce'.

Venturi's inclusive architecture matches in its forms the richness and ambiguity of 20th century experience. The complexity and contradiction he advocates are recognized as valid in painting and in poetry and even in mathematics where there are such things as Gödel's proof (see Hofstadter, 1979): that in the long run, the most logical of statements in mathematics can neither be proved nor disproved. Why then should we not recognize the inherent complexities and contradictions of architecture?

Even Vitruvius's architecture was complex and contradictory comprising three conflicting conditions: 'Commodity, Firmness and Delight'. If they conflicted even in Roman times how much more they conflict late in the 20th century when 'program, structure, mechanical equipment and expression' all make contradictory demands. That is true even for a single, simple building. And as buildings get bigger, as the urban context becomes increasingly complex, so architecture too becomes more complex than ever.

So, unlike Mies and others who sought to simplify, Venturi: 'welcome(s) the problems and exploit(s) the uncertainties'. What is more by embracing 'complexity and contradiction, he also sets his sights on further qualities: vitality *and* validity.

So Venturi presents the catalogue of things he likes, such as (p. 22):

the Compromising rather than the Clean
the Distorted rather than the Straightforward
the Ambiguous rather than the Articulated
the Boring as well as the Interesting
the Accommodating rather than the Excluding

Venturi is for 'richness of meaning rather than (for) clarity of meaning', for 'the implicit function as well as the explicit function'. He prefers 'both-and' to 'either-or', 'black *and* white, and sometimes gray, to black *or* white' (my emphases). For Venturi, a valid architecture 'evokes many levels of meaning and combinations of focus' in ways which simple and excluding architecture cannot hope to do.

For all this variety, however, Venturi's 'architecture of complexity and contradiction has special obligations toward the whole', which he goes on to call 'the *difficult* whole' (again my emphasis). Venturi's whole 'must embody the difficulty of inclusion rather than the easy unity of exclusion'.

So Venturi articulates his two-part programme:

1. Firstly, to re-examine the medium of architecture itself. We should look at our complex goals to see how these can be used to increase the scope of our architecture. The variety inherent in our visual perception, with all its ambiguities, must also be acknowledged and exploited;
2. Secondly, we must acknowledge the 'growing complexity of our functional programs such as those for research laboratories (and) hospitals'. We should recognize also our problems at city and regional scale. Even a single house, whilst simple in scope turns out to be complex in purpose if we are to express the ambiguities of contemporary experience.

Ambiguity as Venturi emphasizes is of fundamental importance in the arts as a whole. He draws, as one might expect, on William Empson who argued (1955) that far from being *deficiencies* in poetry, ambiguities are the very stuff of which good poetry is made.

Thus ambiguity is necessary for: 'giving us an insight which preserves the unity of his experience and which . . . triumphs over the apparently contradictory and conflicting elements of experience by unifying them into a new pattern'.

Venturi senses similar contradictions-within-unity in various kinds of painting he admires: Abstract Expressionism, Pop Art, Optical Art and so on.

Venturi suggests that in architecture, complexity and contradiction may be expressed in two ways. One is based on our perceptions: caused by contradictions between what an image *is* and what it seems to be.

The other relates to the form and content of the building, to discrepancies between its 'program and structure'.

He finds discrepancies of both these kinds in the work of some of the greatest architects including: Vanbrugh, Bernini, Lutyens and others. He finds them even in the work of Le Corbusier in the ground floor plan of the Villa Savoye (Fig. 9.20). Is it, he asks, a *square* in plan, as suggested by the grid of columns, or a U-shape as contained by the glass and stuccoed walls?

He starts with perceptual ambiguities, in matters such as scale, direction openness or closedness, symmetry or asymmetry.

He looks for, and finds, dualities, ambiguities, 'both-and' modes of planning and other contradictions between physical fact and psychic effect.

Venturi then goes on to examine complexity and contradiction in his 'form and content as manifestations of programme and structure'. He is looking for what he calls: Double-Functioning Elements and finds them at various scales including Construction and Detail: 'drip mouldings which become cills, windows which become niches, architraves which make arches'.

There is, too, the Multi-Functioning Room. Thus, according to Kahn, a gallery can be 'directional and non-directional, a corridor and a room at once'. Indeed according to Venturi: 'The multi-functioning room is possibly a truer answer to the Modern architect's concern with flexibility. The room with a generic rather than a specific purpose, and with moveable furniture rather than moveable partitions, promotes a perceptual flexibility. He finds them also in the Multi-functioning Building such as the Ponte Vecchio in Florence, the Château de Chenonceaux (Fig. 9.21), or even Sat' Elia's City of the Future that the

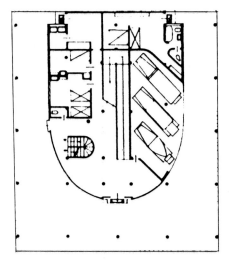

Fig. 9.20 Le Corbusier (1929) Villa Savoye, ground floor plan (from Overmeire, 1986).

Fig. 9.21 Château de Chenonceaux: bridge by Philibert de l'Orme *et al.* (1556–1559) (author's photograph).

buildings themselves serve several functions: Bridge *and* Shops, Bridge *and* Château and so on.

In their cult of the minimal Modern architects dismissed rhetoric. Indeed they have been afraid of it. But rhetoric is needed for underscoring meaning. Vanbrugh, for instance, underscores the meaning of entrance with his disengaged columns and pilasters flanking the archway to his kitchen court at Blenheim (Fig. 9.22). Even Mies underscored the meaning of structural frame with his equally redundant I-sections at Lake Shore Drive, Seagram and elsewhere (Fig. 9.23).

Having explored the contradictions which arise from the actual process of building, Venturi goes on to consider those generated by the program. Mies, he says, wanted to 'create order out of the desperate confusions of our time' whereas he, Venturi, looks for meaning in them. Which leads him specifically to look, not for overreaching order, but for the limitations of systems.

As he says, one can start with a consistent order and then modify it against whatever needs contradict it: 'Here you build up order and

Fig. 9.22 John Vanbrugh (1705–24) Blenheim Palace: Archway to Kitchen Court, left (author's photograph).

then break it down'. He calls this 'Contradiction accommodated'. Or one can start with 'the inherent complexities and contradictions of living' and somehow attempt to synthesize from them what he calls 'the difficult whole'.

To be valid, he says, order must accommodate 'the circumstantial contradictions of a complex reality' for thereby it admits: 'control *and* spontaneity', 'correctness *and* ease' – 'improvisation within the whole'. So the designer must decide: 'what must be made to work, and what it is possible to compromise with, what will give in, and where and how'. Above all: 'When circumstances defy order, order should bend or break'.

Naturally enough, the Classical orders give order but there are other kinds, *conventions* by which he means both the elements of building and the methods by which those elements are disposed. The elements may be everyday things, commonplace: 'in their manufacture, form and use . . . the vast accumulation of standard, anonymously de-signed products'. These he calls conventional elements to which he wants to add those 'commercial display elements which are positively banal or ugly in themselves'. Being banal and ugly, they are rarely used by architects.

Venturi wants to add such things to the architectural repertoire quite simply because they exist. Architects ignore them, bemoan them, try to suppress them, even have them taken away. But other people use them anyway whatever architects may think. In which case architects would do well to pre-empt those who might spoil their buildings later by incorporating 'banal and ugly' elements into their designs in the first place.

He is delighted by the way in which regular, symmetrical, Italian Palazzi have been able to accommodate, in their ground floors, each generation's concept of what 'frankly stylish contemporary bars' should be. As he says: 'Our buildings must survive the cigarette machine'.

Of course historians and critics committed to the Modern Movement deplore the ways in which 19th century architects ignored develop-ments in technology, taking refuge instead in the Gothic Revival and Academic Revivalism in general, not to mention the Arts and Crafts.

The pioneers of the Modern Movement looked to industrial vernacu-lar and, given such examples, it is hardly surprising that the Moder-nists of the 1960s should be thrilled by the prospects of more recent industrial innovation.

There was much innovation in the 60s, stemming from industrial and electronic research, air transport systems, communications and

Fig. 9.23 Mies van der Rohe (1954–58): Seagram Building (now 375 Park Avenue, New York); redundant I-section (author's photograph).

'the vast enterprises of war' – not to mention the space program. Since society gave priority to these, few of the innovations were applicable to architecture. So rather than playing with what Venturi calls: electronic expressionism architects should accept their more modest roles as: 'combiner(s) of significant old clichés, valid banalities – in new contexts'.

By doing which, moreover, they could 'ironically express' their legitimate distaste for the ways in which society was pursuing its 'inverted scale of values'.

He refers to Kenneth Burke's 'perspective by incongruity' suggesting that this also is found in Pop Art which gives: 'uncommon meaning to common elements by changing their context and increasing their scale'. As he says: 'old clichés in new settings achieve rich meanings . . . ambiguously . . . old and new, banal and vivid'.

Having described this approach to architecture, Venturi extends it to the larger urban scale. For just as individual buildings cannot be freed of the honky-tonk elements which others stick on them, neither can the landscape nor the townscape.

Architects and planners who try to get them removed 'flaunt their impotence' and put at risk any further influence they might have had as experts. They ought, instead, by slight adjustments, 'modifying or adding conventional elements . . . gain a maximum of effect through a minimum of means . . . make us see the same thing in a different way'.

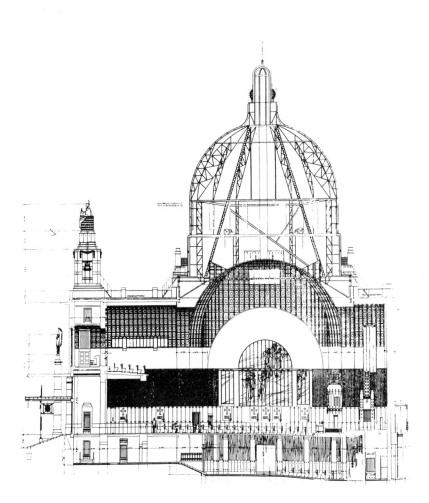

Fig. 9.24 Otto Wagner: Church at Steinhoff, Vienna showing external and internal domes (from Geretsegger and Peintner, 1979).

Fig. 9.25 St Basil's Cathedral
Circulation space between chapels and
external wall (author's photograph).

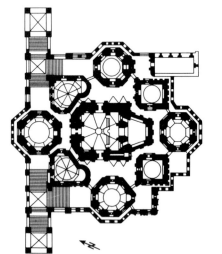

Fig. 9.26 Postnik and Barma (1555–61)
St Basil's Cathedral, Moscow. Plan
showing arrangement of chapels as
'detached linings' with circulation
spaces between them.

He finds precedents for what he calls 'contradictions adapted' in the Piazza di San Marco of which he says:

> The consistent spatial order . . . is not without its violent contradictions in scale, rhythm, and textures, not to mention the varying heights and styles of the surrounding buildings.

He then makes what many people see as a surprising, if not indeed shocking comparison:

> Is there not a similar validity to the vitality of Times Square (New York) in which the jarring inconsistencies of buildings and billboards are contained within the consistent order of the space itself?

Contained and consistent honky-tonk he suggests has its own validity and excitement. Only when it spills out into the no-man's land of roadtown does it become banal.

He goes on to challenge the Modern Movement idea that the internal spaces of a building should be expressed by its external form. In extreme cases, indeed, such as Mies's Barcelona Pavilion external space flows into the building to the extent that exterior and interior are one.

But Venturi suggests: 'Designing from the outside in, as well as (from) the inside out, creates necessary tensions, which help make

Fig. 9.27 St Basil's Cathedral 18th century external wall containing the chapels each of which is 'expressed', externally, by its own spire (author's photograph).

architecture. Since the inside is different from the outside, the wall – the point of change – becomes an architectural event'. And what is of crucial importance: 'by recognising the difference between the inside and the outside, architecture opens the door once again to the urbanistic point of view'. In other words, it makes urban design possible again!

Curiously enough, Venturi fails to quote the most obvious examples: the domes of the great Renaissance cathedrals such as Saint Peter's and St Paul's. For each of these is layered in a very particular way. Each has an internal dome, in scale with the building's interior, and a structure above this to support a higher, external dome in scale with the surrounding city (Fig. 9.24).

He finds many more examples of the 'unattached lining which produces .. . . additional space(s) between the lining and the external wall' and even Russian-doll like nestings of spaces within the external form, in, say, the great Baroque Churches and even Soane's Breakfast Room.

Detached linings obviously leave spaces between themselves and the containing walls and even between each other. In St Basil's Cathedral in Moscow, for instance (Figs 9.25–9.27), the chapels are so separated by linings and circulation spaces that one perceives a central Chapel surrounded by eight separate ones in octagonal formation.

Frank Lloyd Wright of course insisted that the external forms of his buildings should grow organically out of the interior spaces. Which of course is what happened in his Guggenheim Museum – a vast, spiral

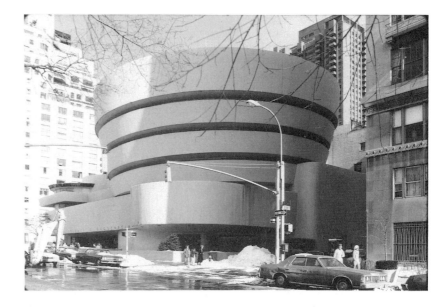

Fig. 9.28 Frank Lloyd Wright (1956) Guggenheim Museum, New York. The internal spiral is 'expressed' externally thus destroying the street line (author's photograph).

ramp, expressed directly by the external form, highly disruptive to the street (Fig. 9.28). But the Morris Shop in San Francisco has a similar, if smaller, spiral ramp contained within a rigid square (Fig. 9.29). Which leads to the most important of Venturi's urban insights:

> Contradiction, or at least contrast, between the inside and the outside is an essential characteristic of urban architecture.

In the last theoretical chapter of his book Venturi addresses the most intractable of all his problems: how to discharge his Obligation Towards the Difficult Whole. He is, of course, looking for a 'difficult unity through inclusion rather than . . . easy unity through exclusion'. Venturi's difficult whole includes 'multiplicity and diversity of elements in relationships that are inconsistent' or, at least, are, in terms of perception 'among the weaker kind'.

He has some fairly conventional views on how unity may be achieved although he does not go into quite so much detail as, say, Christian Norberg-Schultz (1963) or Rob Krier (1988).

The easiest kind of unity, of course, is achieved by using large, pure and simple elements, as Boullée did, such as a sphere, a cube or a pyramid but, paradoxically, unity can also be achieved by extreme multiplicity of some kind. Venturi could have cited, although he doesn't, Action Painting, of the kind which Jackson Pollock used to do in which there are so many tiny dribbles of paint, complex and contradictory in form and direction, that one reads the canvas as a *whole*. And of course one may read a labyrinthine plan as a unity of this kind not to mention a complex elevation. Such readings, or so Venturi suggests, will occur 'through a tendency of the parts to change scale, and to be perceived as an overall pattern or texture'.

Fig. 9.29 Frank Lloyd Wright (1948) Morris Gift Shop, San Francisco. The brick wall to the street line masks the internal planning around a circular ramp (author's photograph).

He looks at Heirarchies in which one part dominates the others. Indeed one element – such as the dome of St Peter's – may be a dominant binder. But an element a good deal less dominant than this might well be used to hold a duality together. Or two elements, each complete in itself, may be inflected towards each other (Fig. 9.30).

Since these – and other compositional devices – are available (see, for instance Norberg-Schultz, 1963), any building, however complicated, can be unified if that is what one wants. But Venturi is by no means sure that all buildings should be unified anyway.

Poets and playwrights often leave their characters in unresolved situations. We may well prefer a late, unfinished Michelangelo in which the figure is not quite released from the stone to one of his earlier, completed and smoothly polished works. So why should buildings – or urban layouts – always be complete?

Venturi had been stung into writing as he did by Peter Blake's photographic Essay on *God's Own Junkyard*. In which, among many other things, Blake had contrasted the splendid, calm orderliness of Jefferson's Campus for the University of Virginia with the 'chaos of commercial Main Street'.

Which for Venturi was quite irrelevant. So he posed his fundamental questions: '. . . is not Main Street almost alright? Indeed, is not the commercial strip of Route 66 almost alright?'

He thought they were and all they needed were slight twists of context, giving, for instance 'more signs more contained' within a given area. Venturi points out that in some of Blake's photographs or, rather, in their composition as photographs, 'there is an inherent sense of unity not far from the surface'. The crucial point, of course, is that this 'is not the obvious or easy unity derived from the dominant binder or the motival order of simpler, less contradictory compositions'. It is, rather: 'that derived from a complex and illusive order of the difficult whole'.

Or, again in Heckscher's (1962) words, it is the unity which:

> maintains, but only just maintains, control over the clashing elements which oppose it. Chaos is very near; its nearness, but its avoidance, gives . . . force.

Pop art has a great deal to teach us, with its contradictions of scale and context as, for instance, in Jasper Johns's laying of three American flags, at different scales, on top of each other. . . . These, in themselves, should have 'awakened architects from prim dreams of pure order' (Fig. 9.32).

And so Venturi concludes:

> it is perhaps from the everyday landscape, vulgar and disdained, that we can draw the complex and contradictory order that is valid and vital for our architecture as an urbanistic whole.

Venturi 2

Learning from Las Vegas

In *Learning from Las Vegas* (1972) Venturi, Scott Browne, Izenour and their Class of 1968 at the University of Pennsylvania sought, among other things, to apply certain principles which they had outlined in an Essay (1968) on *A Significance for A & P Parking Lots*. They took the view that, since for years, architects had been looking outside architecture for formal inspiration: the 18th century Romantics had looked at rustic cottages, Le Corbusier at grain elevators and steamships, Mies at American steel factories, and so on, they might look at the popular architecture of their time to see what *that* had to offer.

Since popular vernacular at its most exuberant was to be found along the commercial strips which line the approaches to many American cities, Scott Brown decided that her students should analyse the most exhuberant of them all: the Las Vegas Strip. The Strip is lined, not only

Fig. 9.30 Carlo Rainaldi Piazza del Popolo, Rome (1662–78) including, with Bernini (left) S Maria di Monte Santo and with Fontana, (right) S Maria de' Miracoli. Each church is 'unified' within its own symmetry and 'inflected' by its spire towards the other (author's photograph).

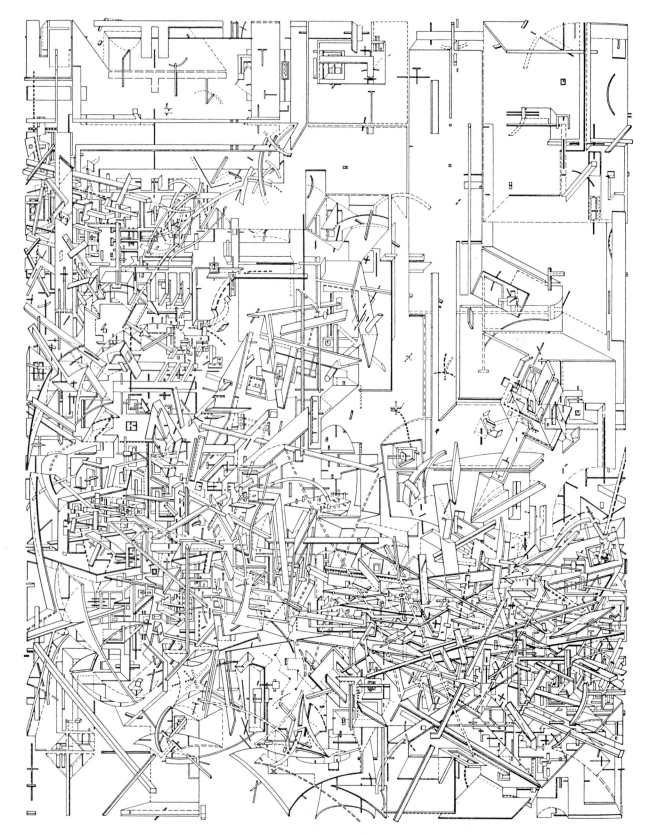

Fig. 9.31 Daniel Libeskind (1979) Arktische Blumen: Arctic Flowers. Although none of the conventional unifying devices is used, such as symmetry or one dominating element complexity extends across the whole surface in such a way as to produce a rich unity of diversity.

with shops, restaurants, motels and even wedding chapels but also with large hotels, their lobbies containing large casinos (Fig. 9.33).

Strip architecture in general, of course, had been villified by Peter Blake in *God's own Junkyard* (1964) which, indeed he subtitled: *The Planned Deterioration of America's Landscape*.

Scott Brown, however, argued that there was rather more to The Strip than that, which is why she had her students analyse it as 'a phenomenon of architectural communication'. The students were not to be concerned with the morality of commercial advertising, gambling interests and the competitive instinct any more than the engineer, analysing Gothic structures, need concern himself with the morality of medieval religion.

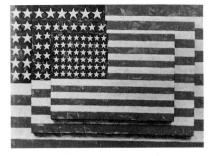

Fig. 9.32 Jasper Johns (1958) Three Flags. These, superimposed at three different scales produce a further kind of unity.

It was to be a study, not of content, but of method and indeed, one of the required texts was my own account of the *Conference on Design Methods* which we had held at Portsmouth in 1967!

Scott Brown found it strange that architects:

> who can accept the lessons of primitive vernacular . . . so (easily) take in an exhibit like Architecture without Architects . . . industrial vernacular architecture . . . adapt to . . . electronic and space vernacular as elaborate neo-Brutalist or neo-Constructivist megastructures, do not (as) easily acknowledge the validity of the commercial vernacular. (Source: Venturi, Scott Brown and Izenour, 1972)

They were obsessed by the idea of space, bewitched by the Italian piazza as a 'pedestrian-scaled . . . intricately enclosed space' and simply could not take in the fact that traversing Route 66, at automobile speed, was also a rewarding spatial experience. Nor, seeing space as, they did, as the essential ingredient of architecture, could they tolerate the idea of architecture as painting or even architecture as sculpture.

Architecture, for them, was supposed to consist of 'space and form at the service of program and structure'. Which meant that the eclectic architecture of the 19th century dressed as it was in historical styles evoking: 'explicit associations and Romantic allusions to the past to convey literary, ecclesiastical, national, or programmatic symbolism' was anathema to them.

Fig. 9.33 Las Vegas Strip: as rich in its complexity as Libeskind's drawing but by no means so evenly distributed and therefore not so unified (author's photograph).

Yet throughout the history of architecture, from Egyptian times to the early 20th century, there had been 'a tradition of iconology' in which 'painting, sculpture, and graphics were combined with architecture'.

The pure, abstract forms of Modernism were supposed to convey whatever meaning was necessary 'through the inherent, physiognomic characteristics of (their) form(s)'.

In truth, of course, their forms *had* been derived from current art movements – abstract painting and machine-forms – whilst more recent Modernists, such as Archigram, had turned 'while similarly protesting' to Pop art and the space industry.

So the Modernists, after all, encouraged the expression of meaning as long as the right meanings – abstract or machine-form – were conveyed. For which reason they refused to tolerate 'representational architecture along (the) highways'.

The Las Vegas team call the roadside architecture of styles and signs antispatial. As they say, 'it is an architecture of communication *over* space; communication *dominates* space as an element in the architecture and in the landscape' (my emphases).

That landscape, so they say, is new in scale. Nineteenth century eclecticism 'evoked subtle and complex meanings' which could be savoured 'in the docile spaces of traditional landscape'.

But the roadside strip, in its new eclecticism: 'provokes bold impact in the vast and complex setting of a new landscape, (a landscape) of big spaces, high speeds, and complex programs'. As one speeds across this landscape one makes connections between a great different styles and signs 'far apart and seen fast'. What unites them, of course, are the messages they convey which are all 'basely commercial'. There is nothing new in displaying that kind of message, but: 'the context is basically new'.

As Banham suggested (1973) the driver on the freeway *may* have a sense of direction. He may know that his destination lies to the left of his present route. But to reach it he has to follow, not his own knowledge of where his destination lies, but the *signs* which tell him that *in order to go left* he must, in fact, start with a turn to the right.

This dominance of signs over space is also true at pedestrian scale – and speed – in such large and complex buildings as airports. Which of course conflicts with the Modernist view that: 'If the plan is clear, you

Fig. 9.34 Las Vegas Strip (author's photograph).

can see where to go'. Thus according to the team who went to Las Vegas:

> complex programs and settings require complex combinations of media (far) beyond the purer architectural triad of structure, form, and light at the service of space. They suggest an architecture of bold communication rather than one of subtle expression.

Arriving in Las Vegas with such thoughts in mind the team found that the signs 'hit' them even before they landed at the airport. They found that the message systems were of three kinds:

1. heraldic signs such as those at the kerbside
2. physiognomic signs in which messages are given by the face of the building itself; the balconies and regularly spaced windows which say *hotel*; the spire added to a bungalow which says *wedding chapel* and so on
3. locational signs by which service stations are found on corner lots, casinos in front of the hotels, and valet parking in front of the casinos.

Among other things they point out that whereas according to Information Theory there would be far too much 'noise' along the Las Vegas Strip, most people actually *do* find what they are looking for!

The Las Vegas team plot a hierarchy of persuasive devices, from the Arab *souk* in which there are no *signs* of these Western kinds; buyers are persuaded by the smell and feel of the goods on sale, not to mention explicit oral persuasion by the salesmen (Fig. 9.35). But as the scale of signage increases to that of the medieval street, the (American) Main Street, the Commercial Strip, the Las Vegas Strip to the Shopping Center; so (verbal) signs become increasingly important. What is more, on the whole, pedestrian signs are parallel with the street – along the frontages of buildings; above shops, behind their windows, and so on. Whereas signs for drivers have to be larger in scale and, on the whole: 'at right angles to the street'.

They suggest that as our speed increases so our cone of vision diminishes; that as we pass under overhead signs these increase our sense of speed and that moving objects are more likely to attract our attention than static ones.

The buildings along the American Strip of course have their vast A & P Parking Lots which the Las Vegas team compare in more than scale to Versailles. They see the parking lot as 'a current phase in the evolution of vast space since Versailles'. It lies somewhere between the scale of the high-speed highway and the low, sparsely distributed buildings which provide no sense of enclosure and not much in the way of direction either. The parking lot, they say:

> is the *parterre* of the asphalt landscape. The patterns of parking lines give direction much as the paving patterns, curbs, borders, and *tapis vert* give direction at Versailles; grids of lamp posts substitute for obelisks, rows of urns and statues as points of identity and continuity in the vast space.

Clearly they wrote that tongue-in-cheek but they go on to point out that:

> the highway signs, through their sculptural forms or pictorial silhouettes, their particular positions in space, their inflected

Fig. 9.35 Pharmacist in the souk in Jeddah. He has no need of lettered signs. The sights and smells of the goods he sells, not to mention his presence, are suffficient to attract his customers (author's photograph).

shapes, and their graphic meanings that identify and unify the megatexture.

These signs make 'verbal and symbolic connections through space', they communicate 'a complexity of meanings through hundreds of associations'. And, what is more, they do this 'in a few seconds from far away'. So it is that: 'Symbols dominate space. Architecture is not enough'.

The most important spatial relationships along the Strip are not those between the buildings. They are, rather, those between the *signs*. So: 'The big sign and the little building is the rule on route 66'.

So the space of Las Vegas is neither confined by buildings, as medieval space had been. Nor was it balanced and proportioned in the manner of Renaissance space; swept up in 'rhythmical ordered movement' like Baroque space nor free-flowing around the urban space markers – the separated pavilions of the Modern Movement.

So, they ask, how can one use the tools developed for analysing traditional urban space in this completely new kind of space?

Once the sign becomes more important than the building itself, it swallows up most of the budget: 'The sign at the front is a vulgar extravaganza, the building at the back, a modest necessity'.

Sometimes, of course, the building itself *is* the sign as in the case of the 30 foot, Big Duck which Peter Blake (1964) discovered at Riverhead on Long Island (Fig. 9.36b). The Duck was designed, in 1931, by William Collins for Martin Maurer, a highly successful commercial producer of ducks. Given the quality of his product, and a convenient location, Maurer felt that the only way to increase his – very respectable – sales was to have a gimmick of some kind (Andrews, 1984).

Anyone seeing Maurer's Duck, of course, recognizes it as looking like a duck and, given its location, would be likely to read it for what it is – a building for selling ducks and eggs.

The Las Vegas team therefore chose Maurer's Duck as their perfect example of a building which looks 'like' what it is *for* and therefore they used it as the paradigm of all buildings which look like what they are or what they are for. Which enables them to distinguish between three quite different ways of displaying function: the Las Vegas way, of placing a Big Sign at the kerbside in front of a Little Building; the

Fig. 9.36 (a) Duck and decorated shed (from Venturi *et al.*, 1972). *(b)* William Collins (1931): The Big Duck, Riverhead, Long Island (from Blake, 1964).

alternative Las Vegas way of designing an efficient building and then covering the façade with signs – they call this a Decorated Shed; and thirdly the making of a building which looks like what it is for; they call all such buildings Ducks (Fig. 9.36a).

Having described these three ways of giving meanings to buildings, the team then looked at various ways of analysing two quite different parts of Las Vegas, The Strip where the major Casino-Hotels are located and Fremont – the Downtown Street consisting largely of close-spaced casinos. This close-spacing on Fremont of course means that the buildings, and the lights, are packed rather more densely than such things are on The Strip (Fig. 9.37).

They plotted both of these places on plan; in the manner of Nolli (see p. 268 and endpapers) as external and internal public spaces, in terms of land use, transportation – movement and stopping – intensity of signification – including illumination levels – and so on.

In their Nolli Plan of Fremont, for instance, the solid parts of the buildings, forming the *poché* are formed, not just of walls and structural columns, but of gambling machines since these define the public internal spaces much more than the buildings themselves do. The public, after all, have to thread between the machines.

As they point out, whilst the Street and the Strip are both lined with casinos, Fremont and The Strip are rather different in character. Since Fremont is Downtown, where land-values are high, it is lined continuously with casinos – with an occasional cross-street. Thus the Golden Horseshoe, The Mint, the Golden Nugget and the Lucky Casino can all be encompassed in a single photograph.

By contrast on The Strip land-use is far less intensive. Not only are there parking lots in front of the casinos and hotels, there are also rather large gaps in which the desert, literally, comes right to the road side.

From which the Las Vegas team concluded that Fremont – almost as dense as an Arab market – is a pedestrian-scaled street – whereas The Strip, with its long frontages – and gaps – is scaled for driving at automobile scale, and speed.

Which presents a certain problem. As they say, the façade of the Stardust Hotel is covered by a 600 foot computer-animated neon sign. This works through a five-minute sequence, as does the kerbside sign.

Fig. 9.37 Las Vegas: Fremont. The far greater density of signs than one sees on The Strip mean that this is a pedestrian street (author's photograph).

So, literally, to see the whole sequence one has to stand and stare for five minutes which is quite impossible for the motorist. No doubt the Las Vegas team would argue that all one needs to see, as one drives past, is that the sign *is* changing; that it is by no means important to see whole sequence. But having watched the sequence, many times, I disagree.

The second part of *Learning from Las Vegas* is devoted to more general questions to do with: Ugly and Ordinary Architecture and the Decorated Shed. Indeed these are defined as two main manifestations:

1. where the architectural systems of space, structure, and program are submerged and distorted by an overall symbolic form; this kind of building-becoming-sculpture they call the *duck*
2. where systems of space and structure are directly at the service of the program, and ornament is applied independently of them; this they call the *decorated shed*.

They compare in great detail two housing blocks: Paul Rudolph's Crawford Manor (1962–66) and their own Guild House for old people (1960–63) to elaborate on the differences, describing Guild House as 'An architecture of meaning' and Crawford Manor as 'An architecture of expression'.

They point out that most great buildings in history, in one way or another, have been Decorated Sheds. The west end of a Gothic cathedral, with its porches, towers and spires, in no way expresses the section of the nave which lies immediately behind. The front is a kind of Bill Board, decorating the cathedral itself although this, consisting of nave, transepts and sanctuary, with their external expression of structure may indeed, in itself, be a Duck.

The Renaissance palazzo also, with its sturdy stone walls pierced by arched or flat-lintelled windows, often has architecture carved on to it, in the form of pilasters and string courses. The latter, not to mention pediments and cornices, *may* help to protect the wall surfaces from the weather but these horizontal elements cannot form a complete *architectural* system in themselves. They need totally non-structural columns or pilasters carved on *as decoration to the shed* (Fig. 9.38). Mies van der Rohe, having designed a structural steel frame of columns and beams encased in concrete, then had I-sections in steel, or even bronze, fixed to the outside for structural expression. Seagram too is a Decorated Shed.

Unlike, say, Le Corbusier's more sculptural buildings which are, unequivocally, Ducks.

So Venturi and Scott Brown conclude what they and their students learned from Las Vegas:

> When Modern architects righteously abandoned ornament on buildings, they unconsciously designed buildings that *were* ornament (in themselves). In promoting Space and Articulation over symbolism and ornament, they distorted the whole building into a duck . . . substituted for the innocent and inexpensive practice of applied decoration on a, conventional shed the rather cynical and expensive distortion of program and structure to promote a duck; mini-megastructures are mostly ducks. It is now time to re-evaluate the once-horrifying statement of John Ruskin that architecture is the decoration of construction, but we should append the warning of Pugin: it is all right to decorate construction but never (to) construct decoration.

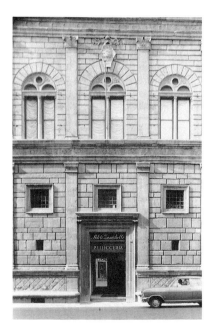

Fig. 9.38 Leon Battista Alberti (from 1453) Palazzo Rucellai, Florence. The 'architecture' of pilasters, string courses and joints, carved into the plain stone surface make this a prototype 'decorated shed' (author's photograph).

Robert Stern

Venturi presents a comprehensive argument for rethinking architecture and urban space design in 'Complex' and 'Contradictory' terms. Robert Stern (1977) has more specific things to say about the forms of the buildings by which urban spaces are enclosed in terms of their character. He articulates three principles, or at least attitudes, which he sees as basic to Post-Modern design. They are:

1. Contextualism, in which the individual building is seen as part of a larger whole. 'Contextualism is a slogan of affirmation in the belief that buildings (which) refer and defer to (those) around them gain strength over those that do not . . .'. Contextualism 'holds out the possibility', may even insist 'that the form, colour, and scale of the new building' may – perhaps even should – be closely related to that of any existing building it abuts;

2. Allusionism, in which architecture is 'an act of cultural and historical response'. It is not to be confused, says Stern with simplistic eclecticism based on pat, predigested images from the past. It suggests, rather, 'that there are lessons to be learned from the history of architecture . . . from engineering and (the) behavioural sciences'. Above all allusionism suggests: 'that the history of buildings is the history of meaning in architecture'. Postmodernist allusionism can take many forms: the (scenographic) recapturing of an entire mood . . . the incorporation into new work of recognizable fragments from the past 'for semantic or empathic purposes'. Indeed, 'Recognisable elements from different moments in the past can be mixed up to heighten the viewer's perceptions of the architect's – and the client's – intentions';

3. Ornamentalism, in which the wall is used 'as the medium of architectural meaning'. Allusionism of course may determine that ornament of a certain kind be used but for Stern: 'the decoration of the vertical plane need not be justified in historical or cultural terms . . . the decorated wall responds . . . to. . . . An innate human need for elaboration and an instinct to measure building-size in relation to human-size'.

Charles Moore

Whilst Venturi and Stern display an implicit Empiricism in their work, Charles Moore articulates his interest. The fullest presentation of his views from this point of view occurs in *Body, Memory and Architecture* (1977) which he wrote with Kurt Bloomer.

Having described our intuitive responses to architecture, they discuss the limitations of a functionalist, mechanistic approach suggesting that we might break away from this by studying the philosophy of perception of the kind outlined here in Chapter 2. They also explore the psychology of perception, as it has developed during the 20th century. They examine Body-Image Theory; Body, Memory and Community. Robert Yudell contributes a chapter on Body Movement, drawing, naturally enough, on Dance.

Dancers, they suggest, speak of 'feeling' space. They learn to think of it as real 'stuff' which they can 'hold, push, pull, and touch'. More than the rest of us they 'feel a critical relationship to the space outside their bodies'. Above all they understand the significance of movement in terms of front/back; left/right and up/down. Thus: Movement upward can be interpreted as a metaphor of growth, longing, and reaching, and movement downwards as one of absorption, submersion and compression. Similarly movement in a horizontal plane is identified, by the great choreographer Laban as 'the zone of communication and' social interaction' (Bloomer and Moore, 1977).

The choreographer, of course, plans and directs the three-dimensional movements which dancers will make on a – usually – horizontal stage. The architect designs a three-dimensional stage around which people are obliged to move. Buildings, in other words, 'can encourage a choreography of dynamic relationships among the persons moving within their domains'. So the architect, too, whether he likes it or not, is a choreography of other people's movements in space. Since this is inevitable, he might as well do it with conviction, providing sequences of movement which people find interesting and enjoyable.

There is much more to this slight but stimulating book including analyses of Human identity in Memorable Places, including the Acropolis of Athens; Stonington, Connecticut; Wright's Winslow House; Zimmermann's Baroque Church of die Wies; Moore's own Burns House and Kresge College.

Kresge College (1966–74)

As one might expect of Empiricist designers; Moore and Turnbull; Kresge College is a serious response to user needs, climate, economics (hence the cheap construction) and so on. Indeed one has to criticize the construction; balloon-frame vernacular, with exposed board surfaces, which even in the California climate can soon look tatty. But freshly painted as it was before our 1980 visit it looked just as bright and cheerful as one expected from photographs taken when it was new (Fig. 9.39).

William Turnbull had drawn up a Master Plan for the University of California at Santa Cruz in 1967. This included a number of residential colleges, one of which (no. 6) was located to the west, where the site was bounded by steep ravines with rocky knolls and groves of redwood.

Moore and Turnbull had completed their plan for a college on this site by 1969 but State funds were available only for classrooms, laboratories, administration and faculty offices. But a private donation

Fig. 9.39 MLTW/Moore-Turnbull (with Buchanan, Calderwood and Simpson) (1966–74): Kresge College, University of California at Santa Cruz: entrance arch (author's photograph).

had been received from the Kresge family for reading-rooms, common rooms, conference rooms, residential accommodation and so on. The college had existed for two years as a body of people housed in temporary accommodation and the Assistant Provost, Michael Kahn, had taught at the Institute of Behavioural Studies in Southern California; he and the Provost, Robert Edgar, believed that the fundamental unit of the social and learning environment should be the encounter-group, that is the 'kin-group' of about 25 students who lived and worked together with a faculty leader. Once the idea of kin-groups had been established, certain large facilities were broken into smaller units, thus the main dining-room was abandoned to be replaced by a co-operative food shop and 'family' kitchens for the students in residence and a coffee shop for those who commute.

In 1970 they established a course on 'Creating Kresge College' which drew enthusiastic responses from the students. One particular group of students, Ashbaugh, Palmer, Wulfing and Kramartz attempted to define the students' environmental needs, using survey techniques; these included types of accommodation, furniture, attitudes towards public space and privacy, eating facilities and so on. These suggested that the various kinds of accommodation: administrative, academic, residential and social facilities ought to be interspersed, whilst instead of the 'dorms' which are the normal units of residence on American campuses, there ought to be a mixture of eight-person units, and four-person units in the various apartment buildings. There was a demand also for octet units, that is two-storey open living spaces each for eight (very friendly) students. In the event, four of these were built.

Moore and Turnbull worked with great ingenuity to accommodate these 'needs' and designed a college which, instead of being grouped around a conventional quad which in any case would have been difficult on this particular site, takes the form of a 1000 foot L-shaped street along which administrative, academic, residential and social accommodation are interspersed (Fig. 9.40).

They devised a highly flexible system of residential accommodation in which each student would be provided with knock-down, space-making elements which could be used as required on a simple do-it-yourself basis. This proved unacceptable to the various bureaucracies but still Moore and Turnbull produced a certain flexibility. Indeed, architects and students together decided on a modular system, a Finnish one, based on cubes which could be built up in many configurations. In addition to a basic set of cubes, each student was given a desk top, a bedboard, foam mattress and a director's chair. They also decided on the mix of residential unit-forms – including the required octets – and on the unit furniture which can be put together in various configurations.

In one respect they overdid their provision for user needs. The students of the late 1960s who participated in the design had a particular concept of togetherness, which centred on the washrooms. They felt there was nowhere quite like the showers for getting to know each other. But the students who actually moved into Kresge took quite a different view of these things. For them, the kitchen was the centre of socialization, and the original kitchens were too small. They were, in fact, later extended but each at the loss of a study-bedroom. I know of no clearer example of the basic problem underlying partici-pation – that the (extreme) tastes of one generation might well be in conflict with (extreme or even normal) tastes of the next.

As for the overall layout, the idea of a street, as distinct from an open quad, was adopted for a number of reasons; firstly because it provides a clear and understandable structure, within which the various

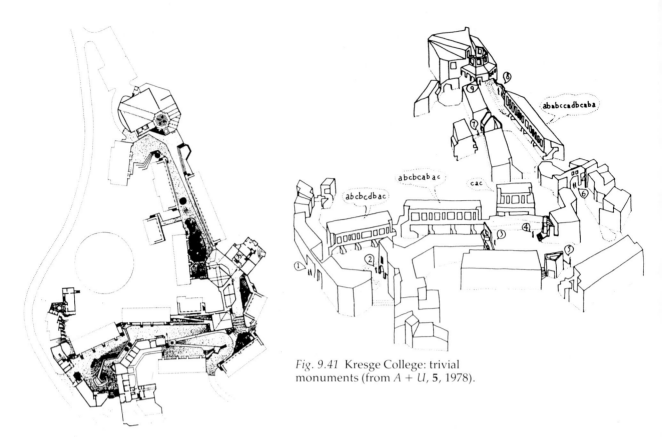

Fig. 9.41 Kresge College: trivial
monuments (from *A + U*, **5**, 1978).

Fig. 9.40 Kresge College: plan (from
A + U, **5**, 1978).

components of the College might be organized; secondly because its
linear form established an easy link for pedestrians from one part to
another of the College and to other parts of the University; and,
thirdly, because the street itself, like any village street, is a focus for
communal activities. The buildings also have backs which face on to
the forest, thus offering privacy and quiet. But the forest itself is so
thick and the buildings themselves so closed on that side that one
cannot really move along the backs. The students, indeed, are forced to
use the street as their major circulation route and this, together with
the fact that most buildings have balconies looking on to the street,
made them feel that they were 'on show'. The octets and the 'on stage'
nature of being in the street means that Kresge is no place for
introverts.

At first sight, the buildings which actually line the street are in
conflict with the picturesque intentions. For, in their general forms,
they look like nothing so much as those stark, white, linear houses
which Le Corbusier built for the Weissenhof Siedlung in Stuttgart
(1927). Yet in a sense the starkness of the buildings reinforces the point
that, in picturesque planning, it is the urban spaces themselves that
have the greatest effect, rather than the buildings which line them. It
would, indeed, have been interesting if, Nogues, Reventos and their
colleagues in Barcelona, Moore and Turnbull had lined their street
with measured reproductions from the American West. But then the
streets of the American West tend to be straight and wide, with no
particular sense of enclosure. We can see what an assemblage of
measured reproductions from the West might have looked like in the
two Main Streets, USA built for the California Disneyland (1955) and
the Florida Disneyworld. Somehow this is the wrong architecture to be
grouped around the picturesque street which Moore and Turnbull had
planned.

The buildings themselves take that characteristic Moore and Turn-bull form of pierced parallel white-painted plates, layered in front of each other. The front layer contains large, unglazed openings, arched or rectangular in form, with open access to galleries between them and the actual façades, with their smaller, rectangular window openings. The inner faces of the outer plates are colour coded, bright red at the bottom of the street shading through orange to yellow at the top. The rear façades of the various buildings, facing on to the forest, are painted in a dark ochre colour for camouflage against the forest. As Woodbridge (1974) says, the actual construction – in timber frame – is akin to the basic low-cost building contractor's vernacular, which almost certainly will deteriorate with time. But she supposes that the buildings themselves will inspire a certain affection, whilst the architects' encouragement of do-it-yourself may well inspire a continuous process of rebuilding. Certainly they looked well, repainted after some ten years of use.

The street itself is punctuated by a number of incidents (Fig. 9.41), starting at the lower end with a monumental gateway which opens on to an arena with a system of steps which spiral down to a central drain. There is a post office – administrative offices (Fig. 9.42) – to the right of the arena and, beyond that, the Provost's house. The Main Street, lined with student residences, ascends past the post office to a laundry – surmounted by an observation platform – a pair of telephone booths, reached by monumental steps and celebrated by a rainbow arch (Fig. 9.43) a student speakers' rostrum which stands, approached by steps, over the garbage cans (Fig. 9.44). Indeed, it faces the viewing platform

Fig. 9.42 Kresge College: Post Office – Administration Building (author's photograph).

thus inviting a dialogue of speakers. The street turns left and levels out at this point. One passes under another triumphal arch and reaches, finally, an octagonal courtyard which used to have a fountain and which gives access to a (Viennese) restaurant.

Turnbull comments on these markers:

> The octagonal court at the upper (northern) end provides an entry to the town hall/assembly and restaurant building.

> The library is denoted by a two-storey gateway. The laundry, a symbolic town watering hole, is emphasized by a rather large triumphal arch (cleanliness is next to godliness). It is echoed across the space of the middle plaza by a raised bandstand, situated to conceal the main trash box.

Moore himself thought of this as a podium or pulpit for student orators, noting its physical location vertically over the garbage. Turnbull continues:

> Other importances, such as telephone booths, are enlarged as street markers to serve as commentary on the importance of communications in student and faculty life.

As Turnbull himself puts it:

> The street creates a center for the College, a place where people meet. It establishes a unique character and identity, setting the place apart from its traditional quadrangle-inspired neighbours. It is a space which organizes and enriches the life of the College in much the same manner that a street does for a village or a small town.

Fig. 9.43 Kresge College: Main Street, telephone booths (author's photograph).

Fig. 9.44 Kresge College: rostrum for student orators (over the garbage cans) (author's photograph).

The architects' encouragement of do-it-yourself does *not* extend to the trellising, with creepers, which students have fixed to the east side of the northern street; an obvious comment on what they saw as architectural blandness (Fig. 9.45). But on the whole they seem very well satisfied, indeed suspiciously so. And then one learns that it is policy for students entering the Santa Cruz campus to be given psychological tests and to be allocated to the college, indeed to the very rooms and room-mates, which have the best chance of suiting their personalities.

So despite Sitte's pessimistic predictions, despite Gaudet's subli-mating of his own picturesque tendencies in favour of more teachable, axial compositions, the Pueblo Espagñol, Cullen's (unbuilt) Mary-culter, Spoerry's Port Grimaud and Kresge College show that, in skilled hands, picturesque planning *can* be achieved.

Kurt Bloomer, with Moore has gone on to describe in their *Body Memory and Architecture* (1977) the principles, based on Empirical philosophy, on which the latter bases his designs. He thinks in terms of sensory inputs – especially those haptic sensations of up/down, back/front, left/right and, above all, in a ballet-dancer-like sense of movement.

Fig. 9.45 Kresge College: Upper Street (author's photograph).

Fig. 9.46 Charles W. Moore Associates and Urban Innovations Group with August Perez Associates (1975–78): Piazza d'Italia, New Orleans: perspective drawing (from *Progressive Architecture*, April 1978).

My own view, which should be perfectly clear by now, is that such an Empirical approach is not only subtler, and more profound intellectually than the simple-minded Rationalist view, but that it has a greater potential – which indeed has been borne out in practice – for generating the kinds of spaces which Sitte, Gaudet, I, and, I suspect, you, find infinitely better to inhabit than the bleaker sterilities of axial planning.

Piazza d'Italia (1975–78)

Whatever the Picturesque intricacies of their planning the urban spaces of Kresge College (*Progressive Architecture*, May 1974) were lined with smooth-faced white walled buildings; as white as anything built by the Modern Movement architects of the 1920s. But the Piazza d'Italia in New Orleans (1977–78) is quite a different matter for here Charles Moore, with his Urban Innovations Group, August Perez and Associates built the full-blown, perhaps one should say full-flooded, St Joseph's Fountain.

This came about because whilst everyone knew what contributions the French, the Spanish and the Blacks had made to the culture of the city, the Italians, somehow, felt less esteemed. And then in a single four-month period during the middle 1970s some 100 buildings were demolished in the Central Business District (Filler, 1978). So the city decided to develop a single block it owned in that area as a 'new symbolic focus – part gathering place and part memorial – (for) the Italian community'.

So a Competition was set up, won by Perez and Associates, who suggested strategies for various 19th century commercial buildings but their scheme lacked the requisite focus. Charles Moore had gained second place by concentrating on such a focus; a fountain, designed as a map of Italy in relief, some 80 feet long, stepping up towards the Alps at the Swiss end and with Italy herself stepped according to her contours in slate, marble, cobblestones and mirrored tiles with (small) cascades of water for the Arno, the Po and the Tiber. He hoped to represent the volcanoes too with perpetual flames but these were impractical (Fig. 9.46).

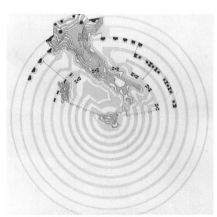

Fig. 9.47 Piazza d'Italia: plan (from *Progressive Architecture*, November 1978).

Italy is set in a Pool, representing the Adriatic and the Tyrrhenian Seas and since most of New Orleans's Italians come from Sicily, a rostrum in the form of Sicily is placed at the centre of a system of concentric circles from which the paving patterns and, more important, colonnades and walls, are generated in concentric circles (Fig. 9.47).

These colonnade-walls are layered much like the balcony-fronts at Kresge except that there are more layers. They are also stepped outwards in radius and increased in height as the radius increases. Thus the innermost of the walls, which crosses the Adriatic, is Tuscan. It steps outwards over the Tyrrhenian Sea to Doric and behind the Tuscan wall is an Ionic one stepping outwards to a Corinthian one and, further out still, behind the Doric there is a Composite one (Fig. 9.48).

Where Italy steps up to Switzerland there is a Triumphal Arch – intended as the entry to a Delicatessen – for which Moore invented a Delicatessen Order, Corinthian, but with hot dogs for the corner volutes. Not that Moore's Corinthian has proper Acanthus leaves. His capitals are stainless steel with tiny jets of water for leaves. But then Moore's Ionic has similar jets in place of egg-and-dart mouldings. His Tuscan has 'wetopes' rather than metopes whilst the very columns of this Tuscan are formed of tiny, downward-spurting water jets to form the flutings of the columns. As Filler says, overwhelmed by all this (1978): 'Moore and his colleagues have manipulated water in ways that one scarcely would have thought possible. But here it is, washing sensuously over the stainless steel arch of the Doric wall, sliding down stucco surfaces surprising richness of texture, dancing in the sunlight in thousands of permutations in the course of a sultry Southern summer afternoon'.

Not surprisingly, after that, Filler describes the Fountain as 'the richest expression of the historical revival in contemporary architecture' comparing it, much to this latter's disadvantage, with Philip Johnson's AT & T. But the question, of course, is why in the last third of the 20th century, Moore, Johnson and others should be designing Classically at all?

The answer, perhaps, is to be found in the 'astonish me' syndrome! In 1919 Sergei Diaghilev instructed the two figures who, more than any others, had changed the nature of their arts in the 20th century; Pablo Picasso and Igor Stravinsky, to do exactly that, to astonish him. They

Fig. 9.48 Piazza d'Italia (author's photograph).

did so by producing music (Stravinsky), settings and costumes (Picasso), unequivocally neo-Classical. For what could be more astonishing, more shocking, than for these two pioneers of the Modern to turn, as it were, full circle?

The only Modern architect to have done that in the 1930s was Giussepe Terragni who, having produced the most significant (Italian) Rationalist buildings, the Novoconum and the Casa del Fascio (both in Como) went on, towards the end of his life, to produce the neo-Classical Pirovani Tomb (1936) in the Cemetery at Como.

The 'astonisher' in the case of American architecture was not so much Moore, or any other practitioner as Arthur Drexler, Curator of Architecture and Design at the Museum of Modern Art in New York who, prompted no doubt by Johnson, mounted an Exhibition late in 1975, of great rendered drawings from the Ecole des Beaux Arts in Paris – the kind of work for which Antoine Gaudet had been responsible in the early years of the century. But Drexler's Exhibition was arranged at a time when architects, world wide, were realizing that the simple geometries of Modernism, the even simpler geometries of Neo-Rationalism, really could not work Pragmatically.

As Drexler (1977) says in his Preface to the lavish book he published after the Exhibition Johnson had actually declared in 1952 that the 'battle of modern architecture has long been won'. Unfortunately, according to Drexler, this was so true that by 1975, 'the theoretical basis of modern architecture is as much a collection of received opinions as were the (Beaux Arts) doctrines it overthrew'.

That theoretical basis of course emerged from the Bauhaus where:

> social concern was reinforced by a preference for treating form as simple geometric elements of unchanging value, at last enabling man's artifacts to be free of the shifting values of historical style. The immutable nature of pure geometry was supposed to make it peculiarly well-suited to the demands of machine production, although there is nothing about machinery that inherently limits it to the replication of simple geometric forms.

The result of this geometric fixation, he says, is 'a brilliant historical style' highly suitable for furniture but in architecture 'its moralizing fixation on utility and industrial technique led to an anti-historical bias'.

Its consequences, according to Drexler, 'have yet to be fully understood' but 'they are all too painfully obvious wherever modern architecture has dealt with the urban environment', for 'to be anti-historical is to be anti-urban'.

But by 1975, so many Beaux Arts buildings had been destroyed that if architects agreed on one thing 'enough to sign manifestos and march on picket lines it is the need to preserve what is left of Beaux-Arts architecture . . .'.

Louis Khan's buildings, and writings, had reminded them that Beaux Arts, like (axial) planning had its virtues and aspects of Beaux Arts education had continued in (American) schools up to the late 1940s.

But whilst they could see virtues in such planning, Modernists could not understand 'the apparent unrelatedness, or independence, of elevation and section from the . . . plan, despite . . . that . . . favourite Beaux-Arts theme . . . correspondence of a building's exterior to its internal organisation'. They were puzzled too by 'the eclectic use of historic styles'. Yet the Beaux-Arts was no more monolithic about such things than the Bauhaus had been about others! So:

Some Beaux-Arts problems, (such as) how to use the past may . . .
be seen . . . as liberating rather than constraining. . . . A more
detached view . . . might . . . provoke a more rigorous critique of
. . . assumptions underlying the architecture of our . . . time.
Now that modern experience . . . contradicts modern faith, we
would be well advised to reexamine our architectural pieties.

Thus Drexler articulated what many seemed to be thinking. Indeed
only five years later, at the Venice Biennale of 1988, some two-thirds of
the architects exhibiting showed Classical influences in their work.

Rowe and Koetter

Collage City

Colin Rowe and Fred Koetter first published their Collage City in 1975.
Like Rossi, the Kriers and others before them they had been greatly
disillusioned by the Utopian schemes of Le Corbusier, not to mention
his many predecessors, from Sir Thomas More onwards. Indeed they
trace an intriguing history – they say cinematic – of the Utopian ideal,
and the various philosophies behind it.

For, as they point out (p. 33) by the late 1940s, Modern Architecture:
'had certainly arrived but the New Jerusalem was not exactly a going
concern; and slowly it began to appear that something had gone
wrong'. Two different oppositions were emerging: 'the cult of townscape and the cult of science fiction'.

They see townscape as 'a cult of English villages, Italian hill towns,
and North African casbahs . . . a matter of felicitous happenings and
anonymous architecture'.

Indeed, they suggest, it had begun to emerge in *The Architectural
Review* in the early 30s. They draw attention, particularly, to two
articles in the *Review* by Amédée Ozenfant, Le Corbusier's erstwhile
associate, who, living in London at the time, urged that rather than
sketching hypothetical plans for the year 3000 – for London or Paris –
architects should accept 'the present, the actual condition of the
English capital! Her past, her present and her immediate future'.

Instead of Utopian visions, Ozenfant was concerned with 'what is
immediately realizable'. He was, in a sense, applying Duchamp's idea
of the ready-made to existing buildings in the city much as he and Le
Corbusier had applied it, fifteen years earlier, to the products of
mass-production: industrial windows, Thonet bentwood chairs and so
on.

Rowe and Koetter found this highly significant for Ozenfant himself
represented a direct connection to Cubist and post-Cubist tradition
within which, of course, collage, the pasting of newspaper cuttings
and other, more-or-less flat objects on to the picture, had played such a
crucial part.

So Townscape itself could be seen, as it were, through collage-
coloured spectacles. It could, in other words, be interpreted 'as a
derivative of the late eighteenth century Picturesque; and, as it
implicated all that love of disorder, cultivation of the individual,
distaste for the rational, passion for the various, pleasure in the
idiosyncratic and suspicion of the generalised which may, sometimes,
be supposed to distinguish the architectural tradition of the United
Kingdom'.

Their other alternative to Modernism, Science Fiction, 'identifies itself with mega-buildings, lightweight throwaways, plug-in variability, over-city grids . . . linear cities, integration of buildings with transport, movement systems and tubes'.

Rowe and Koetter characterize certain works of Superstudio as representing the ultimate Science Fiction city. And they characterize Main Street in the Florida Disneyworld as the ultimate application of Townscape. Naturally enough, they find both of these wanting; sometimes for the same – Utopian – reasons and they conclude their analyses by asking three questions which, paraphrased, are:

1. Why should we be obliged to prefer a nostalgia for the future to a nostalgia for the past?
2. Could not the model city which we carry in our minds allow for our known psychological (they might have added physiological) constitutions?
3. Could not this ideal city behave, at one and the same time, quite explicitly as both theatre of memory and theatre of prophecy?

Given Le Corbusier's very intention, of ensuring sun, space and greenery for everyone, Rowe and Koetter see his *Ville Radieuse* as a setting for Rousseau's noble savage. Indeed Le Corbusier's individual buildings, raised, as they are, on *pilotis*, seem to exist in themselves whilst offering the least possible interaction with the surface of the earth!

Since Le Corbusier's buildings hardly touch the ground, however, they can hardly enclose urban spaces. Rowe and Koetter present a telling comparison, with figure/ground illustrations, between the centre of Parma and that Plan for Saint-Dié by Le Corbusier which, for many years, adorned the dust-covers of English editions of *Towards a New Architecture* (Figs 9.49 and 9.50).

In these figure/ground plans the buildings are black, the spaces between them white and whilst one can read off the Parma plans the streets, squares and courtyards of the medieval city, all one reads from Le Corbusier's Plan are vast open spaces between his abstract buildings. Such streets, squares and paths as there are consist, merely, of level-paved surfaces meandering across the landscape and in no way enclosed by the buildings.

Comparing Le Corbusier's Plan Voisin – his application of the Ville Radieuse to Paris – with Asplund's contemporary (1922) Plan for a

Fig. 9.49 Rowe and Koetter (n.d.): figure/ground plan of Parma (from Rowe and Koetter, n.d.).

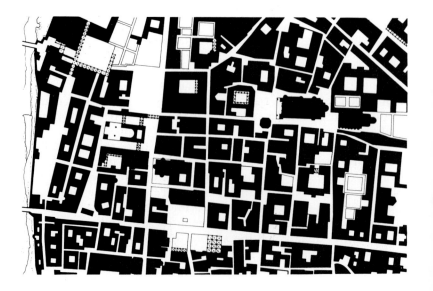

Royal Chancellery in Stockholm they find the latter far more responsive to the grain of the city. Thus they see Le Corbusier's Plan as a statement of historical destiny – design for a reconstructed society, and Asplund's as a statement of historical continuity.

Yet Rowe and Koetter do not dismiss Le Corbusier out of hand. They find that both these ways of looking at the city have their values – spatially as well as sentimentally. Their aim, therefore, is to reconcile the two.

They find clues as to how this might be done in the Palazzo Farnese in Rome and the Hotel de Beauvais in Paris where, in each case, buildings which in themselves are fairly regular are crammed on to quite irregular sites by the use of regular and irregular courtyards.

Like Venturi before them (1966) Rowe and Koetter revive the idea of poché to define 'the imprint upon the plan of the traditional heavy structure' and in these cases also it serves to disengage the principal spaces of the buildings from each other.

Rowe and Koetter attach great importance to the apparent opposition between all-of-a-piece design such as Versailles and the assemblage of fragments such as one sees in Hadrian's Villa at Tivoli. Which leads them to other dichotomies; between design using scientific analysis and design by public participation, between the engineer, who calculates everything precisely and the 'bricoleur' who improvises with whatever happens to be at hand.

They continue with their dichotomies; between, for instance, 17th century Rome and London. They see Rome as:

> . . . that collision of palaces, piazze and villas (surely it should be ville?) . . . that inextricable fusion of implosion and accommodation, that highly resilient traffic jam of intentions, an anthology of closed compositions and *ad hoc* stuff in between, which is, simultaneously, a dialectic of ideal types plus a dialectic of ideal types with empirical content.

This Rome, with its 'assertive identity of subdivisions' leads to an equivalent interpretation of ancient Rome, 'where forum and thermae pieces lie around in conditions of inter-dependence, independence, and multiple interpenetrability'.

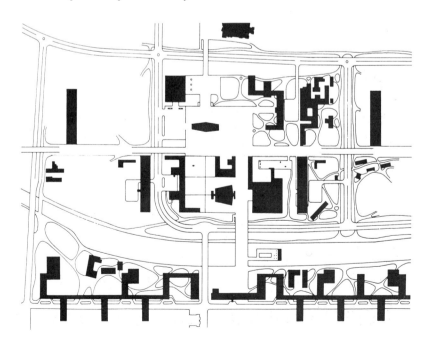

Fig. 9.50 Rowe and Koetter (n.d.): figure/ground relationships in Le Corbusier's Plan for Saint-Die (from Rowe and Koetter, n.d.).

Rowe and Koetter offer Rome, in these and other manifestations, as an alternative to the 'disastrous urbanism of social engineering and total design'.

So again they see an opposition, between 'an abstract, would-be scientific idealism and a concrete, would-be populist empiricism'.

What is more they see Rome as an imploded version of London. Given a much blander topography, enlarging the set-pieces and diluting their impact, they see parallels between the Forum of Trajan and Belgravia, the Baths of Caracalla and Pimlico, the Villa Albani and Bloomsbury, the Villa Giulia and Westbourne Terrace. So the 'bricolage' of Rome, Imperial and Papal, find their 19th century, more or less bourgeoise equivalents in: 'a compilation of rationally gridded field, mostly corresponding to estate structure, with conditions of confusion and picturesque happening in between, mostly corresponding to stream beds, cow tracks, etc. . . . which could only help . . . qualify the virtues of order with the values of chaos'.

So how to reconcile the dichotomies they find!

Rowe and Koetter, of course, are very clear. The dichotomies can only be resolved by what they describe as collage. As they say (p. 144):

> . . . a collage approach, an approach in which objects are conscripted or seduced from out of their context, is – at the present day – the only way of dealing with the ultimate problems of, either or both, utopia or tradition;

They approve collage because as they say of Picasso's Bicycle Seat (1944) – in which the seat forms the head and the handlebars form the horns of a bull's head – Picasso himself, having effected this first translation from bicycle to bull, looked forward to another in which his sculpture, thrown on to a scrap heap, might encourage someone else to put the elements to their original use again.

As Rowe and Koetter say:

> Remembrance of former function and value (bicycles and minotaurs); shifting context; an attitude which encourages the composite; an exploitation and recycling of meaning . . . desuetude of function with corresponding agglomeration of reference; memory; anticipation; the connectedness of memory and wit; this laundry list of reactions to Picasso's proposition; and, since it is a proposition evidently addressed to people, it is in terms such as these, in terms of pleasures remembered and desired, of a dialectic between past and future, of an impacting of iconographic content, of a temporal as well as a spatial collision, that resuming an earlier argument, one might proceed to specify an ideal city of the mind.

What is more:

> the provenance of the architectural objects introduced into the social collage need not be of great consequence. It relates to taste and conviction. The objects can be aristocratic, or they can be 'folkish', academic or popular. Whether they originate in Pergamum or Dahomey, in Detroit or Dubrovnik, whether their implications are of the twentieth or the fifteenth century, is no great matter. Societies and persons assemble themselves according to their own interpretations of absolute reference and traditional value; and, up to a point, collage accommodates both hybrid display and the requirements of self-determination.

10

The competitions

The new and different attitudes to urban space which had been emerging in the 1960s and 1970s were to become quite coherent by the end of the 1970s.

Roma Interrotta

Roma Interrotta was the title of an Exhibition held in Rome in 1978. Michael Graves (1979) traces its origins to a discussion with Piero Sartogo who had been asked to propose the theme for an Exhibition of Urbanism, to be held in Rome (IIA, 1978). They looked at the various historic plans of Rome, published by Frutaz, and decided that, of these, the most interesting by far was one by Nolli (Fig. 10.1).

Graves himself had lectured on the Nolli Plan – actually one of two which Nolli published in 1748 – which he found interesting because:

> . . . it records that sense of figure and void not only in the public domain, but also the semi-public conditions of the major pieces of architecture in the city. He was interested, it seems, in describing not only the plan/surface relationships of street and square but also the ambiguities held in the ground plane by virtue of one's passage from the public external enclosure gesture of public rooms within the buildings.

Nolli, in other words, showed the inside spaces of the larger public buildings in exactly the same way as he showed the public streets and squares; that is to say white, against the general urban texture which he shaded with fine diagonal lines. Or, as Graves puts it: 'The vast housing and commercial stock of the city have been rendered as urban *poché*, while the religious, civic, and state structures have been described in a level of detail which encourages the understanding of the city as a spatial sequence of successive rooms'. By drawing his Plan at ground floor level 'Nolli's description captures more accurately . . . the relationships of piazza to threshold to internal public room with a sense of *marche* or promenade that would be unimagineable using other graphic assumptions'.

Given the problems of printing anything larger in the 18th century, Nolli divided his Rome into three horizontal sections from west to east and four rows from north to south, that is twelve sections in all. Since Nolli's Plan was published in this way the organizers of the Exhibition decided to give one section each to twelve participants.

Some of these sectors, of course, contain some of the finest urban spaces in the world, and some of the world's great monuments. So, starting in the top north-west corner, the most important of these,

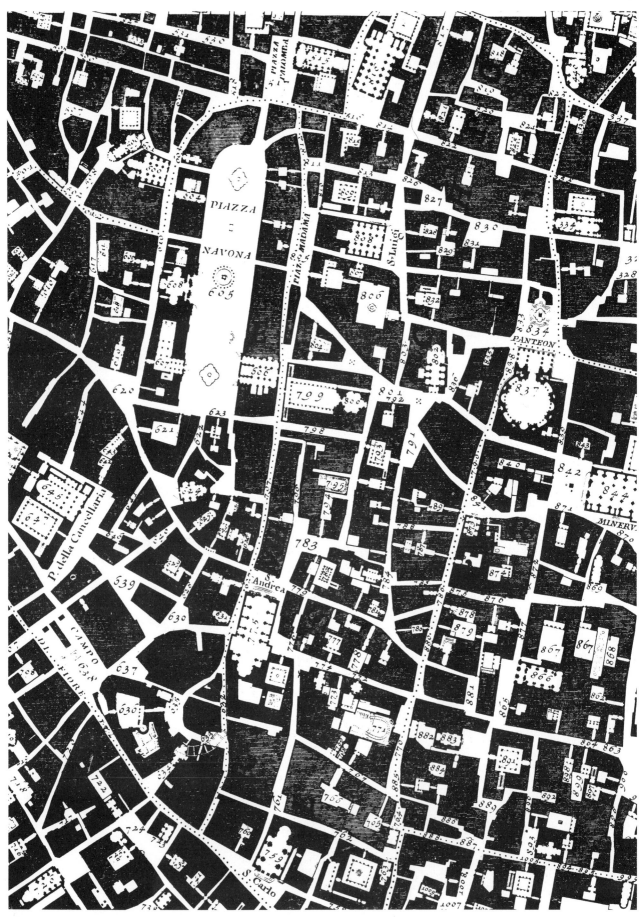

Fig. 10.1 Giambattista Nolli (1748) Rome at the time of Benedict XIV: the Plan of Rome. Sector V including the Piazza Navona and the Pantheon (from Nolli, 1748). *See also* endpapers.

sector by sector, are, moving eastwards: (1) the Vatican and the Castel S. Angelo: Piero Sartoga kept this Sector for himself; (2) had the Mausoleum of Augustus, the Piazza del Popolo, the Piazza de Spagna, the Trevi Fountain and the Quirinale. This they gave to Constantino Dardi; (3) being largely outside the walls had very little building in Nolli's time: but it had the Baths of Diocletian and S. Maria dei Angeli (Antoine Grumbach).

The sectors in Nolli's second row are: (4) the Janiculum which again had very little building in Nolli's time (James Stirling); (5) had the Piazza Navona, the Pantheon, S. Maria sopra Minerva, the Forum of Trajan (Paolo Portoghesi); (6) had the Quirinale. This too was largely outside the walls but it had the vast Baths of Diocletian (Romaldo Giurgola).

And in Nolli's third row: (7) Trastevere, again, was mostly outside the walls and Nolli's drawings in the margin took up about one-third of it (Venturi and Rauch); Sector (8) contained the ancient core of the city, with the Campidoglio, the Forum Romanum and the Colosseum (Colin Rowe); Sector (9) was on the eastern fringes of the city but it had St John Lateran (Michael Graves).

Most of Nolli's fourth row is taken up with a decorative border which, as Aurigemma says (1979) quoting Zänker (1973) includes, in Sector 10 . . . ancient Rome . . . including the Tiber at the Campidoglio, the She-Wolf and the Twins . . . three columns of the Tempio dei Dioscuri, the Colosseum, the Basilica of Maxentius, the arches of Titus, Septimus Severus, and Constantine, the columns of Trajan and Marcus Aurelius, the obelisks of the Lateran and the Esquiline. This Sector was allocated to Rob Krier.

Sector (11) was taken up largely with Nolli's Dedication of the Map to Pope Benedict XIV. But it also contained the Baths of Caracalla. It was allocated to Aldo Rossi.

And finally Sector (12), like Sector (10), was taken up largely with Nolli's marginal drawing, in this case of modern Rome, or at least the Rome which was modern in Nolli's day, represented by a tiarra with, in the background, the Campidoglio and the then new façade of St John Lateran. Leo Krier was given this Sector.

So what did the contributors make of their various sectors in terms of urban space, not to mention the heritage of Rome from various periods?

Given the holiest site of all, Sartoga set out to shock by imposing on to the area colliding buildings of a kind more extreme than anything seen in Rossi. He then devoted some of the major buildings to shocking uses devised, in large part, from Fourier's description of his Phalanstèrie; thus St Peter's and the buildings crashing across it became an Opera House, with Dance, Visual Arts, Poetry, Song, Music and other studios. The Castel S. Angelo became an Orgy Museum and so on.

Dardi in Sector (2) left most of the Rome that Nolli knew but replaced most of the more recent constructions with stratified housing.

Grumbach's contribution to Sector (3) consisted, he says, of reverse archaeology, in which projects designed for the Sector which remained unbuilt, or built only in part, by Winckelman, Ledoux, Pierre Chareau, Bruno Taut, Le Corbusier, Terragni, and J. J. P. Oud were reinstated. Since little had actually been built in this Sector by Nolli's time, these interventions hardly harm his Plan and would indeed have made subsequent developments more coherent, not to say more intriguing.

Stirling, too, proposed a number of interventions for his Sector (4); based almost entirely on his own projects both built and, in rather greater quantity, unbuilt. Since most of this sector, the Janiculum, west of the Tiber, was largely unbuilt – apart from the old city's walls, Stirling hardly violated the Rome of Nolli's time; he recouped the line of the old City Wall with a vastly multiplied length of his student housing for Selwyn College (1959), connected to the Tiber by housing of the kind he had built in Runcorn, crossing the river itself with a Ponte-Vecchio-like platform, based on Stirling's unbuilt scheme for Siemens (1969) leading straight into a bridgehead in the city centre based on his scheme for a Museum in Cologne (1975). Altogether Stirling used some 30 of his buildings or projects each placed, as far as it could be, according to the context offered by Nolli's Rome, the actual topography and so on.

Given Sector (5) one of the most critical in Nolli's Plan, Portoghesi, unlike Sartoga, proposed the slightest of interventions. He took the eastern slope of the Quirinale and tried to reconstruct the ancient topography, on to which he then designed a pattern of winding streets 'tree-like, branched, structures found in northern Latium served as models' and lined them with faceted buildings some four storeys high, of almost Reptonian Picturesqueness.

Giurgiola, in Sector (6), proposed a highly efficient city immediately to the west of the Aurelian Wall with parallel buildings running east–west in serried ranks, whilst outside the wall the open landscape was reinstated to provide, among other things, for the growing of food:

> The walls, which do not have to defend anyone any longer, feed the city. Within them, computerised pipelines have been built to feed food and materials needed by the markets and the workshops uninterruptedly along the perimeter of the whole city. The service has been integrated with large rotating booms supported by aerostats, thus reducing the need for vehicles with heavy loads on the streets

Venturi's sector (7) was largely outside the walls of Nolli's Rome. It also contained part of his marginal drawing showing Trajan's Column, the Temple of the Dioscuri, the Coliseum, the Baths of Caracalla and other monuments of ancient Rome. Venturi touched nothing of Nolli's Rome. He simply replaced Nolli's engraving with one of his own collages from *Learning from Las Vegas*. Even this had a fragment of a colonnade, supporting the sign for Caesar's Palace, whilst Venturi's written text – one of the shortest – merely drew parallels between Rome and Las Vegas. As he says, young Americans, used to the anti-urban scale of the gridiron city, visited Rome in the late 1940s and discovered the scale of the piazza: 'the traditional urban spaces, the pedestrian's scale, the mixtures, yet continuities, of styles . . .'. And two decades later, Venturi suggests, architects 'are perhaps ready for similar lessons about large open space, big scale, and high speed'. For 'Las Vegas is to the Strip what Rome is to the Piazza' (Fig. 10.2).

Venturi discovers other similarities between the two cities: in their siting, for instance, the Campagna and the Mojave Desert. He sees each city also as an archetype rather than a prototype – or Quatremèrean Model – from which others may be derived since each is an exaggerated example of its kind. Each city, he suggests, has elements which are suprarational in scale; churches in the case of Rome, casinos in the case of Las Vegas and just as Rome's churches are open to the public 'off streets and piazzas', so the Las Vegas casinos are open off the Strip. In Rome the pilgrim, religious or architectural, can walk from church to church and in Las Vegas the gambler or the architect similarly can take in a variety of casinos along the Strip.

And much as the Roman monuments of Nolli's Plan contain large but enclosed public spaces, so too do the Casinos of Las Vegas!

Colin Rowe and his team in Sector (8) make the implicit assumption that for the purposes of Roma Interrotta everything built since Nolli's time is quite unworthy to be there. Nor can they see their way to replacing whatever *is* there with anything modern.

As they say:

> We could have proposed that on the Palatine be erected a fragment of the *ville radieuse*, on the Aventine a figment of Ludwig Hilbersheimer's imagination, over the Colosseum and the Circus Maximus as space frame; but in the name of mere amusement or dubiously *avant garde* proclamations, to protract the errors and the later irresponsibilities of modern architecture does not appear to us to be a very useful procedure. We assume that, on the whole, modern architecture was a major catastrophe – except as a terrible lesson – best to be forgotten. . . .

So instead of presenting Modernist schemes they draw on the work of a Father Mulcahy, whom they presume to have written the Catalogue for an Exhibition on Rome: The Lost and the Unknown City. Thus they see the Villa which the 18th century Cardinal Albani built for himself on the Palatine as an early forcing house of neo-Classicism. They also draw extensively on the projects which Valadier prepared for Napoleon Bonaparte including complete reconstructions of the Palatine, the Circus Maximus, a monumental cemetery, a *sistemazione*

Fig. 10.2 Venturi and Rauch (1978): Roma Interrotta Sector VII (from *Architectural Design*, **49** (3/4), 1979; IIA, 1978).

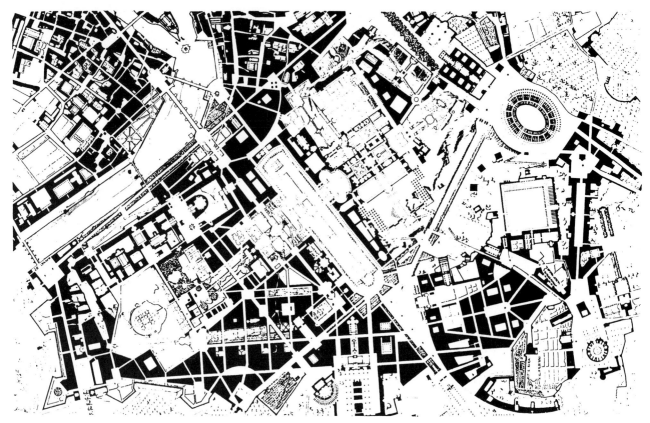

Fig. 10.3 Colin Rowe (1978): Roma
Interrotta, Sector VIII (from
Architectural Design, **49** (3/4), 1979; IIA,
1978).

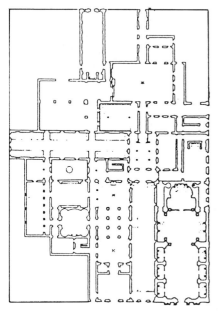

Fig. 10.4 Michael Graves (1978):
Church of the Trinita de'Pellegrini
from Roma Interrotta Sector IX (from
Architectural Design, **49** (3/4), 1979; IIA,
1978).

of the Aventine, an Egyptian Temple and an *Arco Napoleonico* as a
pendant to the Arch of Constantine (Fig. 10.3).

Rowe and his team take these as their inspiration for perhaps the
most coherent sequence of urban spaces of any in the Exhibition,
interlinked by streets with a seriousness of purpose that none of the
other entrants even tried to match. They show this in their figure-
ground plans of black buildings against white backgrounds. So, as
Chimacoff (1979) says: 'this project calls directly into question the
continuing efficacy of modern architecture, modern zoning and
building laws, and established modern building types'.

In Sector (9) Michael Graves himself was designing for what, in
Nolli's time, had been largely a virgin site. Graves raised important
theoretical issues by taking four buildings of Rome and assigning to
each of them a role in his scheme of things. Thus he sees the Temple of
Minerva Medica as an object in the landscape, emphasizing its exterior
volumes as figure. He contrasts this with the Villa Madama which has a
series of modelled interior spaces, thus emphasizing the idea of void,
rather than solid, as figure. Then Hadrian's Villa represents for Graves
a series of internal spaces disposed about a series of clearly defined
routes whilst, given that it has no less than five parallel progressions of
rooms, each symmetrical within itself, the Church and Hospice of the
Trinita de' Pellegrini represents for Graves a more ambiguous network
of movement (Fig. 10.4).

Having identified these four building forms, Graves suggests that
they also provide tendencies for urban landscape design. Thus he uses
them in his Sector, no. (9), containing, as it does, the Porto Maggiore
and the Church of St John Lateran. Graves's scheme, in fact, is a huge
garden, much like that for his Crooks House (1976) blown up very

many times and containing buildings according to his four tendencies or, in some cases, fragments of them. As Chimacoff says in his Review of the Exhibition, 'If size and scale are taken as a measure of interest and concern, then it is quite apparent that Graves's preferences are for a world of urban landscape. In the context of the scale of Rome, however, his garden is too vast'.

Although he was allocated Nolli's Sector 10 – consisting largely of Nolli's historical drawings – Rob Krier felt that, however distinguished the contributors, the whole idea of redrawing and reinterpreting Nolli's Plan had seemed rather absurd from the beginning.

He therefore contemplated the various ways in which man undertakes the art of building: by carving the landscape into geometric forms, or quarrying stones and building walls. He analysed the properties of walls, of columns, of towers, of bridges, of interior space, the house as an actual building, its interior spaces, the part the house plays in enclosing the spaces of the city, and so on.

Having symbolized each of these in some drawn form, Krier then went on to draw them over the architectural elements of Nolli's drawing, leaving his human figures, and his actual plan intact.

Half of Aldo Rossi's Sector (11), of course, was taken up with Nolli's Dedication and Rossi draws over this a selection of his own buildings such as his Housing at Gallaretese, in Milan, and his Monument to the Partisans at Segrate. There is also a Statue of Liberty-like Caryatid which symbolizes Rossi's intentions.

His Plan was to rebuild the great Antonine Baths and to add fountains, tea rooms with promenades, and trampolines, cabins for changing – a favourite Rossi building-type, this – or to provide shade and or shelter and, finally, a house of water.

Rossi's scheme includes a seminary, a market, a gymnasium and academy, and a vast swimming pool, which, because it is so well supervised, 'may protect the invalid from a possible risk of drowning (yet) subjects him at the same time to a sense of inferiority *vis-à-vis* the skilled swimmer and sportsman' (Fig. 10.5).

Rossi's house of water of course was to contain the cooling and heating installations. At the same time it was to be both fantastic and symbolic, cool and mysterious. As Rossi says:

Fig. 10.5 Aldo Rossi (1978): Roma Interrotta Sector XI (from *Architectural Design*, **49** (3/4), 1979; IIA, 1978).

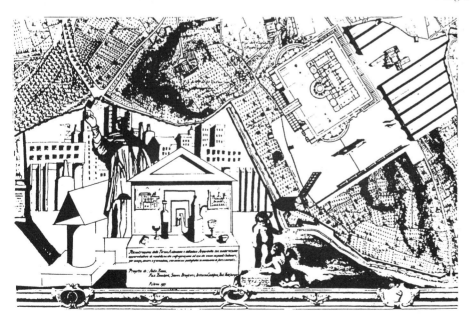

It can be traversed by boat like a terrifying ravine, or explored by underwater swimmers, who can carry out an unprecedented kind of scientific/technological investigation among the depths of its foundations and the convolutions of its pipework.

The less audacious could visit the house of water on foot by way of an iron bridge.

But above all Rossi's scheme seems to have been a declaration of certain predilections. He says:

> . . . the real interest of the authors – manifestly not an innocent one – as will not escape the alert critic – is in the bathing installations themselves.

His reconstruction of the Baths may or may not be historically accurate for even the best of reconstructions is a corruption. Nevertheless, he says:

> . . . a certain relationship with Rome does exist. . . .

> For it is certain that in this impure arrangement of spaces the relation between Eros and athletic training, which was the glory of many ancient civilisations, is lost sight of. Even a dispassionate analysis of the spatial organisation of the Thermae reveals that Love, be it in the highest meaning of the word, was for sale there.

Leon Krier's Sector (12) consisted largely of Nolli figures with Michelangelo's Campidoglio in the background. Krier replaced this with one of his own covered squares, a building type which, he says, grew out of the need for cities to be decentralized.

London has its postal districts, Paris its arrondissements and Rome its *riones*. Krier sees these as about the right scale for an urban

Fig. 10.6 Leon Krier (1978): Covered Square from Roma Interrotta Sector XII (from *Architectural Design*, **49** (3/4), 1979; IIA, 1978).

community in that they can contain all the necessities of day-to-day existence, the pedestrian can traverse them easily, and so on. The centre of each *rione* would be marked by one of Krier's covered squares, which would be super social centres, with restaurants, clubs, rooms for games and artistic performances all stacked up within those favourite Krier devices, buildings-as-columns. The upper parts of these would be given over to artists and craftsmen, all working for the adornment of their *rione* and the square itself would be covered by a vast, timber-trussed roof.

Krier shows such buildings in various locations: replacing Michelangelo's Campidiglio, terminating the Piazza Navona – this was to be a semi-circular one – and, most dramatic of all, a vast triangular one closing the Via della Consolazione – which itself would be built over – from the Piazza in front of St Peter's (Fig. 10.6).

St Peter's and the other basilicas would be converted into vast thermae and social centres – competing in splendour with those of ancient Rome, and The Piazza itself would be converted into a large elliptical lake for swimmers!

Les Halles

But theorizing is one thing, and the solution of practical design problems quite another. It is true to say, as Leo Krier did (1980b), that it was the specific problem of the Les Halles wholesale market site in Paris which, above all, focused international attention on the problems of urban space design.

Access to Les Halles had become a problem shortly after World War II. Its very centrality (immediately north of the Seine at the Île de la Cite and Notre Dame), which had been such an asset in the 19th century, clearly, with rising amounts of road traffic, made things difficult both for those bringing in goods for sale and those taking goods out again for distribution. By 1953 it had been decided in principle that the Market should be moved to a suburban site, that is La Villette at Rungis. Matters were further complicated by the decision to locate a vast new transport interchange at Les Halles, from the Metro to the new rapid transit (RER/RATP), so in 1967 the decision was finally taken not only to move the Market but also to demolish Baltard's cast-iron and glass pavilions which had housed it.

They had extended eastwards, or rather east south-east, some 450 metres from the Halle au Blé (Wheat Market) of Le Camuscle Mezieres (1762). This had been rebuilt in 1806–11 as Bellanger's circular, iron-and-glass domed Bourse de Commerce, which fortunately survives to this day and forms an important focal point of the neighbourhood, surpassed in quality only by the 16th century Gothic and Renaissance church of St Eustache which lies to the north and east of it, breaking the northern (rue Rambuteau) line of the site.

Baltard's pavilions were arranged with strict symmetry about their more southerly axis. The first six of these were started in 1854 at the eastern (Innocents) end of the site. They were grouped, with strict symmetry, as two sets of three about their own cross axis so that on each side a central square Halle, 50 m × 50 m, was flanked by the rectangular ones, each 50 m × 40 m. The six Halles were separated from each other by a central roofed aisle and cross aisles. The total width of the site, including the rue Rambuteau to the north and the rue Berger to the south, thus amounted to some 200 metres.

The site was crossed, immediately west of this first group, by the north–south Boulevard des Halles, beyond which a second group was started, in 1856, extending towards the Halle au Blé. There were four Halles in this second group: two square and two rectangular to precisely the same arrangements and dimensions as the original six and finally, in 1936, the Bourse was embraced by two semicircular ones.

Once the decision had been taken to demolish Les Halles, their replacement was entrusted to APUR, an Atelier Parisien d'Urbanisme, in 1967 but the council of Paris refused their designs. By this time there was much public protest over the demolition of Baltard's pavilions, which indeed were put to a wide variety of uses: theatre, circus, jazz concerts, contemporary music concerts, exhibitions of painting, sculpture, crafts and an ice-skating rink was constructed. But despite this evidence of flexibility in use, and after much public protest, the demolition of Baltard's pavilions was started in 1971.

Once the site of Les Halles had been cleared, the space which was ripe for development proved to be somewhat irregular, compromised to the north and west of the Boulevard des Halles by St Eustache and to the south by what remained of the semicircular Place des Halles. There had, in fact, been further clearances at the eastern (rue des Innocents) end of irregular, triangular tracts to north and south thus leaving something between a 'T' and an Apollo Command Module in shape, some 350 metres in each of its major dimensions.

By 1971 a project by APUR had been adopted and SEMAH (Société d'Economie Mixte pour l'Arrangement des Halles) constituted to develop it. At the same time the decision was taken to build the Centre National d'Art de Culture Contemporaine – later to be called the Centre Pompidou – on the Plateau Beaubourg, which is close to the site

Fig. 10.7 Jean Pattou (1981): Plan for Les Halles in Paris (from ACIH, 1981).

635

of Les Halles, across the Boulevard Sebastopol. In 1972 a final APUR project was accepted, within which there was to be a Forum, stepping down to the Metro, which project was entrusted to Vasconi and Pencreac'h. It was opened in 1979.

But still there were problems over the site as a whole and, after Giscard d'Estaing's election as President of France in 1974, nine different teams of (French) architects were consulted, including Vasconi and Pencreac'h. By 1975 the contenders had been whittled down to three: ARC, Bernard de la Tour d'Auvergne and Visconi-Pencreac'h – with Ricardo Bofill and the Taller di Arquitectura. The latter's scheme at this stage centred on an oval arena surrounded by (Classical) colonnades.

Of these the public preferred the ARC scheme, but Giscard preferred Bofill. So in May 1975 Aillaud was named co-ordinating architect, to be assisted by Bofill and de la Tour d'Auvergne. It is hardly surprising that no common solution emerged from such different personalities but, confident of Giscard's backing, Bofill and the Taller went on to produce further designs (see *Architectural Design*, **50**(9/10), 1980) including a colonnaded square linked to a tree-lined rectilinear space by triumphal arches and containing an open air theatre (all second project 1975), a further permutation on the oval arena linked to a Nancy-like hemicycle (third project 1976), and one grouped round a formal lake (fourth project, 1976–77).

Work was started on this latter project in 1978 in the form of a monumental, not to say neo-Classical, apartment block on the rue Rambuteau just to the east of St Eustache. But in March 1977 Jacques Chirac had been elected Mayor of Paris and he had different ideas. By October 1978 he had named himself chief architect for the Les Halles site, dismissed Bofill and ordered demolition of the building which had been started.

Chirac's response to Bofill's Classical Monumentality, of course, is explained in part by the fact that Giscard himself had promoted it as part of *his* vision for a revival of past French Glories. But whilst one regrets this large-scale demonstration of what neo-Rationalist planning, neo-Classical forms and prefabricated (large panel) systems finally *could* have achieved, there are echoes of what might-have-been,

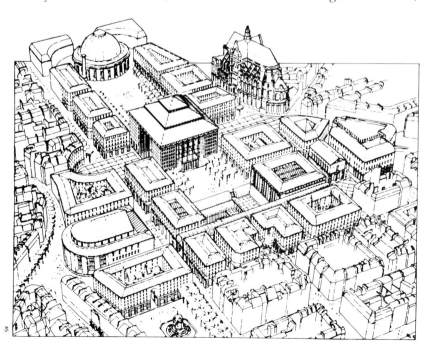

Fig. 10.8 Leon Krier (1981): Plan for Les Halles (from ACIH, 1981).

as we have seen, at St Quentin en Yvelines, Marne la Vallée and Zac Guilleminot-Vercingétorix in Montparnasse.

As for the future of Les Halles, Chirac's thoroughly characterless scheme has been built, despite the fact that in 1979 ACIH (Association pour la Consultation International pour l'Amenagement de Quartier des Halles) set up an international competition which attracted some 2000 registrations – at $60 a time – and 690 actual entries. When these figures are compared with the 3000 registrations and 600 entries for the Palhevi Library in Teheran, not to mention the 1058 registrations and 455 entries for the Mosque in Madrid, one gains some idea of how important the urban-space scale of design now seems to the international community. The names of some of the entrants, too, indicate their variety and quality. They included Don Appleyard and Associates, Claude Chabrol, Greggotti Associates, Leo Krier, Charles Moore (with Grover, Harper), Luigi Moretti, Jean Pattou, Franco Purini and Aldo Rossi, although the five equal prize winners were Richard Ness, Greg Walton and Steven Peterson (all Americans), Michael Bourdeau and Franco Purini, each working with an Italian team.

The programme for the ACIH competition took into account changes which had occurred in the neighbourhood since the destruction of Les Halles and the building of the Centre Pompidou. It also took into account various elements of Chirac's programme which already had been commissioned and, indeed, were nearing completion, such as the vast underground RER/RATP station and the hugh, rectangular concrete block on the rue Rambuteau containing its HVAL plant, also Vasconi and Pescreac'h's shopping Forum which steps down to the station, underground parking and so on.

Fig. 10.9 Moore, Grover, Harper (1981): Plan for Les Halles (from ACIH, 1981).

The programme looked for a sense of identity with the neighbour-hood and an image of centrality in a large, international city.

As far as new building was concerned, the ACIH programme required future planning: a telephone exchange, sports facilities (a swimming pool, gymnasium, skating rink, etc.) below ground level, exhibition space or a large auditorium partially below and partially above ground level, and at or above ground level, 35 000 sq m of housing, a 300 room hotel, shops, workshops and a market, various social facilities and some 40 000 sq m of gardens and urban spaces.

The entries ranged in scope from Pattou's amazing, 3-dimensional Disneyworld, stepping up from a lake almost at RER level (Fig. 10.7), to Matsui's plain, rectilinear campus lined symmetrically with buildings, almost in the manner of Jefferson's Charlottesville campus. The ACIH's report on the competition (1981) shows 600 of the entries, but there is a well-chosen selection in colour in *Architectural Design*, **50** (9/10), 1980.

In terms of Urban Design Theory, the competition was notable for having presented, for the first time, a direct confrontation between those who – designing for the same site – took a neo-Rationalist approach and those who took a neo-Empiricist one. The extremes, as one might expect, were represented at that time by Leo Krier and Charles Moore respectively.

Krier initially was invited on to the Jury, who then decided that it might be more important for him to present a project. It is, of course, a typical Krier, with a main axis centred on the Halle au Blé, with a typical Krier covered square – some 75 × 75 × 30 m – to the east and a cross axis further to the east, centred on Vasconi and Pencreac'h's existing Forum. The four large buildings-as-columns at the corners of Krier's covered square, supporting its roof, actually are his International Hotel, the Hotel des Quatre Continents (Fig. 10.8).

Moore's scheme is very much more complex. It is centred on an irregular lake, which of course provided for boating and contained, as it were, islands of housing. There was further housing at the western end of the lake – towards the Halle au Blé – and this was seen as the quiet end compared with the eastern zone, devoted to culture and entertainment, with a Mansard-roofed hotel between the two (Fig. 10.9).

As one might expect, the irregular forms of this project were derived, as it were, from 'what is' – by taking the lines of the various streets which converge on the site of Les Halles and projecting them further into it. By looking at the monumental 'givens' – the Halle au Blé and St Eustache and containing spaces about them, there are hints, almost, of a piazza like that of St Peter's in Rome, with colonnades converging from the Halle au Blé towards an oval piazza, but all rendered somewhat irregular. There is attention also to imagery, drawing on waterfront environments from such diverse places as Dayton, Ohio; Springfield, Massachusetts; and Bushkar in Rajasthan.

There are references, too, to those Loire châteaux which themselves are reflected in water: Azay-le-Rideau and Chenonceaux.

As for the place of the ACIH competition in the development of public consciousness concerning the importance of Urban Design, let us sympathize with Leo Krier when he says (1980):

> Could this be a revolution occurring in the heart of an insane
> profession? For given the monstrosities built or planned by the
> last three generations, starting with Le Corbusier and ending with
> Taillibert or Rogers, one can well understand the anguish of the
> Mayor of Paris . . . what better proof could there be of the

profession's inability to restore an urban fabric than the 15 years of debacles, intrigues, plans and counter-plans and the fact that what was being sought was not the best solution, but the least bad.

But, as he goes on to say:

> Analysing the projects submitted, it becomes clear that, in contrast to what might have occurred a few years ago on a similar occasion, a good third of the projects tried, with varying degrees of success, to reconstruct a fabric of streets and squares on the Paris scale. Leaving aside the folklore, idiocies, acrobatics and pipedreams . . . we must recognise that the most important tendency is towards the construction of a tradition and familiar urban fabric. The rebirth of that difficult *metier* was an undeniable and revolutionary fact of this competition.

11

Treatment of urban space

Halprin and Moore; Johnson

It is one thing to design an urban space, leave such a space between buildings, or even make such a space by demolishing buildings as Mies van der Rohe proposed to do to form the Mansion House Square in London (1965). Given such a space, clearly, one can do as Mies intended: that is pave most of it whilst leaving traffic routes, not just around the perimeter but in this case also cutting across the urban square.

Paving is the obvious answer but there are many possibilities. One can pave it, roughly, as in some of the Cambridge courts whilst laying smooth-stone paths on the major pedestrian routes. One can make a central lawn, which only fellows can cross, with pathways round the sides for mere mortals. One can landscape it like many London squares and fence the landscaped part so that only residents of the square have access. No doubt they will want to park their cars outside their doors so the landscape will be surrounded by paved roads.

These are common ways of treating urban spaces but of course there can be many others. Even that least promising of urban spaces, the American City Block, can, given sufficient imagination, be transformed into a pleasant, even a tranquil place. Lawrence Halprin and Charles Moore showed one way with their Lovejoy Fountain (1965) using cascades of water to bring a little of the Oregon wilderness into the centre of Portland, Oregon (1965) (Figs 11.1 and 11.2). Philip Johnson went a stage further with the Fort Worth Water Gardens

Fig. 11.1 Lawrence Halprin and Associates with Moore, Lyndon, Turnbull, Whitaker and Urban Innovations Group (1965–) Lovejoy Fountain, Portland, Oregon: plan (from Johnson, 1986).

Fig. 11.2 Lovejoy Fountain (from Johnson, 1986).

(1970). Johnson himself says of them (1985): 'Vine terraces must be as old as Babylon. Running-water parks certainly predate Hadrian's Villa. Groves of trees are as old as Academe. All of this for Texas was the impetus . . . of the Fort Worth Water Garden'.

As one approaches through the groves one hears the sound of running water which soon overrides the sounds of street traffic. And then, at the centre, water cascades over and between the (concrete) rocks of a jagged, angular, man-made quarry into a maelstrom some 30 feet below the surface. As one steps down and into the quarry the effect, literally, is sensational for in addition to one's sense of seeing; one's senses of movement, equilibrium and most certainly hearing are stimulated thoroughly; indeed the sound of the rushing water is so magnified by reflections that one is reminded of Niagara, Victoria and the other great waterfalls (Figs 11.3 and 11.4).

Johnson's Thanks-giving Square in Dallas (1970–75) – actually triangular – is more consciously architectural, centred as it is on a spiral Shrine, a place for meditation with, below it, a Hall of Thanksgiving in which the story of that all-American occasion is told through religion, art, music and literature (Johnson and Burgee, 1971).

Bofill and the Taller de Arquitectura

These, of course, are splendid built examples of townscaped urban spaces but the most creative attempt to explore *possibilities* was that of Bofill and the Taller de Arquitectura when – in rather a different context – they looked at what might be done to Fort St Cyr, a redundant Army Fort outside Paris (1972) (Fig. 11.5). This, paraphrased, and applied to urban space generally, opens up new vistas for the treatment of urban space which, once the space has been defined by surrounding buildings, might include:

1. Leaving the surface substantially flat
   (a) with continuous paving
   (b) paved but with defined pedestrian paths

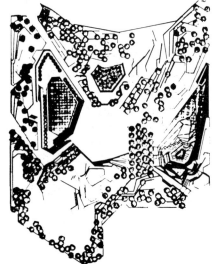

Fig. 11.3 Philip Johnson/John Burgee (1970) Fort Worth Water Garden, Fort Worth, Texas plan (from Johnson and Burgee, 1985).

(c) paved for pedestrians but with vehicular routes:
    (i) around the perimeter ⎫ with parking
    (ii) across the middle   ⎭ without parking

(d) landscaped in the middle: formally or informally

    (i) with grass   ⎫ open
    (ii) with trees   ⎬ closed
    (iii) with flowers etc. ⎭ by change of level
                        by railings etc.

2. Building on to the surface

(a) walls	(g) towers	(m) fountains
(b) seats	(h) terraces	(h) raised pools
(c) pavilions	(i) staircases	(o) planters
(d) flagpoles	(j) steps	(p) moats
(e) triumphal arches	(k) colonnades	(q) sculpture
(f) follies	(l) arcades	(r) clocks
		(s) pergolas

3. Digging into the surface
    (a) for pools
    (b) grottos
    (c) quarries
    (d) cascades
    (e) canals

4. Suspending over the surface
    (a) lights   (on poles)
    (b) mobiles (on cables)
    (c) flags   (on towers)
    (d) streamers (on pergolas)

Fig. 11.4 Fort Worth Water Garden
(author's photograph).

There was a zany surrealism about some of the Taller's proposals which might trigger further ideas. This was presented by means of examples including:

1. abandoned appearance, romantic. . . .
2. ruin after an explosion
3. Maginot Line, Atomic Shelters, Journey to the centre of the earth, Dante's Inferno, Catacombs, Buried City, Deserted City
4. find oneself at the bottom of a crater
5. directional landscape
6. partial perspective, real or false
7. artificial mountain
8. very open, terraced city, watch tower, etc.
9. city of Flash Gordon
10. surrealist city (Escher)
11. romantic city
12. garden city in space
13. city in the French (Classical) style
14. medieval city, etc.
15. encrusted Coliseum
16. foundations for Tower of Babel
17. domed city
18. platform city
19. suspended rock city
20. crater
21. Futurist city
22. inflorescence (enormous flower, cloud, fog)
23. bombed city (ruins)
24. triumphal arches

Fig. 11.5 Ricardo Bofill and the Taller de Arquitectura (1972): project for Fort St Cyr (from original sketch).

25. great ruins (Gothic, Baroque)
26. Eiffel towers
27. cathedrals
28. towers
29. Surrealist city
30. labyrinth
31. Cape Canaveral
32. camouflage by landscape (banks, trees, water)
33. curtain wall (mirrored, floodlighting, ivy etc.)
34. luminous panels
35. surrealist (paint woods on walls)

They also had ideas on multi-sensory inputs within the space using such elements as:

1. landscape (or urban) sounds:
   (a) of woods (jungle, storms)
   (b) military (march past, battle)
   (c) marine (calm, stormy, rain)
2. music:
   atmosphere: Classical, Pop, montages
3. speaking voice:
   poetry, literature, announcements, information, orders.
4. colour:
   (a) posters, super graphics
   (b) projected images or colours
   (c) colour applied (by pigment or light) to the atmosphere, to the trees, to water

The Taller also had ideas on sculpture which could be taken from some museum or produced especially for the purpose. The sculpture itself could be static: carved in wood or stone, cast in bronze, or it could be dynamic. Dynamic forms for the Taller included Gothic clocks with moving figures striking the hours, Calder mobiles, water-wheels, windmills, and so on. They envisaged sculpture at human scale: such as life-sized figures, at small scale like sophisticated gnomes or enormous, like the Trojan Horse, a Sphinx with Napoleon's head and so on.

Miguel Angel Roca: Cordoba

There is a similar exuberance in the urban improvements initiated in the Argentine City of Cordoba by Miguel Angel Roca, during his period (1979–80) as Secretary of Public Works to the City Council; a short time, indeed, to carry out so much work! Apart from refurbishing a number of 19th century, cast-iron and glass markets – to serve as community centres – Roca also undertook a considerable amount of urban (space) renewal (Guisberg and Bohigas, 1981).

This falls generally into three groups: urban sculpture, geometric concrete constructions which reveal the influence of Roca's Master Louis Kahn, pergolas to articulate shopping streets over a distance of some nine blocks, between the Streets 27 April and 9 July and paving, or rather repaving patterns.

The markets, especially the San Vincente and the General Paz (Fig. 11.6) have all the glitter of the Centre Pompidou overlaid by Magritte-like surrealist touches and, since all this is inside the original, cast-iron and glass structures, there are no problems at all of the kind the

Fig. 11.6 Miguel Angel Roca (1980): Refunctionalisation of the Mercado General Paz, Cordoba, Argentina (author's photograph).

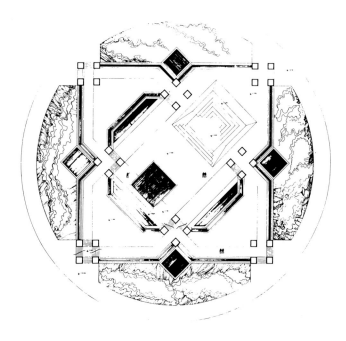

Fig. 11.7 Miguel Angel Roca (1969)
Plaza España, Cordoba, Argentina.
Plan (courtesy Miguel Angel Roca).

Beaubourg has in terms of solar heat gain, of wear, weathering and
maintenance of materials. The Mercado General Paz is wrapped by a
two-storey, L-shaped extension with a wave-form plan. It is glazed
from ground to roof but unlike Foster's Willis Faber Office in Ipswich it
is by no means vulnerable to solar over-heating because it is shaded by
the original Market. The resultant reflections, of glass into glass,
interior structure, trees and so on really *do* form surrealist images,
ever-shifting as one moves along the narrow, undulating spaces

Fig. 11.8 Plaza España (courtesy
Miguel Angel Roca).

Fig. 11.9 Miguel Angel Roca (1979) 'Shadow' of the Cathedral formed in the paving of the Plaza de Armas, Cordoba, Argentina (courtesy Miguel Angel Roca).

between the cast-iron Market and its extension. Here, one feels, Roca has achieved the kind of zany surrealism which the Taller de Arquitectura were exploring in their Brainstorming of Fort St Cyr.

Roca's Urban Sculptures are built on a huge roundabout: the Plaza España (1969), on urban squares such as the Plazoleta Ambrosio Funes (1980) and the Plaza Civica (1980) and even on an urban triangle, the Plaza Italia of 1980. They are treated in various ways; the Piazza España for instance consists of a large square inscribed within a circular roundabout and enclosing a smaller diagonal square (Fig. 11.7).

There are various changes of level so that the lower parts are remarkably tranquil and, marking the corners of the squares, there are concrete pylons of various heights which, year by year are being covered with low reliefs designed by successful sculpture students (Fig. 11.8). The Plaza Italia has geometric sculptures, interplays of cubes at various scales in the three corners of the triangle with a central circle in the form of a relief map.

Roca's pedestrian Mall system is defined in part by pergolas, light steel structures curved to support semicircular vaults of planting whilst the paving is planned to respond to the adjacent buildings. In the case of the University, for instance, the paving represents its elevation, full scale and 'cast' as a 'shadow' from the actual façade at the angle that would have been cast on the day, and at the time, the University was founded.

The paving outside the Cabildo – City Hall – represents the plan of the debating chamber itself so the Cordoban one can locate his representative's seat and stamp on it to criticize his performance! Most dramatic of all however – because it is laid out in an open square – is the paved 'reflection' of the Cathedral façade, again at an appropriate angle like the 'shadow' of the University (Fig. 11.9).

Bohigas: Barcelona

An even larger scale application of such ideas was undertaken by Bofill's great rival in Barcelona, Oriole Bohigas, in his position as Delegate for Urban Services (1981–82). He commissioned some 50 architect-planners – largely of the Barcelona Minimalist School – to

Fig. 11.10 Plaça Reial, Barcelona. Tarrago, S. (1974).

undertake the redesign of some 130 open places in the city, ranging in size from the whole of Barceloneta – the Port area of Barcelona – to tiny urban spaces, such as those by the churches of Santa Caterina, Sant Pere and Santa Maria i La Ribera in the older part of the city (see Bohigas *et al.*, 1983).

Some are simply exercises in paving and/or steps; that is true of the three church squares. Others are vast remodellings in three-dimensional space, such as the Parc de l'España Industrial. The latter, by Peña-Ganchegui, steps down, very steeply, some six metres from street level to an artificial lake. The space thus defined is rather dramatic but it is spoiled by a row of rather crude lighthouses which mark the edge of the Parc.

Several of the schemes are landscapings of streets, or at least include streets together with some kind of park. These include: Freixes' Parc del Clot; Quintana's Avinguda Gaudí; Mestras with Sanabria, Barragán and de Solá's Avinguda Rio de Janeiro; Amadó and Domenèch's Passeig Picasso; Cantallops and Simon's Passeig Reina Maria Cristina; Sanmartí's Renfe-Meridiana and Solá-Morales' Moll de la Fusta. Most

Fig. 11.11 Correa and Mila (1981–82) Plaça Reial remodelling (author's photograph).

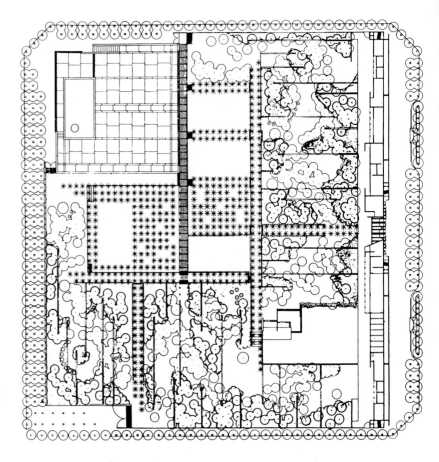

Fig. 11.12 Salonas, Arriolqa, Gali and Quintana (1981–82) Parc de l'Excorxador, Barcelona. Plan (from Bohigas *et al.*, 1983).

of these include palm trees in serried ranks; indeed there are six such rows on the Moll de la Fusta not to mention neo-Classical balustrades.

Apart from the Moll, and the Passeig Picasso, three schemes in particular have attracted international attention. They are Correa and Milá's remodelling (1981–82) of Francescs' Plaça Réal (1843–59), Solanas, Arriola, Gali and Quintana's Parc de l'Escorxador and Piñón with Viaplana's Plaça de l'Estació de Sants.

The Plaça Réal is a splendid urban space, some 84 metres by 56 and lined with fine, four storey neo-Classical buildings of uniform height including arcades at ground level. Originally it had a central fountain, surrounded by a railed garden around which the four sides were used for parking (Fig. 11.10). Whilst one sympathizes with Correa and Milá's desire to get rid of the parking, their solution seems a little drastic. For they have taken away the railings, and the garden, moving even Gaudi's lamp posts. The whole Plaça now is paved at the same level, allowing for drainage falls through which highly disciplined palms are supposed to grow. Which gives the whole thing a bleak and forbidding air (Fig. 11.11). What is more it destroys the scale of what was once one of the finest urban squares in Europe.

The Parc de l'Escorxador by Solanas, Arriola, Gali and Quintana takes up four blocks of Cerda's extension to Barcelona. It is laid out rather like a Mondrian painting with parallel ranks of palm trees taking the place of Mondrian's black lines (Fig. 11.12). The north-western rectangle is higher than the rest and it is paved to provide a setting for a vast and colourful sculpture by Joan Miró, the *Dona amb ocell* and the main north–south line along its eastern edge takes the form of a raised pergola. There are minimalist pavilions in the lower parts of the Parc and also a minimalist childrens' playground.

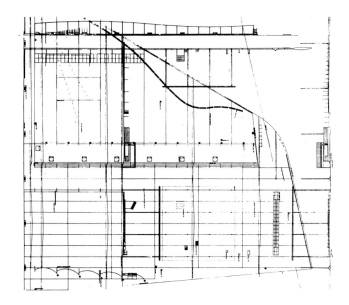

Fig. 11.13 Pinon and Viaplana (1981–82) Plaça l'Estacio de Sants, Barcelona. Plan and section (from Bohigas *et al.*, 1983).

Pinon was faced with a difficult problem indeed when he was designing the Plaça de l'Estació de Sants, that is the Sants Station Square (1981–82). For it is built over underground parking and therefore his structures had to be relatively light. The chief ones are a large expanded-metal canopy supported on very slender columns, high fences of the same materials and a pergola, wave-form in section, also of expanded metal. Beneath this there are concrete tables-cum-benches intended for chess-players and others. Low benches and lines of posts, undulating in height, also are planned to wave-form curves. There are stone cannon balls too, arranged in wave-forms so the whole thing is an interesting exercise in applying equivalent wave-forms in plan and section (Fig. 11.13). Which no doubt looked rather good on the drawings. But these subtleties have very little impact on the mere pedestrian observer (Fig. 11.14). The Square *can* be made to look particularly impressive in night-time photographs – provided that the street lights are turned off and one uses an exposure of several minutes.

Otherwise it is simply too delicate to register in one's consciousness. Barcelona's Minimalism clearly represents some kind of reaction – in their own city – to the richness of Gaudi, Domenech and others of the

Fig. 11.14 Plaça l'Estacio de Sants (author's photograph).

Modernismo. But that very richness makes Minimalism look even more poverty-stricken than it might in some more austere places.

Correa and Milá as we have seen destroyed the sense of place and certainly the sense of scale, in their remodelling of the Plaça Réal. Others have destroyed to rather more positive effect. Daniel Buren's treatment of the Cour d'Honneur at the Palais Royale in Paris caused quite a scandal at the time (1986). His candy-stripe black and white columns, ranging in height from two or three centimetres to two or three metres certainly came as something of a shock.

And yet the rhythmic games he plays with their heights, the patterns of the paving, and so on, have their own fascination defining, as it were, complex, intersecting diagonal planes across their tops and a peopling of the Cour by columns – which in turn attract real people – far removed in effect from Correa and Milá's impoverishment of the Plaça Réal. But of course, if in due time, either seems too disruptive it can be restored to its original form!

Isosaki: Tsukuba Civic Centre

Isosaki's Civic Centre for Tsukuba (1980–83) was intended, as he says (1984b) to mark the centre of an amorphous New Town, or rather Science City of Tsukuba. Isosaki felt he was expected to do this with 'a tower standing on the city axis' or at least 'symmetry as a sign of monumentality'. But Japan had a reputation for copying, rather well, Western designs; Tsukuba was to be the place where the Japanese initiated her own new kinds of technology. So Isosaki saw his role as symbolizing, not just the aspirations of the Science City itself, but of the Japanese nation as a whole.

He did not feel he could do that with traditional Japanese forms; these had been outmoded by neo-Classicism. That too had been outmoded by Modernism, yet Modernism itself, literally, was too transparent to be monumental.

But there were more fundamental problems. As Isosaki says (1984a): 'In the 1970s (an) amalgamation of emperor, state, and capital

Fig. 11.15 Arata Isosaki (1978–83): Centre Building, Tsukuba, Japan: plans (from *Japan Architect*, January 1984 and *Building Design*, May 11 1984).

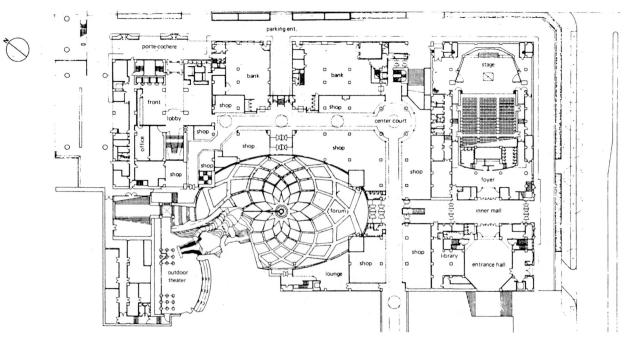

generated a prevailing structure (elsewhere he calls it Japan Incorporated) in which architecture became commercial merchandise'. So, as he puts it (1984b) he had been hired 'not by a king but by a state, and requested to produce a portrait of the state . . . and yet the countenance of the state is not as clear as that of an existing ruler, and even if it were. . . I would rather it didn't emerge too clearly'.

So: 'In order to deal with this ambivalence, I made the centre simply a space – a void; I portrayed a metaphor in which all the usual spatial arrangements are reversed or inverted'.

He got the idea from *Las Meninas* of Velasquez; a painting of, ostensibly, the King and Queen of Spain. Yet what one sees is Velasquez himself, the back of his canvas, the Princess and several Ladies in Waiting. Then behind them one notices a tiny convex mirror in which the King and Queen are reflected. Which means that the painting is not *of* them but rather of what *they* saw as they were being painted.

Isosaki tried to build inversions of this kind into his Tsukuba Civic Centre. There is a rectangular terrace, a pedestrian deck some 120 metres by 72. It is paved with brown tiles across which there is a heavy tartan grid in white and yellow tiles with narrower stripes interwoven in red.

The L-shape of buildings: a concert hall to the south and an hotel to the east hardly enclose the terrace and since the screens of trees to the north and west are interrupted by wide pedestrian decks the space leaks out in these directions (Fig. 11.15).

The buildings themselves are geometric collages of Ledoux, Giulio Romano, Otto Wagner, Michael Graves, Richard Meier, Charles Moore, Aldo Rossi, Hans Hollein, Peter Cook, Adalberto Libera, Philip Johnson, Leon Krier, Ettore Sottsass and many others in gleaming white, grey or silver aluminium, glass block, ceramic tile, granite, artificial stone and so on (see also Popham, 1984 and Jencks, 1987).

But above – or rather below – all this as Isosaki says (1984b): 'When you visit the building you will come upon the oval-shaped (plaza) sunken (into the terrace). One portion is wrinkled and misshapen as if it had been gnawed at.' (Fig. 11.16).

One's descent is marked – at the 'gnawed' part – by a bronze laurel tree draped with a golden tunic which, as Isosaki says (1984a) derives symbolically from the legend of Daphne. The tree itself, of course,

Fig. 11.16 Tsukuba Centre Building: paving (from *Japan Architect*, January 1984).

Fig. 11.17 Tsukuba Centre Building: cascade (from *Japan Architect*, January 1984).

derives from palm trees of Hans Hollein's Travel Agencies in Vienna, which in turn derive from Nash's in the Kitchen of the Brighton Pavilion! One descends between Lucien Kroll-like rubble walls with, to one's left, a Piazza d'Italia-like stepped cascade (Fig. 11.17).

Once down there one finds Isosaki's most extreme inversion. As he says (1984a):

> I . . . used this sunken plaza as metaphoric expression of the hollowness of the centre. The minute I learned that, by coincidence, the oval plaza is the same size as (Michelangelo's) piazza on the Capitoline . . . I immediately set (about) inverting icons.

In Rome one walks *up* to Michelangelo's Piazza where, at the very middle of his oval there is, or was, a statue of Marcus Aurelius. So, says Isosaki: 'At Tsukuba a flight of steps leads down into the plaza which has a concave surface for the drainage of water from the cascade'. His paving is black where Michelangelo's is white; and vice versa. Thus there is deliberate 'iconographic confusion'.

Isosaki also says: (1984b): 'I made the centre simply a space – a void (Jencks calls it a Black Hole); I portrayed a metaphor in which all the usual spatial arrangements are reversed or inverted. . . . Everything is situated around a void. It is Michelangelo in reverse'.

Clearly Tsukuba is an extreme example but between them Halprin and Moore, Johnson, Bofill, Roca, Bohigas and Isosaki present some of the more adventurous treatments of urban spaces many of which could be applied, with appropriate local variations, in urban spaces round the world.

PART FOUR

APPLICATIONS

12

General urban texture and monuments

Aldo Rossi suggested (1966) that the fabric of a city consists of two things; the general urban texture of buildings lining streets and squares which, of course, will change over time, and the monuments, large-scale buildings whose very presence gives each city its particular character, embody, as Rossi says, the memory of the city.

Curiously enough, in the 1980s, two cities in particular, Berlin and Paris, demonstrated, with remarkable clarity, these two modes of city building.

In Berlin the IBA – the International Bauausstellung – of 1987 resulted from explorations in the 1970s as to how the frayed general texture of the city should be rebuilt or rehabilitated.

Berlin: general urban texture

Interbau (IBA)

As far as the IBA is concerned, of course, there had been previous Exhibitions, especially in the German-speaking countries, of what might be called 'the present state of housing'. The dwellings thus built had been retained and, in most cases, are still occupied. These included the Artists' Colony at Matildenhöhe in Darmstadt (1900), the Weissenhof Siedlung in Stuttgart (1927) the Internationale Werkbundsiedlung in Vienna (1932) and the Siedlung Babi in Prague (1931). In Berlin itself there had been the Interbau of 1957 which left as its monument the Hansaviertel of typical high-rise flats by such well-known masters of the Modern Movement as Aalto, Gropius, Jacobsen, Niemeyer and elsewhere le Corbusier's *Unitée d'Habitation*. So in 1975 the Berlin Senate's Director of Architecture, Hans Christian Müller, decided that it was time to plan another such Exhibition in the Diplomatic Area which runs east/west between the Tiergarten – a vast park – and the Landwehrkanal which runs more or less parallel to its southern edge (Lampugnini, 1984, Davey and Clelland, 1987b).

In 1965 indeed Fritz Hitzig had proposed a group of large villas for the Diplomatic Quarter on the grounds that such villas, once built, could be used as older villas can in various ways: by families – even diplomats – with servants, divided into large apartments, or sub-divided further to provide units of social housing.

The idea of building on this scale in the Diplomatic Quarter was opposed by a publisher, Wolf Jobst Siedler and an architect, Josef Paul Kliehues, who argued that, rather than simply building a ghetto of new work – a City of the Future – the occasion of the Exhibition should be taken to bring together the rather disparate parts of which West Berlin is formed. Berlin, of course, is divided, by the highly sinister Wall and since the original City Centre, with its Palace, its Cathedral, its main Square, the great museums and the University lies completely to the east of the Wall, West Berlin is a city with no heart. It has, rather, a series of sub-centres in a great swathe, running westwards, south of the Wall, from the old Postal District SO 36 to the Diplomatic Quarter. The eastern parts in particular, Postal District 96 and Luisenstadt have been greatly ravaged over time, by such things as the coming of the railways, the provision of roads for the motor car, wartime bombing, post-war planning and so on. They were occupied largely by immigrant workers and as far as Siedler and Kliehaus were concerned, these depressed areas in particular were most in need of improvement.

West of these in Southern Friedrichstadt, there were the Kulturforum (at which point the Wall swings northwards) and west of that again – that is south of the Park bearing that name – the Southern Tiergarten including the Diplomatic Quarter. These presented rather different problems in that much of what existed was in good condition but, as in so much post-war planning, there was not much sense of urban enclosure.

In the Kulturforum, for instance, there were large, prestigious but unrelated, showpieces for the Western way of life such as Scharoun's Philharmonie, home of the Berlin Philharmonic, Scharoun's equally sculptural National Library, Mies van der Rohe's National Gallery and Gutbrod's Arts and Crafts Museum. There was no need here for renewal. What was needed, rather, was some way of urbanizing the Kulturforum in the way that Perez d'Arce had urbanized Chandigarh.

So Siedler and Kliehues argued that given these different kinds of problems, the character of each centre should be reinforced where possible by urban conservation or renewal and, where necessary, by building new. So rather than simply building new in the Diplomatic Area, attempts should be made to integrate the past, the present and the future of West Berlin as a whole, by a whole series of schemes which amounted, eventually, to 90.

Siedler and Kliehues's cause was taken up early in 1977 by the *Berliner Morgenpost* in which were published a series of articles entitled Models for a City. Siedler and Kliehues worked towards an Exhibition in which they sought to come to terms with Berlin, its existing structure and what would be needed in terms of restoration, repair and supplements to it.

Other architects were brought into the debate, including Carlo Aymonimo, Heinrich Klötz, Robert Krier, Charles Moore, Wolfgang Pehnt, Aldo Rossi, Peter Smithson and James Stirling.

Then, by October 1977, as Lampugnani reports (1984), Dietmar Grötzembach and Bernd Jansen, had articulated a comprehensive programme for an International Building Exhibition (the IBA) to be held in Berlin. Their proposals formed the basis of a Senatorial Bill which was passed in June 1978 on the: 'Preparation and Implementation of an International Building Exhibition in Berlin in 1984.' And thus the IBA was set in train.

The Bill contained various propositions. West Berlin indeed was polycentric, but this should be seen as an advantage which encouraged differences in character between the various zones. At the same time, however, there were differences in living conditions within the advantaged and disadvantaged areas and these, most certainly, should be ended. The polycentric nature of West Berlin, however, meant that it lacked a central area 'as a spatial reference for Berlin civic consciousness' and somehow there would have to be compensation for this. So the aim was to make the city as a whole more attractive; to give all West Berliners some way of identifying with their city. The Kurfürstendam – centre of, among other things, Berlin's rather sleazy nightlife – was by no means an adequate symbol.

The Bill too suggested that the historic plan of the city be used as a basis for future development. In this way there would be 'a future for our past'. Relationships too between social norms and individual freedom would have to be re-thought and reformulated. Requisite individuality, variety and capacity for change could all be achieved by regarding 'the city as a constant, the building as a variable'. There was to be emphasis too on the quality of housing and, above all, a kind of productive tension was to be developed, or, rather, redeveloped between 'social requirements and the individual, artistic responsibility of the architect'.

All this was to be expressed, and, indeed, concentrated within an area of 250 hectares into which some 9000 dwellings – and their necessary infrastructures – were to be inserted.

According to the Bill, the central aims of the IBA were to restore the 'Inner City as living space' and 'rescuing a clapped-out city'.

Once the Bill had been passed, a Planning Association was set up and in 1984 the envisaged Exhibition was held.

Further discussion made it clear that the various sections of Berlin would have to be treated in different ways. The old Quarter SO 36, for instance – part of the Kreuzberg Quarter – needed careful, sensitive restoration and sensitive redevelopment (Fig. 12.1); Luisenstadt – also part of old Kreutzberg – had been laid out in the mid-19th century by Peter Joseph Lenné and whilst the layout was still intact, individual buildings needed considerable renovation. Nor was there a proper infrastructure of services.

Southern Friedrichstrasse had been built to an elegant, Baroque layout by Philipp Gerlach and even up to 1939 it had been a cultural and political centre of Berlin. But it had been subject to wartime destruction and the later depredations of planners (Figs 12.2 and 12.3). Also with the building of the Wall it was no longer connected to the historic centre, so in this case careful additions were needed.

As for the southern Tiergarten, whilst the Kulturforum was relatively new, other parts of the area, including the Lützowplatz as the historic Gateway to the Tiergarten and parts of the Diplomatic Quarter itself

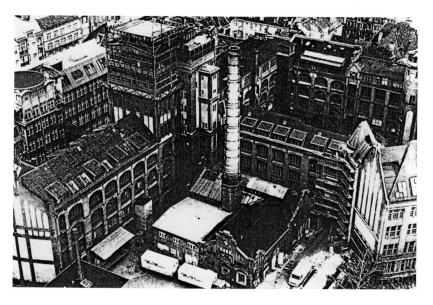

Fig. 12.1 19th century Berlin Block (from Girouard, 1985).

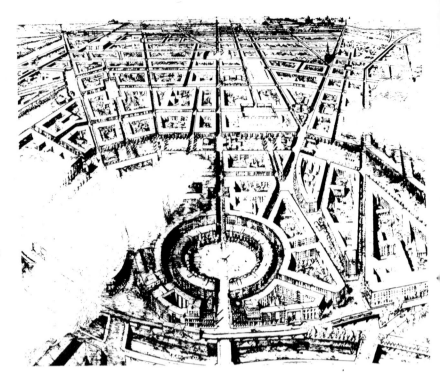

Fig. 12.2 Rob Krier (1977) Stadliche
Friedrichstadt, Berlin: Ideal plan (from
Krier, R. 1982b).

had deteriorated into ruins and wasteland. Here the city would have to
be stitched together whilst maintaining, at the same time, the large
existing green spaces including the Tiergarten.

Elsewhere in Berlin, as Clelland says (1987) there was 'another
detached fragment of Neubau responsibility': the Prager Platz – a 19th
century urban square – had become a formless frayed traffic intersection. This would have to be reconstructed as a proper urban space.
And elsewhere also, quite outside the city, the old harbour on the
Tegel Canal – as Lampugnani says a 'much loved, delightful rural
recreation centre for Berlin' would have to be redesigned for recreation
and housing. Here, too, there was the ecological problem of water
purification.

Nor was Hitzig's proposal for urban villas entirely forgotten. Indeed
it was developed at a series of Summer Academies held in Berlin
during the mid-1970s by Josef Paul Kliehues, Oswald Mathias Ungers

Fig. 12.3 View of Stadliche
Friedrichstadt along the
Friedrichstrasse from Werner
Duttmann's Mehringplatz (1968–75) to
a concept of Hans Scharoun's
(author's photograph).

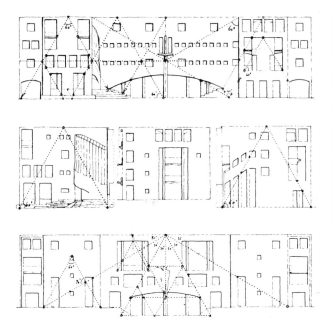

Fig. 12.5 Housing on the Ritterstrasse
(author's photograph).

Fig. 12.4 Rob Krier et al. (1977–80):
Housing on the Ritterstrasse, Berlin
(from Krier, R., 1982b).

and others who took the view that a four-storey house, square on plan, could indeed be used, whole or subdivided, in the various ways which Hitzig had proposed. Apart from the urban villa, Rob Krier had shown already with his Housing on the Ritterstrasse (1977–80) that low-density perimeter housing could be very effective (Figs 12.4 and 12.5).

So as Clelland points out (1987) the slabs and tower blocks of the Hansaviertel were to be replaced in the IBA by two quite different kinds of development: urban villas and perimeter housing, that is housing which encloses a complete urban block leaving a courtyard in the centre.

Kliehues was appointed Director for the desolated areas in which much new building (Neubau) would be needed, whilst Hardt-Waltherr Hämer became director of rehabilitation for old buildings, called in Berlin 'Altbau'.

Originally they intended that by 1984 some 9000 dwellings would be completed as Altbau or Neubau. But soon this was seen as unrealistic and it was agreed that by 1987 – 750 years after the founding of the city – some 3000 dwellings each of Neubau and Altbau should be ready.

The areas for Neubau included Tegel on the River Spree, the Prager Platz, the Southern Tiergarten area and the Southern Friedrichstrasse. The Altbau areas were to include Luisenstadt and those areas which remained in West Berlin of the old Postal District SO 36.

Competitions were held for developments at various locations within these areas. These included the planning of Residential and Recreational Facilities on the site of the Tegel Docks (1980), not to mention the design of individual buildings in this area; Urban Surveys and buildings designs for the Karolinenstrasse (1983–85), the Prager Platz (1979); various projects for the Lutzowplatz and the Lutzow-strasse (1979–81); Urban Villas for the Kurfurstenstrasse (1982); housing for Am Karlsbad (1983–84); a new Science Centre on the Tiergarten (1979–80); various embassies and housing to unite and urbanize the Kulturforum on the Rauchstrasse (1980) (IBA, 1987; Nakamura, 1987).

The entrants for these various competitions read like a veritable
international *Who's Who* of architects in the 1980s. They include such
European Rationalists as Aymonimo, Botta, Grassi, both Kriers,
Reinhard and Reichlin, Rossi and Ungers; members of the New York
Five, including Eisenman, Hejduk and Meier, other American archi-
tects such as Moore, Robertson and Tigerman; Austrians, such as
Hollein and Peichl, British such as Clelland, Cook and Hawley, the
Smithsons and Stirling; Dutch, such as van Eyck and Hertzberger,
Japanese such as Isosaki, Kurakawa and Ushida; and others somewhat
more individual such as Martorell, Bohigas and Mackay, Böhm,
Gregotti, Grumbach, Kliehues, Portoghesi, Valle, and Zenghelis.

Schemes with a high content of Urban Space Design include that for
the Tegel Docks which was won by Moore (1980); but Leon Krier also
was awarded a Special Prize; that for the Magdeburger Platz, won by
Nielebock and Grutzke, that for the Science Centre, won by Stirling
and Wilford, that for an International Cultural Forum, with notable
entries by Hollein (1983–87) and Ungers (1984), that for the Rauchstrasse won by Robert Krier, those for the Prince Albrecht Palace site by
Hejduk, that for South Friedrichstrasse by the OMA – the Office for
Metropolitan Architecture – by Eisenman for the Wilhelmstrasse, by
Hejduk and Hadid. The more notable of these included Gustav
Peichl's Plan for the Tegel area as a whole, James Stirling's formation of
a Science Museum around existing buildings in the Kultur Forum.

The Kultur Forum

Stirling's Science Centre lies immediately behind, and is attached to
the 19th century Law Courts just north of the Landwehr Kanal.
Immediately to the north there is Gutbrod's Kunstgewerbemuseum
(1978) and east of that there is the Mathei Church. Mies van der Rohe's
Staatsgallerie (1965–68) lies south and east of the Church, and
therefore east of the Science Centre. Eastwards again, beyond Mies's
Gallerie is Scharoun's gilded, Expressionist Staatsbibliotek and,
further to the north, his equally gilded and Expressionist Philharmonie.

Mies's square black box, standing on a rectangular plinth, was
designed initially as an Office Building for the Bacardi Rum Company
in Havana and his self-contained form has made any kind of extension
virtually impossible. Scharoun's Philharmonie by contrast has
spawned a Hall for Chamber Concerts and the Museum of Musical
Instruments almost like natural growths.

Hollein's scheme for unifying, if not exactly urbanizing, the Kulturforum consisted of paving a large, rectangular area between the
Church and the Philharmonie with a Bible Museum in the form of a
tower and other buildings providing some sense of urban enclosure.
Ungers's scheme was somewhat more dramatic with a colonnade
square in front of the church linked on a diagonal axis to two L-shaped
buildings back to back beyond the Philharmonie and quite a high
Tower beyond the Bibliotek.

As for Stirling's Science Centre, this is planned around a courtyard
behind the old Law Courts. Stirling's courtyard is as irregular as
anything in Sitte and, at first sight, it seems to have been planned in a
Sitte-like way. The Centre consists largely of small offices and these
line double-banked corridors within buildings which, on plan at least –
working anti-clockwise behind the old Law Courts – look like a
(Romanesque), cross-shaped Church, a linear building with a two-
storey, glass-roofed Stoa open to the courtyard, an octagonal Cam-

panile and an Amphitheatre also open to the courtyard where its stage normally would have been. Beyond this Amphitheatre and attached to it, almost touching the old Law Courts, there is a Fortress or Castle, square on plan and with circular corner towers which proves in three-dimensional reality to be a garden.

Yet the courtyard is unlike Sitte in the way that, apart from the Campanile, which is eight storeys high, all the other new buildings are five storeys high and flat roofed, although in 1987 only one floor of the Basilica had been built.

As Buchanan points out (1980) the planning was by no means determined by Sitte-like decisions as to how things would look in three dimensions. It was planned, rather, by regulating lines or perhaps, as Buchanan calls them: leylines (Fig. 12.6).

If one walks out of the Law Courts along its central axis and crosses the courtyard towards the Stoa, one comes to a point, somewhat in front of it, where two other axes meet: the centre line of the Church and the centre line of the Theatre.

Once one has spotted this, then as Buchanan says:

> Further investigation reveals that every face, centrepoint and other important crossing is generated by lines, either connecting significant points on the existing building and then projected; or connecting a point on this building with a significant point on the site; or connecting significant points of the new building. . . .

So:

> a line connecting one corner of the central portico of the existing building with a corner of the site generates the front face of the theatre and the point where the walkway of the stoa ends; a point connecting the other corner of the portico with a re-entrant corner at the back of the building defines one face of the fort; the centres

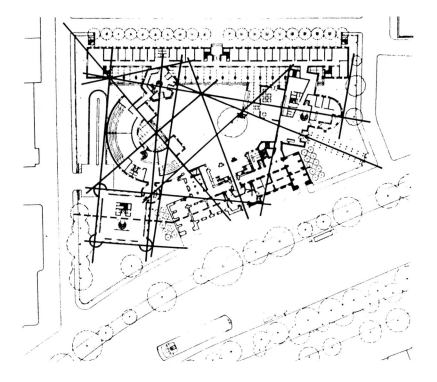

Fig. 12.6 James Stirling and Michael Wilford (1979–80) Science Centre, Berlin showing planning by 'ley lines' (Buchanan, 1980).

Fig. 12.7 Rob Krier (1980) Layout of
Urban Villas for the Rauchstrasse
(author's photograph of IBA model).

of the campanile, theatre and two of the towers of the fort fall one
line; and their tangents on another. . . .

and so on.

There are several other such co-ordinates in and around the
courtyard but in one case only does the building indicate its function.
The (amphi) theatre actually contains fan-shaped lecture theatres but
despite the strict symmetry of the building as a whole, the internal
planning is quite asymmetrical at ground floor level. Externally the
stage appears as a slot between two towers which, at five storeys, are
far too high to frame any kind of stage. This too has a glazed canopy.

Fig. 12.8 Rob Krier (1982–84)
Apartment Block for the Rauchstrasse
(author's photograph).

The buildings themselves are stuccoed with horizontal bands of red and blue marbling, all rather high for the width of courtyard they enclose but at least there *is* clearly the sense that an urban space *has* been contained between them. Except that instead of paving, it has a floor of grass!

West of this again, at the further end of the Diplomatic Quarter there is the best known, perhaps, of all the IBA developments; a group of urban villas planned by Robert Krier (Konopka, 1985). Krier won an IBA Competition for such houses to be built behind the old Norwegian Embassy, on the Rauchstrasse which, curiously enough, lies opposite the Hansaviertel on the Tiergarten. His scheme retained the L-shaped Embassy with a mirror image of it across a new central axis. About which also there are urban villas of the Kliehues/Ungers variety, four to each side with the last pair linked across the axis by a concave block intended to terminate the new vista and to contain the central court formed between the villas (Fig. 12.7).

It was crucial to Krier's philosophy that others should be involved in the realization of his scheme so that whilst he kept this three-part building for himself, and designed one of the other villas also, the L-shaped villa, mirroring the Embassy, was allocated to Aldo Rossi and others were allocated to Mario Botta, Brenner and Tonon, Herman and Valentiny, Georgio Grassi, Nielebock and Partner and Gianni Braghieri. Botta withdrew, on the grounds that he could not work within the cost limits, and his villa was re-allocated to Hans Hollein.

It is interesting to see the effects which building in Berlin had on the various designers. The concave side of Krier's Terminal Building, facing into the central court is faced largely in brick; indeed with banded brickwork at ground level and window details which might well have come from the 19th century brick vernacular of Berlin. The convex side, however, is faced in stucco; at least the central portion, and as at Ritterstrasse there is a heroic sculpture – a portrait bust, above the wide-but-shallow entrance arch (Fig. 12.8). The planning of the apartments is quite complex; indeed Krier uses internally the kinds of geometric form he analysed in his book on Urban Space. So many of the apartments have central vistas of geometric forms in enfilade.

Krier's critics have pounced on this internal planning as evidence that he is concerned with geometric manipulation at the expense of

Fig. 12.9 Rob Krier and Hans Hollein; Urban Villas nos 8 and 9 for the Rauchstrasse (author's photograph).

Fig. 12.10 Aldo Rossi Apartment block for the Rauchstrasse (author's photograph).

human comfort and convenience. But as Krier himself points out (1987, personal communication) prospective users were offered open plans – open, that is, apart from the structure and service-related rooms, such as kitchens and bathrooms – and then offered choices of various geometric arrangements or whatever else they chose to do in terms of internal planning. In one case, Krier's chief opponent in the Berlin Senate was persuaded by his wife to buy one of Krier's apartments!

The most flamboyant of designs for the Rauchstrasse Villas was Hans Hollein's with more complex planning geometries even than Kriers' (Fig. 12.9). This means that each facade curves in a series of facettes and bays painted grey, pink or yellow with a deeper pink over most of the ground floor and the wide overhanging eaves.

Krier himself felt challenged by Hollein and his villa too is rather complex. Unlike his Terminal Building it is completely stuccoed with Hollein-like pinks and yellows around certain windows; de Stijl-like reds and blues around others.

But the biggest surprise, perhaps, was Aldo Rossi who abandoned the white, geometric sterility of his Gallaretese Housing in Milan and his Modena Cemetery for rugged construction in banded brick (Fig. 12.10). The fact that his building, L-shaped, turns a corner – mirroring the old Norwegian Embassy – meant that he could mark this turn with a tower with an octagonal turret and a pyramidal copper roof. Rossi, what is more, used brick again for his housing of the Wilhelmstrasse in which the staircases which divide the apartments into pairs are surmounted by (very tall) pediments.

Whilst the Rauchstrasse developments can be counted successful on many levels; several of Krier's most cherished ideas were sacrificed on economic grounds. His four-storey villas were raised to five storeys and all the non-housing uses he had planned, such as shops, workshops and a kindergarten were eliminated. Thus Krier's idea of the central space contained by the villas as a kind of 'social condenser' was lost. Whatever Social condensing function it serves is provided by the childrens' playground.

Fig. 12.11 Moore, Ruble, Yudell (1980) Residential and Recreational facilities at Tegeler Hafen, Berlin (from Kliehues and Klotz, 1986).

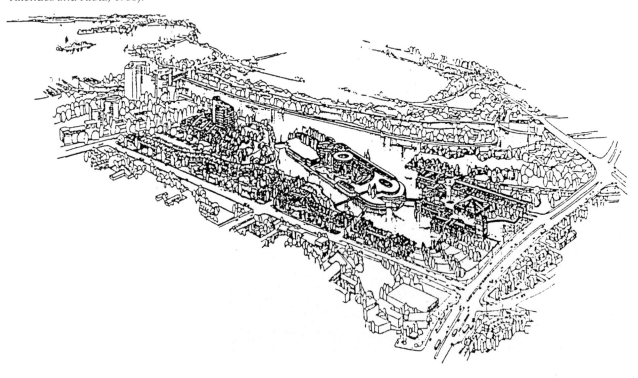

Given sequences of almost cubic villas down each side, separated by cubes of space almost as big as the villas themselves, one would expect a fairly leaky urban space. But the empty cubes are occupied by trees which contribute considerably to the sense of *being* in an urban space.

The other major area of Neubau is to be found in the Southern Friedrichstrasse. As Davey and Clelland suggest this was first laid out in the 18th century by Philipp Gerlach as a series of Baroque urban spaces. These had been eroded over time by the coming of the railway and the Landwehrkanal, not to mention wartime bombing. So Kliehues's aim for the area was a critical reconstruction of the original layout, or at least a reinterpretation with modern terraces lining Gerlach's boulevards and enclosing his urban blocks.

As Davey and Clelland also point out, the Berlin block is very large compared with the urban blocks of other cities. Which enabled the Berliners to plan hierarchies of spaces from the most public realm of the street, through ranges of increasingly private spaces as one penetrates into the block, to the most private spaces of all within individual dwellings.

There were many variations on how such blocks can be enclosed and how the boulevards between them could be lined.

So the problems in South Friedrichstrasse were the design of insertions intended to line the streets, proposals for the articulate site of the former Prince Albrecht Palace (1984); housing for the Kochstrasse/Friedrichstrasse area (1981); the Koch/Wilhelm/Puttkamerstrasse area (1983–84); 'Living near the Berlin Museum' (1985); high-rise apartments for the Wilhelmstrasse (1981); not to mention schools, a centre for the deaf, the Bessel Park (1986) and various urban renewal projects, such as the junction of Koch and Friedrichstrasse, the Wilhelmstrasse, and so on, in ways by which the original plans of these areas could be reinstated. Rossi, Reichlin and Reinhart, Martorell, Bohigas and Mackay, Eisenman and Robertson all gained prizes for their entries to the Koch/Friedrichstrasse area.

Of those completed by 1987 the most interesting in terms of offering precedents for urban space planning elsewhere are probably the large complex adjacent to the Berlin Museum, the Schinkelplatz on the northern Rauchstrasse and Moore's housing at Tegel.

Of these the Museum Area is the largest in scale, with a vast, six-storey courtyard surrounding Isozaki's nine-storey apartment

Fig. 12.12 Tegeler Hafen: Housing (author's photograph).

Fig. 12.13 Tegeler Hafen: Housing (author's photograph).

Fig. 12.14 Leo Krier (1980–83) 'New Block Quarter' for Berlin-Tegel (from *Architectural Design*, **54** (7/8), 1984).

block. South of this there are two rows of urban villas, six to a row, and separated by a space which is hardly wider than the villas themselves. Thus there is a strong sense of urban *enclosure* but not much of urban *space*.

The largest single Neubau site was at the Tegeler Hafen, the old docks on the Tegel Canal, some 10 kilometres north west of the Diplomatic Quarter. The Competition for housing and leisure facilities was won by Charles Moore's Grover, Harper Office and they proposed a series of urban villas, with eight-storey terraces behind them, radiating from an octagonal courtyard and undulating, more or less in parallel lines along the Canal in a series of long, S-shaped curves (Figs 12.11–12.13).

Moore's leisure facilities were to be accommodated on a rectangular island, with semicircular ends, in a basin open to the canal.

The terraces are Post-Modern Classical in detail, finished in plasticized stucco whose style is to be matched in the urban villas. Moore designed a model villa to which other architects, such as Grumbach, Stern, Tigerman, Portoghesi and Hejduk were invited to respond.

But the most surprising scheme was Leo Krier's. His schemes for Echternacht, Royal Mint Square, and La Villette had been strongly axial but in the 1980s he changed direction in two specific ways. His plans became much more informal and his architecture became more Classical.

These changes became extremely clear in his designs for Tegel (1980–83) (Krier, 1984). Krier found the site, bounded by the River Havel, the Borsig Factories, an Autobahn and the Tegel Forest to be as big as medieval Amsterdam or Renaissance Florence. Yet Tegel consisted of little more than a modest urban centre with 'frayed fringes'.

Krier naturally wanted to make a proper city with the streets and squares, public and private buildings of self-contained Quartiers (Figs 12.14 and 12.15). The requirement for a Sports Centre suggested part of his programme to which were added Public Baths, an (Odeon) Theatre, a Library, a Grammar School, a Nautical Club, an Art Gallery and so on (Fig. 12.16).

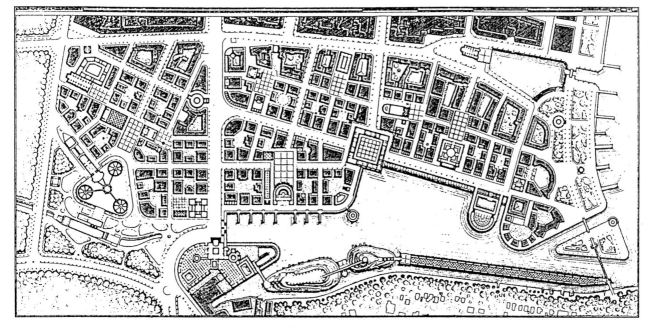

Fig. 12.15 'New Block Quarter' Berlin-Tegel (from *Architectural Design*, **54** (7/8), 1984).

He started his urban design by extending streets as they existed in Tegel to form his cross streets of the site and increased by excavation the length of the waterfront. His main street runs somewhat diagonally to this and his public buildings, of course, each have their urban spaces of streets and squares (Fig. 12.15).

Most of the housing takes the form of two- or three-storey blocks grouped around small squares to form insulae. As Krier says: 'The proportions, dimensions and materials should be those used in Berlin's best residential buildings. Energy-wasting materials such as concrete, aluminium and plastic should not be utilised, nor indeed are they needed!'.

As for the public buildings, they: 'must be erected to the highest standards of craftsmanship and technology. Classical architecture has fully met all these requirements'. They include a splendid Covered Square in the form of a Belvedere, a (roofed) Roman Theatre (Fig. 12.16), the Odeon, a vast Public Baths with two groupings of Frigidarium. Tepidarium and Caldarium on the Roman pattern around

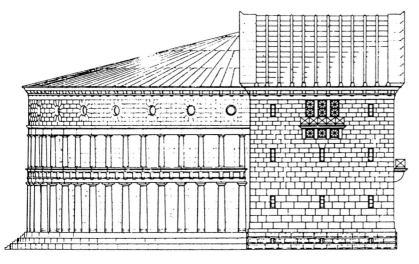

Fig. 12.16 'New Block Quarter' Berlin-Tegel: Odeon (from *Architectural Design*, **54**, (7/8), 1984).

a central Aula, a Public Library formed of diminishing squares, a cylindrical Public Library with a conical roof, a great Gymnasium with an open Greek-Theatre-like Arena.

All these are presented in meticulous, Classical detail and located with consummate skill within the plan to give intricate but unified views of the City from whatever viewpoint. It is quite a breathtaking concept!

And for the Tegel area too, Gustave Peichl designed a long, ship-like Phosphate Elimination Plant by which drinking water could be extracted from the Tegeler Lake.

The largest urban spaces designed for the IBA are those around the Prager Platz in Schöneberg Platz. This was once a (rather open) circus but wartime bombing and planners' depredations had destroyed any sense of urban enclosure. Rob Krier, Aymonimo and Böhm each did schemes to show how housing up to six storeys or so designed as segments of the circus could ensure that it was defined again. In addition to contributing to the circular space, Böhm's segment also has a bathing and leisure complex behind it.

As for the north Rauchstrasse the Schinkelplatz was planned by Rob Krier who, as he had already at the Ritterstrasse (1973), invited others to design the individual houses. The Schinkelplatz itself is quite a small square, some eight bays wide on each side with, in principle, four larger squares – each some 14 bays along each side, disposed diagonally about it (Ferlenga, 1983) (Fig. 12.17). Thus there are urban spaces, open at their far ends, radiating along both axes from the central Platz.

Most of this development is four storeys high, which has all the advantages predicted by the various advocates of this limit. The enclosed courts too are beautifully landscaped whilst the houses themselves have the variety one would expect with some 20 architects involved (Fig. 12.18). Since the site had contained a Villa by Karl Friedrich Schinkel, destroyed during World War II Krier rebuilt its elevation on one of his central blocks; hence the name: Schinkelplatz.

There is underground parking or, rather, parking half storey underground which means that a proper urban density can be achieved without the wide open spaces that parking on the ground requires.

Fig. 12.17 Rob Krier (1977) Schinkelplatz as the Focus of Four Blocks (from Krier, 1982).

All in all the IBA seems to have provided the first large-scale demonstration of viable alternatives to the towers and the slabs of the 1960s; very human in scale yet dense enough to give a real sense of urbanity. What is more it seems exceedingly popular, yet Clelland expresses disappointment. As Clelland says (1987) most of the architects involved with IBA in its early days subscribed to the Rationalist tradition. They sought to break free from the banality of much post-war architecture – housing in particular – and to re-establish the city itself as the context for Architecture. So they began to re-use the spatial typologies of the city which had been tested by history; of streets, public spaces, urban blocks, public monuments – using these as theoretical anchors by which the dignity and value of architecture could be restored.

Having analysed the various typologies, for a particular city, as Clelland says, each architect then went on to claim that, since he had analysed the history of the site, using graphic techniques, *his* interventions would be justified because, given that specific method of working, they were bound to work within the structure of the place.

But, as Clelland goes on to point out, 'in example after example, one is left wondering why the resultant buildings are often crude and stark': why there should be such a 'yawning chasm between the good intentions of the theory and the practical results'.

So, according to Clelland, the 'Rationalist school has begun to fail'. He suggests that the buildings ended up diagrammatic and crude because Rationalist theory in itself was diagrammatic and crude.

The problem, one suspects, was endemic to the nature of IBA itself (Rowe, 1984). For, as Rossi points out, a city, to be a city, needs, in addition to its general texture, monuments which give it identity. Since *all* the historic monuments of Berlin, with the possible exception of the Reichstag, lie in the Eastern Sector, West Berlin would have to build its own. Which it did, in the Kulturforum, in the form of Scharoun's Philharmonie and Bibliotek, Mies's Museum, and so on.

But these, literally, are not enough, either in number or in distribution; West Berlin needs more if it is to feel like a real city in Leon Krier's sense.

There were few monuments in the IBA programme. Certainly Peichl made his Phosphateliminationsanlage at Tegel into one when it need

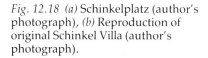

Fig. 12.18 (a) Schinkelplatz (author's photograph), *(b)* Reproduction of original Schinkel Villa (author's photograph).

(b)

(a)

not have been but apart from public buildings around the Prager Platz the only serious monument in the IBA programme was Stirling's Science Centre!

But in the months leading up to the opening of the IBA, so Clelland suggests, a 'New Spirit' was beginning to emerge.

Several winners of the later competitions presented designs different in kind from most of the IBA work. They were Eisenman and Robertson, Zaha Hadid and Daniel Libeskind.

Eisenman's Housing for Friedrichstrasse (1982–84) stands at the very 'gateway' to East Berlin: 'Checkpoint Charlie'. He responded to the ghastly symbolism of his site by planning the entire Block, around three existing buildings, as a three-dimensional park: 'The City of Excavations', for which he 'constructed' an imaginary history (Doubilet, 1987 PA4/87), conforming to the regular street grid of Berlin, as does much of Eisenman's new block.

But the tragic history of Berlin was played out on that grid so Eisenman 'challenged' it with another one, Mercator's projection: 'upon which so much Enlightenment history has been acted out'. The Berlin grid diverges from it by 3.3 degrees.

So Eisenman planned the basic masses of his building to the Berlin alignment and clad it with a square-gridded, glass wall system. He then planned 'Mercator masses' projecting out of the basic masses – angled at 3.3 degrees – with white and grey walls, a 'red brick' grid and so on. He planned 'Mercator' walls in his Park, too, to 'challenge' the Berlin Wall.

Zaha Hadid had sprung to international attention when she won the Hong Kong Peak Competition (1982–3). She had a vast, man-made 'landscape' of abstract, polished granite 'rocks' into which she thrust four 'beams' of accommodation (Wigley, 1988) piled over each other at dramatically clashing angles.

A ramp curves up and between them to the Reception and the car park whilst various bits of Club accommodation 'hover' between her 'beams' like flying saucers.

There are family resemblances between this Hong Kong scheme and Hadid's entries to the Berlin Competitions. But given the restricted Berlin sites, and the very ordinary briefs, she could not rise to such splendid heights!

Fig. 12.19 Daniel Libeskind (1987) The City Edge. A 450 metre 'beam' containing residential, commercial and other accommodation, cantilevered at an angle of six degrees along the Flottwell strasse (author's photograph of IBA model).

Her Kurfürstendam Office Block (corner of Lewishamstrasse), is long and narrow. She covers it with one of her 'beams' over which the office floors billow out, behind a huge 'sail' of curtain walling. She covers her Stresermanstrasse site with a three storey 'beam' of housing and a seven storey 'sail' at the corner of Dessauerstrasse (see Hadid 1987, 1988).

It seems unlikely that either of these will be built but in 1987, Daniel Libeskind designed an even larger 'beam' of housing, offices, public administration, a kindergarten, commercial premises, light industry, a cinema and so on which still seemed viable in January 1989. Libeskind's 'beam' is some 450 metres long, 10 metres wide and 20 metres high, rearing over Flottwellstrasse as a huge cantilever, six degrees to the horizontal, to a height of 56 metres (Fig. 12.19).

Libeskind's drawings show networks of fine lines clashing at disparate angles and he has an external lift, rising and falling on a 20 metre rotating disc. Wigley (1988) describes Libeskind's interiors as:

> a jumble of folded planes, crossed forms, counter reliefs, spinning movements, and contorted shapes. This apparent chaos actually constructs the walls that define the bar; it is the structure. The internal disorder produces the bar even while splitting it, even as gashes open up along its length.

So the IBA's final gesture is a monument after all, albeit a strange one. What is more it will define, under itself, a new and unfamiliar kind of urban space! So Clelland was right in suggesting that a 'New Spirit' was emerging towards the end of the IBA.

No doubt he took the term from an earlier *Architectural Review* (August, 1986) in which L. M. Farrely, announcing a 'New Spirit' in architecture had proclaimed the 'death' of 'Post-Modernism', which seems a little premature given the many journals devoted to 'Post-Modernism', the 30 or so monographs on 'Post-Modernist' architects, the major books by Jencks (1987) and Stern (1988) which have all been published since Farrely pronounced!

Her 'New Spirit' was based on 'the thrusting, dynamic imagery of Constructivism and . . . Futurism's savage beauty'. It was a 'state of mind' derived from Dada, but it had many other precursors, especially the Russian Constructivists. And among the work of many (still) unknowns she shows the work of architects who have loomed larger in the scheme of things than she could have known in 1986: Frank Gehry, Zaha Hadid, Daniel Libeskind and Co-op Mimmelblau, which is interesting because in 1988 they were chosen to represent yet another new 'tendency', 'Deconstruction'. But since its major monument is in Paris, Bernard Tschumi's Parc de la Villette, we should consider the Parisian context before looking, specifically at Deconstruction.

Paris: the monuments

As we have seen, Aldo Rossi suggested (1966) that the fabric of a city consists of two things; the general urban texture and the monuments. We have seen also that in the 1980s, two cities in particular, Berlin and Paris, demonstrated, with remarkable clarity, these two modes of city building, and that Paris set its sights on 1989, the Bicentenary of the French Revolution, to initiate a programme of building – and conserving – urban monuments.

Architectures Capitales

Nine of these were identified as the Architectures Capitales (Mitterand *et al.*, 1987). They are von Spreckelsen's Grande Arche de la Défense; I. M. Pei's Pyramide for le Grand Louvre; Bardon, Colboc and Phillipon's conversion of the Gare d'Orsay into a Museum with Gae Aullenti's interiors; Jean Nouvel – with Architecture Studio's – Institute for the Arab World; Chemetov and Huidobro's Ministère des Finances; Carlos Ott's Opéra de la Bastille; various developments at La Villette including Bernard Tschumi's Parc with its Folies, Reichen and Robert's conversion of the old meat market into a Grande Halle, Le Zénith, an inflatable hall for Pop Concerts by Chaix and Morel, Fainsilber's Cité des Sciences et de l'industrie and de Portzamparc's Cité de la Musique.

Whilst important in themselves for the life of Paris, the reconstructions and rehabilitations in themselves, literally, cannot add to the monuments of Paris. The old Gare d'Orsay looks much as it did – apart from the signs – in its previous incarnation as a railway station and similarly the Grande Halle at La Villette is substantially the structure that it was as a meat market although its presence, naturally, affected Tschumi's planning of his Parc. Nor can one conceive of an inflatable, such as Le Zénith as a monument in Rossi's sense. His whole point about monuments is their permanence. Even Fainsilber's Cité takes its form from the structural frame of the abattoir which was started and left incomplete on the site.

The most monumental gestures amongst all these 'Architectures Capitales' clearly are the two which provide full stops at either end of the Champs Elysées, von Spreckelsen's Arche at the Tête de la Défense and Pei's Pyramide at the Louvre.

The point of von Spreckelsen's Arche was to mitigate the gap-toothed effect which the towers of the 1960s at La Défense give from the Cour Napoléon at the Louvre and along the Champs Elysées. To which end von Spreckelsen designed an enormous hollow cube – 105 metres in each dimension, open front and back – and tilted away from the major axis of the Champs Elysées by some six degrees; exactly, or so von Spreckelsen says, the angle at which Cour Napoléon of the Louvre itself is tilted away from that same axis (Fig. 12.20).

Fig. 12.20 Johnann Otto von Spreckelsen (1982–88) Grande Arche: Tête de la Défense, Paris (author's photograph).

The side walls of the Arche contain offices, some 20 metres deep and tapering towards the front and back to give very sharp edges, rather like I. M. Pei's East Wing at the National Gallery in Washington DC. The wedge-shaped taperings are faced with Carrara Marble whilst the glazed facades, facing into and outwards of the arch, are clad with grids of curtain walling in 21 metre bays, framed at every seventh storey in the height and every seventh bay in their width by bands of marble.

von Spreckelsen says of them (1987):

> The façades of the open cube appear with a bright and smooth surface, symbolising a micro-chip, showing the lines of communication; an abstract graphic work inspired by the most brilliant invention of modern electronics.

The floor of von Spreckelsen's Cube contains links with the various transport systems: 'bus, Métro, RER and train, not to mention a shopping centre and an International Data Processing Market'. The sides, as we have seen, contain offices, and the roof is dished to form a garden reached by lifts which rise in a 'column' made of tensioned cables.

Of his overall intentions von Spreckelsen says:

> An open cube
> A window in the world
> As a temporary Grande Finale to the avenue
> With a view into the future.
> It is a modern Arc de Triomphe,
> Celebrating the triumph of mankind,
> It is a symbol of hope for the future,
> That all people can meet freely,
> Here under The Triumphal Arch of Man. . . .

To which one can only respond: 'How very Parisian!'

As for the other end of the axis, the Cour Napoléon at the Louvre, this has been enhanced by Ioeh Ming Pei's Pyramide (Fig. 12.21).

Fig. 12.21 Ioeh Ming Pei (1981–88) Pyramid Entrance to Le Grand Louvre (author's photograph).

Which, almost literally, is the tip of the iceberg since most of Pei's constructions are below ground. So are the considerable remains of the original Louvre, Philipe Auguste's 12th century Castle not to mention Charles Vs 14th century residence.

Anyone faced with the prospect of getting into the Louvre during the 1980s must welcome the idea of a central entrance hall with tunnels to the three main wings. Especially since Pei's entrance hall contains an information desk, an auditorium, a reception area for children, a café-restaurant and the various museum shops all linked to car parks and the station for tourist buses.

The only point of contention, obviously, is Pei's Pyramide, 33 metres square on plan and 21 metres high.

At first sight it seemed like sacrilege; a Modernist glass pyramid in the middle of one of the finest Renaissance courts in the world. The materials, too, seemed unacceptably High Tech consisting, as they do, of steel tubes, some five centimetres in diameter, forming a fine mesh with eight millimetre tension cables, the two together looking rather like a spider's web.

Yet nothing of the old Louvre is destroyed, indeed as we have seen, much of earlier Louvres is recovered. Given so much underground circulation there had to be *some* surface marker of the entrance. Which could only be made with a structure of some kind, in which case Pei's Pyramide seems to be a good deal less offensive than most other conceivable forms.

A neo-Classical pavilion, however small, would have been crushed by the real thing. A Miesian glass box, with its rectilinear geometry, would have conflicted with the verticals and horizontals of the Renaissance Cour. A dome however delicate, would still be too substantial.

Pei's Pyramide refuses to compete and if, in the long run, it proves offensive, then of course, like the gossamer which it so resembles it can be blown away!

The other monuments built in Paris for the Bicentenary, whilst more or less impressive in themselves, have much less to offer in terms of urban design. Both Ott's Opéra and Nouvel's Institute . . . Arabe simply fill difficult sites with Late-Modernist curvilinear forms whilst Chemetov's Ministère des Finances (1982) is clustered behind a huge linear form of which the chief claim to fame is that it, literally, 'dips its toes' into the waters of the River Seine (Fig. 12.22).

Fig. 12.22 Paul Chemetov and Borja Huidobro (1982–): Ministère des Finances (author's photograph).

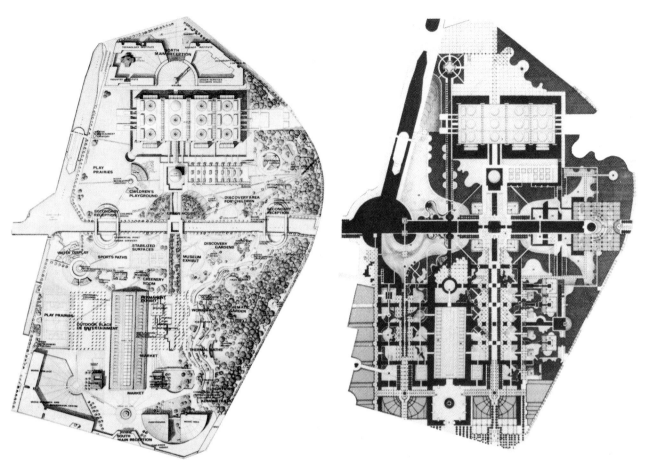

Fig. 12.23 Kisho Kurokawa (1982–3)
Project for the Parc de la Villette, Paris
(from Barzilay *et al.*, 1984).

Fig. 12.24 Alain Provost (1982–83)
Project for the Parc de la Villette, Paris
(from Barzilay *et al.*, 1984).

Parc de La Villette

As early as the late 1940s it had been decided that the old Meat Market
of Paris, housed in cast iron and glass Pavilions by Baltard: Les Halles
was no longer adequate and alternative sites were suggested. It was
decided in 1959 that the new site should be at La Villette, at the
north-west periphery of Paris, where already there was an old cattle
Market, also by Baltard. In 1966 a Competition was launched for new
Abattoirs to be built north of that old Cattle Market.

There was much discussion as to how appropriate this might be but
work was started on the Abattoirs. Discussion continued, however,
and, since cattle could no longer be walked to the Market, it was closed
in March 1974. There was much discussion as to its future use and
eventually the idea emerged that it should be used as a Grand Hall for
Exhibitions and Entertainment.

Then in 1976, the Atelier Parisien d'Urbanisme and the Préfecture
organized an open Ideas Competition for all 55 hectares of the Villette
site. This attracted 167 entrants including Antoine Grumbach, Bernard
Huet, Henri Ciriani, Leon Krier (see pp. 196–9), Diana Agrest and Mario
Gandelsonas. Adrien Fainsilber's entry was selected and this included
a number of propositions – some of which had been suggested in
earlier discussions of the site.

So Fainsilber's scheme included the Grand Hall idea for the Market –
it was opened for its new uses in 1985 – a City of Science and Industry

to be housed in the vast but incomplete Abattoir building – this was opened in 1987 – a vast new City of Music to the south of the Grand Hall and a formal landscaped Park between the two existing buildings.

As at Le Halles however various power struggles continued; there were many scandals and whilst Fainsilber's scheme for the City of Science was retained, his design for the Parc was not. A new Competition was set up in 1982–83 for L'Invention du Parc (Barzilay, Hayward and Lombard-Valentino, 1984). This attracted 472 entrants including Emile Aillaud, Carlo Aymonimo, Jean Baudoin, Zaha Hadid, Rem Koolhaas, Kisho Kurokawa (Fig. 12.23), Richard Meier, Rodrigo Pérez d'Arce, Cedric Price, Moore, Grover, Harper, Alison Smithson and Alain Provost (Fig. 12.24).

The organizers detected seven families of entries: the garden in the city . . . the poetic and plastic concept . . . a diversity of facilities and spaces . . . to reconcile natural and imposed constraints . . . the garden . . . between nature and the city and so on.

They ranged, as one might expect, over the whole gamut from extreme formality to extreme informality. Aymonimo's scheme, for instance, is a vast, formal linear structure of which he says: 'A great architectural structure (a . . . concept . . . like that of an ancient viaduct) crossing the park from north to south, rests on an artificial terrain. It links the new park to the system of 19th century parks.' Rossella Marchini also designed 'a great non-religious basilica, with the same role as a cultural reservoir and a matrix for the urbanisation and production that had formerly been played by the Cluniac and Benedictine monks'. Michel Corajoud, on the other hand, treated the park as an 'ancient palimpsest' in which 'one piece of writing is laid over another, no longer clear; as if an English garden had been superimposed over the French one underneath', and, given the size and complexity of the site, the two left side by side. Kurokawa, for instance, says of his scheme: 'A dividing line between the geometrical to the west and the disordered to the east, the north–south axis also becomes a meeting point.'

The winner was Bernard Tschumi with a scheme which, physically and metaphorically is many-layered (Tschumi, 1984). Tschumi lays out his ground plan by using those age-old devices: the square, the triangle and the circle, so disposed that the square encloses the City of Science, the circle lies south of this and the triangle further south, east of Baltards's Great Hall. Tschumi sees this as a system of planes or surfaces. Then he lays a 120 metre grid over the site, some eight squares North to South and five from East to West which he sees as a system of points. And at every point of intersection he places a folie. Then between and around his folies soar and swoop a multiplicity of paths. Some of them respond to the square, the circle and the triangle, others take free forms through his folies, over and around his 'thematic' gardens. Tschumi sees these walkways as a system of lines, a 'promenade cinématique' of the kind he developed in the Manhattar Transcripts (1981, 1983) (Fig. 12.25).

So, Tschumi superimposes three geometric systems: of points, of lines and of surfaces. Each system is clear and coherent in itself but, superimposed, they affect each other. Sometimes one reinforces another, sometimes they interfere to produce distortions and sometimes they simply co-exist (see Tschumi, 1985, 1987 and 1988) (Figs 12.26a–c).

The folies themselves are 36 foot cubes (10.8 metres) divided three dimensionally into 12 foot cubes forming 'cages'. Then, as Tschumi says (1987) 'The cage can be decomposed into fragments of a cage or extended through the addition of other elements'. Every part of the

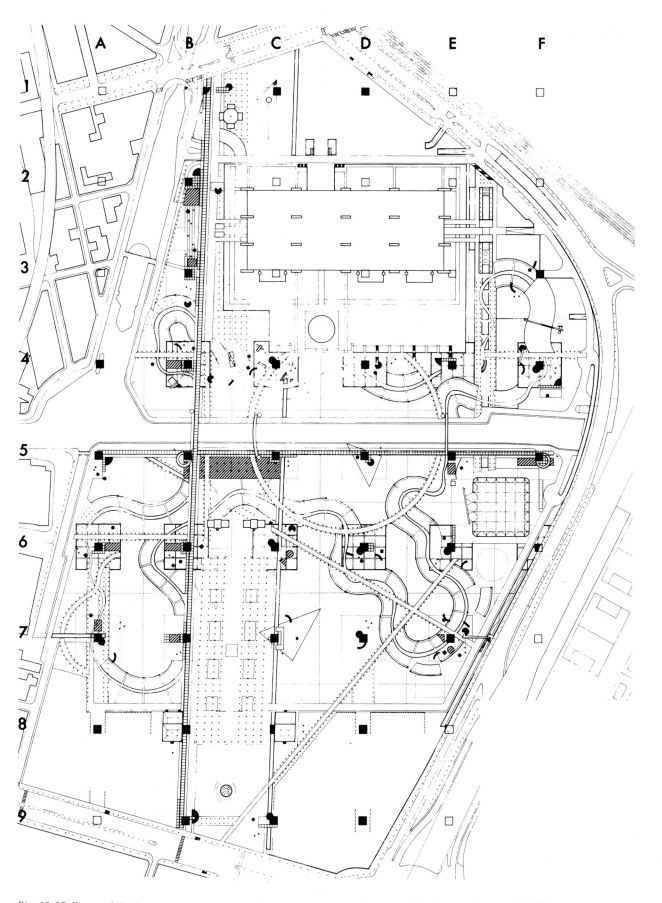

Fig. 12.25 Bernard Tschumi (1982–83) Project for the Parc de la Villette (model) (from Tschumi, 1982–3).

(a)

(b)

(c)

Fig. 12.26 Bernard Tschumi: Parc de la
Villette (1987): Folies under
construction *(a)* (Constructivist) Folie
p. 7 . *(b)* Gallery between Folies. *(c)*L5
with restaurant/bar (author's
photographs).

structural frame, is covered by a bright red-enamelled steel envelope. There may be stairs, ramps or even walkways passing through.

The forms of the 'other elements' are determined by combinatory rules. They may be cylinders or triangular prisms, one or two storeys high and clad in grey granite. They may have specific functions: cinema, restaurant, piano bar, video threatre, observatory, shop or whatever and of course there may be clashes between function and form.

Tschumi has allocated certain folies, and certain spaces between them to other designers, such as John Hejduk, Peter Eisenman with Jacques Derrida (the Choral Work) and so on (see Derrida, 1987; Tschumi, 1987; Eisenman, 1988).

Spaced as they are to his large grid, Tschumi's small folies cannot enclose space in the way that four-storey terraces would. Rather they punctutate space, draw space around themselves and if we seek parallels, in terms of openness, the nearest may be those the Venturis found so intriguing (1968, 1973) in their A & P Parking Lots.

Deconstruction

Like Hadid, the Libeskind in Berlin – not to mention Eisenman – Tschumi at La Villette, offers new and exciting ways of designing in space, hardly known before the mid-1980s. So what is his – what is their – motivation?

This question was explored in some detail by an Academy Symposium at the Tate on Deconstruction (March, 1988), associated issues of *Architectural Design* and *Art and Design* (both 3/4 1988) and at an Exhibition of Deconstructivist Architecture held – at Philip Johnson's behest – by MoMA (the Museum of Modern Art) in New York during the Summer of 1988. So what was there in the Symposium, the Magazines and the Exhibition?

We have seen already Mark Wigley's description of Libeskind's City Edge for Berlin. Elsewhere, Wigley (1987) finds metaphors for such things in the writings of Jacques Derrida who, he says 'deconstructs aesthetics by demonstrating that the constructional possibility of form is precisely its violation by a subversive alien, foreign body that already inhabits the interior and cannot be expelled without destroying its host'.

Jacques Derrida

So what is Derrida driving at? That's difficult to say, given his mercurial way of thinking but he offers an explanation. For some time, he says (1986), a 'de-constructive procedure' has been establishing itself, an attempt to free philosophy from its inbuilt constraints, the 'takings-for-granted' which for centuries have stultified thinking, above all such 'binary-oppositions' as: God/man; science/technology; philosophy/architecture' and so on.

So what does Derrida do? He reads the work of others, such as Ferdinand de Saussure, and 'deconstructs' it by taking the author's own premises and pushing them further than he did, thus 'subverting' the text from 'within'. Derrida does this in three books (all 1967): *De la Grammatologie*; *L'Écriture et la Différence*; *La Voix et le Phénomènone*. He aims to 'deconstruct' three things: 'Onto-Theology' (belief in God's existence); 'Logocentrism' (the belief that one can get 'to the bottom of things' by logic, rational argument, Divine Revelation or whatever) and 'Phonocentrism' (Saussure's belief that all thinking depends on language, and that language itself derives from speech).

Derrida attacks Saussure in *Grammatologie*. When we speak, he says, our language is 'transparent' to our thoughts; our words express our ideas directly as we have them. Once we write them down, we can *see* the words, but there's no direct access to the thoughts behind them. So words on paper are 'opaque' to our thoughts, so are numbers, diagrams, drawings, paintings, buildings or whatever. So if we want to use language as a model for these other ways of signifying, we'd better use written rather than spoken language.

That's a tiny fragment of Derrida and of course there's very much more. As Hirsch says (1983), he joins those who attacked, and finally destroyed 'the myth of the given': Wittgenstein, Heidegger, Quine and Sellars who 'proved' there are not, and cannot be 'ultimate foundations' to our knowledge. Empiricists have always known that. Only Rationalists looked for fundamental 'truths'; for as David Hume put it (1739–40):

> The understanding, when it acts alone . . . according to its most general principles . . . subverts itself and leaves not the lowest degree of evidence in any proposition.

So Derrida's great achievement is to show by applying Rationalist methods that Rationalism does not and cannot work.

Derrida's Deconstruction 'stuns' Rationalism with a blow from which it may never recover. Clelland may have been right when he declared that Rationalism is dead, not just in architecture. So what does Deconstruction offer? For many Derrida's inspiration lies, not only in what he writes but also in the way he writes it, with many verbal games: alliterations, metaphors and puns. Architectural equivalents may be found in Tschumi's handling of his folies.

Venturi 3

The parallels are more than superficial. As one of Derrida's English translators, Geoff Bennington, points out (1987) Derrida, in *Grammatologie* writes of 'The Outside and the Inside', 'The Outside should be the Inside' and so on.

More architectural metaphors but, as Bennington also points out, Venturi had written – a year earlier, in *Complexity* . . . – of 'The Inside and the Outside'. So Bennington allows himself a 'cautious analogy'.

Venturi likes walls to be good and solid; obvious containers, protectors of internal space with transparent holes for windows. He cannot abide the Modern Movement idea of 'flowing space'; of outside and inside opening into each other through glass walls which 'can be discounted by the eye'. Inside and the outside are and must be different. Which is exactly what Derrida says of words. Spoken words, he says, are too 'transparent' – like Venturi's glass walls – which is why he, Derrida, gives such priority to writing.

So, says Bennington, Derrida demonstrates 'the impossibility of conceiving the inside prior to the outside. Only an outside can define an inside'! So whilst Derrida may have 'stunned' Rationalism, he gives even more authority to Venturi's kind of Empiricism!

13

The future of the city

Post IBA

The major IBA competitions were held in, or around, 1980 so anything designed or written by neo-Rationalists – or neo-Empiricists – since then, can be described as Post IBA.

Such work has taken many forms. Bofill and Spoerry, for instance, have both been building characteristic designs along the New Jersey shore line, the latter in conjunction with Ezra Ehrenkrantz, pioneer, in the United States, of prefabricated building systems.

And there have been theoretical developments.

Alexander: New Theory of Urban Design

Alexander's *Pattern Language* (1977) was prescriptive right down to levels of fine detail whereas the *New Theory of Urban Design* which he and colleagues published (Alexander *et al.*, 1987) is devoted to Seven Detailed Rules of Growth. These are:

1. piecemeal growth: to 'guarantee a mixed flow of small, medium and large projects' – preferably in equal quantities by cost
2. the growth of larger wholes: 'Every building increment must help to form at least one larger whole. . . .'
3. visions: 'Every project must first be experienced, and then expressed, as a vision which can be seen in the inner eye (literally)'
4. positive urban space: 'Every building must create coherent and well-shaped public space next to it'
5. layout of large buildings: 'The entrances . . . main circulation, main division . . . into parts . . . interior spaces . . . daylight, and . . . movement within the building, are all coherent and consistent with the position of the building in the street and in the neighbourhood'
6. construction: 'The structure of every building must generate smaller wholes in the physical fabric . . . in its structural bays, columns, walls, windows, building base etc. . . . in its entire physical construction and appearance'
7. formation of centres: 'Every whole must be a center in itself, and must also produce a system of centers around it.'

Having described these rules in detail, Alexander and his colleagues then present a worked example, for an area just north of the Bay Bridge in San Francisco. Interestingly enough what amounted to an (eroded) part of the San Francisco grid is converted by the application of these Rules into a Picturesque layout rather in the manner of later Robert Krier – of which more later – with a Gateway, an Hotel, a Café, a

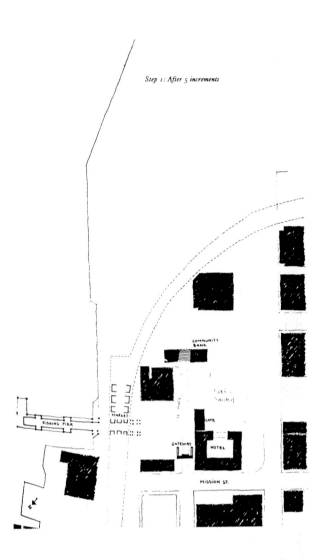

Step 1: After 5 increments

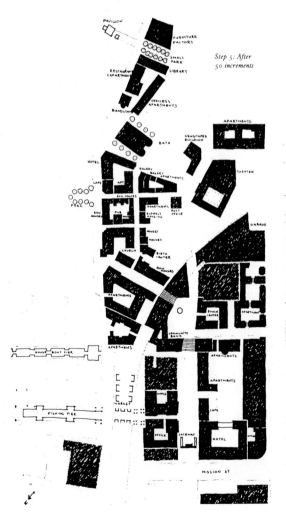

Fig. 13.1 Alexander, Neis, Annonou and King (1987): Mission Street, San Francisco, development after 5 increments and after 50 (from Alexander *et al.*, 1987).

Step 5: After 50 increments

Market and Fishing Pier, a Community Bank, Apartment Buildings, a Parking Garage, an Educational Center, even a Fountain and a Kiosk. As the whole started to come together, they added a Swimming Pool – contained in a Crystal Palace, Trees, a Church, and some 30 other buildings not to mention the – consciously designed – spaces between them. Which once again gives the lie to the Sitte-Gaudet idea that one cannot design informality (Fig. 13.1).

Alexander and his colleagues present some general rules applicable, as it were, to the universe.

Duany and Plater-Zyberk: Seaside

Duany and Plater-Zyberk (1983) were even more prescriptive, and rather more specific, in their Urban Code for the New Town of Seaside in Florida (Ivy, 1985) (Fig. 13.2).

Having analysed carefully the more attractive towns of the American deep South they laid out a Master Plan, including a Central Square, with roads radiating from it, a Town Hall, a School, a Post Office, an Hotel, a Beach Pavilion, a Club for swimming and tennis and so on. They then allocated plots for eight different types of development: Type I lots, for instance, are those which surround the central square intended for shops with residential uses – probably hotels – up to five storeys above them. Type II lots, in the Square in front of the Town Hall are zoned for Offices, rather like the Vieux Carré in New Orleans; Type III are intended to generate Workshops, Car Repair, Warehousing and so on; Type IV large private houses and apartment buildings based on Greek Revival Antebellum Plantation Houses, Type V mixed uses in coherent groups of buildings; Type VI houses with views towards the sea, Type VII smaller houses, like those of Charleston, with no direct views of the sea and Type VIII special buildings to mark gateways and so on.

Having laid down their general strategies, Duany and Plater-Zyberk then worked out the details. Variances to their Types are granted on the basis of architectural merit; the spatial definition of a street or square must be maintained by building a specified minimum of the frontage and lots with deep front yards must have picket fences. Houses must have porches for specified lengths of their frontages, so must commercial arcades since these are 'essential to the southern town as a type, and a positive influence on the social use of the street'.

Outbuildings are encouraged at the rear to 'create a secondary level of urbanism' and cars must be parked within individual lots; maximum and minimum heights are specified for roofs, as they are for porches, and towers of small 'Footprint' (200 square feet) are encouraged everywhere 'so that even the most landlocked house may reach for a view of the sea'. Boundaries are drawn mid-block between the different zoning Types, to encourage the development of streets and squares which are coherent spatial entities in themselves (Fig. 13.3). Having worked out the code for seaside, Duany and Plater-Zyberk have now done equivalent but different codes for some 20 other places.

Clearly such permissive rules are a far cry from the 'thou shalts' and 'thou shalt nots' of, say, the *Essex Design Guide* (1973). Indeed the whole point of the Seaside legislation is to permit, and even to encourage idiosyncrasy. What is more it seems to work, for the result, as Ivy says, is a 'Community of delightful amenities'.

So Empiricism – with a touch of Pragmatism – continues to develop. What of Rationalism?

Clelland suggests that IBA itself showed the poverty of Rationalism,

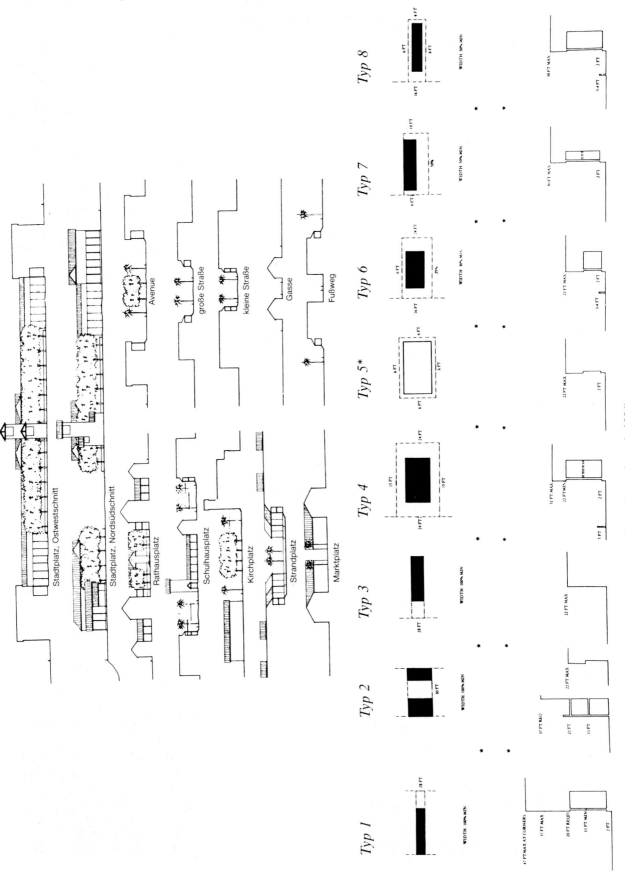

Fig. 13.2 Duany and Plater-Zyberk (1983): Seaside: urban codes (from *Baumeister*, **9**, 1986).

its impotence in dealing with real problems. Yet some of the housing is very fine in concept, if not in construction. If one wants to live at urban density, then Robert Krier's Ritterstrasse, Rauchstrasse and his Schinkelplatz provide highly humane environments at the kind of scale which the Cambridge research (see Chapter 7) proved to be some kind of optimum.

Quatremèrian Types clearly work in such cases and so do Quatremèrian Models. Early Rationalism failed, not so much because of these approaches but because in true 18th century manner, it tried to reduce architecture to the pure, abstract geometry of pure cones, spheres, cylinders, circles, squares, cubes and so on. Historically, these have never worked in architecture and it was naïve of architects, late in the 20th century, to think that somehow they could be made to work for them. It was incredibly naïve of architects such as Rossi to suppose that plain, white, painted plaster surfaces, could endure better for them than they had for Le Corbusier in the 1920s.

But like Le Corbusier, Rossi too realized how unrealistic he had been and in his Berlin buildings, on Friedrichstrasse and Rauchstrasse turned to good, honest, Berlin brick with all its advantages in terms of wear, weathering and aging gracefully.

In other words he abandoned the gross abstraction of Rationalism and compromised, not only with the physical realities of Pragmatism but also with the human realities of Empiricism. His Rationalism did not fail; he accommodated it to reality. As he went on to do in his later work.

Fig. 13.3 Seaside: typical street scene (from Duany and Plater-Zyberk, 1985).

Rossi post IBA

As early as 1972, indeed, Aldo Rossi's preoccupations were beginning to change. There were indications that he, too, might move away from the strict, plain geometry of Rationalism in an Architectural Collage (Rossi, 1972b) in which a rather solid tower, possibly a stage tower has, in front of it, a full-blown Classical Pediment over a typical, if inverted set of Gallaratese/Modena windows (Fig. 13.4a). And then in a project for Venice: Canareggio West (Arnell and Bickford, 1985) he had set, within typically Rossian courtyards, a large Hotel, in brick, with typical Rossi windows to the first two floors and tiny Boullée windows higher in the façade which terminates in a Classical cornice (Fig. 13.4b). He wanted to make a 'great large building' on the Grand Canal of which he says (1985):

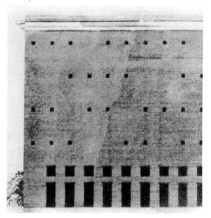

Fig. 13.4(a) Aldo Rossi (1972): Architectural Collage (from *A + U*, 5: 1976). *(b)* Aldo Rossi (1980): Carneggio West: a hotel on the Grand Canal, Venice (from Arnell and Bickford, 1985).

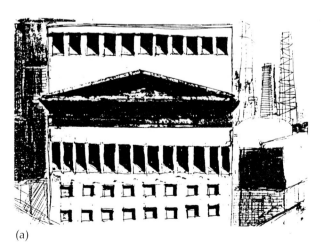

(a)

(b)

Fig. 13.5 Aldo Rossi with William
Stead (1981): (Moltini) Funeral Chapel
Brianza/Giussano (from Arnell and
Bickford, 1985; Rossi, 1987).

> When I was making a cornice for . . . Canareggio, I looked at the
> designs for the cornices of the Palazzo Farnese, to copy them and
> to make them as alike as possible, because I think that architecture
> is something that carries continuity, something that relates to
> what preceded it.

Curiously enough Rossi's Classical explorations continued in very
much more detail with another House for the Dead; the Molteni
Chapel at Brianza (1981) (Fig. 13.5). Internally, at least, the Classicism
is complete for as Arnell and Bickford say:

> Rather than an exploration of romantic images of mourning, the
> project was seen as a design for a monument, in keeping with the
> historic continuity and identity of tombs and memorials of urban
> architecture. The exactitude of the classical orders was taken as a
> model of architecture as a collective enterprise, communicable by
> the precise codes of the discipline.

Other projects, such as the Housing for Viadana (1982) seem to
compromise Rossi's growing interest in Classicism with his earlier
Rationalist forms – themselves compromised against the realities of
construction in brick.

But two projects in particular show the Classicising ascendent; the
Congressional Palace for Milan (Rossi *et al.*, 1982) and the Carlo Felice
Theatre in Genoa (1982) designed by Rossi with Gardella, Reinhart and
Sibilla. The Congressional Palace has a Gallaratese-like plan with
office-fingers projecting from a central spine – which of course has a
glazed, equilateral atrium roof – with, at one end, a large cubic building
for the Congress Halls themselves and, at the other, a circular tower
with a slender, conical spire. The cube, like the Venice Hotel has a
cornice (Savi and Lupano, 1983) (Fig. 13.6).

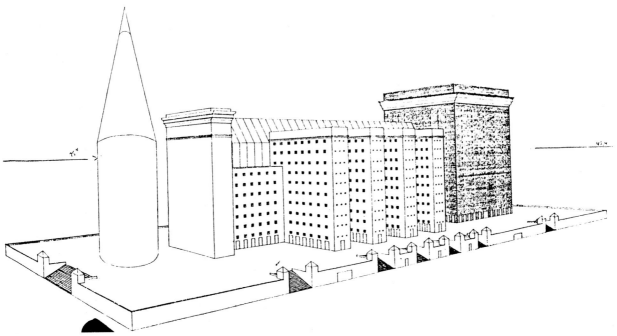

Fig. 13.6 Aldo Rossi with M. Adjini and G. Geronzi (1982): Congressional Palace for Milan (from Savi and Lupano, 1983; Arnell and Bickford, 1985).

Curiously enough similar forms are displayed in the Carlo Felice Theatre (1982) (Fig. 13.7). Whilst this looks like a piece of skilful conservation of Barabino's 18th century neo-Classical Theatre this is entirely new. Rossi's most obvious addition is a Congressional Centre-like Cube with full-blown cornice, string courses, rustication and Boullée-like windows. This of course encloses the fly-tower. And then hardly visible from outside another Rossi Cone expands downwards through four or five levels of foyers at the back of the auditorium.

Fig. 13.7 Ignazio Gardella, Aldo Rossi, Fabio Reinhart and Angelo Sibilla (1982): Carlo Felice Theatre, Genoa (from *Lotus*, 42).

The most significant declaration of withdrawal from his former, abstract, Rationalist position is to be found in the comments by Rossi and his colleagues which accompany their drawings (in *Lotus*, 42, 1984). They say:

> The main material of the building is stone, then plaster and iron. The 'new materials' have decayed in a short time; what was thought an innovation was often dictated by pure speculation. The unplastered concrete, great glass surfaces and metals that were supposed to convey the image of a new, perfect and efficient building have shaped objects that are nothing but the corpses of the so-called modern architecture today. So the use of stone is not a technical sacrifice or a formalistic choice, but a carefully thought-out decision.

They go on to say in passing that in the 'most technologically advanced country' – the USA – new skyscrapers are clad in granite and stone.

One cannot get much more pragmatic than that!

Rob Krier: later theories

Whilst he was applying his Typologies of Urban Space to the Ritterstrasse, the Rauchstrasse and the Schinkelplatz in Berlin Rob Krier was effecting similar analyses to internal spaces, not to mention the Elements of Architecture as a whole. He did so in *Rob Krier on Architecture* (1982a).

Naturally enough whilst most internal spaces are rectangular, he finds examples which match his three major Urban Types: square, circular and triangular with equivalent combinings and distortions. The rectangle, after all, is an elongated square! He detects ten Elements of Architecture such as the Wall, the Column, the Bridge, the Roof, the House, the Interior, the City, and so on; then shows how his Types

Fig. 13.8 Rob Krier (1977) Burgenland, a new village for Austria (from Krier, 1982).

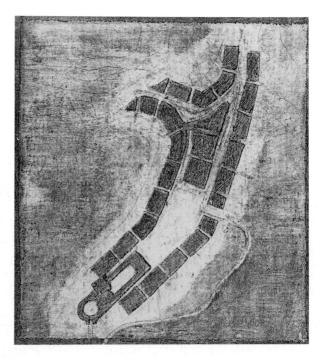

have been incorporated into his own designs with further sets of variations on Façade Compositions, the Treatment of Corners, and the application of his room-plan Types into actual apartment plans.

Krier took these analyses a stage further in the *Elements of Architecture* (1983 and, *Architectural Composition*, 1988). Here he starts with four Ground Figures, the square, the triangle, the circle and an irregular form. Like his Urban Spaces these too are subject to distortions such as Addition, Penetration, Buckling, Segmentation, Perspective and rather less determinate Distortion.

He shows how these can be projected into the third dimension by walls and columns, given flat roofs, pitched roofs, vaulted roofs; combined to form octagonal, cross-shaped, circles-within-squares, squares-within-circles, circles elongated to form ovals and so on.

Then of course individual spaces can be composed together, strung along axes, balanced about one or more axes, rotated about a central point.

Krier then presents a fascinating analysis of architectural detailing – much of it Classical – but this is beyond the scope of a book on urban space design!

All this is clearly the work of a man who, having been seduced for a while by the abstract geometric simplicities of Rationalism, wishes to penetrate much closer to the heart of architectural design.

Rob Krier: Empiricist

Whilst up to and including his various projects for Berlin Rob Krier had been working with the pure geometries of Rationalism, at least in his planning forms, which were then projected into the third dimension by his façade and section Typologies, another way of designing began to emerge after his Roma Interrotta submission.

There had of course been examples of irregular planning in *Urban Space*, especially in the 'stitchings' of the Wilhemsplatz and the Österreichische Platz in Stuttgart by Hummerich and Böhm, but these

Fig. 13.9 Rob Krier with B. Dewez and M. Geiswinkler (1985) Project for restoring the Urban Tissue of Amiens (from Krier, R., 1987a).

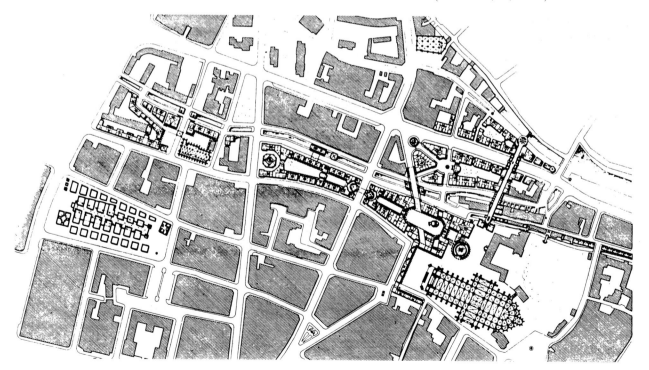

were conditioned by the medieval layouts into which they were designing.

And in 1977, Krier presented designs for a Village in the Burgenland, Austria which, responding to the site, curves gently along the crest of a hill (Fig. 13.8). Indeed it follows the traditional plan for villages in that region with two streets, coming in from the north stopping to open up a Village Square which is closed again at the southern end by a cluster of public buildings, including a Castle.

Although most of his schemes continued to be rather regular, Rationalist in their planning, Krier also developed his ideas of informal space culminating with his studies for Amiens where of course the medieval street pattern encourages, even determines, irregularity (Garcias, 1985) (Fig. 13.9). Which by no means inhibits him from lining the streets and squares with housing according to his Types which, with their pitched roofs and other details, are sympathetic to the context of Amiens.

Here, indeed, Empiricism is at work!

Leon Krier post IBA

As for Leo Krier's work in the 1980s, he was critical of IBA: suggesting that a golden opportunity was missed when, in 1978, it was decided to abandon any idea of a Master Plan. His idea of a Master Plan, of course, is developed out of the planning Principles he had described for Luxembourg. As he says:

> The first task of a truly pluralist building exhibition would be to commission different master-plans for clearly defined and separate project areas, laying down densities and distributions of functions, built masses and public spaces, in plan and silhouette. Such master-plans would then constitute the *inviolable legislative* and ideological basis for all further design decisions. For example, modernist aesthetics, principles of construction and zoning could only be applied within an uncompromisingly modernist master plan. Traditional architecture would remain the privilege of a purely traditional master-plan and so on.

In this way it would be possible to create a true plurality of city models. For: 'It is good to divide what cannot be united; to divorce what cannot be reconciled. Democracy should do more than encourage everyone to grind their differences.' Each city would have its Modern zones, its Classical zones and so on. Indeed he saw divisions of this kind as offering the only chance for Classicism to be re-established in the city.

His project for Tegel of course had been a zone, or quartier exactly of that kind but since that could not be built he developed similar ideas, on a smaller scale, but with greater complexity in his visionary design for Pliny's Villa at Laurentum (1982). Having read, like many others, Pliny's description, Krier envisaged a promontory or peninsula for the site. Which of course meant that he had to work at different levels. Indeed there is a marvellous cascade of buildings at the seaward end of his promontory.

As at Tegel so at Laurentum Krier envisages simple, domestic buildings, an Atrium, Winter Quarters, a Garden Pavilion, contrasted with the more public buildings such as a Cryptoportus, a Triclinium and a Monopteros. He sees the complex as 'most certainly . . .

embellished with rich statuary and numerous frescos'; with the 'deep mouldings of the monuments . . . heightened by vibrant colours'.

Leon Krier on Speer

The most controversial aspect of Krier's Classicism has been his commentary on the work and advocacy of Albert Speer (L. Krier, 1985e). Krier finds himself in an equivocal position: defending Speer's architecture against those who suggest that because Adolph Hitler chose Classical, rather than Modernist, buildings to symbolize the power of his Reich, therefore *all* Classicism since the 1930s has been Fascist.

Which, of course, accounted for the tired old syllogism:

> Hitler loved classical architecture
> Hitler was a tyrant
> Hence classical architecture is tyrannical

A belief so deep-rooted that as Krier says (p. 218):

> . . . many effigies of concrete, steel and glass, which disfigure the German land were executed for the explicit purpose of showing that liberty and progress had at last taken root in the tyrant-battered Fatherland.

As Krier points out (p. 221) the true architecture of National Socialism was the industrial architecture of the factories (with their slave labour) and the concentration camps (in which people were processed mechanically). Indeed he quotes Speer himself to the effect that 'without having to think about it, Industry is right, *there is no going back* (his italics). What is more Krier quotes Hitler who declared: 'I am, to speak frankly, crazy about Technik.' And as Krier says: (p. 222) '. . . this side of his madness . . . brought infinitely more suffering upon humanity than his love for classical architecture.. . . . His barbaric crimes were, after all, not perpetrated in a monumental environment but in degrading industrial sheds and camps'.

As far as Krier is concerned, 'This criminal element of Nazism not only resides in its racism but in equal measure in its industrialist-socialist-centralist-collectivist-modernist *Sturm und Drang*.'

But since the Allies – East and West – gained so much from Nazi industry: from rocket design to the VW Beetle, they were by no means going to denigrate Nazi industry!

Nevertheless, Classical architecture *was* a 'successful and reliable means of Nazi propaganda' a 'civilised and well mannered face on an empire of lies' (Fig. 13.10).

Which, according to Krier, is a confusion of *political ends* with *cultural means*. Nevertheless, as he says, the greatest human institutions, to this day, are symbolized by classical monuments, the basic classical principles of 'harmony-firmness-utility' are as relevant now as ever they were, 'concordant with the fundamental ideals of significant human establishments'.

It is simply a fact that: *'Classical architecture has been the noblest instrument of politics* and of civilising propaganda for thousands of years and throughout all great cultures and continents.' Of course it has been used by tyrants but it: 'transcends the purpose of tyrannical abuse'. Supra-national bodies, such as the United Nations, the EEC, UNESCO and NATO which have chosen *not* to use Classical forms are, so Krier

Fig. 13.10 Albert Speer with Adolph Hitler (1937–43) North–South Axis for Berlin (from Krier, 1985).

Fig. 13.11 Paulick, Leucht, Hopp *et al.* (1952–58) Karl-Marx Allee, East Berlin (from Bonfanti *et al.*, 1973) Compare with *Fig. 13.10.*

says, lacking vision and moral authority *as one would expect* from their architecture.

As Krier says:

> Industrial civilization is incapable of building cities or villages. It is unable to create meaningful or beautiful places. It builds suburbs, zones and transport-systems, dumping grounds and concentration camps. There are always forms of mass-housing, mass-transport, mass-communication, mass-elimination. Auschwitz-Birkenau and Los Angeles are children of the same parents. They are reifications of social placelessness, of the incapacity to give human work and commonwealth dignified and pleasing forms.
>
> *Architecture is not political, it is an instrument of politics, for better or worse.*

And Krier reminds us in his next major scheme, the *Completion of Washington DC* (1985b) that Classicism was by no means confined, even in the 1930s, to Fascist dictatorships. In Moscow alone the Lenin Library, the Council of Ministers, the Moscva Hotel, the Red Army Theatre and the Intourist Building all give the lie to that (so does the Karl-Marx Allee in East Berlin (Fig. 13.11)). So in Washington itself do the Jefferson Memorial, the (original) National Gallery of Art and the Supreme Court.

So it is fitting that Krier should have chosen Washington to make a number of further points. In that he concentrates on the Mall: Krier's Completion of Washington, in a sense, is the apotheosis of his axial manner.

Krier intended to urbanize what he saw as a too-empty city in much the same way as Rodrigo Perez d'Arce had urbanized Chandigarh. Krier sees the whole complex of monumental Washington as far too vast to make a single, unified city – such a city, of course, being for him one that pedestrians can encompass. As with Luxembourg so Krier wanted to divide Washington into a series of quartiers: Lincoln Town; Washington Town, Jefferson Town with Capitol Town in the centre. He looks at each of these in turn and proposes, in most cases, a denser development than there is already.

Central to Krier's scheme is his much enlarged Tidal Basin by which the Reflecting Pool, in front of the Bacon's Lincoln Monument, would be widened out, in a wedge, to be even more reflecting from more directions (Fig. 13.12). He proposes a new setting for the White House by which buildings are reflected either side of the ellipse in front of it to give it a proper framing and the Tidal Basin too is opened up to the Ellipse so that the whole ensemble, including the White House, will be reflected.

Krier's boldest idea, however, is to open a Canal from the Reflecting Pool towards the Capitol Building. Certainly those who have spent hours trudging between the various Museums which line the Mall in the furious heat of the Washington summer, or the bleak, rainswept mudscape of the Washington winter, would prefer to cross the Mall by gondola, as Krier suggests, than to wander, wilting, on foot!

In many ways this Washington scheme is an apotheosis of Krier's general urban thinking. He is concerned, obviously, with relationships between the Monuments, the Public Spaces and the general urban texture of the city. As he says, both 'public space and monumental architecture are like precious jewelry. Too much of it is a false luxury, too little of it is a false economy'.

A good city, he says, is made of streets and squares and squares provide natural settings for people to meet. But the square also provides the 'choice location of all things public'. It is, in other words, the proper location for monumental buildings.

Krier reinforces the point by showing the monuments without any city around them and the city without any monuments, suggesting that the *true* city is one which combines the two in judicious balance.

He repeats his castigations of Modernism in saying: 'there is little to be saved. It is but a negation of those ideas, values, and principles which made architecture worth having: no walls, no columns, no arches, no windows, no streets, no monumentality, no individuality, no decoration, no craftsmanship, no grandeur, no history; no tradition!'

So:

Man must be returned to the privilege to use his legs for a better purpose than walking to his car, subway or plane.

It should be man's constitutional right to perform all daily and habitual deeds without the use of mechanical means of transport; to walk to his place of work, his club, his church, his restaurant, his clinic, his school, his library, his gym, and park. (Now it is but the rare privilege of a few.)

Including, it should be said, this author!

Krier elaborates on these points in the Manifesto which he wrote for the Skidmore, Owings and Merrill Architecture Institute (SOMAI) (1986) he says: 'the good City provides the totality of urban functions within comfortable and pleasant walking distance', which of course gives a limit to its overall size: 'It cannot grow by extension of width or height'. The only way it can grow is by 'multiplication', that is by building other, adjacent cities.

So the city as it stands:

. . . is a complete and finite urban community, member of a larger family of independent urban quarters, of cities within the city, of cities within the country. The traditional city is economical in the use of *time, energy* and *land*. It is by its nature *ecological*.

Such ideas finally came to fruition a year later in one of Krier's most ambitious designs. Before we look at this, however, we ought to

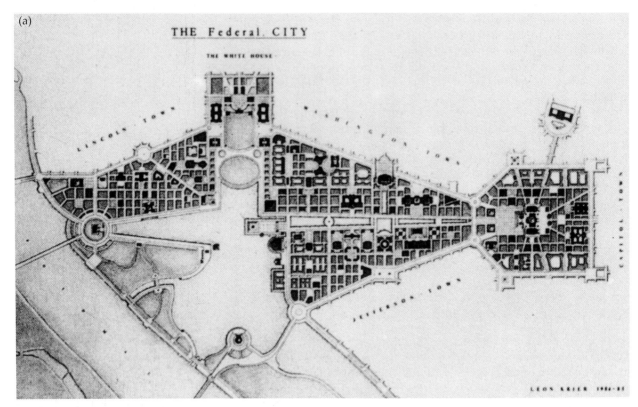

(a)

Fig. 13.12 Leon Krier (1986)
Completion of Washington DC with
the monumental centre urbanized and
the mall converted into a grand canal
(from *AMM*, **30**, 1986).

(b)

consider the most lavishly contained of neo-Rationalist urban spaces was designed, not by Rossi, Aymonimo or by either of the Kriers but by Jones and Kirkland for the Mississauga City Hall (1986).

Jones and Kirkland: Mississauga City Hall

Mississauga lies west of Toronto and there is an urban wasteland between them. The site lies within this wasteland, next to the parking-lot of a regional shopping centre, itself set within a superblock surrounded by 12-storey office towers (Fig. 13.13).

So in this case, Jones and Kirkland were not so much inserting their organism into the existing city as placing it in the hope that a truly urban city would grow round it! (Jones, 1987). The brief, as developed, required not only a City Hall but also an Art Gallery and a Municipal Library. Thus they planned a north/south axis running to Lake Ontario with a Picturesque Park to the north; 'simulating the idea of the wilderness', the City Hall itself, around three sides of a court; a further court to be flanked by the cultural buildings and beyond that again another court for a large pyramidal monument (Fig. 13.14).

The City Hall is united – one cannot say unified – by a wide pediment-as-building across the major axis – Jones calls it the Great Arch – which, as Maxwell points out (1988) is much like Leo Krier's Restaurant for his School at Cergy Pontoise. Behind this, from west to east are a 14-storey office block with a stepped-pyramidal roof, a 100 metre Rossi-like clock tower with an open steel frame to its upper parts, a square Great Hall with a glazed pyramidal roof, and a circular, Asplund-like Council Chamber. The Great Hall is linked eastwards to the Council Chamber, southwards to a Conservatory and thence to Jones's Great Arch, and westwards to the Office Block by way of Bernini-like tapering Scala Regia.

Southwards of the Great Arch, open colonnades enclose the first of the open courts – the Civic Square – east and west of which are, respectively, an open Amphitheatre and a fairly formal Garden. Of course it is early to judge how this will work as an urban space since it clearly leaks out to the south. Once the next court is built, contained by the Cultural buildings, this Square may become truly Civic.

Much has been made of the City Hall's Canadian vernacular connotations with the Great Arch as a barn, the Council Chamber as a

Fig. 13.13 Jones and Kirkland (1987): Mississauga City Hall near Toronto (from *A + U*, December 1987).

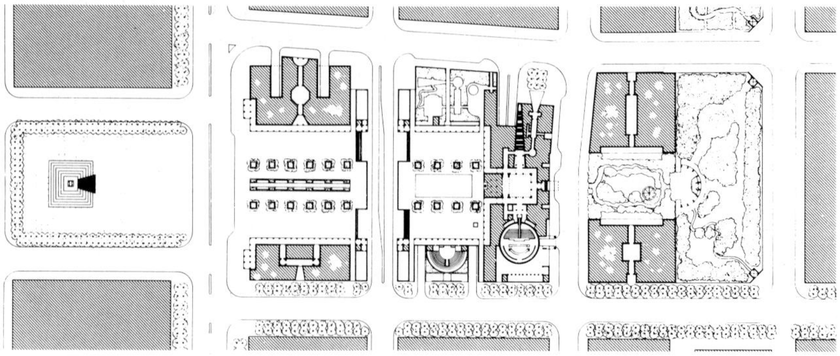

Fig. 13.14 Mississauga City Hall: plan including future extensions (from *A + U*, December 1987).

grain-silo and so on (Jones, 1987; Maxwell, 1987; and also Cawker, 1987). Jones himself is happy to acknowledge what Boddy calls Regional and Jencks calls Post Modern Vernacular. He accepts 'strong rationalist tendencies . . . a persistent coincidence between form and function', whilst also confirming that: 'a typological design has always been a characteristic of my work . . .'. What is more he: 'puts a high value on its distinction as a public building (a Monument!) from the City fabric'.

He accepts, also, that the Council Chamber, in particular, may be Nordic Classicism and since he uses so many Classical elements: 'the Loggia, the Peristyle, the Scala Regia, the Piano Nobile, the rotunda, etc.' he agrees, absolutely, with Leon Krier that: 'we have ample proof of classicism as a broad and generous body of ideas controlling composition and typological experiment. Within these limited ideas it is possible to fabricate an infinite number of real or imaginary buildings'.

Clearly the City Hall could not have been built as it was if there had been no neo-Rationalism in the 60s and 70s. But since Rossi and the Kriers moved away from its abstract geometries (although Grassi seems intent on retaining them) towards the Pragmatic use of materials, and increasingly to Classical detail, Jones and Kirkland sprang to international attention fully armed with these things. There are signs at Mississauga too that Jones and Kirkland paid attention also to the Empirical realities of multi-modal human sensory needs.

Leon Krier: Atlantis

There are no doubts that Leon Krier did in designs for what may turn out to be the most complete architectural development by any of the neo-Rationalists moving towards Pragmatism and Empiricism; his design for *Atlantis* on Tenerife (L. Krier, 1987b; Porphyrios, 1988). It was commissioned by H. J. Müller as 'an international place of encounter and research for the arts, sciences, politics and business' and completion is expected in the year 2000! (Figs 13.15 and 13.16).

As Krier suggests, given this brief, certain architects would have packed everything into one vast megastructure with all that this implies in terms of: 'rambling and labyrinthine complexes . . . oppressive, confusing, depressing and overpowering'. Instead of that he has designed and located:

> . . . more than a hundred buildings, both large and small, each of which can be simplified to its typologically irreducible core: church, baths, gallery, library, theatre, restaurant, workshop, house, etc.

As he says, these represent the 'hierarchic components of the city' and they are grouped around 'some 31 external streets, alleyways and stairways, and 19 squares, some small, others large'.

Whereas for Pliny's Villa Krier had to imagine a site, the topography of Atlantis is real indeed. The site rises from 595 metres above sea level to 635, so he located a corniche promenade along the lower edge – some 350 metres long – and halfway up the slope an Agora. And at the top an Acropolis, in precisely the relationship to the Agora that the Ancient Greeks would have enjoyed.

At the west end of the Corniche are Hanging Gardens, with a swimming pool, tennis courts, baths, a fitness centre, a gymnasium, a solarium and laboratories whilst at the east there is an open air Theatre with a Library, a Music Studio and a Monopteros.

The narrow streets and alleys are lined with 'plain-fronted houses, garden walls and pergolas', but the houses all have garden terraces with views over the countryside. As for Tegel so at Atlantis the public buildings open on to squares and they have monumental qualities 'which both qualify and dominate the lines of sight within the city'.

The Agora has a 24-columned Stoa, a Hotel, a Restaurant and shops whilst the Acropolis is reserved for an Art Museum, in 17 differentiated pavilions, a Greek Cross Church and a four-towered Atrium Carrée at the foot of a 42 metre Great Tower.

Fig. 13.15 Leon Krier (1987) Atlantis, Tenerife. Painting by Carl Laubin (from *Archives d'Architecture Moderne*, 1988; *Architectural Design*, **58**, 1987).

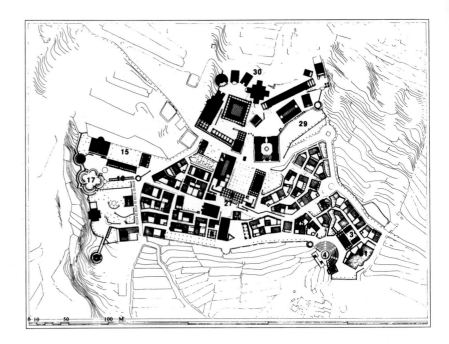

Fig. 13.16 Leon Krier (1987) Atlantis: plan (from *Archives d'Architecture Moderne*, 1988; Krier, L., 1988; *Architectural Design*, **58**, 1987).

As Krier says:

> Nowadays picturesque street patterns and organic urban structures are frequently thought to have grown as unconsciously as flowers in a field. People like to forget that the plasticity, perspective, and symbolic precision of these apparently free-formed stone masses are not the fortuitous product of a spontaneous zeal for building but represent, on the contrary, the attainment of the highest sense of ordering, the realisation and consolidation of the highest ethical and artistic consciousness. . . .

So with this project in particular, one of the most influential neo-Rationalists formally embraces the Empiricist view!

Indeed Krier went into close, meticulous detail as to the different kinds of lighting which would be needed for displaying different kinds of art in the different galleries; no designing could be more Empirical than that!

Atlantis may yet be realized, not in Tenerife, but in Andalucia, but still as a rather special place for intellectuals to meet. Leon Krier's extensions for Dorchester, however come much closer to his ideal of the urban *quartier* in a place for everyday living. His designs were prepared (1989) for the Prince of Wales, as Duchy of Cornwall, to be built on the Poundbury Farm Estate.

As one might expect, Krier's designs allow for urban-scale streets and squares to which other architects will be invited to contribute individual public buildings, and sections of the general urban texture, shops, housing for different income groups and so on.

So at Poundbury, Leon Krier offers south-west England the kind of scenic adaptable model which Duany and Plater-Zyberk offer for the southern United States at Seaside.

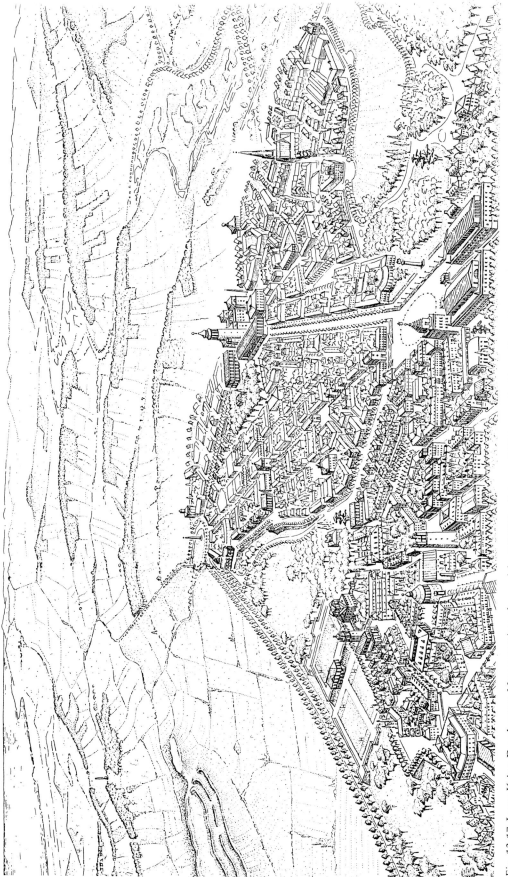

Fig. 13.17 Leon Krier: Dorchester. New *quartiers* planned for HRH the Prince of Wales on the Poundbury Farm Estate of the Duchy of Cornwall.

Cities of the future?

There are those who still see New York as *the* prototype City of the Future but clearly the initiative has passed elsewhere first to Los Angeles, then to Houston and now to many North American cities. Like Los Angeles, Houston is younger than New York. It was founded some 200 years later, in August 1836, when two New York speculators, the Allen Brothers, paddled up Buffalo Bayou and landed where it turns south and eastwards. Tradition has it that there and then, Augustus Allen sketched the plan for a settlement, a gridiron, five blocks by five: 'using his hat as a table'.

A year later, 1837, the Government of Texas had been moved from West Columbia to Houston and the city eventually became the third largest port within the United States.

So Downtown now extends some 16 blocks by 20, bounded not by streets but by freeways. Within them the new commercial core is a couple of blocks south of Texas, centred on Tranquility Park which commemorates the first Lunar Landings and is surrounded by that cluster of skyscrapers, Late Modern and Post Modern, which make Houston's skyline so different from New York's. These include One Shell Plaza (1971), Penzoil Place (Johnson and Burgee, 1985), their Republic Bank Center (1981) the Texas Commerce Tower (1982) and Allied Bank Plaza (1983).

Most of these are connected underground by a system of tunnels which almost rivals Montreal's in extent and complexity. Like Montreal's it was built for climatic reasons – equal and opposite – for Montreal can be desperately cold and dry in the winter: Houston hot and humid in the summer.

But Downtown alone is by no means enough to distinguish Houston as one kind of City of the Future. Already in the 1920s residential subdivisions were being established around the commercial core, such as the exclusive River Oaks. As these prospered, so the city was expanded to incoporate them.

Such developments were boosted by the vast freeway system, started in the 1950s with North, South, East and West Loops enclosing, roughly, a rectangle some nine miles by seven. Around this an Outer Belt has been started seven miles east of Downtown and planned to turn west twelve miles to the north. But already a series of spectacular suburbs or, rather, satellite cities, has been developed on the freeways to the south, the west and beyond the West Loop.

These include the Texas Medical Center which, as Barrington suggests, is 'a city unto itself' and the Astrodomaine of Astroworld, Astrohall and Astrodome. And of course there is NASA, the prototype of all science parks.

Then there are commercial centres, such as Greenway Plaza which Barrington describes as satellite cities, to which must be added the Post Oak Shopping Sector, the Town and Country Shopping Area and Greenspoint Mall. Then again there are residential areas which, in addition to River Oaks, include the Memorial Area.

The 127 acres of Greenway Plaza (1967 onwards) include 10 office buildings, apartment blocks, and a Stouffer's Inn, not to mention sports and entertainment facilities.

But most spectacular of all is the Magic Circle which lies west of the West Loop in an area which as late as the 1950s was still open fields. Then Sakowitz and Joske's opened stores there, followed by Neiman Markus. By 1965, the Galleria was under way; a vast complex centred on a skating rink surrounded by three storeys of shops, a luxury hotel and so on all totally enclosed and air-conditioned.

This was completed in 1971 and five years later, a second Galleria was started including a second hotel, not to mention Marshall Field and the Lord and Taylor stores. These, with the Post Oak Commercial Center, comprise the Magic Circle which is now, as Barrington says, 'a destination in itself'.

Houston is by no means the only American city to have had new centres develop around it which in size and facilities rival and even surpass the original downtown. As Goldensohn points out (1986), a new urban form which he calls the instant city of the suburbs or the pseudo-city is appearing across the United States.

They range from the Forrestal Center outside New York at Princeton in New Jersey to the Irvine Spectrum in Orange County, California. Some simply grew, as Goldensohn puts it, 'helter skelter' around the freeways as at Houston whilst others were planned with great care to become literally, substitute cities.

Even in Atlanta which, thanks to John Portman, has had a massive downtown revitalization, instant cities offer strong competition. From 1980 to 1985 downtown Atlanta gained some 4.3 million square feet of office space. But Perimeter Center to the North gained 7.6 million and Cumberland/Galleria, to the north east, gained 10.6 million. At which rate both Perimeter and Cumberland/Galleriau will have surpassed downtown Atlanta in office space by 1990.

What is more, space usage becomes increasingly specialized. Downtown retains the highest concentrations of government, professional services, finance, the wholesale trade and conventions. Perimeter Center and Cumberland/Galleria however have become prime locations for accountants, lawyers and other professionals whilst Perimeter Center also houses multi-national corporate headquarters.

Forrestal, New Jersey, founded by Princeton University in 1976 had, in the first ten years, attracted IBM, Grammon, Dow Jones, RCA, Merrill Lynch and some 45 other corporations. And late in the 1980s Forrestal was growing at such a rate that it was expected, by 1992, to contain some 120 to 125 million square feet of office space; more than the whole of downtown Milwaukee or downtown Newark.

Forrestal has hundreds of luxury town houses and apartments. Princeton Forrestal Village, for instance, is to have a 300-room Marriott Hotel, a shopping centre containing some 125 units: shops, restaurants, banks, a day-care centre and a health club. What is more Forrestal has seeded other developments along Route 1 such as Whispering Woods.

Yet Merrill Lynch plan to add more offices such that their development has been described as 'a World Trade Center on its side'.

Leinberger and Lockwood (1986) see Los Angeles as the fastest growing city of them all with such urban village cores as Century City, Costa Mesa/Irvine/Newport Beach, Encino, Glendale, the Airport, Warner Center, Ontario, Pasadena, Universal City/Burbank and Westwood.

For whilst in 1960 60% of all the office space in Los Angeles was downtown in the city itself, the figure, in 1986, was only 34%. The rest was contained in the instant cities.

Many of these have specific identities; with the aerospace industries concentrated around the Airport and Torrance, entertainment having moved from the Hollywood/Hills to Universal City/Burbank, insurance from Wilshire Boulevard to Pasadena. Pasadena's decaying core has been restored, with restaurants, expresso bars and shops whilst the run-down family housing which used to be within walking distance of the core has been replaced by new condominiums and town-houses. Houses in nearby residential areas have been renewed for young professional families.

Nor, unlike downtown, do these instant cities consist of high-rise clusters. Instead they consist of separated towers with parking, and landscaped spaces between them.

Few of them, it must be said, show much sense of urban space design. In most of them plots have been developed with little consideration for the buildings next door or the spaces between.

One extraordinary exception to this rule is Ben Carpenter's Las Colinas 15 miles along the Airport freeway out of Dallas. Already, in 1986, it contained more office space than the City of Dallas itself in the early 1970s. By 1986 the working population of Las Colinas was 51 000 and Carter estimated that by the year 2000, it would have risen to 180 000 of whom 50 000 will live there.

The offices are grouped along the shore of an artificial lake from which a 'Venetian' Grand Canal loops between them. There are picturesque shops along one side, 'town houses' on the other which, on closer inspection, turn out to be façades to a multi-storey parking garage. Free gondolas are available for those who wish to see Las Colinas from the water and the office complex itself has become a (minor) tourist attraction!

Few other cities can match the scale of such developments, nor, as Goldensohn (1986) said, 'the Texas gift for creating reality out of fantasy'.

In general, then, it seems that the days are gone, in North America, at least, when everything was focused on a single downtown area with its central business district, its shops, cinemas, theatres and other places of entertainment. Instead of that many American cities are surrounded by instant cities, each with its core of office buildings 'where the buildings are tallest, the daytime population largest, and the traffic congestion most severe'. And this core is surrounded by shopping malls, condominiums, town houses, suburban houses, movie theatres, restaurants, hotel/conference centres and so on.

Most of them were too new when Goldensohn was writing even to appear on the maps but, as he says, the free-wheeling American consumers knew very well where to find them.

So how did all this happen? As Muller points out (1976 and quoted Goldensohn 1986): 'A mass of economic activity was building in the suburbs, now it's gone critical. The idea of a metropolitan area no longer dominates. We must think of polycenters and (an) urban realism in which the old city is but one center.'

Two generations of planners have been brought up on Christaller's view (1933), modified by Lösch (1938, 1954) that settlements cluster naturally in hexagonal formations, about a central place in which the exchange of goods and services is facilitated by 'adjacency'. But 'Now we are living in a culture in which the idea of the central place is radically transformed. The central place to which an isolated office park responds is not a physically central place. Adjacency is not important. The big dish on the roof provides the links. We are talking about a . . . global city.'

Since the late 1960s, indeed, industry itself had been changing with much more emphasis on information systems and much less on actual manufacture. The communciations revolution means that people can be dispersed in ways which had been quite unthinkable – except by visionaries such as Marshall McLuhan – even 20 years earlier.

Leinberger and Lockwood (1986) see post-war suburban sprawl as 'merely a transitional phase between the traditional, compact, pre-war city and today's metropolitan area'.

Leinberger and Lockwood detect five reasons for the growth of these instant cities of which the first four were causes of urban sprawl in the first place.

Firstly as the basis of the economy shifted from manufacturing to service and knowledge-based industries so the forms of urban development are bound to change. Whilst manufacturing accounted for one-third of all employment in 1920 by the middle 1980s it accounted for only one-sixth. Many of the new service industries: retailing, fast food catering and so on need new outlets – such as shopping malls – whilst the computer-based professions need increasing amounts of office space.

And whilst factories were unwholesome neighbours – which meant that they were zoned away from housing – office buildings, not to mention high-tech business parks are acceptable in middle class and even exclusive suburbs.

Secondly, the growth of road transport, at the expense of rail, means that neither commuters nor goods have to go to a station. They can be taken from door to door along the freeways *around* the city rather than into and out of it.

Thirdly, advanced telecommunciations, including cheaper long-distance calls, means that far fewer people need to travel at all. In addition to telephones, of course, telecopiers, facsimile systems, telexes, Zap Mail, and computer modems are available, ever more cheaply, as the relative costs of calls come down.

Fourthly, whilst construction costs are similar for city centre and suburban sites, land costs are very different. Leinberger and Lockwood quote figures of $50 to $1000 per square foot for urban sites against $10 to $50 for suburban ones.

What is more offices need parking, which, downtown, might well have to go underground. Multi-storey car parks would be cheaper, and there would be room for these in the suburbs. In many suburbs indeed land values may be such that parking could be sustained at surface level. So suburban office space, even in prestigious high-rise blocks, can be rented for some $15 to $24 per square foot whilst their downtown equivalent might cost anything from $18 to $42.

Such economic factors have encouraged the building of instant cities but Leinberger and Lockwood detect a fifth one which, in their view, finally determined that families move. Most Americans, they say, *like* city life, or such urban facilities as a good selection of shops, restaurants, hotels and so on. Each, to be viable, needs a certain critical mass of people. A modest regional shopping mall, for instance, may need a catchment of 250 000 within a radius of three to five miles. These people, in their turn, need accessible employment and housing. The critical mass for a decent restaurant, might be 20 000 people and so on. So for quite sophisticated services, the critical mass may be a good deal smaller than used to live pre-war in downtown.

What is more people want their facilities close at hand. They do not want to drive very far and the optimum locations evidently are those which can be seen from the highway and are easy of access from it.

Which means that the better located instant cities attract more and more office buildings and hotels, increasingly sophisticated shops, and high-density housing. As this goes on, so the old city centres themselves become, as it were, increasingly suburban.

They may be turned into tourist attractions such as the South Street Seaport in Lower Manhattan, Harbour Place in Baltimore, Fisherman's

Wharf in San Francisco and so on. And these in their turn may attract so many people that shopping malls, on the suburban model, will be built as close as possible to them!

What is more the old urban centres had become so 'dangerous and inefficient' a generation ago that families had felt obliged to flee them for the refuge of the new, wholesome and hygenic instant cities.

Yet as Leinberger and Lockwood point out, instant cities too have their social problems. They are growing, on the whole, as white, upper middle-class areas for the very obvious reason that the managers and other executives who decide on their location do so for their own convenience. Which is time and energy-efficient for them and for anyone else who can afford the nearby houses and the cars needed to move them over fairly short distances.

Which does not include the majority of office workers, clerical staff, cleaners, caretakers; those who serve in the local stores, restaurants, gas stations and so on. They simply cannot afford executive-prices so they face long and costly journeys by car or by bus – often having to change downtown – to the suburbs which they can afford.

The obvious solution would be low-cost housing in the instant cities but that, precisely, is what the residents do not want. They have, as Leinberger and Lockwood put it, 'raised the drawbridge' against housing for the working classes. Indeed many of them live in fenced or walled communities guarded, gated and secure.

Urban villages have developed within the United States largely because of the way local government is organized. Greater Los Angeles, for instance, contains over a hundred cities and five counties, whilst metropolitan Atlanta has 46 cities and seven counties. Many of these are anxious to expand their tax bases, to generate employment and to welcome 'progress'. So they compete with each other in offering the most liberal zoning legislation, tax abatements – at least on a temporary basis – and improvements to roads, sewers and other parts of the infrastructure. Even if the residents in one area resist, they will still be affected by developments which their immediate neighbours have welcomed as sources of profits for themselves.

Leinberger and Lockwood finally ask if the urban village is good or bad for the city. They see the question itself as irrelevant since the trend seems to be so well established – in America – as to be quite irreversible. Not that they would wish to reverse it anyway, for, as they say:

> . . . it is hard to imagine the ideal urban village as being anything but very good. The opportunity for all kinds of Americans to live, work, shop, and play in the same geographic area – while retaining easy access to other urban village-cores with specialized features that their own district lacks – seems almost too good to be true.

Goldensohn is much less sanguine. For despite, or even because of, their sophistication such instant cities simply lack the very features which, for Jane Jacobs and others, are the essence of the city. As Goldensohn puts it:

> One missing ingredient is history, megacenters have no past, no rich diversity of architecture or neighbourhood built layer upon layer over time. The ethnic and economic mix is narrow.

He goes on to suggest that according to some urban theorists, instant cities will separate American society even further by class and race. As prosperous Americans flock to these new suburban cities so the poor, already left behind, will be completely forgotten.

Most of those who move in, of course, will be products of the suburbs, having grown up with fathers who commuted to work in the city centre whilst they – and their wives – will be commuting to other suburbs. Already, 70% of all Americans live in suburbs, as against the 39% who still live in cities. As Goldensohn says, 'The high-tech labor pool necessary to a service economy is culturally prepared for the megacenter. They are, in general, a flexible, youthful group, willing to relocate, and very much at home in a car culture.'

So, Goldensohn suggests, the children of those who move into these instant cities will have no contact with the *city*; they simply will not know what urban life can be like and thus will not know what they are missing. Unless, as he suggests, they visit the real Venice and *then* realize that Las Colinas is merely a fake. Even then he suggests they might prefer their fake.

So whilst the instant cities cannot be stopped, at least in North America, they are by no means the solution to all our urban problems. And how much better they would be if their design could be informed by the kind of urban thinking which has been developing elsewhere.

The future of the city

So what does all this tell us about the future of the city? Cities, no doubt, will have many futures. Old cities, and the older parts of cities will survive more cherished than they were in the heady days of the Modern Movement when so many of them were crucified against the Corbusean vision of the 'Ville Radieuse'. Many of them had contained perfectly good housing, of the kinds which Jane Jacobs and Nicholas Taylor loved so much, demolished to make way for the tower blocks and the motorways. It is unlikely that so much good urban fabric will ever again be sacrificed to (empty) Corbusean space and the great god motor car.

We shall learn from cities such as Siena and Venice, that great urban spaces designed for pedestrians should be kept for their use and not cluttered with cars like, for example the Circus in Bath or the Place Stanislas in Nancy.

Rossi's lessons too will be heeded; that the 'memory' of the city resides in its monuments, that without them it is no longer that particular city. We might even learn that the monuments themselves are at their best when we see them looming out of the general urban texture – as the Coloseum used to do out of Medieval Rome until Mussolini had it 'freed', so it now stands in rather unsplendid isolation. Wren himself designed a Piazza closely around St Paul's, no less than five storeys high, that rises up to the first cornice of the Cathedral itself and is far denser than any of the entries for the 1988 Paternoster Square competition. How pleased the developers would have been with Wren's own solution!

Perhaps we shall learn from Leon Krier that cities ought to be zoned again: not in the sense of separating places of work from places for dwelling, places for services and so on but in terms of *quartiers* each containing, within easy walking distance, the necessities of day-to-day life. We might agree with him too that they should be zoned in terms of architectural and planning styles. Krier sees this as the only way of building coherent groups of Classical buildings again. Curiously enough Hugh Wilson used a similar technique to get a Modernist Zone built in Canterbury after World War II, which means that in Canter-

Fig. 13.18 Chamberlain, Powell and Bonn (1966–83) Barbican, London (author's photograph).

Fig. 13.19 Rogello Salmona (1968): El Parque, Bogota (author's photograph).

bury we can now enjoy the old medieval sector around the Cathedral quite unmolested by the out-of-keeping, out-of-scale, out-of-character buildings of the 1950s. They have their own zone – or ghetto – which we can choose to take or leave.

We might learn also from Duany and Plater-Zyberg's Seaside that such zones or quartiers can force variety if each has its own internal rules of development.

Nor should it be too much to hope, as Halbwachs, Rossi and the Kriers do, that more and more people will be able to live again literally 'over the shop' as Medieval craftsmen used to. That will be encouraged by the growth of information processing, for clearly the computer is a less disturbing neighbour than the lightest of industry; less disturbing even, than the Medieval carpenter's saw, the blacksmith's – or even the shoe-maker's – hammer!

Some kind of consensus also emerges from the work of Jane Jacobs, Christopher Alexander, the Kriers and many others: that overlapping, interlocking uses make for lively and even for safe city places. Their concept of mixed-uses can be stretched in scale.

However appalling one finds the architecture, however gross the scale of the towers, however squalid the streaked concrete and brick, Chamberlin, Powell and Bon's Barbican in the City of London (1959–1983) has a great deal of interest to offer (Fig. 13.18). There is no doubt that some people, particularly the old very much enjoy living high up, looking out over the City with its memories and being able to take a lift straight down to the foyer of the Arts Centre to hear and see the London Symphony Orchestra or the Royal Shakespeare Company.

One is also reminded of Salmona's El Parque in Bogota (1968–71) in which three massive residential towers are grouped around a bullring (Fig. 13.19). Of course there are further possibilities.

Some of these were described by Ricardo Bofill and the Taller de Arquitectura in their entry to a competition for Monaco which they called *Le Cheval de Monaco* (Broadbent 1975a, b). It consisted of an 'urban arena' surrounded by multi-storey 'pluri-functional' buildings (Fig. 13.20). These, as their name implies, could be fitted-out as apartments, bars, boutiques, cafés, galleries, offices, restaurants, shops and so on whilst the arena itself could be used for cinema, circus, concerts, dancing and other kinds of leisure activities. There would be equipment for basket ball, boxing, fencing, hockey, judo not to mention sound–light projections and so on.

If living in such a place, then, at any moment, one could choose whether to stay in one's apartment, listening to records, watching television or whatever, look out of the window to see what was happening in the arena, stay at the window as a spectator, merely watching, go down and join in or even go down and start something new.

Le Cheval de Monaco was intended as an essay in urban freedom, as exemplified by the Taller's various slogans: 'Time for each and time for all,' 'Happiness is a cultural value,' 'Time to love,' 'New sensibility,' and so on. Of course it had deeper implications. If such a variety of leisure pursuits were to be found, literally outside one's window then one's need to travel in search of diversion would be greatly diminished.

Not that 'pluri-functional' building was exactly new. Roman urban villas, for instance, had shops along their street frontages. Medieval craftsmen, literally lived 'over the shop' as did their 19th century successors.

On a larger scale of course, Le Corbusier's Unité d'Habitation' in Marseilles has a deck of shops, a supermarket and a hotel halfway up, a

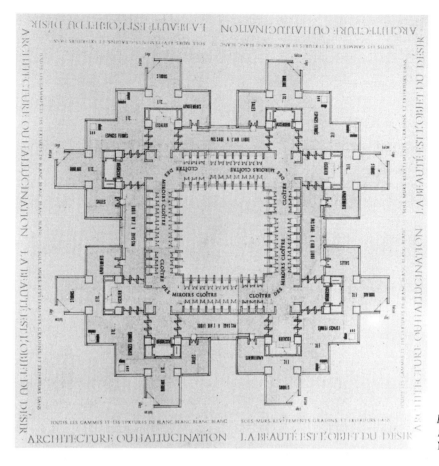

Fig. 13.20 Bofill and the Taller de Arquitectura (1975) Le Cheval de Monaco (from the original drawing).

school, a gymnasium and other facilities on the roof (Fig. 13.21). Lucien Kroll's student housing for the University of Louvain (at Woluwe St Lambert, outside Brussels) is a mix of students' rooms, bars, shops, social facilities, an ecumenical centre and restaurants distributed amongst its various blocks.

However, Le Corbusier's Unité shows one kind of problem. Kroll's residences another. For the Unité of 337 apartments is not really big enough to sustain a supermarket or even great variety of shops. Most of them indeed seem to be used as offices by the various professionals, architects, doctors, lawyers, who have chosen to live as Le Corbusier intended. Clearly if one is planning 'pluri-functionality' of that kind one has to know – as the 'instant-city' builders know so well, that each function, be it bar, restaurant or shop needs a specific catchment area or, rather, catchment population, if it is to be viable.

Kroll's intention in the case of his residences was that the various kinds of accommodation should be 'mixed in', which, somewhat to his chagrin, proved impossible in the case of the restaurants which, with their serveries, kitchens, food stores and so on, proved too big as units to be 'squeezed' into his blocks. Which of course would have been true for many other kinds of activities (Fig. 3.22).

Supposing each city had a number of places; architectural and planning 'improvements' on the Barbican – less brutal and rather smaller in scale – where instead of living 'over the shop' one lived as Bofill suggested 'over' one's leisure pursuits: concerts, theatre, opera, aerobics, bowling, computing, dance, disco, drawing, gymnastics, jazz, painting, sculpture, skating, swimming, tennis and so on, each place occupied by people particularly active in these areas. It would save them a great deal of travelling time and others, less zealous about

Fig. 13.21 Le Corbusier (1952) Unité d'Habitation, Marseilles (author's photograph).

347

Fig. 13.22 Lucien Kroll (1968): Student Residences, Medical Faculty, University of Louvain, Woluwe St Lambert near Brussels (author's photograph).

these particular pursuits but wanting to engage in them occasionally, could come and enjoy them as they pleased from time to time.

Then one could decide where to live on the basis of what one expected to be doing most often. Which of course would reduce the need to travel, the need for cars, therefore for roads and parking places. Which would save much space within the city, thereby reducing travelling distances even further.

Some of these 'specialist' centres no doubt would become urban monuments in the Rossi sense. One agrees with him too that between them the city needs an ever-changing general grain or texture. Again Berlin has shown the way with the IBA housing, much of which is based on March and Trace-like forms (see Chapter 7).

But it seems to me that in addition to these Rossi-like 'monuments' and 'urban texture' each city needs a third component which, for the moment, we might call 'out-of-town' housing. Most cities have this in the form of suburbia. Edwards, an ardent advocate, describes this (1981) as:

> a neutral world . . . an area of houses . . . a hybrid. It possesses something both of the countryside and of the city. It has trees, grass, hedges and flowers, but it also has buildings, streets and pavements. It is a place whose inhabitants are broadly of a similar social class, where the breadwinner sleeps but does not work, where houses are set in gardens, but where the streets have kerbs.

It results, he says, from the activities of an estate-developer, 'which may be a city council, a new-town corporation, a speculative builder, or perhaps a farmer who finds bungalows a more profitable crop than corn'.

A suburb however, is not a garden city, still less an 'instant' city. Each house has its garden, which may be used, in part, for growing food but there are no shops, no industrial estates nor even any large blocks of flats. Unlike the instant-city dweller, the suburbanite depends on the city for virtually everything, apart from a place to sleep. Given the low densities of suburbia, of course, there cannot be much sense of urban enclosure between the buildings. The only way,

Fig. 13.23(a) Self-built housing: El Abanico, Santo Domingo, Dominican Republic. Having built a very basic shelter the owners are building a permanent house around it (author's photograph).

indeed, of getting enclosure will be by skilful planting of trees, large and small, hedges, fences and so on.

No doubt suburbia will continue to spread. As farmers are discouraged by the European Community from over-producing food many of them clearly will want to 'plant' this more profitable 'crop'. Some of them will no doubt want to provide rather more than housing; shops, places for leisure and so on, aspiring indeed to build European versions of the 'instant city'.

But there is another form of housing-outside-the-city which, it so happens, is far better known in the developing world. It consists of self-built housing, or rather self-built communities of houses, schools, shops and so on. As one sees in Brazilia and Chandigarh such developments often have a far greater vitality than anything that has been formally planned.

In many cases, having built a basic dwelling the 'owner occupier' then begins to build around it concrete block walls, asbestos cement roofs and so on. This 'hardening' process seems to be occurring everywhere in the emerging world as the shanty-dwellers build up their resources. They can be encouraged of course, by schemes in which sites and services' are laid down onto which they can then build their dwellings.

Indeed the justifiable pride which many shanty-dwellers take in the houses they have built is itself a form of condemnation, in the eyes of Marxist theorists, such as Roberto Segre (1975) who see them as incipient capitalists on however small a scale. Segre and like-minded theorists would rather see the very poor housed in sub-standard, government-provided housing on the grounds that this housing in itself will enforce a form of social cohesion and thus trigger 'the urban revolution'.

Such building clearly is expensive to build and few Third World countries can afford it. Nor can the poor afford the rents, or even the heating bills which living in such dwellings incurs.

Self-build can by contrast be cheap. Indeed by definition it is the cheapest possible kind of dwelling since the labour costs are literally zero. Given the personal satisfaction which it engenders in the self-builder, it seems to have many advantages, even in London where Walter Segal instituted a self-build scheme at Lewisham.

Fig. 13.23(b) Self-built housing, Caracas, Venezuela. This concrete floored, brick, tile and asbestos cement housing is planned much as Hillier and Hanson predict that 'informal' housing will be (see pp. 21–3) (author's photograph).

How much richer the cities of the developed world would be if zones were given over to self-build with the minimum of planning, and even constructional constraints. In time, no doubt, such areas would acquire an equivalent vitality to that which is so noticeably present in, for example, the 'free-cities' around Brazilia.

So one can see building of three kinds emerging. Rossi-like 'monuments' which clearly will be the work of professional designers; developments within the more general urban texture which again, on the whole, will be the work of professionals, perhaps on the lines of Héré's Nancy, with coherent urban spaces defined by façades with self-design, if not self-build at the back, and 'free' zones in which self-build is encouraged and even facilitated by 'sites and services' schemes.

As for the forms of the general urban texture, clearly there is much to be said for patterns of streets of the kind which Jane Jacobs described but one would hope to see alternatives of various kinds. London, for instance, certainly has its streets but it also has its squares. Many of these are surrounded by four-storey terrace housing, in fair-faced brick or stucco. Not only do they look attractive, they are also remarkably efficient. The efficiencies of such housing, of course, have been realised by the Taller di Architectural in, for example, Les Arcades du Lac or Antigone, not to mention many of the IBA schemes in Berlin. Significantly in many of these developments cars are accommodated where they should be: underneath the squares, with staircase or elevator access to the actual apartments.

The crucial point about this kind – and scale – of development of course, is that it matches precisely the prescription which March and Trace developed out of their research (Chapter 7) for the most efficient urban housing. The Georgian square was such a form writ large; and as we also saw in Chapter 7, the Georgian town house contained many rooms of the size which Peter Cowan showed (1964) to be highly adaptable to different uses.

Since Georgian houses were planned to contain quite a lot of rooms of, or around, this significant size, and since Georgian window-spacings enable larger rooms to be subdivided into rooms more or less of this size, it is hardly surprising that the basic Georgian form has proved so eminently useable for so many purposes. But the Georgian house around-the-square has many other advantages. It was designed for the 'season' in a particular town with large rooms at the front facing the square, in which 'the family' could receive their guests and smaller rooms for services – and servants – at the back. It so happens that such a distribution of room sizes, often over four floors and a basement, makes such houses useable for very many purposes. They can be retained as rather grand houses, converted into apartments, colleges, hotels, nursing homes, offices and even schools of architecture. Indeed the Architectural Association occupies three such houses, opened sideways to each other, at 66–68 Bedford Square in London.

The 'Urban Villas' of IBA share some of these advantages of course. They have internal flexibility but lack the ultimate flexibility of terrace housing, that as purposes expand, one can knock holes through the party-wall from one terrace house to another.

It is largely a matter of choices. As the 'instant city' builders realize whilst cities in the past were built for the production and exchange of goods, cities in the future will have to respond to the pressures for exchanging information. Given our sophisticated equipment, this can all be done electronically and much of it can be done from home.

A few, no doubt, will want to get away from the city altogether. They will hide themselves in their 'electronic cottages' in the woods. But

Fig. 13.23(c) Self-built housing: Hydra, Greece. Several hundred years of lime wash have given this informal housing the qualities of a picturesque tourist attraction! (author's photograph).

most of us need human contact, not to mention choices of which humans to make our contacts with, which is our main reason for living in the city.

Several built forms seem to offer more choices than most, much as Jane Jacobs's 'safe' streets and Bofill's 'arenas'. A city built of these in judicious balance, containing Rossi-like 'monuments' surrounded by a general 'urban texture' of the kinds which IBA provides and surrounded, as appropriate, by suburbs, 'instant cities' on the Houston model, some of them devoted to self-build, seems likely to offer the widest possible range of urban choices, to more people, than many of our current cities do.

References

Note: **bold** type indicates buildings and projects.

AAM (1978) *Rational: Architecture: Rationelle* with Essays by Delevoy, R. L., Vidler, A., Krier, L., Scolari, M., Huet, M., Krier, R. and many projects. Archives d'Architecture Moderne, Brussels.

ACIH (1981) Association pour la Consultation International pour l'Aménagement du Quartier des Halles: **600 Contreprojets pour les Halles.** Editions du Moniteur, Paris. See also *Architectural Design* **50** (9/10) 1980.

Addison, J. (1712) On the Pleasures of the Imagination. *The Spectator* No. 412, June 1712 to No. 421, July 3 1712. Reprint edited by G. G. Smith (1897–98) as *The Spectator*, Dent, London.

Akurgal, E. (1978) *Ancient Ruins and Civilizations of Turkey*, Haşet Kitabevi, Istanbul.

Alberti, L. B. [c. 1485) *De Re Aedificatori, Libri Decem*, trans. Leoni, J. (1726, 1739 and 1755) as *The Ten Books of Architecture* (ed. J. Rykwert) (1955) Tiranti, London.

Alexander, C. (1964) *Notes on the Synthesis of Form.* Harvard University Press, Cambridge, Mass.

Alexander, C. (1966) A City is Not a Tree. *Architectural Forum*, April 1966; reprinted in *Design*, No. 6 February 1966. Revised (1986) for *Zone* 1/2, New York; revised version reprinted in Thakara, J. (1988) *Design After Modernism*, Thames and Hudson, London.

Alexander, C. (1975) *The Oregon Experiment*, Oxford University Press, New York. Center for Environmental Studies Vol. 3.

Alexander, C. (1979) *The Timeless Way of Building*, Oxford University Press, New York. Center for Environmental Studies Vol. 1.

Alexander, C. (1981) **The Linz Cafe; Das Linz Café**, Oxford University Press, New York; Löker, Wien. Center for Environmental Studies Vol. 5.

Alexander, C., Ishikawa, S. and Silverstein, M. (1968) *A Pattern Language: Towns, buildings, construction*, Center for Environmental Studies, Berkeley, California. Republished (1977); Oxford University Press, New York. Center for Environmental Studies Vol. 2.

Alexander, C., Neis, H., Anninou, A. and King, I. (1987) *A New Theory of Urban Design*, Oxford University Press, New York. Center for Environmental Studies Vol. 6.

Alison, A. (1790) *Essays on the Nature and Principles of Taste*, Edinburgh. Fourth edn (1815) Edinburgh.

Andrews, J. J. C. (1984) *The Well-Built Elephant and other Roadside Attractions.* Congden and Webb, New York.

Anson, B. (1986) Don't Shoot the Graffiti Man. *Architects' Journal*, **184** (27), 2 July 1986.

Ardrey, M. (1967) *The Territorial Imperative*, New York.

Edition consulted (1969) Collins, London.

Aristotle (n.d.) *Politics*, trans. Rackham, H. (1932), Loeb Classical Library, Heinemann, London.

Arnell, P. and Bickford, T. (compilers and eds) (1985) *Aldo Rossi: Buildings and Projects*. With an Introduction by Vincent Scully, a Postscript by Rafael Moneo and Project Descriptions by Andrews, M. Rizzoli, New York.

Ashcraft, N. and Scheflin, A. E. (1976) *People Space*, New York.

Aurigemma, G. (1979) Giovan Battista Nolli. *Architectural Design*, **49** (3/4).

Ayer, A. J. (1956) *The Problem of Knowledge*, Penguin Books, Harmondsworth (Reprinted by Penguin Books, 1984.)

Aymonimo, C. (1967–9) **Housing Complex for the Gallaratese Quarter of Milan:** Project of 1967–9: Axnmetric Sketch in Bonfanti *et al.* (1973).

Aymonimo, C. (1973) *L'Abbitazione Razionale: Atti dei Congressi CIAM 1929–30*, Ed. Mesilio, Padua.

Aymonimo, C. and Rossi, A. (1969–74) **Housing Complex at the Gallaratese Quarter Milan, Italy**. Edited and photographed by Futigawa, Y., with text by Nicolini, P. *GA*, 45 (1977); Conforti, C. (1981).

Bacon, E. N. (1967) *Design of Cities*, Thames and Hudson, London.

Bacon, F. (1620) *The New Organon*, London (ed. F. H. Anderson, 1960), Bobs-Merrill, New York.

Balestracci, D. and Piccini, G. (n.d.) *Siena nel Trecento*, Ed. Clusf, Florence.

Balfour, A. (1978) **Rockefeller Center:** *Architecture as Theatre*, McGraw Hill, New York.

Banham, R. (1962) Kent and Capability. *The New Statesman*, 7 December.

Banham, R. (1969) *The Architecture of the Well-Tempered Environment*, Architectural Press, London.

Banham, R. (1975) *Mechanical Services*, Unit 21 of the Arts Third Level Course: History of Architecture and Design. Open University, Milton Keynes.

Banham, R. (1981) *Megastructures:* Urban Futures of the Recent Past. Thames and Hudson, London.

Barley, M. W. (ed.) (1977) *European Towns: their archaeology and early history*, London.

Barthes, R. (1953) *Le Degrée Zéro d'L'Écriture*, Editions Seuil, Paris. Trans. Lavers, A. and Smith, C. (1967) as *Writing Degree Zero*, Jonathan Cape, London.

Bartolotti, L. (1983) *Siena*, Ed. Laterza, Rome-Bari.

Barzilay, M., Hayward, C. and Lombard-Valentino, L. (1984) **L'Invention du Parc: Parc de la Villette;** *Con-*

cours International; International Competition 1982–1983, Ed. Graphite, Paris.

Bassegoda, M. (1929) quoted in Voltes Bou, P. (1971).

Baudelaire, C. (1863) Le Peintre de la Vie Moderne, trans. Charvet, P. E. (1972) as The Painter of Modern Life, in Baudelaire: Selected Writings on Art and Artists, Cambridge University Press, Cambridge.

Bayón, P. and Gasparini, P. (1977) Panorámica de la Arquitectura Latino-Americana, Ed. Blume, Barcelona; UNESCO, Paris.

Benevelo, L. (1960) Storia dell Città, Ed. Laterza, Bari, trans. Culverwell, G. (1971) as History of the City, Scolar Press, New York.

Benevolo, L. (1963) Le Origine dell'Urbanistica Moderna, Ed. Laterza, Bari. Trans. Landry, J. (1967) as The Origins of Modern Town Planning, MIT Press, Cambridge, Mass.

Benjamin, W. (1955) Schriften Suhrkamp Verlag, Frankfurt, trans. Zohn, H. and ed. H. Arendt (1973 as Illuminations, Fontana, London).

Bennington, G. (1987) Complexity without contradiction in architecture. In AA Files, No. 15, Summer 1987, Architectural Association, London.

Beresford, M. (1967) New Towns of the Middle Ages: Town Plantation in England, Wales and Gascony, London.

Berkeley, G. (1709) An Essay Towards a New Theory of Vision. Intro. Lindsay, A. D. (1910) Everyman's Library, Dent, London; Dutton, New York.

Blake, P. (1964) God's Own Junkyard: The planned deterioration of America's Landscape, Holt, Rinehart and Winston, New York.

Bletter, E. H. and Robinson, C. (1975) Skyscraper Style: Art Deco New York. Oxford University Press, New York.

Blomeyer, G. **Rob Krier: The White House, Berlin-Kreutzberg** 1977/80 (Ritterstrasse Housing) in Architectural Design, **52** (1/2) 1982.

Bloomer, K. C. and Moore, C. W., with Yudell, R. J. (1977) Body, Memory, and Architecture, Yale University Press, New Haven and London.

Boase, T. S. R. (1967) Castles and Churches of the Crusading States, London.

Bocchi, F. (1967) Attraverso le Città nel Medioeva, Ed. Grafis, Casalecchio di Reno.

Bofill, R. and the Taller de Arquitectura (1974–78) **Projects for Les Halles: 1974–78**. Architectural Design, (9/10), **50**, 1980.

Bofill, R. (1978) L'Architecture d'un Homme, Arthaud, Paris.

Bofill, R. (1985) Ricardo Bofill: Taller de Arquitectura with an Introduction by Norberg-Schultz, C. Rizzoli, New York.

Bohigas, O., Puigdomènech, Acebillo, J. and Galofré, J. (1983) Plans i Projectes per a Barcelona 1981/82, Ajuntament de Barcelona.

Bonfanti, E., Bonicalzi, R., Rossi, A., Scolari, M. and Vitale, D. (1973) Architettura Razionale, France Agneli, Milan.

Bordini, G. F. (1588) **Sketch Plan of the Streets of Sixtus V** from Giedion (1962)

Borghesi, S. and Banchi, E. L. (1898) Nuovi Documenti per la Storia dell'Arte Senese, Enrico Torrini, Siena.

Bortolotti, L. (1983) Le città nella storia dItalia. Siena, Editori Laterza.

Bottomore, T. (ed.) (1983) A Dictionary of Marxist Thought, Blackwell Reference, Oxford.

Boullée, E.-L. (n.d.) Architecture: Essai sur l'Art, Paris. Ed. Pérouse de Montclos, J.-M. (1968), Paris.

Braghieri, G. (1981) Aldo Rossi, Ed. Zanichelli, Bologna.

Broadbent, G. (1973a) Design in Architecture. John Wiley, Chichester. Republished with a Postscript (1987) David Fulton, London.

Broadbent, G. (1973b) The Taller of Bofill. Architectural Review, **CLIV**, (921), November.

Broadbent, G. (1975a) Taller di Arquitectura Architectural Design, **XLV**, 7/1975.

Broadbent, G. (1975b) The Road to Xanadu – and Beyond. Progressive Architecture, September.

Broadbent, G. (1977) A Plain Man's Guide to the Theory of Signs in Architecture. Architectural Design, **47** (7/8) 1977.

Broadbent, G. (1981a) Bofill and the Taller. A A Files, **1** (1), 1981–82.

Broadbent, G. (1981b) Architects and their Symbols. Built Environment, **6** (1). Reprinted (1983) in Piplin, J. S., La Gory, M. E. and Blau, J. D. Remaking the City, University of New York Press, Albany, New York.

Broadbent, G. (1987) On Reading Architectural Space. Espaces et Sociétés, Société Semiotique Hellenique.

Broadbent, M. (1973) Wine Tasting, Christie's Wine Publications, London. 1979 edn consulted: Mitchell Beazley, London.

Buchanan, P. (1980) Stirling Magic. Architectural Review, **CLXVII**, (998), April.

Bullock, N. (1978) Housing in Frankfurt: 1925–1931. Architectural Review, **CLXIII**, (976), June.

Burke, E. (1757) A Philosophical Enquiry into the Origin of our Ideas of the Sublime and the Beautiful: with an Introductory Discourse Concerning Taste, and Several Other Additions, in The Works of the Right Honourable Edmund Burke, The World's Classics, Vol. 1, London, Oxford.

Burke, G. (1975) Towns in the Making, Arnold, Leeds.

Cantor, N. F. and Werthman, M. S. (1972) Medieval Society 400–1450, Thomas Y. Crowell, New York.

Cappon, D. (1971) Mental Health and High Rise. Canadian Public Health Association, April.

Carreras Candi, F. (1929) Pueblo Espanol, in Las Noticias. Trans. and reprinted in Voltes Bou, P. (1971) Spanish Village of Barcelona, Corporation of Barcelona.

Carter, P. Mies van der Rohe at Work, Pall Mall, London.

Castell Esteban, R. (1985) **Guía de el Pueblo Español, Mointjuich, Barcelona**, Es. Castell, Barcelona.

Castells, M. (1972) La Question urbaine, François Maspero, Paris. Trans. Sheridan. A. (1977) as The Urban Question: A Marxist Approach, Edward Arnold, London.

Cataneo, P. (1554) L'Architettura, Venice.

Cawker, R. (1987) Between the Lines in A + U No. 207, December.

Chadwick, E. et al. (1842) Report on the Sanitary Conditions of the Labouring Population and on the Means of its Improvement, Poor Law Board, London.

Chadwick, H. and Evans, G. R. (1987) Atlas of the Christian Church, Book Club Associates in association with Macmillan, London.

Charvet, P. E. (1972) Baudelaire: Selected Writings on Art and Artists, Cambridge University Press, Cambridge.

Chaslin, F. (1985) Les Paris de François Mitterand: Histoire des Grands Projets Architecturaux, Gallimard, Paris.

Chemetov, P. and Huidobro, B. (1982–) **Ministère des Finances, Paris**. See Mitterand *et al.* (1987).

Chimacoff, A. (1979) Roma Interrotta Reviewed. *Architectural Design*, **49** (3/4).

Choay, F. (1965) *L'Urbanisme, Utopies et Réalités: Une Anthologie*, Éditions du Seuil, Paris.

Chomsky, N. (1957) *Syntactic Structures*. Mouton, The Hague.

Christaller, W. (1933) *Die zentralen Orte in Suddeutschland: Eine ökonomisch-geographische Untersuchung über die Gesetzmassigkeit der Veerbreitung und Eintwicklung der Siedlungen mit städtischen Funktionem*. Jena. Trans. Baskin, C. W. (1966) as *Central Places in Southern Germany*. Prentice-Hall Engelwood Cliffs, New Jersey.

Cipolla, C. M. (1976) *Before the Industrial Revolution: European Society and Economy 1000–1700*. London.

Clark, K. (1969) *Civilisation*, BBC Publications and John Murray, London.

Clelland, D. (1987) In our times. *Architectural Review*, **CLXXXI**, (1082), April.

Coleman, A. (1985) *Utopia on Trial*, Hilary Shipman, London.

Collins, G. R. and Collins, C. C. (1965) *Camillo Sitte and the Birth of Modern City Planning*. Revised edn (1986), Rizzoli International, New York.

Colquhoun, A. (1975) Rational Architecture. Review of an Exhibition offshoot of the Milan Triennale Architettura Razionale Exhibition held at Art Net in London. In *Architectural Design*, **XLV**, 6/1975.

Conant, K. J. (1939) **The Third Church at Cluny**, in *Medieval Studies in Honour of A Kingsley Porter*, (2 vols), Cambridge.

Conant, K. J. (1954) Medieval Academy Excavations at Cluny, VIII. *Speculum*, **29**, also **38** (1963).

Conant, K. J. (1959) *Carolingian and Romanesque Architecture*, Penguin, Harmondsworth.

Condit, C. W. (1964) *The Chicago School of Architecture: A History of Commercial and Public Building on the Chicago Area*, 1875–1925. University of Chicago Press, Chicago and London.

Conforti, C. (1981) **Il Gallaratese di Aymonimo e Rossi**, Ed. Officina, Rome.

Correa and Mila (1981–82) **Plaça Reial, Barcelona**. See Bohigas *et al.*, 1983.

Cowan, P. (1964) Studies in the Growth, Change and Ageing of Buildings. *Transactions of the Bartlett Society*, No. 3, Bartlett School of Architecture, London.

Cramer, S. (1906) Lecture on Air Conditioning quoted in Ingels, S. (1952) *Willis Carrier, Father of Air Conditioning*, Garden City.

Crombie, A. C. (1972) *Medieval Science and Technology*, in Cantor, N. F. and Werthman, M. S. (1972).

Crouch, D. P. and Mundigo, I. L. (1977) The City Planning Ordinances of the Laws of the Indies Revisited II. *Town Planning Review*, **48**, October, pp. 397–418.

Crouch, D. P., Carr, D. J. and Mundigo, A. L. (1982) *Spanish City Planning in North America*, MIT Press, Cambridge, Mass.

Cullen, G. (1959) *Townscape*. Architectural Press, London.

Cullen, G. (1966) *The Scanner*. Alcan Industries Limited, London.

Cullen, G. (1971) *The Concise Townscape*. Architectural Press, London.

Culot, M. (1977) Portrait de François Spoerry. *Archives d'Architecture Moderne*, No. 12, November, pp. 4–22.

Culot, M. (1988) Une Ile: An Island, in *Leon Krier: Atlantis* Archives d'Architecture Moderne, Brussels.

Daniel, N. (1975) *The Arabs and Medieval Europe*, Longmans, London. Librairie du Liban, Beirut.

Dardi, C. (1978) **Roma Interrotta: Sector II**, in *IIA Catalogue* (1978). Reprinted in *Architectural Design*, **49** (3–4), 1979.

Darwin, C. (1859) *The Origin of Species*, John Murray, London. 1968 edn consulted, Penguin Books, Harmondsworth.

Davey, P. and Clelland, D. (1987a) Berlin: Origins to IBA. *Architectural Review*, **CLXXXI**, (1082), April.

Davey, P. and Clelland, D. (1987b) 750 Years of Berlin. *Architectural Review*, **CLXXXI**, (1082), April.

Davies, W. H. (n.d.) *Leisure*, in Gardner, H. (1972) *The New Oxford Book of English Verse*, Oxford University Press, Oxford.

Delevoy, R. E. *et al.* (1978) *Rational: Architecture: Rationelle: The Reconstruction of the European City*, Archives d'Architecture Moderne, Bruxelles.

de Quincy, Quatremère (1788) Imitation. In Pancoucke: *Encyclopédie Métodique*, Paris. Reprinted in Krier, L. and Porphyrios, D. (eds) 1980.

de Quincy, Quatremère (1823) *Essai sur La Nature, le But et les Moyens de l'Imitation dans les Beaux Arts*, Treuttel et Würtz, Paris. Reprinted in Krier, L. and Porphyrios, D. (eds), 1980.

de Quincy, Quatremère (1832) 'Architecture', 'Construction', 'Copier', 'Invention' and 'Type', all in his *Dictionnaire de l'Architecture*, Paris.

Derrida, J. (1967a) *De la Grammatologie*. Trans Spivak, G. C. (1976) as *Of Grammatologie*, John Hopkins University Press, Baltimore.

Derrida, J. (1967b) *L'Écriture et la Différence*. Trans with introduction and additional notes by Bass, A. (1978) Chicago University Press, Chicago.

Derrida, J. (1967c) *La Voix at le Phénomènone*. Trans (1973) as *Speech and Phenomena*, Northwestern University Press, Evanston.

Derrida, J. (1972) *Positions*. Trans (1981) as *Positions*, University of Chicago Press, Chicago, (1987) Athlone Press, London.

Derrida, J. (1978) *La Vérité en Peinture*. Trans Bennington, G. and MacLeod, I. (1987) as *The Truth in Painting*, Chicago University Press, Chicago.

Derrida, J. (1985) Point de Folie – maintenant architecture. In *La Case Vide: La Villette* (ed. B. Tschumi). Reprinted in *AA Files*, No. 12, Summer 1986, Architectural Association, London.

Derrida, J. (1986) Architetture ove il desiderio puu abitare – Interview by Eva Meyer. In *Domus*, No. 671, April, 1986.

Derrida, J. (1987a) Cinquante-deux aphorismes pour un avant-propos. In *Psyché*, Galilée, Paris. Trans Benjamin, A. (1988a) as Fifty-Two Aphorisms for a Foreward for *Deconstruction: Academy Forum at the Tate*, 28 March 1988, Academy Editions and Tate Gallery, London.

Derrida, J. (1987b) Pourquoi Peter Eisenman écrit de si bons livres. In *Psyché*, Galilée, Paris. Trans (1988) as Why Peter Eisenman writes such good books. *A + U* 1988/8.

Derrida, J. *et al.* (1987) *Mesure pour mesure: Architecture et Philosophie*, Cahiers du CCI, Centre Georges Pompidou, Paris.

Derrida, J. (1988) Filmed interview with Norris, C. for *Academy Forum at the Tate*.

Descartes, R. (1637) *Discourse de la Méthode pour bien Conduire sa Raison et Chercher la Vérité dans les Sciences*. 1941 edition consulted, Manchester University Press, Manchester; also trans. and intro. Wollaston, A. (1960) as *Discourse on Method*, Penguin Books, Harmondsworth.

Descartes, R. (1641) *Méditations sur la Philosophie Première dans laquelle est Démonstrée l'Existence de Dieu et l'Immortalité d l'Âme*. Trans. and Intro. Wollaston, A. (1960) as *Meditations*, Penguin Books, Harmondsworth.

Descartes, R. (1644) *Principles de la Philosophie*. Preface translated Wollaston, A. (1960) as *Principles of Philosophy*, Penguin Books, Harmondsworth.

de Seta, C. and di Mauro, L. (1980) *Palermo*, Ed. Laterza, Rome-Bari.

Dewey, J. (1908) Does Reality Possess Practical Character? in *Essays, Philosophical and Psychological, in Honor of William James*, Longmans Green, New York. Reprinted (1934) as The Practical Character of Reality, in *Philosophy and Civilization*, Minton, Balch, New York and in Thayer, H. S. (1970).

Dewey, J. (1922) La Dévelopement du Pragmatisme Américain, in the *Revue Métaphysique et de Morale*, **29**, 1922. Translated (1925) as The Development of American Pragmatism, in *Studies in the History of Ideas*, Columbia University Press, New York. Reprinted (1931) in *Philosophy and Civilization*, Milton, Balch, New York and in Thayer, H. S. (1970).

Diaz, B. (*c.* 1568) *Historia verdadera de la conquista de la nueva España*, Trans Cohen, J. M. (1963) as *The Conquest of the New Spain*. Penguin Books, Harmondsworth.

Dilke, O. A. W. (1971) *The Roman Land Surveyors: an Introduction to the Agrimensores*, London.

Doré, G. (1872) **Carter Lane** and **A City Thoroughfare**, in *London: A Pilgrimage*, reprinted (1987) as Jerrold, B. and Doré, G., *The London of Gustave Doré*, Wordsworth Editions, London.

Doubilet, S. (1987) The Divided Self: **Social Housing, West Berlin** by Peter Eisenman. In *Progressive Architecture*, March, 1987.

Doxiadis, C. (1972) *Architectural Space in Ancient Greece*, MIT Press, Cambridge, Mass.

Drexler, A. (ed.) (1977) *The Architecture of the Ecole des Beaux Arts*, based on an Exhibition held at the Museum of Modern Art in New York; October 1975 to January 1976. Museum of Modern Art, New York; Secker and Warburg, London.

Duany, A. and Plater-Zyberk, E. (1983) *The Town of Seaside:* Master Plan for the Town of Seaside, Florida. (See also Ivry, in *Architecture* Magazine, June 1985) and

Abrams, J. (1986) The form of the (American) city: two projects by Duany and Plater-Zyberk. *Lotus International*, **27**, 1980/II.

Eisenman, P. (1982–86) **Berlin Housing** see Eisenman, P. (1983) The city of artificial excavation. *Architectural Design*, **53** (7/8), 1983: Doubilet (1987); Eisenman, P. *et al.* (1988); Eisenman, *A + U*, 1988/8.

Eisenman, P. (1988) Interview by Charles Jencks. *Architectural Design*, **58** (3/5), 1988.

Eisenman, P. and Derrida, J. (1986) **Oeuvre Choral: Choral Work**, see Tschumi (1987); Auricoste, I. and Tonka, H. (1987); Derrida, J. (1987b); Eisenman, P. (1988a) and (1988b) Choral Works: Parc de la Villette. *A + U*, 1988/8.

Eliot, T. S. (1932) *Selected Essays: 1917–32*, Harcourt Brace, Jovanovich, New York.

Eliot, T. S. (1933) *The Use of Poetry and the Use of Criticism*, Harvard University Press, Cambridge, Mass.

Empson, W. (1955) *Seven Types of Ambiguity*, Meridian Books, New York.

Engels, F. (1845) *The Condition of the Working Class in England*. Revised trans. 1962, Foreign Languages Publishing House, Moscow.

Engels, F. (1883) Speech at the graveside of Karl Marx, in Tucker, R. C. (1978) *The Marx and Engels Reader*, W. W. Norton, New York.

Ennen, E. (1977) *The Medieval Town*, Trans. Fryde, N., London.

Essex County Council (1973) *A Design Guide for Residential Areas*, County Council of Essex.

Evenson, N. (1969) *Le Corbusier: The Machine and the Grand Design*, Studio Vista, London.

Fanning, D. M. (1967) Families in Flats. *British Medical Journal*, November, No. 198.

Farrell, T. (1985) South Bank, London, Improvement Scheme. See Finch, P. (1985) South Bank Lifeline. *Building Design*, October 11.

Farrell, T. (1986) *Charing Cross Development: An Urban Proposal*, by the Terry Farrell Partnership for Greycoat Group PLC in association with the British Railways Board, London.

Farrell, T. (1987) *Terry Farrell in the Context of London*. Catalogue by Rowan Moore of an Exhibition at the RIBA Heinz Gallery, London, 14 May–13 June 1987.

Farrelly, E. M. (1986) The New Spirit. *Architectural Review*, **CLXXX**, (1074), August.

Ferlenga, A. (1983) **Rob Krier Schinkelplatz**. *Lotus International*, **39**, 1983/III.

Ferriss, H. (1922) The New Architecture (Including **Ferriss' drawings of Building Envelopes**), *New York Times*, March 19, 1922. Reprinted in Corbett, H. W. (1923) Zoning and the Envelope of the Building, in *Pencil Points*, April 1923 and in Ferriss .Leich, J. (1980) *Architectural Visions: the Drawings of Hugh Ferriss*, Whitney Library of Design, New York.

Filarete, A. A. (n.d.) Trattato d'Architettura (cited Rosenau, 1983) for numerous manuscripts, the most important being the *Codex Maglia-becchianus*, Biblioteca Nazionale, Florence.

Filler, M. (1978) The Magic Fountain: **Piazza d'Italia, New Orleans**. *Progressive Architecture*, November, pp. 81–7.

Finch, P. (1985) South Bank Lifeline (Terry Farrell's scheme for improving the South Bank complex in London). *Building Design*, October 11.

Fleming, I. (1959–60) Thrilling Cities serialized in *The Sunday Times*. Reprinted (1963) as *Thrilling Cities* vol. 1: From Hong Kong to New York and vol. 2: From Hamburg to Monte Carlo. Jonathan Cape, London and (1965) Pan Books, London.

Fontana, D. (1590) *Della Transportazione dell'Obelisco Vaticana et delle Fabriche di Nostro Signore Papa Sisto V, fatto dal Cav. Domenico Fontana, Architetto di Sua Sandita*, Rome. Trans. for Giedion, S. (1962) by Ackerman, J. S.

Francesc, Daniel and Molina (1848–59) **Placa Reial, Barcelona**. See Bohigas *et al.* (1983).

Frontinus, J. (n.d.) *de Limit*. 1 ed. Thulin.

Futigawa, Y. (ed.) (1986) *Architect: Zaha Hadid*. Introduction by Isosaki, A. and an interview with Boyarsky, A. G A Architect **5**, ADA Edita, Tokyo.

Gabrielli, F. and Scerrato, V. (1979) *Gli Arabi in Italia*, Scheiwiller, Garzanti.

Games, S. (1985) *A Magnificent Catastrophe*. In *Behind the Façade*, BBC, London.

Garcias, J.-C. (1985) Urbano, troppo urbano: **un progetto por Amiens**, with entries by Martorell, Bohigas, Mackay, Krier, R. with Dewez, B. and Geiswinkler, M., Dollé, B. and Henry, G. AUSIA; AARP; and Naizot, G. *Casabella*, **513**, May 1985.

Gardella, I., Rossi, A., Reinhart, F. and Angello, S. (1982) **Carlo Felice Theatre, Genoa;** *Lotus International*, **42**, 1984/2.

Gaudet, J. (1902) *Éléments et Théorie de l'Architecture: Cours Professé a l'École Nationale et Spéciale des Beaux Arts*, Librairie de la Construction Moderne, Paris.

Gayle, M. and Gillon, E. V. (1975) *Cast Iron Architecture in New York*, Dover, New York.

Geddes, P. (1949) *Cities in Evolution*, Ernest Benn, London.

Geretsegger, H. and Peintner, M. (eds) (1964) *Otto Wagner, 1841–1918*, Residenz Verlag, Salzburg, trans. Onn, G. (1979) Academy Editions, London.

Giedion, S. (1941) *Space, Time and Architecture* (1962 edition consulted), Harvard University Press, Cambridge, Mass.

Gilpin, W. (1748) *A Dialogue upon the* **Gardens . . . at Stowe** *in Buckinghamshire*, J. and J. Rivington, London.

Gilpin, W. (1768) *An Essay upon Prints: Containing Remarks upon the Principles of Picturesque Beauty, the Different Kinds of Prints, and the Characters of the Most Noted Masters*, London.

Gilpin, W. (1794) *Three Essays: On Picturesque Beauty; On Picturesque Travel; and On Sketching Landscape: to Which Is Added a Poem, On Landscape Painting*, London. Republished 1972, Gregg International, Farnborough.

Gilpin, W. (1808) *Remarks on Forest Scenery, and Other Woodland Views, Relative Chiefly to Picturesque Beauty*, London.

Girouard, M. (1985) *Cities and People*, Yale University Press, New Haven and London.

Giurgola, R. (1978) **Roma Interrotta: Sector VI**, in *IIA Catalogue* (1979). Reprinted in *Architectural Design*, **149** (3–4), 1979.

Glusberg, J. and Bohigas, O. (1981) *Miguel Angel Roca*, Academy editions, London.

Goldberger, P. (1979) *The City Observed: New York: A Guide to the Architecture of Manhattan*, Penguin Books, Harmondsworth.

Goldensohn, M. (1986) Metropolis Now. *United*, **31** (16), October.

Gosling, D., Cullen, G. and Donaghue, D. (1974) **Development Plan for Maryculter New Town, Aberdeen**, Christian Salveson.

Gosling, D. and Maitland, B. (1984) *Concepts of Urban Design*, Academy editions, London; St Martin's Press, New York.

Grabar, O. (1973) *The Formation of Islamic Art*, Yale University Press, New Haven and London.

Grassi, G. (1970) Project for Restoration and Extension of the **Castello di Abbiategrasso** in Milan as a New Community Palace in Bonfanti *et al.* (1973).

Grassi, G. (1985) **Fixed Stage Project for Roman Theatre at Segundo**. *Lotus International*, **46**, 1985/2.

Graves, M. (1978) **Roma Interrotta: Sector IX**, in *IIA Catalogue* (1979). Reprinted in *Architectural Design*, **49** (2–3), 1979.

Graves, M. (guest ed.) (1979) Roman interventions. *Architectural Design*, **49** (3–4), 1979.

Grumbach, A. **Roma Interrotta: Sector III**, in *IIA Catalogue* (1979). Reprinted in *Architectural Design*, **49** (3–4), 1979.

Guidoni, E. (1971) **Il Campo di Siena**, Ed. Multigrafica, Rome.

Guidoni, E. (1979) La Componente Urbanistica Islamica nella Formazione delle Città Italiane, in Gabrelli, F. and Scerrato, V. (1979).

Hadid, Z. (1981) **Housing, Stresemanstrasse, Berlin**. *Architectural Review*, **CLXXXI**, (1082), April 1987.

Hadid, Z. (1987) **Berlin: Stresermannstrasse à Kreutzberg**. *Architecture d'Aujourd'hui*, No. 252, September 1987.

Hadid, Z. (1988) **Two Recent Projects for Berlin and Hong Kong**. *Architectural Design*, **58** (3/4), 1988.

Hakim, B. S. (1986) *Arabic–Islamic Cities; Building and Planning Principles*. KPI, London.

Halbwachs, M. (1909) *Les Expropriations et le Prix des Terrains à Paris*, E. Cornély, Paris.

Halprin, L. with MLTW and Urban Innovations Group (1965–66) **Lovejoy Fountain: Portland, Oregon**. See Lyndon, F. D. 1966: Concrete Cascade in Portland, in *Architectural Forum* No. 125 July–August 1966; Portland Plaze: It's like WOW, in *Progressive Architecture*, No. 49, May 1968; Laurence Halprin Makes the City Scene, in *Design and Environment*, Fall 1970; Portland Center: Lovejoy Plaza, in *A + U*, 1973/8; also *A + U*, 1978/5 and Johnson (1986).

Hartshorne, C. and Weiss, P. (eds) (1934) *Collected Papers of Charles Sanders Peirce* vol. 5, Harvard University Press, Cambridge, Mass.

Heckscher, A. (1962) *The Public Happiness*, Antheneum Publications, New York.

Hejduk, J. (1985) *Mask of Medusa: Works 1947–1983*, Rizzoli, New York.

Hejduk, J. (1986) Project 11–84, *Residential Building* **Studio Tower South Friedrichstrasse**. *Berlin in Nakamuro, T* (ed.) *1987 International Building Exhibition, Berlin 1987*. A + U extra edn 1985/5.

Hilbersheimer, L. (1964) *Contemporary Architecture: Its Roots and Trends*, Paul Theobalds, Chicago.

Hillier, W. R. G. (1973) In Defence of Space. *RIBA Journal*, November 1973.

Hillier, W. R. G. and Hanson, J. (1984) *The Social Logic of Space*, Cambridge University Press, Cambridge.

Hincmar (n.d.) *Annales Bertiniana* (ed. Waitz, A.) (1883) Hanover. Quoted Daniel (1973).

Hiorns, F. R. (1956) *Town-Building in History: An Outline View of Conditions, Influences, Ideas, and Methods Affecting 'Planned' Towns through Five Thousand Years*, George Harrap, London; Criterion Books, New York.

Hipple, W. J. (1957) *The Beautiful the Sublime and the Picturesque in English 18th Century Theory*. Southern Illinois University Press, Carbondale.

Hippocrates (n.d.) *Aphorisms* III, 4 and 5; also *Airs, Waters*, in trans. Jones, W. H. S. (1923, 1931) and Withington, F. B. (1928) *Hippocrates: Works*, vols 1–4. Loeb Classical Library, Heinemann, London.

Hirsch, E. D. (1983) Derrida's Axioms: Review of Culler, J. (1983) On deconstruction. In *London Review of Books*, 31 July–3 August, 1983.

Hohler, C. (1966) Court Life in Peace and War, in Evans, J. (ed.) (1966) *The Flowering of the Middle Ages*, Thames and Hudson, London.

Hollein, H. (1983–87) **Kulturforum, West Berlin**. *Architectural Design*, **54** (11/12), 1984.

Horn, W. and Born, E. (1979) *The Plan of St Gall* (3 vols), University of California Press, Berkeley.

Hourlier, J. (1964) Saint Odilon, Abbé de Cluny, in *Bibliotèque de la Revue d'Histoire Ecclésiastique*, Louvain.

Howard, E. (1898) *Tomorrow a Peaceful Path to Real Reform*. Revised (1902) as *Garden Cities of Tomorrow*. Edited and with a Preface by Osborn, J. and an Essay by Mumford, L. (1965), Faber and Faber, London.

Hume, D. (1739–40) *A Treatise on Human Nature*. Intro. Lindsay, A. D. (1911) Everyman's Library: J. M. Dent, London.

Hunt, N. (ed.) (1971) *Cluniac Monasticism in the Central Middle Ages*, Macmillan, London.

Hussey, C. (1927) *The Picturesque: Studies in a Point of View*, Putnam, London.

IBA (1987) *Internationale Bauasstellung Berlin 1987*: Projecktübersicht IBA, Berlin.

IIA (1978) *Roma Interrotta Exhibition Catalogue*, Officina Roma, Rome. See also *Controspazio*, No. 4, 1978 and *Architectural Design*, **49** (3/4), 1979.

Isosaki, A. (1983) **Tsukuba Center Building**. *G A Document*, **8**, October 1983; *Japan Architect*, No. 321, January 1984. See also Popham, P. (1984) and Jencks, C. (1987).

Isosaki, A. (1984a) Of city, nation, and style. *Japan Architect*, No. 321, January, pp. 8–13.

Isosaki, A. (1984b) Isosaki on **Tsukuba**. *Building Design*, May 11.

Ivy, E. A. (1985) Building by the Sea: The Southeast. *Architecture Magazine*, June 1985.

Jacobs, J. (1961) *The Death and Life of Great American Cities: The Failure of Town Planning*, Random House, New York. Republished (1962) Jonathan Cape, London and (1965) Penguin Books, Harmondsworth.

James, W. (1896) The Will to Believe. An address to the Philosophical clubs of Yale and Brown Universities. In *New World* (1980) and reprinted in Thayer (1970).

James, W. (1907) What Pragmatism Means. In *Pragmatism: A New Name for some Old Ways of Thinking*, Longmans, Green, New York. Reprinted in Thayer, (1970).

Jeannel, B. (1985) *Le Nôtre*, Fernand Hazan, Paris.

Jencks, C. (1987) *Post-Modernism: The New Classicism in Art and Architecture*, Academy Editions, London.

Johnson, E. (1982) What Remains of Man? Aldo Rossi's **Modena Cemetery**. *Journal of the Society of Architectural Historians*, 1982/1.

Johnson, E. J. (1986) *Charles Moore: Buildings and Projects 1949–1986* with Essays by Krens, T. Moore, C. W., Bloomer, K., Lyndon, D., Stern, R. A. M. and Gastil, R., Klotz, H., Rudolph, D. and T. Song, R. and Johnson, E. J., Rizzoli, New York.

Johnson, P. (1947) *Mies van der Rohe* Museum of Modern Art, New York. Third edition consulted (1978); also Secker and Warburg, London.

Johnson, P. (1959) Whither Away: Non-Mieisian Directions, in Johnson, P. (1979) *Writings*, Oxford University Press, New York.

Johnson, P. and Burgee, J. (1970) **Fort Worth Water Gardens**, Fort Worth, Texas, in Johnson, P. and Burgee, J. (1986).

Johnson, P. and Burgee, J. (1971) **Thanks-giving Square, Dallas, Texas**, in Johnson, P. and Burgee, J. (1986).

Johnson, P. and Burgee, J. (1985) *Philip Johnson/John Burgee: Architecture 1979–85*. Introduction by Knight, C. III, Rizzoli International, New York.

Johnson, P. and Wigley, M. (1988) *Deconstructivist Architecture*, Exhibition Catalogue, Museum of Modern Art, New York.

Jones, E. (1987) Comment: A City Hall in Search of a City. *A + U*, 1987/12.

Jones, E. and Kirkland, M. (1987) **Mississauga City Hall**. *A + U*, 1987/12; *Architectural Design*, **58** (1/2), 1988.

Kant, I. (1758) *The Fundamental Principles of the Metaphysics of Morals* trans. Abbot, T. K. (1987) Prometheus Books, Buffalo, New York.

Keller, H. E. (ed.) and afterword (1978) *Der Markusplatz zu Venedig*, containing Moretti, F. (1831) *Ricinto della Piazza e Piazzetta di San Marco in Venezia*, Karl Hitzegrad, Dortmund.

Keller, H. E. (ed.) (1979) **Der Markusplatz zu Venedig**, with engravings by Moretti (1830) Karl Hitzegrad, Dortmund.

Kenyon, K. (1960) *Archaeology in the Holy Land* (4th edn consulted, 1979), Ernest Benn, London.

Kidder Smith, G. E. (1955) *Italy Builds*. Architectural Press, London, Reinhold, New York.

Kinder, H. and Hilgemann, W. (1964) *dty-Atlas zu Weltgeschichte*, Deutscher Taschenbuch, Munich. Trans. Menze, E. A. (1974) as *The Penguin Atlas of World History*, Penguin Books, Harmondsworth.

Kinsky, C. H. (1978) *Rockefeller Center*, Oxford University Press, New York.

Kliehues, J. P. and Klotz, H. (1986) *International Building Exhibition Berlin 1987: Examples of a New Architecture*, Academy Editions, London.

Knight, R. P. (1806) *An Analytical Enquiry into the Principles of Taste*, London. Reprinted 1972, Gregg International, Farnborough.

Konopka, S. (Intro.) (1985) *Wohnen am Tiergarten: Die Bauten an der Rauchstrasse*. Konopka, Berlin.

Koolhaas, R. (1978) *Delirious New York: A Retroactive Manifesto for Architecture*, Oxford University Press, New York; Academy Editions, London.

Korn, A. (1953) *History Builds the Town*, Lund Humphries, London.

Kostoff, S. (1973) *The Third Rome 1870–1950*, University Art Museum, Berkeley, California.

Kostoff, S. (1985) *A History of Architecture: Settings and Rituals*, Oxford University Press, New York.

Kouwenhoven, J. A. (1953) *The Columbia Historical Portrait of New York: An Essay in Graphic History*, Doubleday, New York. Reprinted (1972) Icon Editions, Harper and Row, New York.

Krier, L. (1968) **University of Bielefeld**. *Architectural Design*, **54** (7/8), 1984.

Krier, L. (1970) **Abbey Extension, Echternacht**. *Architectural Design*, **54** (7/8), 1984.

Krier, L. (1971) **Lewishamstrasse**, in Bonfanti *et al.* (1973).

Krier, L. (1973–78) Analyse et projet d'un ville en péril: **Projet pour la reconstruction de Luxembourg**, in *Archives d'Architecture Moderne*, No. 15, 1978. Also (1979) as Analisi e progetto per una citta in pericolo, *Exhibition Catalogue*, Clea, Rome and (1979) Luxembourg, Capital of Europe, an appeal to the citizens, etc. *Architectural Design*, **49** (1), 1979 and *Lotus International*, **24**, Sept. 1979; *Architectural Design*, **54** (7/8), 1984.

Krier, L. (1974) **Royal Mint Square Housing**. *Architectural Design*, **54** (7/8), 1984.

Krier, L. (1976) **New Quartier of La Villette, Paris** in Bonfanti *et al.* (1973) Paris-Project, Nos 15–16 1976; *Architecture d'Aujourd'hui*, No. 187, 1976; *Lotus International*, **13**, Dec. 1976; *Archives d'Architecture Moderne*, No. 9, 1976; as A City Within a City, *Architectural Design*, **47** (3), 1977; *Arquitectura*, Nos 204–5, November 1977; *Architectural Design*, **54** (7/8), 1984.

Krier, L. (1977) **Rénovation du centre ville de Echternacht**, in Bonfanti *et al.* (1973) *Architecture*, Paris, No. 3, 1977.

Krier, L. (1977–79) **Projet pour une Nouvelle Ecole de Cinq Cents Enfants** in *Archives d'Architecture Moderne*, No. 19, 1980; also as School for 500 Children at St Quentin-en-Yvellines, *Architectural Review*, **CLXVII**, (995), January 1980; *Architectural Design*, **54** (7/8), 1984.

Krier, L. (1978a) La reconstruction de la Ville: The Reconstruction of the City, in AAM (1978); Archives d'Architecture Moderne, Brussels, 1978. Expanded (1984) as The Reconstruction of the European City. *Architectural Design*, **54** (11/12), 1984.

Krier, L. (1978b) **Roma Interrotta: Sector XII**, in *IIS Catalogue* (1978). Reprinted in *Architectural Design*, **46** (3–4), 1979. Also Trois centres sociaux à Rome in *Architecture d'Aujourd'hui*, No. 198, 1978; *Architectural Design*, **54** (7/8), 1984.

Krier, L. (1980a) **Project for Les Halles**. *Architectural Design*, **50** (9/10), 1980; also ACIH (1981).

Krier, L. (1980b) Les Halles: An Everlasting Void. *Architectural Design*, 9/10, 1980.

Krier, L. (1980c) **Leon Krier: Drawings**. Intro. by Culot, M. Archives d'Architecture Moderne, Brussels.

Krier, L. (1980–83) **Project for Berlin-Tegel**, in Krier, L. (1980b) Leone, H. (1982); *Architectural Design*, **54** (7/8), 1984.

Krier, L. (1981) **Project for Les Halles**, in ACIH (1981).

Krier, L. (1982) **Pliny's Villa, Laurentum**. *Architectural Design*, **54** (7/8), 1984.

Krier, L. (1984) The size of a City. *Architectural Design*, **54** (7/8), 1984.

Krier, L. (1985a) The Necessity of Master Plans (with reference to IBA). *Art & Design*, No. 5, June 1985.

Krier, L. (1985b) **The Completion of Washington DC**: A Bicentennial Masterplan for the Year 2000. *Art & Design*, November 1985; *Archives d'Architecture Moderne*, No. 30, 1986.

Krier, L. (1985c) Limits of Growth. *Art & Design*, August.

Krier, L. (1985d) The Light Problem. *Art & Design*, September.

Krier, L. (ed.) (1985e) *Albert Speer: Architecture 1932–42*, Archives d'Architecture Moderne, Brussels.

Krier, L. (1986a) An Architecture of Desire. *Architectural Design*, **56** (4), 1986.

Krier, L. (1986b) **The Completion of Trafalgar Square**: A Masterplan for a National Square. *Art & Design*, April 1986.

Krier, L. (1986c) Project for the **Redevelopment of Spitalfields Market**. *Architectural Design*, **57** (1/2), 1987.

Krier, L. (1986d) Tradition – Modernity – Modernism: Some Necessary Explanations. Extract from Directorship Policy Statement for SOMAI (Skidmore, Owings and Merrill Architecture Institute). *Architectural Design*, **57** (1/2), 1987.

Krier, L. (1987a) Leon Krier: A Profile by Ian Latham. *Architectural Design*, **57** (1/2), 1987.

Krier, L. (1987b) **Atlantis, Tenerife**. *Architectural Design*, **58** (1/2); *Domus*, 694, May 1988; *Archives d'Architecture Moderne*, 1988. See also Culot, M. (1988) and Porphyrios, D.L (1988).

Krier, L. and Porphyrios, D. (eds) (1980) *Quatremère de Quincy: De l'Imitation*, Archives d'Architecture Moderne, Brussels.

Krier, R. (1963) **Haus Siemer** in Bonfanti *et al.* (1973); *Architecture d'Aujourd'hui*, No. 179; *Deutsche Bauzeiting*, 1973; *Architectural Review*, 1973; *Architectural Forum*, 1973; *Bouw*, 49; *Bauen und Wöhnen*; *Lotus International*, 1975; Krier, R. (1982b).

Krier, R. (1964) **Leinfelden City Centre, Stuttgart**, in Bonfanti *et al.* (1973), Krier, R. (1975, 1979) *A + U*, No. 78 June, 1977 and as Cultural and Commercial Center for Leinfelden, Stuttgart, in Krier, R. (1982b).

Krier, R. (1973a) **Tower Bridge Housing, London** in Bonfanti *et al.* (1973); Krier, R. (1982b).

Krier, R. (1973b) **Berlin Ritterstrasse**. *Architecture d'Aujourd'hui*, No. 200.

Krier, R. (1974) Dickes House in Krier, R. (1982b).

Krier, R. (1975) *Stadtraum in Theorie und Praxis*, Karl Krämer Verlag, Stuttgart, (1976) Gustavo Gili, Barcelona. Trans. (1979) as *Urban Space*, Academy Editions, London. (1980) *A + U*, Tokyo, (1981) Archives d'Architecture Moderne, Brussels.

Krier, R. (1977a) **Südliche Freidrichstrasse**, Berlin: Ideal Plan in Krier, R. (1982a) also as Urban Development of South Friedrichstadt, Berlin in Krier, R. (1982b).

Krier, R. (1977b) Proposal 1977 for the Area **Lindenstrasse, Alte Jakobstrasse, and Ritterstrasse in Berlin, with Schinkelplatz at the top**; also 'Schinkelplatz as the Focus of Four Blocks' in Krier, R. (1982). See also Schinkelplatz, Berlin. *Lotus International*, No. 41, 1984/1.

Krier, R. *et al.* (1977–80) Housing on the **Ritterstrasse**. *Architecture d'Aujourd'hui*, Nos 200, 213; *Architectural Design*, **49** (12), 1979; Krier, R. (1982a); *A + U*, 84: 01; *Architectural Review*, **CLXVI**, (1051).

Krier, R. (1977–80) **The Rauchstrasse Houses**. *Lotus*, 44, 1984–85; Housing in the Tiergarten, Berlin, in Krier, R. (1982b); *Architectural Review*, **CLXVI**, (1051), September 1984 and *Konopka*, 1985.

Krier, R. (1977–82) **Schinkelplatz, South Friedrichstrasse, Berlin**, see Ferelenga, A. (1983) in Krier, R. (1982a and b); *Architectural Review*, **CLXVI**, (1051), September 1984.

Krier, R. (1978a) **Roma Interrotta: Sector X** in *IIA Catalogue* (1978). Reprinted in *Architectural Design*, **49** (3–4), 1979.

Krier, R. (1978b) Urban Design for the **Prager Platz, Berlin** in Krier, R. (1982a and b).

Krier, R. (1979) Typological and Morphological Elements of the Concept of Urban Space. *Architectural Design*, **49** (1), 1979.

Krier, R. (1980) New Block Partition Between Lindenstrasse and Alte Jacobstrasse, **South Friedrichstadt, Berlin** in Krier, R. (1982b).

Krier, R. (1980) **Projects for Berlin**. *Lotus International*, No. 28; *Bauen + Wohnen*, June 1980; *Neue Heimat*, October 1980.

Krier, R. (1982a) *On Architecture*, Academy Editions, London; St Martin's Press, New York.

Krier, R. (1982b) *Urban Projects 1968–1982* with Essays by Berke, D. and Frampton, K. Institute for Architecture and Urban Studies and Rizzoli International, New York.

Krier, R. (1983) Elements of Architecture. *Architectural Design*, **53** (9/10), 1983.

Krier, R. (1985) **Project for Amiens** in Garcias (1985); also Krier, R. (1987); *Amiens: the Reconstruction of the Historic Centre*, Archives d'Architecture Moderne, Brussels.

Krier, R. (1987) Personal communication at the Academy Forum at the Tate on 'Post Modernism', October 1987.

Krier, R. (1988) *Architectural Composition*, Academy Editions, London.

Kroll, L. (1968–71) **Medical Faculty, Woluwé-Saint Lambert, La Mémé**, Brussels. See Kroll, L. (1975) The Soft Zone. *Architectural Association Quarterly*, **7** (4); Williams, S. (1976) Do it Yourself. . . . *Building Design*, March 30, 1976; Strauven, F. (1976) L'Anarchitecture de Lucien Kroll. *Archives d'Architecture Moderne*, 1976 No. 8; also in *Architectural Association Quarterly*, No. 2, December 1976.

Kroll, L. (1986) *The Architecture of Complexity*, London.

Kroll, L. (1988) *Buildings and Projects*, with an Intro. by Pehnt, W., Thames and Hudson, London.

Kurokawa, K. (1982–83) *Projet pour le **Parc de la Villette, Paris***, see Barziley *et al.* (1984).

Lampugnani, V. M. (1984) How to put a contradiction into effect. *Architectural Review*, **CLXVI**, (1051), September 1984.

Latham, I. (1987) Leon Krier: A Profile by Ian Latham. *Architectural Design*, **57**, (1/2), 1987.

Laugier, M.-A. (1753) *Essai sur l'Architecture*, Duchesne, Paris. Reprinted (1966) Gregg Press, Farnborough; also Trans. Herman, W. and A. (1977) as *An Essay on Architecture*, Hennessey and Ingalls, Los Angeles.

Lazzaroni, M. and Muñ, A. *Filarete*, Rome. Quoted Rosenau, 1972.

Le Corbusier-Saugnier (1922a) Le Chemin des Anes, le Chemin des Hommes. *L'Esprit Nouveau*, No. 17, 1922. Reprinted in Le Corbusier (1924).

Le Corbusier (1922b) L'Angle Droit and L'Ordre. *L'Esprit Nouveau*, No. 18, 1922. Reprinted in Le Corbusier (1924).

Le Corbusier (1922c) Exhibition at the Salon d'Automne of **Une Ville Contemporaine** Reprinted (1924) as Une Ville Contemporain de 3 Millions d'habitants. *L'Esprit Nouveau*, No. 28.

Le Corbusier (1924) Various articles from *L'Esprit Nouveau*. Reprinted (1924) as *Urbanisme*, Editions Crés, Paris. Trans. Etchells, F. (1929) as *The City of Tomorrow*, John Rodker, London. Reprinted (1947, 1971 and 1987) Architectural Press, London.

Le Corbusier (1925a) **Plan Voisin de Paris** for the Pavilion d'Esprit Nouveau at the Exhibition of Arts Decoratifs in Paris. Reprinted Le Corbusier, 1929.

Le Corbusier (1925b) La Rue. *L'Intransigeant*, May 1929. Reprinted in Le Corbusier and Jeanneret, P. (1964) as La Rue: the Street; Die Strasse.

Le Corbusier (1926) Les 5 points d'une architecture nouvelles. Reprinted in Le Corbusier and Jeanneret, P. (1929).

Le Corbusier (1930) *Précisions sur un état présent de l'architecture et d'urbanisme*, Paris.

Le Corbusier (1935) **La Ville Radieuse**, Paris. Trans. (1967) as *The Radiant City*, Faber, London.

Le Corbusier (consultant) (1937–43) with Costa, L., Leão, C., Moreira, J., Niemeyer, O., Reidy, A. R. & Vasconcelos, E. **Ministry of Education and Health, Rio de Janeiro** in Frank, K. (1960) *The Architecture of Alfonso Eduardo Reidy*, Praeger, New York.

Le Corbusier (1946a) *Quand les Cathédrales Etáient Blanches*, trans. Hyslop, F. E. as *When the Cathedrals Were White* (1964 edn consulted), McGraw Hill, New York.

Le Corbusier (1946b) *Manière de penser l'urbanisme*, Ed. Architecture d'Aujourd'hui, Paris. Trans. Entwistle, C. (1967) as *Concerning Town Planning*, Architectural Press, London.

Le Corbusier (1946c) *Manière de Penser l'Urbanisme: Soigner la Ville Malade*, Éditions de l'Architecture d'Aujourd'hui, Paris.

Le Corbusier (1948) Letter to Senator Warren Austin. *Architectural Review*, July 1950 and Banham, R. (1975).

Le Corbusier and Jeanneret, P. (1929) *Oeuvres Complète*, vol. 1: 1910–1929 (eds O. Stonorow and S. Boesiger). Reprinted (1964) as *Le Corbusier and Pierre Jeanneret: The*

Complete Architectural Works, vol. 1 1919–1929. Editions d'Architecture, Zurich; Thames and Hudson, London.

Ledoux, N.-C. (1804) *L'Architecture Considerée sous le Rapport de l'Art, des Moeurs et de la Législation*, Chez l'Auteur, Paris. Reprinted (1981) Uhl Verlag, Nördlingen.

Leinberger, C. B. and Lockwood, C. (1986) How Business is reshaping America. *Atlantic Monthly*, October.

Lenoine, B. (1980) *Les Halles de Paris*, Ed. L'Equerre, Paris.

Leone, H. (1982) The new traditional town: Two plans by Leon Krier for **Bremen** and **Berlin-Tegel**. *Lotus International*, **36**, 1982/III.

Libeskind, D. (1979) **Arktische Blumen: Arctic Flowers** in Libeskind, D. (1981) Wider die altehwürdige 'Sprach der Architektur': Versus the Old-established 'Language of Architecture'. *Daidalos: Berlin Architectural Journal*, No. 1, 1981.

Libeskind, D. (1987) **City Edge Competition, Berlin**. In *AA Files*, No. 14, Spring 1987, Architectural Association, London. Also as **Berlin Project**, *A + U* No. 215, August 1988 and Richter, A. and Forster, K. W. (1988) Daniel Libeskind: **Edificio per uffici, abbitazione e spazi pubblici**. In *Domus*, July/August 1988.

Llorens, T. (1981) Manfredo Tafuri: Neo-Avant-Garde and History. On the Methodology of Architectural History (Review of Architecture and Utopia: Manfredo Tafuri). *Architectural Design*, **51** (6/7), 1981. Reprinted in Ockman, J. (ed.) (1985) *Architecture: Criticism: Ideology*, Princeton Architectural Press, Princeton.

Locke, J. (1687) *An Essay Concerning Human Understanding* (ed. A. D. Woozley) (1964) Collins Fontana Library, London.

Lorenz, K. (1952) *King Solomon's Ring*, Crowell, New York.

Lösch, A. (1938) The Nature of Economic Regions. *Southern Economic Journal*, **5** pp. 71–8.

Lösch, A. (1954) *The Economics of Location*, New Haven.

Lynch, K. (1960) *The Image of the City*, MIT Press, Cambridge, Mass. and London.

Maggi, G. and Castriotto, I. F. (1564) *Delle Fortificazione della Città*, Venice.

March, L. and Trace, M. (1968) *The Land Use Performance of Selected Arrays of Built Forms*, Working Paper 2, Land Use and Built Form Studies, Cambridge.

Martienssen, R. D. (1958) *The Idea of Space in Greek Architecture*, Wittwatersrand University Press, Johannesburg.

Martin, L. (1958–) **Harvey Court: Gonville and Caius College, Cambridge** in Bonfanti *et al.* (1973) in Martin, L. (1983) *Buildings and Ideas: 1933–83*. Cambridge University Press, Cambridge.

Martin L. and March L. (1972) *Urban Space and Structure*, Cambridge Univeristy Press, Cambridge.

Martini, Fr. di Giorgio (c. 1495) *Trattato di Architectura Civile e Militare*, quoted Rosenau, 1972.

Marx, K. (1844) Economic and Philosophical Manuscripts. Trans. (1975) in Marx, K. and Engels, F. *Collected Works*, Vol. 3: 1843–44.

Marx, K. (1857–58) *Grundrisse der Kritik der Politischen Ökonemie*. Trans. Nicolaus, M. (1973) as *Grundrisse*, Penguin Books, Harmondsworth.

Marx, K. (1867) *Das Kapital*, Vol. 1 Trans. English 1887 and (1894) Vol. III. Trans. English 1909. Revised editions, Progress Publishing, Moscow; Lawrence and Wishart, London.

Marx, K. and Engels, F. (1845–46) The German Ideology trans. 1976 in Marx, K. and Engels, F. *Collected Works*, Vol. 5. Progress Publishing, Moscow; Lawrence and Wishart, London.

Marx, K. and Engels, F. (1848) The Communist Manifesto, trans. Moore, S. (1888) 1967 edition consulted. Penguin Books, Harmondsworth.

Matthew, D. (1983) *Atlas of Medieval Europe*, Phaidon, London.

Maxwell, R. (1988) Critique of **Mississauga City Hall**. *Architectural Design*, **58** (1/2), 1988.

May, E. and Wichert, F. (eds) (1929–32) *Das neue Frankfurt*. See Rodrigues-Lorres and Wichert (1977) for edited selection.

Mellaart, J. (1967) *Çatal Hüyük: A Neolithic Town in Anatolia*, Thames and Hudson, London.

Miller-Lane, B. (1968) *Architecture and Politics in Germany 1918–1945*, MIT Press, Cambridge, Mass.

Mitterand, F. *et al.* (1987) *Architectures Capitales: Paris 1979–89*, Electa Moniteur, Paris.

MLTW with Halprin, L. and Urban Innovations Group (1965–66) **Lovejoy Fountain: Portland, Oregon**. See Halprin (1965–66).

MLTW (1966–74) Moore-Turnbull with Buchanan, M., Calderwood, R. and Simpson, R. **Kresge College: University of California at Santa Cruz**. See Another America, Kresge College, University of California, Santa Cruz, in *Architectural Review*, **CLVI**, (929), July 1974; Whitman Village, Kresge College in *Toshi Jutaku*, September 1974; Kresge College, Santa Cruz, USA, in *Baumeister*, 72, September 1975; School: Kresge College, in *Architecture and Urbanism*, May 1975; Kresge College, University of California, Santa Cruz, in *L'Architecture d'Aujourd'hui*, March 1976. Also *Process Architecture*, No. 3, 1977; *A + U*, 1978/5 and Johnson (1986).

Moneo, R. (n.d.) La Idea de Arquitectura en Rossi y **El Cemeterio de Modena** Ed. ETSAB, Barcelona. Trans. Giral, A. as Aldo Rossi: The Idea of Architecture and the Modena Cemetery. *Oppositions*, **5**, Summer 1976.

Moore, C. W. Associates and Urban Innovations Group with Perez, A. Associates (1975–78) **Piazza d'Italia: New Orleans, Louisiana**. See Davis, J. (1975) The Dazzling Piazza That Might Have Been in *New Orleans States-Item*, January 29, 1975; The Magic Fountain *Progressive Architecture*, **59**, November 1978; Filson, R. (1978) The Magic Fountain of the Piazza D'Italia. *Arquitectura*, **215**, November–December 1978; *A + U*, May 1978; Goldberger, P. New Orleans' New Plaza Is A Wild and Mad Vision, in *New York Times*, February 9, 1979; Moore, C. W. (1980) Piazza s'Italia. *Architectural Design*, **50** (5/6), 1980; Also *A + U*, 1978/5, and Johnson E. J. (1986).

Moore, Ruble, Yudell (1980–) **Tegel Harbour Housing: Berlin**. See Tegeler Hafen Competition: Residential and Recreation Facilities in Berlin. Charles Moore Wins First European Competition. *Architectural*

Design, News Supplement; Wohnen und Freikzeit am Tegeler Hafen, in *Bauwelt*, **42**, November 1980; Moore, C. W. (1982) Schinkel's Free Style Pavilion and the Berlin Tegeler Hafen Scheme. *Architectural Design*, **52** (1/2) 1982; Moore, C. W. Tegel Harbour, Berlin. *Architectural Design*, **53** (1/2), 1983; Johnson (1986) *Architectural Review*, **CLXVI**, (1051); IBA (1987) Nakamura, T. (ed.) (1987).

Moore, Grover, Harper (1981) **Project for Les Halles**, in ACIH, September, 1981.

More, T. (1534) *Utopia: A Dialogue of Comfort*, Intro., Warrington, J. (n.d.), Heron Books, London.

Moretti, F. (1831) **Ricinto della Piazza e Piazzetta di San Marco in Venezia**. Reprinted, with an Afterword by Keller, H. (1978) as *Der Markusplatz zu Venedig*. Karl Hitzegrad, Dortmund.

Morris, A. E. J. (1974) *History of Urban Form: Prehistory to Renaissance*, George Godwin, London. Republished (1979) as *History of Urban Form: Before the Industrial Revolution*. Halstead Press of John Wiley, New York.

Morris, C. (1967) *The Naked Ape*, Jonathan Cape, London.

Morris, D. (1969) *The Human Zoo*, Jonathan Cape, London.

Morville, J. (1969) *Borne Brug af Friarsaler*, Disponering Af Friarsaler, Etageboligomrader Med Saerlig Henblik PaBorns Legsmuligheder, SBI, Denmark. Part translated in Alexander, C., Ishikawa, S. and Silverstein, M. (1977).

Moschini, F. (1979) *Aldo Rossi: Projects and Drawings* 1962–1979, Stiav, Florence, Trans. (1979) Academy Editions, London.

Muller, P. (1976) *The Outer City: Geographical Consequences of the Urbanization of Suburbia*, Association of American Geographers, Washington.

Mumford, L. (1938) *The Culture of Cities*, 1970 edn consulted, Harcourt Brace Jovanovich, New York.

Mumford, L. (1952) House of Glass. Reprinted from *The New Yorker*, in *From the Ground Up*, Harcourt Brace Jovanovich, New York.

Mumford, L. (1954) Crystal Lantern. Reprinted from *The New Yorker*, in *From the Ground Up*, Harcourt Brace Jovanovich, New York.

Mumford, L. (1961) *The City in History*, Secker and Warburg, London. Republished (1966) Penguin Books, Harmondsworth.

Mundy, J. H. and Riesenberg, P. (1958) *The Medieval Town*, Van Nostrand Reinhold, New York.

Mutthesius, S. (1982) *The English Terrace House*, Yale University Press, New Haven.

Nairn, I. (1955) *Outrage*, Architectural Press, London.

Nairn, I. (1957) *Counter Attack*, Architectural Press London.

Nakamura, T. (ed.) (1987) *International Building Exhibition: Berlin 1987*, A + U extra edn, 1987/5. *A + U*, Tokyo.

Nasr, S. H. (1976) *Islamic Science: An Illustrated Study*, World of Islam Festival Publishing Company, London.

Newman, O. (1972) *Defensible Space: People and Design in the Violent City*, Macmillan Co., New York, 1973 edn; Architectural Press, London.

Nicolin, P.-L. (1977) *GA: Carlo Aymonimo/Aldo Rossi: **Housing Complex at the Gallaratese Quarter***, Milan, Italy, 1969–74. Edited and photographed by Futagawa, Y., ADA Eduta, Tokyo.

Nolli, G. (1748) *Roma al Tempo di Benedetto XIV: La Pianta di Roma*, reprinted (n.d.) Biblioteca Apostolica Vaticana, Città del Vaticano.

Norberg-Schultz, C. (1963) *Intentions in Architecture*, Universitetsforlaget, Oslo; Allen and Unwin, London.

Norberg-Schultz, C. (intro.) (1985) *Ricardo Bofill: Taller de Arquitectura*, Rizzoli, New York.

Nuttall, Z. (1921) Royal Ordinances Concerning the Layout of Spanish Towns. *The Hispanic American Historical Review*, **4** (4), November 1921, pp. 743–53.

Nuttall, Z. (1922) Royal Ordinances Concerning the Laying Out of New Towns. *The Hispanic American Historical Review*, **5** (2), May 1933, pp. 249–54.

Oates, J. (1979) *Babylon*, Thames and Hudson, London.

Osborn, F. J. and Whittick, A. (1963) *New Towns: Their Origins, Achievements and Progress*, Leonard Hill. London; Routledge and Kegan Paul, Boston.

Papadakis, A. (ed.) (1988a) The New Modernism: Deconstructionist Tendencies in Art. *Art and Design*, **4** (3/4), 1988.

Papadakis, A. (ed.) (1988b) Deconstruction in Architecture. Architectural design profile. *Architectural Design*, **58**, (3/4), 1988.

Patte, P. (1765) *Monuments érigés à la gloire de Louis XV*, Paris.

Pattou, J. (1981) **Project for Les Halles**, in ACIH, September, 1981.

Pausanius (n.d.) *Description of Greece*, trans. Jones, W. H. S. (1918) 5 vols, Loeb Classical Library, Harvard University Press, Cambridge, Mass.; Heinemann, London, trans. and ed. Levi, S. J. (1971) as *Guide to Greece*, Penguin, Harmondsworth.

Pei, I. M. (1981–88) **Pyramid Entrance to Le Grand Louvre**, see Mitterand *et al.* (1987).

Peirce, C. S. (1878) How to Make our Ideas Clear. *Popular Science Monthly*, January 1878. Reprinted in Thayer (1970).

Peirce, C. S. (1902) Pragmatics and Pragmatism, in Baldwin, J. M. (ed.) (1902) *Dictionary of Philosophy and Psychology*, vol. II, Macmillan, New York. Reprinted in Hartshorne and Weiss (eds) (1934) and Thayer (1970).

Peirce, C. S. (1905) What Pragmatism Is. *The Monist*, **15**, (1905). Reprinted in Thayer (1970).

Pellegrini, E. (1986) *L'Iconografia di Siena nelle Opere a Stampa*. Ed. Lombardi, Siena.

Pennick, N. (1979) *The Ancient Science of Geomancy*, Thames and Hudson, London.

Pérez de Arce, R. (1978) Urban Transformations and the Architecture of Additions (including **Chandigarh and Dacca**). *Architectural Design*, **49** (4).

Pérez de Arce, R. (1978) The Urban redevelopment of the city: **Chandigarh and Dacca**. *Lotus International*, **19**, June 1978.

Pérouse de Montclos, J.-M. (1969) *Étienne-Louis Boullée (1728–1799) de l'Architecture Classique a l'Architecture Révolutionnaire*, Arts et Metier Graphique, Paris.

Pevsner, N. (1976) *A History of Building Types*, Thames and Hudson, London; Princeton University Press, Princeton, New Jersey.

Pinon, H. and Viaplana (1981–82) **Placa l'Estacio de Sants, Barcelona**. See Bohigas *et al.* (1983).

Pirenne, H. (1925) *Les Cités Médiévales*, trans. Halsey, F. D.

(1952) as *Mediaeval Cities, Their Origins and the Revival of Trade* (1974) (edn consulted) Princeton University Press, Princeton, New Jersey.

Pirenne, H. (1937) *Economic and Social History of Medieval Europe*, Harcourt Brace Jovanovich, New York. Chapter on The Impact of Commerce and Urbanization, reprinted in Cantor, N. F. and Wertham, M. S. (eds) (1972) *Medieval Society: 400–1450*, Thomas Y. Crowell, New York.

Plato (n.d.) Theatetos, in Warrington, J. (trans. 1961) *Plato: Parmenides and Other Dialogues*, Everyman's Library, J. M. Dent, London; E. P. Dutton, New York.

Plato (n.d.) Phaedo, in Buchanan, S. (ed.) (1948) *The Portable Plato*, Viking Press, New York.

Plato (n.d.) Republic, trans. Cornford, F. M. (1941) as *The Republic of Plato*, Clarendon Press, Oxford.

Platt, C. (1976) *The English Medieval Town*, Secker and Warburg, London.

Popham, P. (1984) A Hollow Monument (**Tsukubu Civic Centre**). *Building Design*, May 11.

Popper, K. (1959) *The Logic of Scientific Discovery*, Hutchinson, London.

Popper, K. (1963) *Conjectures and Refutations*, Routledge and Kegan Paul, London.

Porphyrios, D. (1984) Leon Krier: Houses, Palaces, Cities. *Architectural Design*, **54** (7/8).

Porphyrios, D. (1988) A Critique of **Atlantis**. *Architectural Design*, **58** (1/2), 1988; also The Meaning of Atlantis et sa Signification, in *Leon Krier* (1988); *Atlantis*, Archives d'Architecture Moderne, Brussels.

Portoghesi, P. (1978) **Roma Interrota: Sector V**, in *IIS Catalogue* (1978). Reprinted in *Architectural Design*, **149** (3/4), 1979.

Provost, A. (1982–84) **Projet pour le Parc de la Villette, Paris.** See Barziley *et al.* (1984).

Price, L. (1982) **The Plan of St Gall**, in *Brief*, University of California Press, Berkeley.

Price, U. (1794) *An Essay on the Picturesque, As Compared with the Sublime and the Beautiful; and, on the Use of Studying Pictures, for the Purpose of Improving Real Landscape*, London. Reprinted 1972, Gregg International, Farnborough.

Reff, T. (1983) Manet and the Paris of Haussmann and Baudelaire, in *Monet and Modern Art*, Exhibition Calogue, National Gallery of Art, Washington. Reprinted (1987) in Sharpe, W. and Wallock: *Visions of the Modern City: Essays in History, Art, and Literature*, Johns Hopkins University Press, Baltimore.

Reichlin, B. and Reinhart, F. (1973) **Villa Tonini at Lugano**, in Bonfanti *et al.* (1973).

Reps, J. (1965) *The Making of Urban America*, Princeton University Press, Princeton, New Jersey.

Repton, H. (1794) Sketches and Hints on Landscape Gardening and Sources of Pleasure in Landscape Gardening, in Loudon, J. C. (ed.;) (1840) *The Landsscape Gardening and Landscape Architecture of Humphrey Repton, Esq, Being his Entire Works on These Subjects . . .*, J. C. Loudon, London. Reprinted by Gregg Press, Farnborough.

Reventós, R., Folguera, F., Nogués, X. and Utrillo, M. (1929) **Pueblo Esapañol: Barcelona**, in Voltes Bou (1972) and Castell Esteban (1985).

Rewald, J. (1946) *The History of Impressionism*, Museum of Modern Art, New York. 4th revised edn consulted, also Secker and Warburg, London.

Roca, M. A. (1979–80) **Plaza España, Cordoba, Argentina**, in Roca, M. A. (1981)

Roca, M. A. (1979–80) **Plaza des Armas: Cordoba, Argentina**, in Roca, M. A. (1981) and *Architectural Design*, **54** (11/12), 1984.

Roca, M. A. (1981) *Miguel Angel Roca*, with texts by Glusberg, J. and Bohigas, O., Academy Editions, London.

Rodrigues-Lorres, J. and Uhlig, G. (eds) (1971) Selections from *Das Neue Frankfurt*, Lehrstuhl für Plannungstheorie, RWTH Aachen, Aachen.

Rörig, F. (1967) *The Medieval Town* (trans. Bryant, D.) University of California Press, Berkeley.

Rosenau, H. (1959) *The Ideal City and its Architectural Evolution*, Routledge and Kegan Paul, London. Republished 1972 as *The Ideal City: Its Architectural Evolution*, November Books, New York; 1974 as *The Ideal City*, Studio Vista, London and 1983 Methuen, London; November Books, London.

Rosenau, H. (1976) *Boullée and Visionary Architecture*, including Boullée's Architecture: Essay on Art, Academy Editions, London; Harmony Books, New York.

Rosenthal, A. W. and Gelb, A. (eds) (1965) *The Night the Lights Went Out*, Signet Book, New American Library, New York.

Rossi, A. (1965) **City Square and Monumental Fountain in Segrate, Milan**, in *A + U*, 1976/5.

Rossi, A. (1966) *L'Architettura della città*, Ed. Marsilio, Padua; trans. Ghirardo, D. and Ockman, J. (1982) as *The Architecture of the City*, MIT Press, Cambridge, Mass. and London.

Rossi, A. (1967) Introduzione a Boullée, in Boullée, E.-L. (trans. Italian) *Architettura: Saggia sull'Arte*, Padua.

Rossi, A. (1971a) **Cemetery of San Cataldo, Modena**. *A + U*, 1976: 5; 1982: 11; Conforti (1981) Johnson, E. (1982); Savi, V. (1983); Savi, V. and Lupano, M. (1983).

Rossi, A. (1971b) L'azzurro del cielo, in entry, with Braghieri, G. for **Modena Cemetery Competition**. Reprinted in *Controspazio*, 10 October 1972; trans. Barsoum, M. and Dimitriu, L. (1976) as The blue of the sky. *Oppositions*, **5**, Summer 1976.

Rossi, A. (1972a) Il gioco dell'oca: Boardgame, **Collage of Modena Cemetery** Drawings, in Moschini, F. (1979).

Rossi, A. (1972b) **Architectural Collage**. *A + U*, No. 65, May 1976.

Rossi, A. (1972c) **Project for an Elementary School at Fagano Olona**, (Varese), in Bonfanti *et al.* (1973).

Rossi, A. (1978) **Roma Interrotta; Sector XI**, in *IIA Catalogue* (1978). Reprinted in *Architectural Design*, **49** (3/4), 1979.

Rossi, A. (1980a) **Canareggio West: Project for the Grand Canal in Venice**, in Rossi, 1985.

Rossi, A. (1984) *Lotus International*, **42**, 1984/2.

Rossi, A. (1987) *Aldo Rossi: Architect*, with texts by

Harrison, P., Rossi, A., Barbieri, U. and Braghieri, B., Ghirri, L. and Ferlenga, A. Catalogue of an Exhibition held at York (20 November 1987–3 January 1988 and London, 20 February–29 March 1988) Electa Spa, Milan.

Rossi, A. and Stead, W. (1980) **Molteni Funerary Chapel, Giussano**, in Arnell and Bickford (1985).

Rossi, A. and Braghieri, G., with Stead, C. and Johnson, J. (1981) Brick Building marked by windows. *Lotus International*, **32**, 1981/III.

Rossi, A., with Adjini, M. and Gerinzi, G. (1982) **Congressional Palace for Milan**, in Arnell and Bickford (1985); Rossi (1987).

Rowe, C. (1978) **Roma Interrotta: Sector VIII**, in *IIA Catalogue* (1978). Reprinted in *Architectural Design*, **49** (3/4) 1979.

Rowe, C. (1984) IBA: Rowe Reflects. *Architectural Review*, **CLXVI**, (1051), September 1984.

Rowe, C. and Koetter, F. (1975) Collage City. *Architectural Review*, **CLVIII**, (942), August 1975. Republished (1979) as *Collage City*, MIT Press, Cambridge, Mass. and London.

Russell, B. (1946) *History of Western Philosophy*, Allen and Unwin, London.

Rykwert, J. (1972) *On Adam's House in Paradise: the Idea of the Primitive Hut*, in *Architectural History*, Museum of Modern Art, New York.

Rykwert, J. (1974) 15 Triennale Esposizione Internazionale dell Arte Decorative e Industriale Noderne e dell'Architettura moderne, Milano 20/9–20, 11, 1973, in *Domus*, January 1974.

Rykwert, J. (1976) *The Idea of a Town*, Faber and Faber, London.

Saalman, H. (n.d.) *Mediaeval Cities*, Studio Vista, London; George Braziller, New York.

Saalman, H. (1971) *Haussmann: Paris Transformed*, Studio Vista, London; George Braziller, New York.

Salmona, R. (1968–71) **El Parque, Bogota**, in Bayón, D. and Gasparini, P. (1977).

Salonas, Arriolque, Gali and Quintana (1981–82) **Parc de l'Excorxador, Barcelona**. See Bohigas *et al.* (1983).

Samonà, G. and A. (1967) **Competition Entry for a New Chamber of Deputies Building in Rome**, in Bonfanti *et al.* (1973).

Samonà, G. *et al.* (1970) **Piazza San Marco:** l'Architettura la Storia le Funzioni, Marsilio Editori, Venice.

Savi, V. (1983) **The Aldorossian Cemetery.** *Lotus International*, 1983/III.

Savi, V. and Lupano, M. (1983) *Aldo Rossi: Opera Recenti*, Catalogue of an Exhibition held at Modena 25 June–5 September 1983 and Perugia, October 1983, Ed. Panini.

Scammozzi, V. (1615) *L'Idea della Architetura Universale*, Venice.

Schevill, F. (1909) *Siena: The Story of a Medieval Commune*, Charles Scribner's Sons, New York. Reprinted (1964) Harper and Row Torchbooks, New York.

Schulz, J. and Gräbner, W. (1987) *Berlin: Architektur von Pankow bis Köpenick*, VEB Verlag für Bauwesen, Berlin.

Schütte-Lihotsky (1927) Razionalisierung im Haushalt. *Das Neue Frankfurt*, **1** (5).

Scully, V. (1974) *The Shingle Style Today or The Historian's Revenge*, George Braziller, New York.

Segre, R. (1975) Communication and Social Participation, in Segre, R. and Kusnetzoff, F. (eds) (1975) *América Latina en su Arquitectura*, UNESCO, Paris, trans. Grossman, E. (1981) as *Latin America in its Architecture*, Holmes and Meier, New York and Greenwich, London.

Siena, Commune de Costituto of 1262; Costituto of 1309 and Statuto dei Viari (1280) all in Balestracci, D. and Piccinni, G. (n.d.).

Siena, Commune di (1292) Ordine . . . nelle nuove casa . . . nella Piazza del Campo, tutte finestre debbano esser costruite a colonnelli, from Archivo di Stato in Siena, in Borghesi, S. and Banchi, E. L. (1898).

Simmel, G. (1902–03) Die Grosstäde und das Geistleben, trans. Wolf, K. H. (1950) as The Metropolis and Mental Life, in *The Sociology of Georg Simmel*, Free Press, New York.

Sitte, C. (1889) Der Städte-Bau nach sienen künstlerischen Grundsätzen trans. Collins, G. R. and C. C. (1965) as *City Planning according to Artistic Principles*, in Collins, G. R. and C. C. (1986) *Camillo Sitte: The Birth of Modern City Planning*, Rizzoli International, New York.

Smith, R. C. (1955) Colonial Towns of Spanish and Portuguese Americas. *Journal of the Society of Architectural Historians*, XIV, No. 4, December 1955, pp. 3–12.

Smithson, A. and Smithson, P. (1972) Signs of Occupancy. *Architectural Design*, **XLI**, 2/1972.

Smithson, A. and Smithson, P. (1973) *Without Rhetoric: An Architectural Aesthetic 1956–72*, Latimer New Dimensions, London.

Spoerry, F. (1963) **Port Grimaud**. See Smithson, A. and P. (1972) also Culot, M. Portrait de Francois Spoerry. *Archives d'Architecture Moderne*, No. 12, Nov. 1977, and Williams Ellis, C. (1978).

Stanislawski, D. (1946) The Origin and Spread of the Grid Pattern Town. *The Georgraphical Review XXXVI*, No. 1, January 1947.

Stanislawski, D. (1947) Early Spanish Town Planning in the New World. *The Geographical Review XXXVII*, No. 1, January 1947.

Stein, C. S. (1957) *Towards New Towns for America*, Van Nostrand Reinhold, New York.

Stern, R. (1977) At the Edge of Modernism: Some Methods, Paradigms and Principles for Modern Architecture at the Edge of the Modern Movement. *Architectural Design*, **47** (4).

Stern, R. A. M. (1988) *Modern Classicism*, Thames and Hudson, London.

Stern, R. A. M., Gilmartin, G. and Massengale, J. M. (1983) *New York 1900: Metropolitan Architecture and Urbanism 1890–1915*, Rizzoli, New York.

Stirling, J. (1978) **Nolli Plan: Sector IV**, in *IIS Catalogue* (1978). Reprinted in *Architectural Design*, **49** (3/4), 1979.

Stirling, J., with Krier, L. (1970a) **Siemens A. G. Munchen-**

Pelach. *Architectural Design*, **XL**, July 1970; *Space Design*, October 1970.

Stirling, J., with Krier, L. (1970b) **Project for Derby Civic Centre**. *Space Design*, November 1971; *Domus*, No. 518, November 1972; Bonfanti *et al.* (1973); *Architectural Design*, **XLIII** 9/1973; Krier, L. (1980).

Stirling, J. and Wilford, M. (1980) **Science Centre, South Tiergarten, Berlin**. See Buchanan, P. (1980) in *Architectural Review*, **CLXVII**, (998), April 1980; *Architectural Review*, **CLXXXI**, (1082), April 1987.

Sullivan, L. (1896) The Tall Office Building Artistically Considered. *Lippincott's*, **57**, March 1896. Reprinted many times including Sullivan, L. (1918) *Kindergarten Chats and Other Writings*. 1979 edn consulted, Dover, New York.

Tafuri, M. (1973) *Progetto e Utopia*, Ed. Laterza, Bari, trans. (1976) as *Architecture and Utopia: Design and Capitalist Development*, MIT Press, Cambridge, Mass. and London.

Tafuri, M. (1974) L'Architecture dans la Boudoir: il linguaggio della critica e la critica del linguaggio, trans. Caliandro, V. (1974) as L'Architecture dans la Boudoir: The language of criticism and the criticism of language. *Oppositions*, **3**, May 1974.

Tarn, J. N. (1973) *Five Percent Philanthropy*, Cambridge University Press, Cambridge.

Tauranac, J. (1979) *Essential New York: A Guide to the History and Architecture of Manhattan's Important Buildings, Parks and Bridges*, Holt, Rinehart and Winston, New York.

Taylor, F. W. (1911) *Scientific Management*. Republished (1974) Harper and Brothers, New York.

Taylor, N. (1973) *The Village in the City: Towards a New Society*, Temple Smith, London.

Thayer, H. S. (ed.) (1970) *Pragmatism: The Classical Writings*, Mentor Book of the New American Library, New York; the New English Library, London.

Thiel, P. (1986) *Notations for an Experimental Envirotecture*, University of Washington, Seattle.

Tod, I. and Wheeler, M. (1978) *Utopia*, Orbis, London.

Toynbee, A. (ed.) (1967) *Cities of Destiny*, Thames and Hudson, London.

Tschumi, B. (1981) *The Manhattan Transcripts*, Academy Editions, London and St Martin's Press, New York.

Tschumi, B. (1983) Illustrated index: themes from the Manhattan transcripts. *AA Files*, No. 4, July 1983, Architectural Association, London.

Tschumi, B. (1982–83) **Projet pour le Parc de la Villette, Paris**. See Barziley *et al.* (1987).

Tschumi, B. (1984) Work in progress. In *L'Invention du Parc*, Editions Graphite, Paris.

Tschumi, B. (1985) *La Case Vide*: twenty plates exploring future conceptual transformations and dislocations of the **Villette** project. With an essay on Bernard Tschumi by Jacques Derrida, an introduction by Anthony Vidler and an interview by Alvin Boyarsky. AA Folio VIII. Architectural Association, London.

Tschumi, B.(1987) *Cinégramme Folie, le parc de la Villette* Champ-Vallon, Paris and Princeton University Press, Princeton, New Jersey.

Tschumi, B. (1988) **Parc de la Villette**, Paris. *Architectural Design*, **58** (3/4), 1988.

Tschumi, B. (1988) Notes towards a theory of deconstruction. *Architecture and Urbanism*, No. 216, September 1988.

Tunnard, C. and Pushkarew, B. (1963) *Man-made America: Chaos or Control: Selected Problems of Design in the Urban Landscape*, with Baker, G. *et al.* Drawings by Lin, P., Pozharsky, V. and photographs by Reed, J. and Schulze, C. R. J. Yale University Press, New Haven.

Turnbull, W. (1977) **Kresge College**, quoted in Chang, C.-Y. (ed.) *Process Architecture*, No. 3.

Ungers, M. (1964) The Forum of Culture: **Proposal for Kemperplatz, Berlin**. *Lotus International*, **43**, 1984/3.

van der Rohe, M. (1967) **A New City Square and Office Tower in the City of London**, in Carter, P. (1974).

Venturi, R. (1953) **The Campidoglio: A Case Study**, in *MFA Thesis*, Princeton University. Reprinted (1953) in *Architectural Review*, May 1953, No. 675, pp. 333–4 and in Venturi, R. and Scott Brown, D., with Arnell, P., Bickford T. and Bergart, C. (eds) (1984) *A View from the Campidoglio*, Harper and Row, New York.

Venturi, R. (1966) *Complexity and Contradiction in Architecture*, Museum of Modern Art, New York. Republished (1977) also Architectural Press, London.

Venturi, R. and Scott-Brown, D. (1968) A Significance for A and P Parking Lots, or Learning from Las Vegas. *Architectural Forum*, March.

Venturi, R., Scott Brown, D. and Izenour, S. (1972) *A Significance for A & P Parking Lots or Learning from Las Vegas*, MIT Press, Cambridge, Mass. Revised (1972, 1979) as *Learning from Las Vegas: the Forgotten Symbolism of Architectural Form*, MIT Press, Cambridge, Mass. and London.

Venturi, R. and Rauch (1978) **Roma Interrotta: Sector VII**, in *IIA Catalogue* 1978. Reprinted in *Architectural Design*, **49** (3/4), 1979.

Vidler, A. (1978) La Troisieme Typologie: The Third Typology, on AAM (1978).

Violich, F. (1962) Evolution of the Spanish City: Issues Basic to Planning Today. *Journal of the American Institute of Planners*, **28** (3), August 1962, pp. 170–79.

Vitruvius (n.d.) *De Architectura*, trans. Morgan, W. H. (1914) as *Vitruvius: The Ten Books on Architecture*, Harvard University Press, Cambridge, Mass. Reprinted (1960) Dover Publications, New York. Also trans. Grainger, F. (1934) as *Vitruvius on Architecture*, vols I and II, Loeb Classical Library, Harvard University Press, Cambridge, Mass. and William Heinemann, London.

Voltes Bou, P. (1971) **Pueblo Español de Montjuich, Barcelona: Spanish Village of Barcelona**, Corporation of Barcelona.

von Spreckelsen, O. (1982–88) **Grand Arche; Tête de la Defense, Paris**. See Mitterand *et al.* (1987).

Wagner, O. (1905–7) **St Leopold am Steinhoff**, in Geretsegger, H. and Peintner, M. (eds) (1964) *Otto Wagner, 1841–1918*, Residenz Verlag, Salzburg, trans. Onn, G. (1979) Academy Editions, London.

Ward-Perkins, J. B. (1970) Roman Imperial Architecture as part of Boethius, A. and Ward-Perkins, J. B. *Etruscan and Roman Architecture*. Republished (1981) as *Roman Imperial Architecture*, Penguin Books, Harmondsworth.

Weller, A. S. (1943) *Francesco di Giorgio*, Chicago. Quoted Rosenau (1972).

Wigley, M. (1987) Postmortem architecture: the taste of Derrida. *Perspecta: The Yale Architectural Journal,* No. 23, 1987.

Wigley, M. (1988) Projects. In *Deconstructivist Architecture* (eds P. O. Johnson and M. Wigley), Museum of Modern Art, New York.

Williams-Ellis, C. and A. (1924) *On the Pleasures of Architecture,* quoted without bibliographical details in Williams-Ellis, C. (1971).

Williams-Ellis, C. (1963) **Portmeirion: The Place and its Meaning**. Revised edn (1973) Portmeirion Limited, Portmeirion.

Williams-Ellis, C. (1978) The Miracle of **Port Grimaud** and **Portmeirion** Grows Up, in *Around the World in Eighty Years*, Golden Dragon Books, Portmeirion.

William-Ellis, C. (1982) **Portmeirion:** *It's What? When? Why and How? Variously Answered*, Portmeirion Limited, Portmeirion.

Woodbridge, S. (1974) How to Make a Place (on MKTW **Kresge College**). *Progressive Architecture*, **55**, May.

Wycherley, R. E. (1949) *How the Greeks Built Cities*, London.

Zdekauer, L. (1967) *La Vita Pubblica del Senese nel Pugento*, Bologna.

Zorzi, A. (1980) *Una Citta, Una Repubblica, Un Impero Venezia 697–1797*, trans. 1983 as *Venice 697–1797: City – Republic – Empire*, Sidgwick and Jackson, London.

Author index

Entries in *italics* refer to figures.

Place index

Entries in *italics* refer to figures.

Subject index

Entries in *italics* refer to figures.